RECENT DEVELOPMENTS IN HEALTH ECONOMETRICS

CONTRIBUTIONS TO ECONOMIC ANALYSIS   VOLUME 297

RECENT DEVELOPMENTS IN HEALTH ECONOMETRICS: A VOLUME IN HONOUR OF ANDREW JONES

EDITED BY

BADI H. BALTAGI
Syracuse University, USA
Leicester University, UK

AND

FRANCESCO MOSCONE
Brunel University London, UK
Ca' Foscari University of Venice, Italy

United Kingdom – North America – Japan
India – Malaysia – China

Emerald Publishing Limited
Emerald Publishing, Floor 5, Northspring, 21-23 Wellington Street, Leeds LS1 4DL

First edition 2024

Editorial Matter and Selection © 2024 Badi H. Baltagi and Francesco Moscone.
Individual chapters © 2024 The authors.
Published under exclusive licence by Emerald Publishing Limited.

Reprints and permissions service
Contact: www.copyright.com

No part of this book may be reproduced, stored in a retrieval system, transmitted in any form or by any means electronic, mechanical, photocopying, recording or otherwise without either the prior written permission of the publisher or a licence permitting restricted copying issued in the UK by The Copyright Licensing Agency and in the USA by The Copyright Clearance Center. Any opinions expressed in the chapters are those of the authors. Whilst Emerald makes every effort to ensure the quality and accuracy of its content, Emerald makes no representation implied or otherwise, as to the chapters' suitability and application and disclaims any warranties, express or implied, to their use.

British Library Cataloguing in Publication Data
A catalogue record for this book is available from the British Library

ISBN: 978-1-83753-259-9 (Print)
ISBN: 978-1-83753-258-2 (Online)
ISBN: 978-1-83753-260-5 (Epub)

ISSN: 0573-8555 (Series)

INVESTOR IN PEOPLE

CONTENTS

Acknowledgements   *vii*

Editorial Introduction   *1*
Badi H. Baltagi and Francesco Moscone

Tracking Pupils Into Adulthood: Selective Schools and Long-Term Human Capital   *7*
Chiara Pastore, Nigel Rice and Andrew M. Jones

Physician Behaviour and Inequalities in Access to Healthcare   *37*
Mylene Lagarde and Anthony Scott

Performance Comparison and Socio-Economic Inequalities in Unmet Need for Medical Treatment and Dental Care in the European Union   *55*
Andrea Riganti, Valerie Moran and Luigi Siciliani

'Beyond the Mean' in Biomarkers Modelling for Economic Evaluations: A Case Study in Gestational Diabetes Mellitus   *85*
Georgios F. Nikolaidis, Ana Duarte, Susan Griffin and James Lomas

Empirical Health Economics for Evidence-Based Policies: Some Lessons From Italy   *111*
Vincenzo Carrieri and Francesco Principe

Types of Inactivity and Depression Among Older Individuals   *127*
Anwar S. Adem, Bruce Hollingsworth and Eugenio Zucchelli

Mental Health, Lifestyle and Retirement   *147*
Silvia Balia and Erica Delugas

The Association Between Medical Cannabis Laws and Flows of Opioids by Dosage Strength to US Pharmacies – Evidence From Detailed ARCOS Data, 2006–2014   *167*
Shelby R. Steuart and W. David Bradford

The Prevalence, Trends and Heterogeneity in Maternal Smoking Around Birth Between the 1930s and 1970s   *201*
Stephanie von Hinke, Jonathan James, Emil Sorensen, Hans H. Sievertsen and Nicolai Vitt

Benchmarking Clinical Practice on Treatment Gain Inequality–Probability Bounds   *229*
Raf Van Gestel, Daniel Avdic and Owen O'Donnell

Hidden Figures: Uncovering Quantities Behind Zeros With Econometrics   *241*
Anirban Basu

Investigating Health Outcomes Defined by Multiple Chronic Conditions   *255*
John Mullahy

ACKNOWLEDGEMENTS

We are grateful to all the authors in this volume for their enthusiastic endorsement of this project in honouring Andrew. We are also grateful to all the reviewers and for the publisher's support.

EDITORIAL INTRODUCTION

Badi H. Baltagi[a,b] and Francesco Moscone[c,d]

[a]*Syracuse University, USA*
[b]*Leicester University, UK*
[c]*Brunel University London, UK*
[d]*Ca' Foscari University of Venice, Italy*

We are immensely honoured to serve as Guest Editors for this special volume of *Contributions in Economic Analysis* by Emerald Publishing as a tribute to the outstanding contribution of Professor Andrew Jones to the field of health econometrics and his extensive dedication to the profession.

Andrew is a long-time friend to both editors and contributors to this volume. He is Professor of Economics at the University of York, United Kingdom (UK), where he also assumed the role of Head of the Department of Economics and Related Studies from 2011 to 2015. His tenure saw the flourishing of the MSc in Health Economics at York, resulting in over 500 graduates coming from more than 70 different nations. In addition, he has diligently supervised 27 PhD candidates, shaping the future of health economics scholarship. Notably, he served as the editor of *Health Economics* from 1995 to 2019, playing a pivotal role in advancing research in the field.

Andrew Jones' research covers the area of microeconometrics and health economics, with specific interests in understanding the determinants of health, investigating the economics of addiction and addressing socioeconomic disparities in health and healthcare delivery. His seminal chapter on 'Health econometrics' in the *Handbook of Health Economics* has acquired remarkable recognition, with 770 citations on Google Scholar. Professor Jones exhibits a profound interest in the practical application and dissemination of econometric techniques in the area of health economics.

In 1992, Professor Jones established the European Workshops on Econometrics and Health Economics, as evidence of his commitment to fostering collaborative academic discourse. This initiative, co-organised with Owen O'Donnell, has significantly contributed to the advancement of interdisciplinary research in this area.

Recent Developments in Health Econometrics
Contributions to Economic Analysis, Volume 297, 1–5
Copyright © 2024 Badi H. Baltagi and Francesco Moscone
Published under exclusive licence by Emerald Publishing Limited
ISSN: 0573-8555/doi:10.1108/S0573-855520240000297001

Andrew serves as the research director of the Health, Econometrics and Data Group (HEDG), leading innovative studies at the intersection of economics, econometrics and health. His dedication to exploring inequality of opportunity in health is exemplified by his Leverhulme Trust Major Research Fellowship, held from 2017 to 2020, which employs cutting-edge biosocial data to shed light on critical issues in health economics.

With a prolific publication record, comprising 96 articles, 15 book chapters and 16 editorials spanning from 1989 to 2023, Professor Jones has made a profound impact on the academic landscape. His authoritative books, including 'Applied Health Economics', 'Applied Econometrics for Health Economists' and 'Data Visualization and Health Econometrics', stand as enduring contributions to the field. Additionally, his editorial endeavours, such as 'Econometric Analysis of Health Data' and 'The Elgar Companion to Health Economics', as well as three edited volumes of 'The Oxford Encyclopedia of Health Economics' reflect his dedication to shaping the discourse in health economics.

Professor Jones' significant accomplishments have been recognized with the prestigious Willard G. Manning Memorial Award for the finest research in Health Econometrics. He is also a distinguished author for the *Journal of Applied Econometrics*, awarded for his numerous publications in that journal. Professor Andrew Jones' enduring contributions to health econometrics continue to inspire and shape the trajectory of research in this vital field.

The influential health econometrics research carried out by Andrew during the past three decades or so is recognized in this volume with 12 peer-reviewed articles, written by some of the leading researchers in health econometrics. The diversity of the topics covered constitutes a tribute to the wide-ranging scope of Andrew's research interests and contributions.

1. CONTRIBUTIONS

Pastore, Rice and Jones investigate how selective schooling, where students are sorted by ability, affects adult health, well-being and labour market outcomes. Leveraging the shift from selective to non-selective secondary schooling in 1960s England and Wales, mixed-ability schools led to changes in school quality and peer ability. This research distinguishes between high-quality school attendance for high-ability students and low-quality attendance for low-ability students. It mitigates bias through entropy balancing and Ordinary Least Squares (OLS) regression. Selective schooling seems to have minimal impact on long-term health and well-being but slightly raises wages compared to mixed-ability systems. It also boosts aspirations for high-ability students. Early cognitive and non-cognitive abilities strongly correlate with adult outcomes, emphasising their lasting influence.

Lagarde and Scott explore how physicians contribute to disparities in healthcare access and use. This research analyses three types of decisions that physicians make that can impact these disparities: where they choose to practice, whether they work in public or private settings, and their behaviour in patient interactions. For each decision choice, they outline the challenges and provide empirical evidence on potential policies to mitigate access disparities. The authors recommend that future research should concentrate on modifying healthcare systems to influence physician decisions, including expanding health insurance, balancing public and private sectors, and implementing financial incentives. Additionally, efforts should be made to diversify the physician workforce through training and policies.

Riganti, Moran and Siciliani's study underscores the need for improved healthcare access in European countries. They use European Union (EU)-developed indicators on self-reported unmet needs for comparison, emphasising the importance of considering factors beyond health systems' control in cross-country assessments. The research focuses on the impact of demographic and socioeconomic adjustments on unmet needs and examines disparities based on socioeconomic status. Findings show that adjusting for age, gender and chronic conditions reduces dispersion of unmet medical needs in the EU. Additionally, controlling for income, primarily due to affordability, further reduces dispersion. Socioeconomic disparities in income and education vary by reason for unmet needs, with income disparities being primarily related to affordability. Affordability emerges as the primary cause of unmet dental care needs. Notably, they report that income and education gradients are more pronounced for dental care than medical care.

Nikolaidis, Duarte, Griffin and Lomas employ flexible parametric models to analyse gestational diabetes mellitus (GDM) biomarkers and predict extreme values. They integrate these distributions into an economic decision model, evaluating cost-effective diagnostic thresholds and strategies. Using data from the Born in Bradford study, they identify optimal distributions and assess strategies like 'Testing and Treating', 'Treat all' and 'Do Nothing'. The latter emerges as the cost-effective approach. However, considering long-term benefits for mothers and offsprings may alter this decision.

Carrieri and Principe pay homage to Andrew Jones' significant contributions in health programme evaluation, risky health behaviour and income-related health disparities by reviewing pertinent empirical studies conducted in Italy. Their chapter begins by analysing the impact of reimbursement systems on healthcare behaviour, particularly the shift from incurred-cost-based to prospective systems in hospitals. The authors delve into incentive-driven practices like up-coding and cream skimming, while also considering the potential benefits of primary care incentives and the mixed outcomes associated with cost-sharing schemes. The chapter concludes by emphasising the necessity of accounting for socioeconomic status-related health disparities in the allocation of resources within the Italian National Health Service (NHS), drawing parallels with the experience of the British NHS.

The study by Adem, Hollingsworth and Zucchelli addresses the economic costs of depression, including reduced productivity and increased healthcare utilisation. While the link between employment and mental health is explored, the impact of different types of economic inactivity on depression in older individuals is less understood. They utilise various models and data from the English Longitudinal Study of Ageing to examine how different forms of inactivity may have varying effects on depression. Their findings suggest that transitions to involuntary inactivity (such as unemployment) do not significantly influence depression, while transitions to voluntary inactivity (like retirement) appear to reduce it.

In their work, Silvia Balia and Erica Delugas delve into the intersection of mental health, lifestyle and retirement. Their work introduces a mediation model designed to differentiate the indirect and direct impacts of retirement on health, taking into account the mediating role of lifestyles. They specifically examine the risk of depression, with physical inactivity serving as a potential mediator of retirement's effect. Their findings reveal a notable indirect effect through the mediator though it is relatively modest when compared to the direct effect. This analysis underscores the significance of delving deeper into the role of lifestyle factors in the connection between retirement and health, offering insights into the potential pathways through which retirement influences well-being.

Steuart and Bradford examined the impact of medical cannabis access on opioid use trends using the Callaway and Sant'Anna (2021) difference-in-differences estimator. Analysing data on all opioid shipments to United States (US) pharmacies from 2006 to 2014, they found no significant change in the total morphine milligramme equivalent (MME) units of opioids shipped after the introduction of medical cannabis dispensaries. However, they observed a decrease in the highest MME dosage strengths across all opioids, particularly with commonly diverted ones. This reduction included a 12.2% decrease in 50–89 MME doses and a 13.8% decrease in 90+ MME doses. Additionally, there was a 6.0% increase in low-to-moderate dose opioids (0–49 MMEs), suggesting patients may be using cannabis alongside opioids to achieve a lower opioid dosage.

von Hinke, James, Sorensen, Sievertsen and Vitt present a study that examines the prevalence, trends and diversity of maternal smoking around birth in the UK, with a particular focus on the war and post-war reconstruction era, where systematic data on maternal smoking behaviour is limited. In this context, they emphasise significant events, the dissemination of new information regarding the dangers of smoking and shifts in government policies targeting smoking reduction. The study reveals substantial shifts in smoking rates over three decades, underscores the emergence of a social gradient in smoking and identifies genetic variations in smoking trends.

Van Gestel, Avdic and O'Donnel investigate concerns about low adherence to clinical practice guidelines and the limited adoption of new medical technologies. They suggest benchmarking clinical practice based on the minimum likelihood of a recommended treatment or new technology leading to better outcomes. This bound can be estimated from outcome distributions. They demonstrate this method by examining Swedish cardiologists' adoption of drug-eluting stents, finding a significant portion falls below the benchmark.

Basu reviews the econometric approaches typically used to deal with the spike of zeros when modelling non-negative outcomes such as expenditures, income or consumption. This research studies how alternate behavioural assumptions may be required to understand the economic rationale for why zeros were generated in the data, how they should be modelled, how the model parameters should be estimated and how the results should be interpreted. This chapter argues that a key distinction is understanding whether the goal is to model the true zeros or some other hidden figures behind the zeros observed in the data. The data generation process for both the true zeros and the hidden figures can have rich behavioural content, which may trigger the use of some multi-part models and hurdles.

Mullahy highlights the importance of multiple chronic conditions (MCCs) as indicators of individual and population health. The paper emphasises that considering both the 'intensity' (count) and 'composition' (patterns) of MCCs is crucial for a comprehensive understanding of MCC health outcomes. The study, based on US Behavioural Risk Factors Surveillance System (BRFSS) data, demonstrates that focussing solely on intensity provides an incomplete picture of MCC health outcomes.

Andrew, on behalf of the community of health economics and econometric scholars, we express our gratitude for all the inspiring work you have given us and look forward to your future contributions.

Badi and Francesco

TRACKING PUPILS INTO ADULTHOOD: SELECTIVE SCHOOLS AND LONG-TERM HUMAN CAPITAL

Chiara Pastore[a], Nigel Rice[b] and Andrew M. Jones[b]

[a]*Boston Consulting Group, Spain*
[b]*University of York, UK*

ABSTRACT

We explore the effect of selective schooling, where students are assigned to different schools by ability, on adult health, well-being and labour market outcomes. We exploit the 1960s transition from a selective to a non-selective secondary schooling system in England and Wales. The introductio3n of mixed-ability schools decreased average school quality and peer ability for high-ability pupils, while it increased them for low-ability pupils. We therefore distinguish between two treatment effects: that of high-quality school attendance for high-ability pupils and that of lower-quality school attendance for low-ability pupils, with mixed-ability schools as the alternative. We address selection bias by balancing individual pre-treatment characteristics via entropy balancing, followed by ordinary least squares (OLS) regression. Selective schooling does not affect long-term health and well-being, while it marginally raises hourly wages, compared to a mixed-ability system, and school aspirations for high-ability pupils. Cognitive and non-cognitive abilities measured prior to secondary school are significantly and positively associated with all adult outcomes.

Keywords: Ability tracking; educational reform; well-being; health; entropy balancing; instrumental variables

1. INTRODUCTION

Education policy may be one of the most effective tools to improve life opportunities for individuals across all backgrounds. A central concern, however, in the

---

Recent Developments in Health Econometrics
Contributions to Economic Analysis, Volume 297, 7–36
Copyright © 2024 Chiara Pastore, Nigel Rice and Andrew M. Jones
Published under exclusive licence by Emerald Publishing Limited
ISSN: 0573-8555/doi:10.1108/S0573-855520240000297002

provision of public education is whether and, if so, how to tailor the curriculum around pupils' ability. Tracking students by ability into different schools at a young age is a controversial policy. On the one hand, it can be seen as a way to improve learning and teaching efficiency, by catering for different abilities separately; on the other hand, such systems have been shown to favour children from affluent backgrounds, who are generally more supported by their families and more prepared to take entry tests (Burgess et al., 2018; Cribb et al., 2013). If less advantaged students are more likely to be excluded from the upper tracks, then selective schooling will reinforce existing inequality gaps in education.

Several countries incorporate selection by ability in their secondary schooling systems, including Australia, England, France, Germany, the Netherlands, Switzerland and the United States. Attending an upper track school is generally linked to better educational outcomes, but the presence of tracking is also associated with higher inequality in education and earnings, often leading to low social mobility (Brunello & Checchi, 2007; Burgess et al., 2017, 2020; Hanushek & Wößmann, 2006). There are, however, several other non-monetary benefits of education, which accrue over time through a variety of pathways, including health and well-being (Grossman, 1972). In this chapter, we assess the human capital effects of selective versus non-selective schooling, by looking at long-term health, well-being and labour market outcomes for a British cohort. We do this by exploiting the comprehensive schooling reform implemented in England and Wales in the 1960s, which caused some areas to transition from a selective to a non-selective system of secondary education earlier than others. The empirical analysis relies on data from the National Child Development Study (NCDS), a British cohort study of individuals born in March 1958, allowing us to follow their lives to date. Depending on the area in which they resided at the time, NCDS children were exposed to either a selective or a non-selective system. In selective areas, an entry test determined whether a pupil was offered a place in a selective grammar school, representing the more academic track, or in a vocational secondary modern school, the main alternative for low-scoring pupils. In the non-selective system, schools were converted into or created as comprehensive schools receiving pupils of all abilities. Attendance at different school types exposed pupils to different curricula, teacher quality and peer ability, thus offering an opportunity to explore the long-term human capital effects of variation in school quality. To assess the impact of selective schooling, our empirical approach exploits the differential ability of pupils within that system by estimating two treatment effects. First, we explore long-term effects of attending grammar, compared to comprehensive, for pupils of high cognitive ability. Second, we investigate the effect of attending secondary modern, compared to comprehensive, for pupils of lower ability. An advantage of separating treatment effects is that for each, we make treatment and control groups more comparable. This chapter builds on the literature exploring health impacts of the comprehensive reform in the 1960s (Basu et al., 2018; Jones et al., 2011, 2012). However, we expand on this literature by splitting the sample by cognitive ability, in order to assess the link of selective schooling to biometric markers for cardiovascular disease and stress, as well as to several dimensions of well-being and human capital in adulthood.

We find that type of secondary school attended does not affect most of our adult health and well-being outcomes, with two exceptions. Attitude towards school is positively linked to grammar attendance and negatively linked to secondary modern attendance, compared to similarly able pupils in comprehensive schools. This could be a channel for educational outcomes, found to be significantly linked to type of school by Burgess et al. (2017) and Guyon et al. (2012). The second exception is labour market outcomes, which are better for grammar school pupils, confirming previous studies on earnings (Burgess et al., 2020; Del Bono & Clark, 2016). Surprisingly, we find marginally better wages for pupils in secondary modern compared to equivalent comprehensive school pupils. We hypothesise that this could be due to the vocational nature of the curriculum at that time and which may not apply today. Overall, a null average effect of selective schooling for long-term outcomes confirms previous findings in the literature (Basu et al., 2018; Del Bono & Clark, 2016; Dustmann et al., 2016). Taken together, the evidence suggests little scope for new selective school places to improve average long-term outcomes. Instead, resources should be targeted to improve childhood cognitive and non-cognitive abilities measured prior to secondary schooling as these appear more important for adult health and human capital. Additional detail of all aspects of the research presented in this chapter can be found in Jones et al. (2018).

2. BACKGROUND

The origins of tracking in the British school system go back to the 1944 Education Act, which established the reorganisation of state secondary schools by Local Education Authority (LEA) in a tripartite system, comprising grammar, secondary modern and technical schools. Pupils could access grammar schools, of highest academic quality, conditional on their performance in the 11-plus test, taken in the last year of primary school, around age 11. The 11-plus was set at LEA level, so difficulty and entry score varied across the country. Grammar schools admitted on average the top 25% of the cognitive ability distribution in their local area (Bolton, 2017). Entry tests consisted of different modules, including mathematics, English and verbal and non-verbal reasoning. The test was usually given to primary schools by LEAs on a given day with no prior notice. Grammar places were then allocated according to test scores, capacity constraints, proximity and other considerations. Pupils not passing the exam attended secondary modern schools, less academically demanding, geared towards trades. A third type, technical schools were for vocational training, did not require an exam and were not prevalent.

Dissatisfaction with the allocation system in state schools in 1965 led the Labour government to promote a phase-out of the selective schooling system (Kerckhoff, 1996). LEAs were encouraged to present plans to create comprehensive schools that catered for all abilities or to convert existing grammar

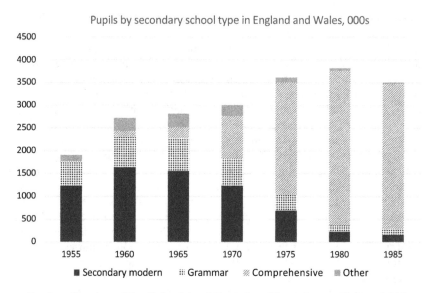

Fig. 1. Number of Pupils by School Type Over Time. *Source:* Bolton (2012). Technical schools included in 'Other'.

schools to comprehensives. Due its non-compulsory nature, the phase-out was gradual (see Fig. 1) and generally slower in areas with a Conservative political majority. In 1998, with the School Standards and Framework Act, the Labour government outlawed the establishment of any new schools that selected pupils by ability. At the time of writing, 163 grammar schools exist in England, attended by approximately 167,000 pupils, while Welsh schools are wholly comprehensive (Bolton, 2017). Selective schooling has recently gained policy attention with the Selective Schools Expansion Fund, launched in 2018, the first phase of which funded expansion projects in 16 existing grammar schools (UK Department for Education, 2019).

The 1960s reform in England and Wales offers an opportunity to evaluate long-term effects of the transition from a selective to a non-selective secondary schooling system. Yet, the lack of a clear roll-out of the reform has made it difficult to isolate the effect of school type on individual outcomes from other confounding factors, particularly individual ability or parental investments. The literature has dealt with this issue in a number of ways, mainly with regard to the effects on earnings and educational achievement. Using NCDS data, Galindo-Rueda and Vignoles (2005) estimate the effect of comprehensive attendance on test scores at age 16, by controlling for prior test scores, in a so-called value-added approach (Todd & Wolpin, 2003), and using instrumental variables (IV) methods. Their results suggest that the comprehensive reform reduced educational achievement for more able children only. The validity of this type of analysis was put under scrutiny by Manning and Pischke (2006), who criticise value-added approaches, comparing outcomes for pupils in selective and comprehensive areas (also found in Harmon and Walker (2000), Jesson (2000) and Kerckhoff (1986), among others). They argue that adding pre-secondary school outcomes as controls is not sufficient to remove endogeneity, since the two groups are too fundamentally different. This is taken as evidence against their results, a conclusion later endorsed by Bonhomme and Sauder (2011), who find that, when using a difference-in-differences approach to correct for unobservables, the effect of selective schooling on test scores in the NCDS cohort disappears.

A number of studies have used alternative methods that are more robust to the criticisms advanced above. Maurin and McNally (2009) use two cohorts of individuals born 12 years apart to compare the effects of selective and non-selective systems of education in England. They find that while attending grammar school is linked to better individual outcomes, the transition to non-selective schooling of the 1960s led to an increase in average educational outcomes, with larger benefits observed for lower socio-economic status (SES) individuals. Burgess et al. (2017) analyse the effects of selection both within selective areas and across areas with different levels of selectivity. Within selective areas, grammar attendance increases pupils' chances of accessing and completing higher education. Secondly, by matching selective and non-selective areas to ensure similarity in area characteristics, they find that high-ability children who do not get into top-tier schools do worse in selective areas. They also show that access to grammar schools is linked to higher socio-economic family background restricting social mobility. Burgess et al. (2020) investigate the impact of selective schooling on area earnings distributions, finding that inequality in average hourly wage is significantly higher in selective areas.

Another strand of the literature has used regression discontinuity methods, estimating the effect of the upper academic track, based on pupils scoring close to the entry cut-off. Using data for the East Riding of Yorkshire, a region in the United Kingdom, Clark (2010) finds small effects of attending grammar school on test scores, while a slightly larger and positive effect is observed for university enrolment. Del Bono and Clark (2016) estimate the impact of Scottish elite schools on educational attainment, income and fertility for the marginal student. Elite schools increase several measures of educational attainment, while small effects on labour market outcomes (positive) and fertility (negative) are found in women, but not in men. Guyon et al. (2012) evaluate the effects of an expansion of grammar school places in Northern Ireland and find that it increased average educational outcomes when considering the whole distribution. However, the expansion also decreased average outcomes for non-grammar school pupils.

Health effects of the comprehensive reform are somewhat less explored in the literature. Jones et al. (2012) find that the association of school type with self-reported health outcomes in NCDS is mostly insignificant when accounting for pre-school characteristics. Further, Jones et al. (2011) evaluate the impact of educational attainment and school attributes on self-reported health behaviours and outcomes in NCDS. They implement a combination of coarsened exact and propensity score matching at the individual level to make pupils more comparable across selective and non-selective system. Although they do not directly look at the impact of type of school on outcomes, they find a stronger association of educational attainment with health behaviours for pupils in low-ability schools and with mental health in high-ability schools. In a more recent study using the NCDS, Basu et al. (2018) explore the effect of selective versus comprehensive schooling on three dimensions of adult health and on smoking. They focus on understanding heterogeneity by ability, by estimating marginal treatment effects along the cognitive ability distribution. Using percentage of comprehensive schools in the individual's LEA in 1969 as a continuous instrument, they find a negative effect of the move to comprehensive schools on depression, magnified for individuals with lower non-cognitive skills. Overall, the literature indicates that accounting for differences in prior ability is key to estimating an unbiased effect of selective schooling.

3. DATA

The NCDS follows the lives of a cohort of individuals born in England, Scotland and Wales in a single week in March 1958. The study started at birth with a sample of over 17,000 individuals, 98% of those born in that week. Following the birth survey, 9 further sweeps have been undertaken at ages 7, 11, 16, 23, 33, 42, 46, 50 and 55, plus the collection of biomedical samples and data at age 45. Approximately, 9,000 were retained at the 2013 wave (Brown et al., 2016). Due to differences in the schooling systems between countries, we only include individuals going to school in England and Wales in the analysis (Welsh individuals overall represent under 5% of our sample). The key variables are described below.

3.1 Pre-Treatment Characteristics

Detailed information from the first three waves of the survey allows us to control for a broad set of pre-secondary schooling characteristics, responsible for the underlying differences cited as the main sources of selection bias when estimating the effect of school quality (Manning & Pischke, 2006). In addition to individual characteristics, family background covariates include mother's interest in child's education (expressed on a 0–4 scale), father's employment status and SES, family composition, financial hardship and council housing during childhood. Rich information is available on infant and child health, which is likely to affect both schooling and long-term health outcomes. We group childhood health conditions from 12 categories under one single indicator of child morbidity, following previous literature (Jones et al., 2011; Power & Elliott, 2006). Maternal smoking during pregnancy, presence of chronic conditions in the family and hospital admissions up to age 7 are included to reflect health endowment. Data collected at age 11 also include whether the child goes to an independent primary school, child's happiness at school reported by parents, whether the child will go to school or study after minimum school-leaving age. Finally, local area characteristics, based on LEA of school attended in 1974, were retrieved from the 1971 Census.

3.2 School

The 1958 cohort started secondary school in 1969, during the transition to the comprehensive system, meaning cohort members experienced one of two different secondary school systems – selective and non-selective. Fig. 2 shows selectivity by LEA at the time, which is inversely proportional to the percentage of comprehensive pupils. Information on the type of secondary school attended at age 16 is retrieved from NCDS wave 3. Schools are classified as grammar (attended by 10% of the NCDS cohort); secondary modern (20.6%); comprehensive (46.6%); non-LEA (20%), including academies, free schools, independent schools; technical (0.5%); and others (2.2%) (including all age and special needs). We consider

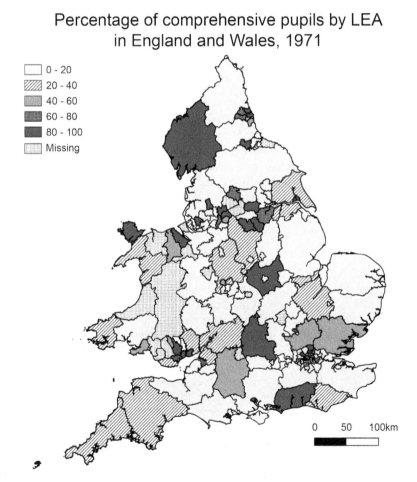

Fig. 2. Selectivity by LEA in 1970. LEAs With Lower Percentages of Comprehensive Pupils Are More Selective and Vice Versa. *Source:* Byrne and Williamson (1976) and Comprehensive School Committee (1971).

attendance for the first three categories of state schools, leaving a sample of 7,694 individuals: 1,040 grammar, 1,991 secondary modern and 4,663 comprehensive pupils. The data on LEA of the school were obtained under special licence.

3.3 Ability

Cognitive skills were assessed through numeracy, reading, verbal and non-verbal tests at ages 7, 11 and 16. Tests were administered during primary, just before secondary and just after secondary school attendance, respectively. Following existing literature, we group test scores to obtain three indicators for cognitive ability, one for each age, by implementing principal component analysis (PCA) (Cawley et al., 1997; Galindo-Rueda & Vignoles, 2005; Jones et al., 2011). For simplicity of interpretation, we then convert the three PCA indices to variables bounded between 0 and 1. As noted by Basu et al. (2018) and Jones et al. (2011), age 11 tests closely resemble the three components of the 11-plus: mathematics, reading, verbal and non-verbal reasoning. We additionally construct a cognitive rank variable, ranking NCDS individuals by their measured cognitive ability at age 11. This is calculated separately for children attending the selective system (grammar and secondary modern schools) and the mixed-ability system (comprehensive schools). Finally, pre-secondary school non-cognitive skills are proxied by grouping teachers' answers on 12 child behaviour dimensions, measured according to the Bristol Social Adjustment Guide (BSAG), administered at age 11. The score is converted to a variable bounded between 0 and 1, so that it is increasing in non-cognitive skills. Due to the way the questionnaire was designed, its distribution is highly skewed towards the right, indicating no behavioural problems.

3.4 Outcomes

3.4.1 Well-Being and Labour Market Measures

In order to assess short-term impact of secondary schooling, we look at aspirations related to school and work measured at age 16, just after secondary school, as potential determinants of future achievements. School aspirations are a dummy variable equal to 1 if the individual intends to stay at school beyond 16, the minimum school-leaving age. Work aspirations are also a dummy variable, indicating whether the individual aspires to personal and intellectual growth through a job. Adult well-being outcomes include life satisfaction, self-efficacy and positive feelings about one's job. These are based on the age 33 survey and are all constructed via PCA, grouping answers to several questions. Contact with police and drug use are retrieved at age 45. The crime dummy indicates whether the individual had any significant contact with police (i.e. whether ever moved by police, received a warning, got arrested, cautioned or found guilty). The drug-use dummy takes value 1 if the individual has ever tried any illegal drug. We also examine two labour market outcomes, each measured twice, at ages 33 and 50. The first is individual gross hourly wage, imputed from weekly, monthly or bi-monthly usual gross pay and hours worked per week, and then log-transformed for regression analysis. The second is a dummy indicating whether the individual is in employment at the time.

3.4.2 Survey Health Measures

The long-term impact of selective schooling is also assessed on a broad range of health dimensions. Self-rated health (SAH) is measured on a 5-point scale: Excellent (1), Good (2), Fair (3), Poor (4) and Very poor (5). A 9-item malaise questionnaire offers a measure of ill-health and discomfort, both physical and mental. For ease of interpretation, in regressions, we use binary variables equalling 1 for excellent or good SAH and for low malaise (scores 0, 1 or 2), measured at age 50. Mental ill-health is also measured by a summary score ranging from 0 to 30 based on 10 different areas: anxiety, appetite, concentration/ forgetfulness, depression, depressive ideas, fatigue, irritability, panic, phobias and sleep, all measured at age 45.

3.4.3 Biometric Health Measures

A body mass index (BMI) measure was constructed as weight in kilograms, divided by squared height in metres, using weight and height measured by a nurse at age 45. A healthy adult BMI ranges from 18.5 to 25 kg/m^2. Individuals with BMI < 18.5 would be classed as underweight, while individuals with 25 < BMI ≥ 30 would be overweight or obese if BMI > 30. High BMI values are correlated with higher risk of cardiovascular disease, stroke and type 2 diabetes (World Health Organisation, 2017).

Blood samples taken at age 45 were used to measure lipids, clotting factors and inflammatory markers. Our outcomes include C-reactive protein (CRP) (mg/ L), fibrinogen (g/L) and triglyceride (mmo/L) levels, as well as cholesterol ratio (mmo/L), constructed as total cholesterol divided by high-density lipoprotein (HDL) cholesterol. All of these markers are positively linked to risk of cardio-vascular disease (Benzeval et al., 2014). CRP and fibrinogen are also associated with higher risk of chronic stress.

3.5 Attrition

A concern when analysing NCDS data is that attrition can be non-random, and we examine differences in average cohort members' characteristics and percent-ages attending each type of secondary school. Treatment status – school type – is observed at age 16. All analyses samples from age 16 onwards present hardly any differences in the average characteristics which provide reassurance that the sample composition does not vary systematically in relation to key characteristics after this point in time, which is in agreement with other literature (Case et al., 2005; Jones et al., 2011). An important feature is that the percentage of pupils attending each type of school does not vary over time.

4. METHODS

4.1 Empirical Framework

Secondary school type, S_i, is the key treatment of interest, and we assume it is a function of pupil's background, B_i, comprising family and individual characteristics, childhood abilities, A_i, and characteristics of the individual's LEA, such as supply of places by type of school, SU_i.

$$S_i = S(B_i, A_i, SU_i) \tag{1}$$

The production functions for adult health and well-being outcomes, Y_i, depend on background, pre-secondary school ability, type of school and local area characteristics. Importantly, we exclude from our framework any post-treatment variables, as these might bias treatment effect in the empirical estimation.

$$Y_i = Y(B_i, A_i, S_i(\cdot), LA_i) \tag{2}$$

In the model, background B_i and ability A_i enter both the school-assignment function, Eq. (1), and the outcome equation, Eq. (2). If there are unobserved factors correlated with either background or ability, the standard OLS estimator of the effect of S_i in the empirical estimation of Eq. (2) will be biased. This issue represents the main challenge for identification of treatment effect in our context. In principle, establishing causal effects requires comparing treated individuals with credible counterfactuals (Heckman et al., 1997; Rubin, 1974). In this spirit, we split the sample into two, thus estimating two separate treatment effects.

Following the Neyman–Rubin framework, we denote two possible counterfactual outcomes for individual i as Y_i^0 in the absence of treatment and Y_i^1 with treatment. On the one hand, we estimate the effect of going to grammar, compared to comprehensive, by comparing outcomes for grammar pupils to their counterfactual. These are comprehensive pupils who would have gone to grammar, had they gone through selection. The effect is an average treatment effect on the treated (ATT), conditional on control individuals providing a reliable counterfactual group:

$$\text{ATT}^G = E[Y_i^1 - Y_i^0 | G_i = 1]. \tag{3}$$

Similarly, we estimate the effect of going to secondary modern, compared to their counterfactual, comprehensive pupils who would have attended secondary modern, had they experienced the selective system:

$$\text{ATT}^{SM} = E[Y_i^1 - Y_i^0 | SM_i = 1]. \tag{4}$$

Since $E[Y_i^0 | G_i = 1]$ and $E[Y_i^0 | SM_i = 1]$ are never observed in practice, we construct two counterfactual groups, one for each treatment. We do this via entropy balancing, aimed at increasing balance in observable baseline characteristics between the treatment and control groups (Angrist, 1998). This first step is followed by parametric regressions based on the model expressed by Eq. (2) and estimated using the weights obtained in the balancing procedure. The advantage of this approach is that it yields 'doubly robust' estimates: treatment effects will be consistently estimated if the first step achieves balance, even though subsequent parametric models are not well specified, or if balancing is incorrect, while parametric models are well specified. The main remaining concern is related to unobservables, possibly confounding the relationship of interest. Estimation of an unbiased treatment effect in this context relies on the conditional independence assumption (CIA), expressed as $Y_i^j \perp S_i | \mathbf{X}_i$, with $j = 0, 1$. This assumption holds if either all characteristics correlated to both treatment and outcomes are observed and controlled for, or by balancing on the observed characteristics, we also achieve balance on the unobserved characteristics. We test this assumption in the placebo procedure illustrated in Section 5.4.

Entropy balancing is implemented for the two separate samples. The first sample includes grammar and comprehensive pupils (GC sample hereafter), with grammar school attendance as treatment. The second comprises secondary modern and comprehensive pupils (SMC sample hereafter), with secondary modern attendance as treatment. Developed by Hainmueller (2012), the procedure assigns weights to the observations in the control group according to pre-specified conditions, in order to emulate the treatment group in terms of the moments and co-moments of specific covariates. The covariates for the balancing procedure are selected based on their expected relationship to both treatment and outcomes (Caliendo & Kopeinig, 2008). The methodological literature highlights that this choice implies a trade-off between bias and efficiency (Imbens, 2004; Rubin & Thomas, 1996). Balancing on a variable that is related to treatment but not outcome will increase the variance of the effect estimate; conversely, balancing on a variable related to outcome but not treatment will bias the estimate. In order to ensure that the variables are not influenced by treatment, which would also bias effect estimates, only pre-secondary schooling variables are used. We take cognitive test scores at age 7, while non-cognitive skills, relative rank by cognitive score, mother's interest in child education and a dummy for high or middle-high father's SES are all measured at age 11, prior to starting secondary school. We prefer age 7 to age 11 cognitive ability scores, since the latter could be biased upwards in selective areas because of 'coaching effects' (Jones et al., 2011), whereby students in selective LEAs score higher because they have been coached for this particular kind of test in view of the imminent 11-plus exam, meaning that age 11 scores do not reflect ability in the same way for pupils from selective and non-selective areas. Since the age 11 rank variable is constructed separately for selective (grammar and secondary modern school) and non-selective (comprehensive) pupils, the bias of coaching effects does not carry over to this variable. By balancing mean, variance and skewness of the five included covariates, as well as their pairwise interactions, we achieved close balance, without compromising the feasibility of the minimisation procedure required for the entropy balancing.

Weights obtained from entropy balancing are then applied to the control observations in parametric regressions. In addition to the five key covariates used

18   *Tracking Pupils Into Adulthood*

in the balancing procedure, we control for the larger set of pre-treatment covariates listed in Table 1. Assuming for each sample, $j = GC, SMC$, a constant average treatment effect α^j, we estimate the following by ordinary least squares (OLS):

$$Y_i^j = \beta_0^j + \alpha^j S_i^j + \beta_1^j \mathbf{A}_i + \beta_2^j \mathbf{B}_i + \beta_3^j \mathbf{LA}_i + \epsilon_i^j, \tag{5}$$

where the binary treatment variable S_i is equal to 1 for grammar attendance in the GC sample, or for secondary modern attendance in the SMC sample, and 0 for comprehensive attendance. Covariates are the vector of ability $\mathbf{A}_i$, including age 7 cognitive skills, age 11 non-cognitive skills and age 11 relative cognitive ability (the rank variable); the vector of individual background characteristics $\mathbf{B}_i$, including sex, ethnicity, family SES, childhood health endowment and primary school characteristics; and finally local authority characteristics $\mathbf{LA}_i$, while ϵ_i is a random error term.

Table 1. Descriptive Statistics for All Covariates by Type of Secondary School.

	Grammar		Comprehensive		Secondary Modern	
	Mean	SD	Mean	SD	Mean	SD
Ability						
Cognitive skills age 7	0.76	0.10	0.61	0.16	0.59	0.15
Non-cognitive skills age 11	0.94	0.08	0.88	0.12	0.86	0.13
Relative cognitive ability age 11	0.79	0.15	0.50	0.29	0.37	0.22
Background Characteristics						
Female	0.55	0.50	0.48	0.50	0.49	0.50
Whether first born	0.36	0.48	0.31	0.46	0.30	0.46
Born in Wales	0.03	0.18	0.09	0.28	0.03	0.16
Not white	0.02	0.14	0.04	0.20	0.04	0.20
Two or more siblings	0.65	0.48	0.73	0.45	0.75	0.43
Twin or triplet	0.01	0.11	0.02	0.15	0.03	0.17
No mother	0.00	0.06	0.01	0.08	0.01	0.09
No father	0.03	0.16	0.04	0.20	0.04	0.20
Family Socio-Economic Background						
Mother interest in child education	2.70	0.77	2.02	1.03	1.88	1.03
Father's SES high/middle-high	0.32	0.47	0.13	0.34	0.11	0.31
Father unemployed	0.01	0.09	0.03	0.17	0.04	0.18
Father job skilled/professional	0.54	0.50	0.47	0.50	0.47	0.50
Council housing	0.19	0.39	0.39	0.49	0.39	0.49
Free school meals	0.03	0.16	0.09	0.29	0.10	0.30
Health Endowment						
Maternal smoking during pregnancy	1.37	0.78	1.59	0.92	1.60	0.93
Child morbidity index	0.06	0.03	0.06	0.04	0.06	0.04
Chronic condition in the family	0.11	0.31	0.15	0.36	0.15	0.36

CHIARA PASTORE ET AL.

Table 1. *(Continued)*

	Grammar		Comprehensive		Secondary Modern	
	Mean	SD	Mean	SD	Mean	SD
Child in Primary School						
Unhappy at school	0.03	0.18	0.07	0.26	0.07	0.26
Independent primary school	0.04	0.19	0.01	0.10	0.01	0.09
Child plans to study after school	0.43	0.50	0.23	0.42	0.17	0.37
LEA Characteristics (1971 Census)						
Proportion comprehensive pupils in LEA	0.29	0.25	0.52	0.32	0.24	0.21
County level proportion unemp. male	0.04	0.02	0.04	0.02	0.04	0.02
Council housing	0.28	0.08	0.29	0.08	0.28	0.08
Owner-occupiers	0.49	0.16	0.48	0.14	0.52	0.11
Manufacturing employee	0.34	0.12	0.36	0.11	0.36	0.10
Agriculture employee	0.02	0.04	0.02	0.03	0.02	0.03
Lone parent families	0.09	0.02	0.10	0.02	0.09	0.02
UK born men	0.91	0.06	0.91	0.06	0.92	0.05
Professional/managerial HOH	0.18	0.08	0.16	0.07	0.16	0.06
Non-manual HOH	0.22	0.07	0.21	0.06	0.20	0.05
Skilled manual HOH	0.27	0.09	0.28	0.08	0.29	0.07
Semi-skilled manual HOH	0.11	0.04	0.12	0.04	0.12	0.03
Non-skilled manual HOH	0.07	0.02	0.07	0.02	0.07	0.02
County borough in 1971 census	0.26	0.44	0.34	0.47	0.27	0.44
London borough in 1971 census	0.11	0.31	0.10	0.29	0.04	0.20
Observations	1,040		4,663		1991	

Source: NCDS. The three ability variables are bound between 0 and 1. Mother interest in child education is on a scale from 1-Little interest to 4-Over concerned. Maternal smoking during pregnancy is on a scale from 1-Non-smoker to 4-Heavy smoker.

4.2 Heterogeneity Analyses and Robustness Checks

We implement a number of additional specifications to further explore the relationship between school type and outcomes and the robustness of our main estimates. First, we include interactions of the treatment and ability variables, in order to explore heterogeneity of treatment effect by cognitive and non-cognitive ability. We estimate:

$$Y_i^j = \gamma_0^j + \alpha'^j S_i^j + \gamma_1^j S_i^j \times C_i^{\text{top}50\%} + \gamma_2^j S_i^j \times NC_i^{\text{top}50\%} + \mathbf{X}' \gamma_3^j + \epsilon_i^{'j} \quad (6)$$

where, for ease of notation, X is the vector of all individual characteristics as in Eq. (5), including the cognitive and non-cognitive skills indicators. The estimated coefficients γ_1^j and γ_2^j reflect the effect of treatment j, compared to comprehensive, for individuals in the top 50% of the ability distribution. We further estimate similar models interacting the school type indicator with sex and high father's SES.

A second additional specification distinguishes between comprehensive schools that were formerly grammar or secondary modern versus comprehensive that were purpose-built. Given the NCDS cohort entered secondary school in 1969, only 4 years after the phase-out of selective schooling, we want to ensure that the effect estimate of school type is not confounded by comprehensive schools that were transitioning from their grammar or secondary modern origin. Moreover, school type is retrieved in 1974, and therefore, schools could potentially have transitioned to comprehensive status between NCDS cohort member entry and data retrieval. For analysis with the GC sample, we set grammar as the base category and two dummy treatment variable indicators: one for attending a comprehensive that is a former grammar CF_i and one for attending a purpose-built comprehensive CB_i. A similar approach is then implemented with the SMC sample as well. We estimate:

$$Y_i^j = \delta_0^j + \delta_1^j CF_i + \delta_2^j CB_i + \mathbf{X}'\delta_3^j + \xi_i^j \tag{7}$$

by OLS, where X is again the vector of individual characteristics. We now distinguish between the effect of attending a comprehensive that could still present characteristics typical of a grammar (or secondary modern) (δ_1^j) and the effect of attending a purpose-built comprehensive (δ_2^j), compared to the base category of attending grammar (or secondary modern).

In a third check, we only include purely selective and purely comprehensive LEAs in the estimation of Eq. (5). We define purely selective LEAs as those with no comprehensive places in 1971, as recorded in Comprehensive School Committee (1971), and purely comprehensive as those with 100% of places in comprehensive schools. Although the estimation sample shrinks significantly, the aim is to provide the analysis for areas where it can be ruled out that comprehensive schools experienced the same 'cream-skimming' of pupils and resources as secondary modern schools.

A final robustness check follows the placebo test procedure implemented by Manning and Pischke (2006). Their procedure consists of estimating the effect of type of secondary school for both pre- and post-secondary school maths test scores, at age 11 and 16, respectively. It is a placebo test because we would not expect secondary school type to be a significant predictor of scores prior to treatment, unless the model is misspecified or the estimation strategy is unable to prevent bias.

5. RESULTS

5.1 Characteristics by Type of School

Average individual characteristics prior to starting secondary school, displayed in Table 1, present some differences by type of school. The largest gap is observed between grammar pupils and the other two groups, while average traits for comprehensive and secondary modern pupils are more similar. Future grammar, comprehensive and secondary modern pupils differ most notably in the three

CHIARA PASTORE ET AL.

measures of ability. Grammar pupils have the highest cognitive and non-cognitive abilities, followed by comprehensive and then by secondary modern pupils. On average, grammar pupils are also more advantaged in terms of socio-economic background. Average local area characteristics are very similar across the three groups, somewhat reassuringly for the identification of an unbiased treatment effect. Table 2 summarises all outcome variables used in the analysis. On average, grammar pupils display higher well-being, better labour market outcomes and better health, while secondary modern students fare worst out of the three groups. The only exception is life satisfaction, where comprehensive pupils score highest and grammar pupils score lowest.

Table 2. Descriptive Statistics for Outcomes by Secondary School Attended.

	Grammar		Comprehensive		Secondary Modern		Range	
	Mean	SD	Mean	SD	Mean	SD	Min	Max
Well-Being Measures								
School aspirations age 16 (dummy)	0.68	0.47	0.28	0.45	0.18	0.39	0	1
Work aspirations age 16 (dummy)	0.93	0.26	0.79	0.41	0.76	0.43	0	1
Life satisfaction age 33 (PCA)	−0.04	1.40	0.04	1.44	−0.02	1.49	−8	2
Self-efficacy age 33 (PCA)	0.21	1.17	−0.02	1.34	−0.06	1.34	−5	1
Positive about job age 33 (PCA)	0.37	1.20	−0.03	1.41	−0.15	1.44	−5	2
Contact with police age 45 (dummy)	0.14	0.35	0.18	0.38	0.18	0.38		
Ever tried illegal drugs age 45	0.19	0.39	0.17	0.38	0.17	0.37	0	1
Labour Outcomes								
Hourly wage at 33	9.33	12.39	7.19	12.52	6.42	10.86	0	357
Employed at 33	0.84	0.37	0.79	0.40	0.80	0.40	0	1
Hourly wage at 50	22.30	30.09	16.33	12.91	15.16	10.97	0	462
Employed at 50	0.92	0.27	0.86	0.35	0.85	0.36	0	1
Survey Health Measures								
Excellent or very good SAH age 50	0.62	0.49	0.52	0.50	0.48	0.50	0	1
Low malaise age 50	0.81	0.39	0.77	0.42	0.76	0.43	0	1
Mental ill-health score age 45	3.02	4.17	3.40	4.68	3.40	4.63	0	30
Biometric Health Measures								
BMI measured age 45	26.41	4.61	27.56	4.88	27.67	5.16	17	64
Cholesterol ratio mmo/L age 45	3.80	1.15	3.97	1.17	4.07	1.18	2	12
Triglyceride mmo/L age 45	1.88	1.46	2.06	1.61	2.15	1.71	0	27
Fibrinogen g/L age 45	2.88	0.56	2.98	0.63	3.00	0.62	1	7
C-reactive protein mg/L age 45	1.84	3.35	2.27	4.93	2.26	4.26	0	152
Observations	1,040		4,663		1991			

Source: NCDS. Details on the use of PCA to construct outcomes can be obtained from the authors. For the wage outcome, we excluded from the analysis 13 individuals with weekly income above £10,000. Healthy ranges for the biometric markers are as follows: < 25 for BMI, < 5 for cholesterol ratio, < 1.7 for triglycerides, 1.9–4.3 for fibrinogen and < 5 for CRP (Fuggle, 2018).

Table 3. Pre- and Post-Matching Moments of Key Covariates.

	Grammar			Comprehensive					
				Raw			Balanced		
	$N = 1{,}040$			$N = 4{,}663$			$N = 4{,}663$		
	Unweighted			Unweighted			Weighted		
	Mean	Var	Skew	Mean	Var	Skew	Mean	Var	Skew
Cognitive skills	0.763	0.010	−0.467	0.618	0.025	−0.404	0.763	0.010	−0.469
Non-cognitive skills	0.940	0.006	−2.288	0.882	0.015	−1.513	0.940	0.006	−2.286
Relative cognitive score	0.795	0.021	−0.944	0.507	0.082	−0.029	0.795	0.021	−0.946
Mother's interest in edu	2.697	0.585	−1.843	2.027	1.057	−0.490	2.697	0.585	−1.842
High father's SES dummy	0.822	0.146	−1.685	0.692	0.213	−0.831	0.822	0.146	−1.683
	Secondary Modern			Comprehensive					
				Raw			Balanced		
	$N = 1991$			$N = 4{,}663$			$N = 4{,}663$		
	Unweighted			Unweighted			Weighted		
	Mean	Var	Skew	Mean	Var	Skew	Mean	Var	Skew
Cognitive skills	0.590	0.022	−0.308	0.618	0.025	−0.404	0.590	0.022	−0.308
Non-cognitive skills	0.867	0.016	−1.363	0.882	0.015	−1.513	0.867	0.016	−1.362
Relative cognitive score	0.376	0.047	0.363	0.507	0.082	−0.029	0.376	0.047	0.364
Mother's interest in edu	1.908	1.065	−0.317	2.027	1.057	−0.490	1.908	1.065	−0.317
High father's SES dummy	0.671	0.221	−0.728	0.692	0.213	−0.831	0.671	0.221	−0.728

Source: NCDS. The top panel refers to the GC sample, while the bottom panel to the SMC sample. Mean, variance and skewness of the pairwise interactions of the five covariates listed are also balanced (not shown). Var = variance; Skew = skewness.

5.2 Selective Schooling and Long-Term Outcomes

We summarise the key contribution of entropy balancing results in Table 3, showing the first three moments of the five key covariates of interest, before and after balancing, separately for the GC and SMC samples. The leftmost columns in both the top and bottom panels show mean, variance and skewness for the treated group, while the three central columns show mean, variance and skewness for the unbalanced comprehensive sample. The last three columns show weighted moments for control individuals from the comprehensive sample, using the entropy balancing weights. In both cases, the weighting procedure achieves almost perfect balance on mean, variance and skewness of key covariates, so that these are similar in the control groups to their respective treated group. The pairwise interactions between covariates are not shown, but close balance is also achieved on their mean, variance and skewness, increasing confidence that the joint distribution of these variables will be more similar in the two groups after matching. Fig. 3 shows density kernel estimates for the three ability measures before and after balancing, separately for the GC and SMC samples. In both samples, applying balancing weights to comprehensive pupils yields a density that resembles more closely that of the treated group, thus strengthening credibility of comprehensive pupils as counterfactual groups for our two separate treatment effects.

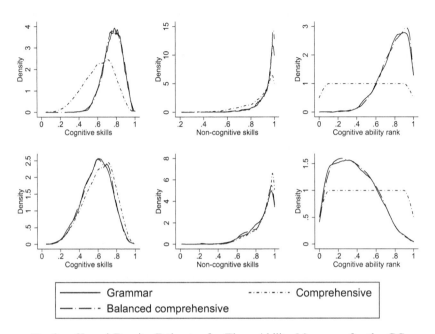

Fig. 3. Kernel Density Estimates for Three Ability Measures, for the GC Sample (Top Row) and the SMC Sample (Bottom Row). Mother's interest in child education and father's SES are not shown, as they are discrete variables. the dashed line (large dash) illustrates density kernels for comprehensive pupils, balanced with the weights obtained via entropy matching so that they are more comparable to treated individuals.

Tables 4–6 report results for the main outcome regressions estimated for the matched GC and SMC samples separately. All continuous variables are standardised for ease of comparison except for logged hourly wage, which can be interpreted in terms of percentages. All models for binary variables are estimated via probit regressions, and marginal effects are shown. Although we only show the coefficients on the treatment and ability variables, all models control for the covariates described in Table 1. Table 4 shows that, for the high cognitive ability sample, attending a grammar school significantly increases school aspirations, the probability that individuals intend to stay at school beyond age 16, by approximately 13 percentage points (pp), but it decreases adult life satisfaction, by 0.13 standard deviations (SD), compared to comprehensive attendance. For the lower cognitive ability sample (lower panel), secondary modern attendance decreases the intention to stay at school beyond minimum leaving age (4 pp), while it increases self-efficacy at 33 (0.08 SD), compared to comprehensive attendance. In Table 5, showing estimation results for labour market outcomes, grammar is

Table 4. Effect of Type of School on Well-being Outcomes.

	School Aspiration	Work Aspiration	Life Satisfaction	Self-Efficacy	Job Positivity	Crime	Drugs
Grammar vs Comprehensive (High Ability)							
Grammar	0.1259***	0.0130	−0.1307**	−0.0535	−0.0014	−0.0142	−0.0103
	(0.0165)	(0.0111)	(0.0460)	(0.0371)	(0.0474)	(0.0171)	(0.0183)
Cognitive Skills	0.1375	−0.0625	−0.0561	0.5919**	0.2390	0.0706	−0.0051
	(0.0943)	(0.0557)	(0.2744)	(0.2164)	(0.2448)	(0.0971)	(0.0911)
Non-cognitive Skills	0.1692	0.0615	1.1847**	1.1133***	0.0421	−0.0450	−0.3070**
	(0.1185)	(0.0663)	(0.3625)	(0.3228)	(0.2596)	(0.0964)	(0.0983)
Relative cogn. Ability	0.6918***	0.1832***	−0.1145	0.3567*	0.8344***	−0.0783	0.1491*
	(0.0623)	(0.0420)	(0.1602)	(0.1622)	(0.1550)	(0.0587)	(0.0608)
Observations	4,197	4,156	3,131	3,083	3,145	3,277	3,279
F			5.3818	7.7965	14.2346		
χ^2 statistic	305.38	52.28				63.44	65.97
Secondary Modern vs Comprehensive (Low Ability)							
Secondary Modern	−0.0420**	0.0179	−0.0069	0.0789*	0.0258	−0.0207	−0.0066
	(0.0129)	(0.0142)	(0.0439)	(0.0362)	(0.0389)	(0.0131)	(0.0142)
Cognitive Skills	0.0393	0.0315	0.2013	0.3840+	0.2571+	0.0840	0.1064*
	(0.0520)	(0.0569)	(0.1581)	(0.1947)	(0.1531)	(0.0551)	(0.0511)
Non-cognitive Skills	0.1413*	0.1341*	0.5838***	0.3905*	0.4602**	−0.1255*	−0.2386***
	(0.0553)	(0.0570)	(0.1631)	(0.1603)	(0.1426)	(0.0543)	(0.0572)
Relative cogn. Ability	0.3449***	0.4142***	−0.2027*	0.2248*	0.6090***	−0.0432	0.0329
	(0.0360)	(0.0413)	(0.0957)	(0.1095)	(0.1164)	(0.0429)	(0.0396)
Observations	4,872	4,818	3,588	3,535	3,597	3,777	3,779
F			5.7861	9.7086	20.4473		
χ^2 statistic	282.59	275.40				206.80	83.91

Source: NCDS. $^+p < 0.1$, $^*p < 0.05$, $^{**}p < 0.01$, $^{***}p < 0.001$. Standard errors clustered at LEA level in parentheses. The top panel is estimated on the entropy-balanced GC sample, while the bottom panel is estimated on the entropy-balanced SMC sample. All continuous outcomes are standardised. Binary outcomes are estimated via probit models, for which marginal effects are displayed. All control variables are included.

CHIARA PASTORE ET AL.

Table 5. Effect of Type of School on Labour Outcomes.

	Log Hourly Wage Age 33	Employed Age 33	Log Hourly Wage Age 50	Employed Age 50
Grammar vs Comprehensive (High Ability)				
Grammar	0.0588[+]	0.0321[+]	0.0879[+]	0.0199
	(0.0308)	(0.0164)	(0.0509)	(0.0144)
Cognitive	0.0082	0.0783	−0.0131	0.0676
Skills	(0.1666)	(0.0970)	(0.2810)	(0.0856)
Non-cognitive	0.4218*	0.0841	0.7541*	0.0963
Skills	(0.2046)	(0.1194)	(0.2990)	(0.0766)
Relative cogn.	0.6533***	0.0585	0.7986***	−0.0165
Ability	(0.1181)	(0.0633)	(0.1563)	(0.0459)
Observations	2,460	3,323	1,551	2,852
F	27.2839		9.6002	
χ^2 statistic		189.20		47.44
Secondary Modern vs Comprehensive (Low Ability)				
Secondary	0.0474	0.0338*	0.0827*	−0.0205
Modern	(0.0324)	(0.0154)	(0.0388)	(0.0132)
Cognitive	0.1868*	0.0422	0.0552	0.1155*
Skills	(0.0835)	(0.0646)	(0.1315)	(0.0550)
Non-cognitive	0.2504*	0.1375**	−0.0229	0.1818***
Skills	(0.1091)	(0.0495)	(0.1808)	(0.0550)
Relative cogn.	0.3710***	0.0566	0.4450***	0.1102**
Ability	(0.0642)	(0.0421)	(0.0795)	(0.0376)
Observations	2,766	3,821	1,689	3,230
F	29.7419		20.8571	
χ^2 statistic		268.53		110.05

Source: NCDS. [+] $p < 0.1$, *$p < 0.05$, **$p < 0.01$, ***$p < 0.001$. Standard errors clustered at LEA level in parentheses. The top panel is estimated on the entropy-balanced GC sample, while the bottom panel is estimated on the entropy-balanced SMC sample. Binary outcomes are estimated via probit models, for which marginal effects are displayed. All control variables are included.

significant at 10% for both age 33 and 50 log-transformed wages, raising average hourly wage by 6 pp and 9 pp compared to attending comprehensive. Grammar also increases the probability of being employed at age 33 by 3 pp, compared to similarly able comprehensive pupils. Secondary modern attendance increases average wage at age 50 by roughly 8 pp and the probability of being employed at age 33 by 3 pp. Table 6 displays results for health outcomes. Grammar attendance is only significantly related to BMI, decreasing it by 0.1 SD, compared to comprehensive, while secondary modern, in the bottom panel, is only significantly and positively related to cholesterol ratio (p-value < 0.1).

Table 6. Effect of Type of School on Health Outcomes.

	High SAH	Low Malaise	Mental Ill-Health	BMI	Chol. ratio	Triglyc.	CRP	Fibrin.
Grammar vs Comprehensive (High Ability)								
Grammar	−0.0055	0.0170	0.0122	−0.1056*	0.0385	−0.0069	0.0031	0.0133
	(0.0301)	(0.0210)	(0.0486)	(0.0528)	(0.0501)	(0.0476)	(0.0449)	(0.0587)
Cognitive	0.2267[+]	0.0699	−0.1821	−0.6314**	−0.5410[+]	−0.5765[+]	−0.1312	−0.0597
Skills	(0.1257)	(0.1107)	(0.2928)	(0.2337)	(0.3019)	(0.2984)	(0.2029)	(0.2834)
Non-cognitive	0.2213	0.0946	−0.6169*	−0.4083	−0.3525	−0.2488	−0.2157	−0.5401[+]
Skills	(0.1558)	(0.1233)	(0.2917)	(0.2819)	(0.3540)	(0.3497)	(0.2149)	(0.3140)
Relative cogn.	0.0948	0.1047	0.2404	0.0119	−0.2163	−0.0790	−0.4670*	−0.4220[+]
Ability	(0.1144)	(0.0764)	(0.1821)	(0.2003)	(0.1811)	(0.2501)	(0.1910)	(0.2408)
Observations	2,875	2,854	2,805	2,759	2,327	2,333	2,302	2,295
F			9.4540	4.9628	56.5408	47.2199	3.5059	3.8530
χ^2 statistic	52.8400	56.4290						
Secondary Modern vs Comprehensive (Low Ability)								
Secondary	−0.0034	0.0060	−0.0302	0.0355	0.0674[+]	0.0241	−0.0231	−0.0281
Modern	(0.0237)	(0.0191)	(0.0372)	(0.0479)	(0.0405)	(0.0447)	(0.0477)	(0.0426)
Cognitive	0.0623	0.0398	−0.1485	−0.0862	−0.0261	−0.0826	−0.2524	−0.0479
Skills	(0.0831)	(0.0738)	(0.1620)	(0.1881)	(0.1991)	(0.2214)	(0.2128)	(0.1731)
Non-cognitive	0.3468***	0.3456***	−0.6103***	0.1171	−0.2685	−0.2160	0.1938	0.0904
Skills	(0.0857)	(0.0808)	(0.1639)	(0.1820)	(0.2452)	(0.2208)	(0.2016)	(0.1957)
Relative cogn.	0.1516**	0.1223**	−0.1603	−0.1411	−0.0989	−0.0803	−0.1599	−0.4420***
Ability	(0.0540)	(0.0466)	(0.1217)	(0.1315)	(0.1302)	(0.1096)	(0.1463)	(0.1183)
Observations	3,250	3,224	3,203	3,145	2,665	2,669	2,634	2,629
F			6.0568	6.2434	17.0289	25.9164	3.9511	6.0538
χ^2 statistic	109.2700	96.6975						

Source: NCDS. $^+ p < 0.1$, $^* p < 0.05$, $^{**} p < 0.01$, $^{***} p < 0.001$. Standard errors clustered at LEA level in parentheses. The top panel is estimated on the entropy-balanced GC sample, while the bottom panel is estimated on the entropy-balanced SMC sample. All continuous outcomes are standardised. Binary outcomes are estimated via probit models, for which marginal effects are displayed. All control variables are included. CHol. = cholesterol, Triglyc. = triglycerides, Fibrin. = fibrinogen.

The ability variables, on the other hand, display a significant association with most outcomes. In Table 4, for both the GC and SMC sample, higher cognitive ability at age 7 is linked to higher self-efficacy in adulthood (0.4–0.6 SD for a one-unit increase in cognitive ability). Age 7 cognitive skills are linked to employment outcomes in the low-ability sample (up to 18 pp increase in age 33 wages). Conversely, they display a significant link with lower biomarkers (BMI, cholesterol ratio and triglycerides), indicative of better health, in the high-ability sample only. In both samples, age 11 non-cognitive skills are linked with higher life satisfaction and self-efficacy (0.6–1.2 SD and 0.4–1.1 SD, respectively), and lower probability of drug use (24–30 pp). The association is stronger in magnitude for the GC sample, of higher cognitive ability. Non-cognitive skills are also significantly associated with the probability of aspiring to personal and intellectual growth at work (13 pp), job positivity (0.5 SD) and a lower probability of committing crime (24 pp) in the SMC sample only. Table 5 shows that non-cognitive ability is also positively and significantly associated with wages (up to 75 pp increase), and with the probability of employment (up to 18 pp). Further, non-cognitive skills are significantly related to better health in the SMC sample, with a 35 pp increase in the probabilities of scoring high self-assessed health and low malaise at age 50 and a reduction of 0.6 SD in mental health problems at age 45. Compared to the GC sample, this result may indicate that higher non-cognitive skills have a protective role for the health of pupils of lower average cognitive ability. Finally, age 11 cognitive ability rank is significantly and positively linked to positive school (35–70 pp increase) and work aspirations (18–41 pp) and job positivity (0.6–0.8 SD). Relative cognitive ability is significantly linked to wages, and coefficients are large, indicating increases of up to 80 pp in the GC sample and up to 44 pp in the SMC sample. Moving from the lowest to the highest rank of cognitive ability is also linked to a decrease in C-reactive protein (0.5 SD) and fibrinogen levels (0.4 SD) in the GC sample. In the SMC sample, higher cognitive rank is significantly associated with the probabilities of scoring high self-assessed health (15 pp increase), low malaise (12 pp increase) and lower fibrinogen levels (0.4 SD).

5.3 Heterogeneous Effects

Interacting treatment with high levels of cognitive and non-cognitive skills, as shown in Eq. (6), did not add any further insights to our main message. We only note that grammar appears to have a larger positive effect on school aspirations and wages for pupils in the bottom half of the cognitive ability distribution for the GC sample. Further interactions with sex indicate that the grammar advantage for school aspirations and probability of employment at the time only applied to boys, while the secondary modern disadvantage for these outcomes only applied to girls. Interactions with SES did not offer additional information.

Secondly, distinguishing between comprehensive schools by origin did not produce significantly different results from our main specification. The main insight is that the wage results are driven by differences between grammar/secondary modern schools and purpose-built comprehensive ones. Conversely, former grammar and

28   *Tracking Pupils Into Adulthood*

secondary modern converted into comprehensive did not produce significantly different wage outcomes in those early years of the transition.

Finally, we conducted a robustness test by including in the estimation procedure only LEAs that were purely selective or purely non-selective. In this further check, sample sizes shrunk significantly, but the main results still apply. Grammar attendance is linked to an increase in the probability of staying in school beyond minimum leaving age and to better employment outcomes (although with lower significance levels), as well as lower BMI. In this specification, coefficients are larger and grammar attendance is also linked to lower CRP and fibrinogen levels, indicative of good health. For secondary modern attendance, the link with school aspirations is negative as in the main specification, although not significant, and the positive links with self-efficacy and employment at age 33 are confirmed.

5.4 Falsification Tests

We conduct placebo checks in the spirit of Manning and Pischke's falsification test (Manning & Pischke, 2006).There are some differences in our procedure, compared to their approach: first, we implement the regressions separately for the GC and SMC samples; second, we include weights obtained by entropy balancing and the set of control variables used in our main specification; third, by varying the balancing algorithm, we try to assess the extent of the potential bias due to unobservables or misspecification. Following their paper, maths test scores are translated into a scale from 0 to 100, so that coefficients are more easily interpreted. The first four columns in Table 7 display results for age 11 maths scores, while the second four do the same for age 16 scores. Results for age 11 scores in columns (1) and (2) for the GC sample confirm the findings by Manning and Pischke. Comprehensive attendance for both groups is a significant and negative predictor of age 11 maths scores when compared to grammar, even after balancing. However, the magnitude of the coefficient is halved after balancing, suggesting that matching is working as expected.

One hypothesis is that the residual 8.76 percentage point difference in age 11 outcomes between grammar and comprehensive pupils is due to coaching effects. Primary schools in selective areas were likely to tutor their pupils in preparation for the 11-plus, and even short-term coaching has been shown to have large positive effects on performance on this type of test (Bunting & Mooney, 2001). For the SMC sample, comprehensive attendance is a significant predictor of maths scores at age 11, but it is positive in the unbalanced and negative in the balanced sample. In this case, entropy balancing potentially eliminates a positive bias from the comprehensive coefficient in the unmatched sample, due to differences in observable characteristics, thus leaving a residual difference that could also be due to coaching effects. Although 4.27 percentage points seems large, it is half the difference of that observed in the GC sample, which is in line with average cognitive ability of future secondary modern pupils being lower than that of grammar pupils. Note, we do not compare our coefficient with Manning and Pischke (2006), since the samples are different, but their estimates range between 3 and 8 pp, depending on the specification.

An alternative explanation is that the coefficients in column (2) reflect pre-treatment differences for which our matching and regression strategy is not

	Age 11 Maths Scores				Age 16 Maths Scores			
	Unmatched		Matched		Unmatched		Matched	
	(1)	(2)	(3)	(4)	(5)	(6)	(7)	(8)
Grammar vs Comprehensive (High Ability)								
Comprehensive	−0.1551***	−0.0876***	−0.0105	−0.0123	−0.0887***	−0.0656***	−0.0664***	−0.0616***
	(0.0083)	(0.0074)	(0.0081)	(0.0081)	(0.0075)	(0.0072)	(0.0071)	(0.0072)
Cognitive Skills 7	0.8174***	0.5230***	0.5173***	0.4836***				
	(0.0217)	(0.0331)	(0.0307)	(0.0333)				
Cognitive Skills 11					0.7535***	0.8565***	0.8926***	0.8917***
					(0.0152)	(0.0302)	(0.0302)	(0.0319)
Non-cognitive Skills	0.2712***	0.0601	0.0651	0.0794+	0.1011***	0.2517***	0.2599***	0.2527***
	(0.0212)	(0.0412)	(0.0473)	(0.0460)	(0.0213)	(0.0456)	(0.0486)	(0.0472)
Matched on Cognitive Skill:								
Age 7	No	Yes	No	Yes	No	Yes	No	Yes
Age 11	No	No	Yes	Yes	No	No	Yes	Yes
Observations	4,166	4,166	4,166	4,166	4,166	4,166	4,166	4,166
F	255.0254	25.7752	28.6748	19.4825	367.1590	84.9778	93.3781	92.6273
Secondary Modern vs Comprehensive (Low Ability)								
Comprehensive	0.0363***	−0.0427***	0.0073	0.0118+	0.0173**	0.0054	0.0098+	0.0087
	(0.0064)	(0.0058)	(0.0060)	(0.0062)	(0.0055)	(0.0054)	(0.0053)	(0.0053)
Cognitive Skills 7	0.8009***	0.6195***	0.6917***	0.6755***				
	(0.0177)	(0.0181)	(0.0174)	(0.0172)				
Cognitive Skills 11					0.7185***	0.6108***	0.6333***	0.6304***
					(0.0138)	(0.0171)	(0.0152)	(0.0152)
Non-cognitive Skills	0.2667***	0.2321***	0.2249***	0.2460***	0.0855***	0.0840***	0.0943***	0.0880***
	(0.0207)	(0.0215)	(0.0231)	(0.0233)	(0.0171)	(0.0199)	(0.0207)	(0.0208)
Matched on Cognitive Skill:								
Age 7	No	Yes	No	Yes	No	Yes	No	Yes
Age 11	No	No	Yes	Yes	No	No	Yes	Yes
Observations	4,847	4,847	4,847	4,847	4,847	4,847	4,847	4,847
F	231.5945	86.1400	144.3652	145.5350	179.1259	67.9224	93.7780	94.5217

Source: NCDS. Standard errors clustered at LEA level in parentheses. Control variables as in main specifications. $^{+}p < 0.1$, $^{***}p < 0.001$, $^{**}p < 0.001$.

adequately accounting. In this case, it is useful to assess whether eliminating these differences would affect treatment effects in order to put bounds on the potential bias. In columns (3) and (4), we include age 11 ability scores to the balancing algorithm. We expect this second step to eliminate differences in age 11 maths scores between treatment and control groups, thus making the comprehensive indicator insignificant, since we are matching on a variable that is highly correlated with the outcome. The purpose of this alternative balancing procedure is to analyse whether it has any effect for the comprehensive coefficient on age 16 maths scores, to understand the role of bias due to unobservables for later outcomes.

Columns (5)–(8) in Table 7 show that the magnitude of the comprehensive coefficient declines in the GC sample, when moving from the unmatched to the matched sample but remains fairly stable around 6 percentage points, even when artificially eliminating age 11 differences. Something similar can be observed for the SMC sample, where the coefficient is initially positive and significant at 1.73 percentage points. This coefficient then decreases to less than 1 percentage point, becoming not statistically significant, after matching, and this result remains stable across the different balancing algorithms. In both samples, eliminating potential unobservable differences at age 11 by matching on that variable produces a variation in the age 16 coefficient of less than 0.005. This is compatible with the coefficients in column (2) picking up a large, although relatively short-lived, coaching effect that biases age 11 maths scores upwards for pupils in selective areas, which would then disappear by age 16. Moreover, to the extent that coaching does not affect outcomes outside of test scores, the range of outcomes presented in this chapter will be exempt from this bias.

6. DISCUSSION

When correcting for pre-treatment differences in pupil characteristics, type of school is not a significant predictor of long-term outcomes, with the exception of some school-related and some labour market outcomes. We find that in the short-term, pupils who attended grammar schools in the 1970s were 13 percentage points more likely to say they intended to stay at school beyond minimum leaving age than comprehensive pupils of similar ability. This effect may translate into better educational qualifications and better employment prospects later in life, which is consistent with the evidence we present on wages (up to 9 points higher) and with a study on the earnings of more recent generations by Burgess et al. (2020). In spite of this, we also find that grammar lowers adult life satisfaction (by 0.13 standard deviations), compared to similarly able pupils in mixed-ability systems. Conversely, secondary modern pupils were about 5 percentage points less likely to want to stay at school beyond 16, maybe due to the vocational nature of the secondary modern curriculum. Better wages (up to 8 points higher) for secondary modern pupils may be linked to the fact they could learn a profession at school, compared to the general education given to low-ability pupils in comprehensive schools. We further find that most of the health outcomes considered are not affected by school type, except for a link between grammar attendance and lower BMI, and secondary modern with higher cholesterol ratio, although magnitudes are small, and significance levels vary by specification.

Our findings corroborate previous literature on the long-term effects of selective schooling. In their analysis of Scottish data, Del Bono and Clark (2016) find no significant effects for most of the adult outcomes considered, except for female income and fertility. Dustmann et al. (2016) find no significant differences by middle-school track for long-term educational and labour market outcomes in Germany. With respect to health effects in the English context, Basu et al. (2018) find no significant average effects of the transition to comprehensive schools for self-assessed health and smoking. We extend their result by adding evidence on biomarkers for risk of Cardiovascular Disease (CVD) and well-being outcomes and by distinguishing between two treatment effects and two samples, in order to build the counterfactual control group more reliably. Taken together with these findings, our evidence sums up to a literature casting doubts over the effectiveness of selective schooling policies to improve long-term outcomes. The clear differences shown in outcomes by school type in Table 2 mostly disappear once we take background into account. We further note that the secondary modern advantage in terms of employment prospects, found for low-ability pupils, may not apply today, since all non-selective schools have moved to more academic curricula, with more emphasis on further education (Crawford, 2014).

A key contribution of our paper is the combination of entropy balancing, an intuitive and effective matching method, with parametric regression, which yields doubly robust estimates, thus helping create a quasi-experimental setting to evaluate an educational reform with no clear roll-out. Criticisms previously advanced by Manning and Pischke (2006) in this literature targeted value-added methodologies and IV regressions used to explore the effects of selective schooling on educational achievement. These were shown to be unable to eliminate selection bias. Our placebo procedures, in the same spirit as theirs, suggest that our methodology nets out some of the pre-treatment differences between compared groups. We argue that the residual placebo effect on age 11 maths scores is likely due to coaching effects. However, we additionally show that, even if the residual effect was due to unobservable differences at age 11, the bias is unlikely to carry over to later outcomes.

Similarly to Jones et al. (2011), we find that childhood non-cognitive abilities are significantly linked with several long-term outcomes and extend this result to our health, well-being and labour market outcomes. We also find that childhood cognitive abilities can be important determinants of our broad range of outcomes later in life, even when accounting for non-cognitive skills, which agrees with the literature on the economics of human capital (Auld & Sidhu, 2005; Bijwaard et al., 2015; Conti & Heckman, 2010). As shown in Fig. 4, the association between all ability measures and outcomes is sizeable, when compared to that between school type and the outcomes. The effect of school type is generally equivalent to moving between 20 and 30 percentiles on the ability distribution. An interesting feature of our findings is that they also suggest that the importance of non-cognitive skills for life outcomes may vary depending on the level of cognitive skills. This is the case for

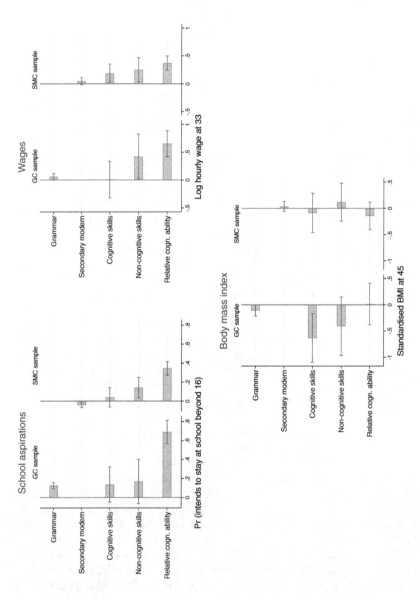

Fig. 4. Coefficient Estimates for School Type and Ability Variables Compared, for the Three Outcomes 'School Aspirations', 'Wages', and 'Body Mass Index'. Point estimates (outer point of shaded bar) and confidence intervals (line bar) taken from Tables 4-6.

the protective role of non-cognitive skills for health, which emerges as significant only in the lower cognitive ability sample.

Building on this finding, a reason why we do not find a significant effect of selective schooling on health and well-being could be that secondary school type does not directly affect the channels leading to better adult well-being. In line with this, Jerrim and Sims (2018) find no effect of attending grammar school on adolescent non-cognitive skills, for a cohort of British individuals born in 2000–2001. Cognitive and non-cognitive skills, together with other general preferences determining our decisions, could therefore be shaped earlier on in childhood (Kautz et al., 2014). If it is true that skills and preferences affect health and well-being in the long-term, then educational policy might have larger spillover effects on health if it channels its resources towards early childhood education interventions, rather than new selective schools. On the other hand, channels that affect these outcomes might also be formed later on, after secondary schooling. Further skill production could occur in adulthood via university attendance, career path, work and residential environment and so on. Understanding the mechanisms and timing of skill production can then be a productive avenue for research, and the theme is in fact very popular in the current literature.

7. CONCLUSION

We add a timely piece of evidence given recent debates on the expansion of selective schooling in England, by looking at long-term health and well-being effects of attending a high- or low-ability school in a selective system, compared to going to a mixed-ability school in a non-selective system. We use data from NCDS, including members from both systems, allowing us to explore health and well-being effects of selective schooling at several points of these individuals' lives over time, in spite of the lack of a clear roll-out of the educational reform. We build our quasi-experimental framework by preprocessing the data through entropy balancing to obtain treatment and control groups with similar distributions and joint distributions of key covariates. We then use the balanced samples in regression analysis.

Our findings suggest that there is no long-term direct impact of high- or low-ability school attendance on well-being measures, self-assessed health, risk for cardiovascular disease and risk of chronic stress at different ages, compared to mixed-ability school attendance. The only exception are short-term schooling aspirations, which are better for pupils in selective schools, and some labour market outcomes, which may be linked. Low-ability pupils attending low-ability schools in selective areas also display better wages than equivalent pupils in mixed-ability schools. However, this result may not be relevant in modern times if it was due to the vocational nature of low-ability schools in the past. We also find that childhood cognitive and non-cognitive ability measured prior to secondary schooling play a significant role as predictors of later health and well-being. Their role as either direct causal predictors of human capital or mediators between education and human capital should be the subject of further research to explore the determinants of differences among individual outcomes, which would be informative for future educational policy.

ACKNOWLEDGEMENTS

This work was undertaken as part of a PhD thesis at the University of York. We thank Thomas Cornelissen, Sandra McNally, Emma Tominey, participants at the HEDG seminars at the University of York, the NCDS 60 Years of Our Lives conference, the RES Junior Symposium 2018 at the University of Sussex, the 4th IRDES-Dauphine AHEPE Workshop and the 3rd IZA Workshop: The Economics of Education for helpful comments. This paper uses data from the National Child Development Study (NCDS), managed by the Centre for Longitudinal Studies at the UCL Institute of Education, and available through the UK Data Service. Boston Consulting Group, the funders, data creators and UK Data Service have no responsibility for the contents of this paper. Andrew M Jones acknowledges support by the Leverhulme Trust Major Research Fellowship (grant number MRF-2016-004) and Chiara Pastore is grateful for support from the Economic and Social Research Council (grant number ES/J500215/1). We declare no competing interests.

REFERENCES

Angrist, J. D. (1998). Estimating the labor market impact of voluntary military service using social security data on military applicants. *Econometrica, 66*(2), 249–288.

Auld, M. C., & Sidhu, N. (2005). Schooling, cognitive ability and health. *Health Economics, 14*(10), 1019–1034.

Basu, A., Jones, A. M., & Rosa Dias, P. (2018). Heterogeneity in the impact of type of schooling on adult health and lifestyle. *Journal of Health Economics, 57*, 1–14.

Benzeval, M., Davillas, A., Kumari, M., & Lynn, P. (2014). Biomarker user guide and glossary. https://www.understandingsociety.ac.uk/sites/default/files/downloads/legacy/7251-UnderstandingSociety-Biomarker-UserGuide-2014-1.pdf. Accessed on 21 September 2017.

Bijwaard, G. E., Kippersluis, H. V., & Veenman, J. (2015). Education and health: The role of cognitive ability. *Journal of Health Economics, 42*, 29–43.

Bolton, P. (2012). *Education: Historical statistics.* House of Commons Library vol. SN/SG/4252 (November), p. 20. http://www.parliament.uk/briefing-papers/SN00620.pdf

Bolton, P. (2017). *Grammar school statistics.* House of Commons Briefing Paper No. 1398. House of Commons Library.

Bonhomme, S., & Sauder, U. (2011). Recovering distributions in difference-in-differences models: A comparison of selective and comprehensive schooling. *Review of Economic Studies, 93*(2), 479–494.

Brown, M., Dodgeon, B., & Mostafa, T. (2016). Webinar: Introduction to the National Child Development Study. http://www.cls.ioe.ac.uk/library- media/documents/NCDS%20Webinar%20May%202016.pdf. Accessed on 17 January 2018.

Brunello, G., & Checchi, D. (2007). Does school tracking affect equality of opportunity? New international evidence. *Economic Policy, 22*(52), 783–861.

Bunting, B. P., & Mooney, E. (2001). The effects of practice and coaching on test results for educational selection at eleven years of age. *Educational Psychology, 21*(3), 243–253.

Burgess, S., Crawford, C., & Macmillan, L. (2017). *Assessing the role of grammar schools in promoting social mobility.* Department of Quantitative Social Science Working Paper No. 17/09, UCL Institute of Education.

Burgess, S., Crawford, C., & Macmillan, L. (2018). Access to grammar schools by socio-economic status. *Environment and Planning A: Economy and Space, 50*(7), 1381–1385. https://journals.sagepub.com/doi/pdf/10.1177/0308518X18787820

Burgess, S., Dickson, M., & Macmillan, L. (2020). Do selective schooling systems increase inequality? *Oxford Economic Papers, 72*(1), 1–24.

Byrne, D., & Williamson, W. (1976). Effect of local education authority resources and policies on educational attainment, 1972–1974. [computer file]. UK Data Archive [distributor] SN: 199. https://doi.org/10.5255/UKDASN-199-1

Caliendo, M., & Kopeinig, S. (2008). Some practical guidance for the implementation of propensity score matching. *Journal of Economic Surveys, 22*(1), 31–72.

Case, A., Fertig, A., & Paxson, C. (2005). The lasting impact of childhood health and circumstance. *Journal of Health Economics, 24*(2), 365–389.

Cawley, J., Conneely, K., Heckman, J., & Vytlacil, E. (1997). Cognitive ability, wages, and meritocracy. In B. Devlin, S. E. Fienberg, D. P. Resnick, & K. Roeder (Eds.), *Intelligence, genes, and success: Scientists respond to the bell curve* (pp. 179–192). Springer New York.

Clark, D. (2010). Selective schools and academic achievement. *The B.E. Journal of Economic Analysis Policy, 10*(1). https://www.degruyter.com/downloadpdf/j/bejeap.2010.10.1/bejeap.2010.10.1.1917/bejeap.2010.10.1.1917.pdf

Comprehensive School Committee. (1971). *Comprehensive education statistics.* 1971 Bulletin of the Comprehensive Schools Committee.

Conti, G., & Heckman, J. J. (2010). Understanding the early origins of the education-health gradient: A framework that can also be applied to analyze gene-environment interactions. *Perspectives on Psychological Science, 5*(5), 585–605.

Crawford, C. (2014). *The link between secondary school characteristics and university participation and outcomes.* CAYT Research Report. Techical Report June. Centre for the Analysis of Youth Transitions.

Cribb, J., Jesson, D., Sibieta, L., Skipp, A., & Vignoles, A. (2013). Poor grammar. Entry into grammar schools for disadvantaged pupils in England. http://dera.ioe.ac.uk/id/eprint/30279

Del Bono, E., & Clark, D. (2016). The long-run effects of attending an elite school: Evidence from the UK. *American Economic Journal: Applied Economics, 8*(1), 150–176.

Dustmann, C., Puhani, P. A., & Schönberg, U. (2016). The long-term effects of early track choice. *Economic Journal, 127*, 1348–1380.

Fuggle, S. (2018). Clinical biochemistry reference ranges handbook. [online]. https://www.esht.nhs.uk/wp-content/uploads/2017/08/Clinical-Biochemistry-reference-ranges-handbook.pdf. Accessed on 3 November 2019.

Galindo-Rueda, F., & Vignoles, A. (2005). *The heterogeneous effect of selection in secondary schools: Understanding the changing role of ability.* Working Paper No. 52, LSE Centre for the Economics of Education. http://search.proquest.com/docview/1018481012?accountid=13042

Grossman, M. (1972). On the concept of health capital and the demand for health. *Journal of Political Economy, 80*(2), 223–255.

Guyon, N., Maurin, E., & McNally, S. (2012). The effect of racking students by ability into different schools: A natural experiment. *Journal of Human Resources, 47*(3), 684–721. www.feem.it

Hainmueller, J. (2012). Entropy balancing for causal effects: A multivariate reweighting method to produce balanced samples in observational studies. *Political Analysis, 20*(1), 25–46.

Hanushek, E. A., & Wößmann, L. (2006). Does early tracking affect educational inequality and performance? Differences-in-differences evidence across countries. *Economic Journal, 116*, C63–C76.

Harmon, C., & Walker, I. (2000). The returns to the quantity and quality of education: Evidence for men in England and Wales. *Economica, 67*(265), 19–35. https://EconPapers.repec.org/RePEc:bla:econom:v:67:y:2000:i:265:p: 19-35

Heckman, J. J., Smith, J., & Clements, N. (1997). Making the most out of programme evaluations and social experiments: Accounting for heterogeneity in programme impacts. *The Review of Economic Studies, 64*(4), 487–535.

Imbens, G. W. (2004). Nonparametric estimation of average treatment effects under exogeneity: A review. *The Review of Economics and Statistics, 86*(1), 4–29.

Jerrim, J., & Sims, S. (2018). The association between attending a grammar school and children's socio-emotional outcomes. New evidence from the Millennium Cohort Study. *British Journal of Educational Studies.* https://www.nuffieldfoundation.org

Jesson, D. (2000). The comparative evaluation of GCSE value-added performance in two-sector models of endogenous growth by type of school and LEA. *University of York Discussion Papers in Economics, 2000*(52). http://cptransform.wordpress.com/2011/02/10/sociotechnicalsystem/

Jones, A., Pastore, C., & Rice, N. (2018). *Tracking pupils into adulthood: Selective schools and long-term well-being in the 1958 British Birth Cohort.* HEDG Working Paper WP18/32. https://www.york.ac.uk/media/economics/documents/hedg/workingpapers/1832.pdf

Jones, A. M., Rice, N., & Rosa Dias, P. (2011). Long-term effects of school quality on health and lifestyle: Evidence from comprehensive schooling reforms in England. *Journal of Human Capital, 5*(3), 342–376.

Jones, A. M., Rice, N., & Rosa Dias, P. (2012). Quality of schooling and inequality of opportunity in health. *Empirical Economics, 42*(2), 369–394.

Kautz, T., Heckman, J. J., Diris, R., Weel, B. T., & Borghans, L. (2014). *Fostering and measuring skills: Improving cognitive and non-cognitive skills to promote lifetime success.* OECD Education Working Paper No. 110.

Kerckhoff, A. (1986). Effects of ability grouping in secondary schools in Great Britain. *American Sociological Review, 51*(6), 842–858.

Kerckhoff, A. (1996). *Going comprehensive in England and Wales: A study of uneven change.* Routledge.

Manning, A., & Pischke, J. S. (2006). Comprehensive versus selective schooling in England in Wales: What do we know? NBER Working Paper No. 12176.

Maurin, E., & McNally, S. (2009). The consequences of ability tracking for future outcomes. Unpublished manuscript (January), pp. 1–38.

Power, C., & Elliott, J. (2006). Cohort profile: 1958 British birth cohort (National Child Development Study). *International Journal of Epidemiology, 35*(1), 34–41.

Rubin, D. B. (1974). Estimating causal effects of treatments in randomized and nonrandomized studies. *Journal of Educational Psychology, 66*(5), 688–701.

Rubin, D. B., & Thomas, N. (1996). Matching using estimated propensity scores: Relating theory to practice. *Biometrics, 52*(1), 249–264.

Todd, P. E., & Wolpin, K. I. (2003). On the specification and estimation of the production function for cognitive achievement. *Economic Journal, 113*, F3–F33.

University of London. Institute of Education. Centre for Longitudinal Studies. (2014). *National child development study: Childhood data, sweeps 0-3, 1958-1974. [data collection]* (3rd ed.). National Birthday Trust Fund, National Children's Bureau, [original data producer(s)]. UK Data Service. SN: 5565. http://doi.org/10.5255/UKDA-SN-5565-2

UK Department for Education. (2019). Selective schools expansion fund: Successful applications, 2018 to 2019. Transparency data. [online]. https://www.gov.uk/government/publications/selective-schools-expansion-fund-successful-applications-2018-to-2019. Accessed 25 November 2019.

University of London. Institute of Education. Centre for Longitudinal Studies. (2008a). *National child development study: Sweep 4, 1981, and public examination results, 1978. [data collection]* (2nd ed.). National Children's Bureau, [original data producer(s)]. UK Data Service. SN: 5566. http://doi.org/10.5255/UKDA-SN-5566-1

University of London. Institute of Education. Centre for Longitudinal Studies. (2008b). *National child development study: Sweep 5, 1991. [data collection]* (2nd ed.). City University. Social Statistics Research Unit, [original data producer(s)]. UK Data Service. SN: 5567. http://doi.org/10.5255/UKDA-SN-5567-1

University of London. Institute of Education. Centre for Longitudinal Studies. (2008c). *National child development study: Sweep 6, 1999-2000. [data collection]* (2nd ed.). Joint Centre for Longitudinal Research, [original data producer(s)]. UK Data Service. SN: 5578. http://doi.org/10.5255/UKDA-SN-5578-1

University of London. Institute of Education. Centre for Longitudinal Studies. (2012). *National child development study: Sweep 8, 2008-2009. [data collection]* (3rd ed.). UK Data Service. SN: 6137. http://doi.org/10.5255/UKDA-SN-6137-2

World Health Organisation. (Sept. 2017). *Body mass index – BMI.* http://www.euro.who.int/en/health-topics/disease-prevention/nutrition/a-healthylifestyle/body-mass-index-bmi. Accessed on 24 September 2017.

PHYSICIAN BEHAVIOUR AND INEQUALITIES IN ACCESS TO HEALTHCARE

Mylene Lagarde[a] and Anthony Scott[b]

[a]*London School of Economics and Political Science, UK*
[b]*Monash University, Australia*

ABSTRACT

This chapter reviews the evidence on the role of physicians in shaping inequalities in access to and utilisation of healthcare. The authors examine three types of physician decisions that can influence inequalities in access and utilisation: location decisions, decisions to work in the public and/or private sector, and decisions or behaviours in the doctor–patient encounter. For each, the authors summarise the issues and empirical evidence on possible policies to help reduce inequalities in access. Future research to reduce inequalities should focus on changes to health systems that influence physician decisions, such as health insurance expansions, the public–private mix and financial incentives, as well as physician training and policies for a more diverse physician workforce.

Keywords: Physician behaviour; inequalities; access; incentives; distribution

1. INTRODUCTION

To improve the health of populations, physicians need to be accessible to those with the highest need for medical care. They also have to be responsive and provide appropriate advice and treatment to patients who visit them. A key finding of many studies that measure inequalities in the utilisation of healthcare with respect to income and heath need is that the utilisation of specialist physicians has a pro-rich distribution whilst inequalities in primary care utilisation are more variable with mixed evidence of pro-poor and pro-rich distributions (Dalziel et al., 2018; Devaux, 2015; Lueckmann et al., 2021; Pulok & Hajizadeh,

---

Recent Developments in Health Econometrics
Contributions to Economic Analysis, Volume 297, 37–53
Copyright © 2024 Mylene Lagarde and Anthony Scott
Published under exclusive licence by Emerald Publishing Limited
ISSN: 0573-8555/doi:10.1108/S0573-855520240000297003

2022; Pulok et al., 2020; van Doorslaer et al., 2000, 2004, 2006). This is the case across many countries and seems to be persistent over time and across study designs and datasets, with some evidence showing that pro-rich inequity may be higher if higher quality methods are used to control for and measure need (Bago d'Uva et al., 2009; Fooken & Jeet, 2022). Richer people, irrespective of age (Dalziel et al., 2018; Halldórsson et al., 2002; Pulok & Hajizadeh, 2022), receive more healthcare compared to poorer people with the same need. Davillas and Jones (2021) and Wouterse et al. (2023) show that such inequities may be exacerbated in times of crisis, such as pandemics.

Inequalities in utilisation are associated with the generosity of health insurance coverage, size of out of pocket payments and the extent of private provision of healthcare (Devaux, 2015; Kaarboe & Siciliani, 2023; Pulok et al., 2022; van Doorslaer et al., 2004). Private medical markets without public health insurance are inherently inequitable because poorer people use less healthcare since they have a lower ability to pay combined with higher average needs for healthcare compared to the rich. Inequalities in access to healthcare are reduced by public health insurance coverage that increases the demand for healthcare which in turn stimulates health workforce supply (Dillender, 2022). Within these schemes, governments can further influence the distribution of physicians and other healthcare resources across geography and different population groups to improve equal access for equal need (Carvalho et al., 2019).

But even in public systems with universal access and equitable geographic distribution, no out of pocket costs and a small private sector, such as Canada, the UK and Sweden, inequalities and inequities still exist (Chen et al., 2022; Cookson et al., 2016; Pulok & Hajizadeh, 2022). Part of the reason is that some population groups find it difficult to access healthcare for a range of reasons that can include language and cultural barriers, low health and financial literacy as well as distance (Levesque et al., 2013). Another related reason is that those who do access healthcare and have identical health conditions may be treated differently depending on their characteristics, including their socio-economic status, race or gender. These disparities may be appropriate if they reflect differences in patients' needs or preferences (vertical equity), but they can drive inequalities (horizontal inequity) if they are caused by physician's preferences and beliefs whilst patients' needs are the same.

By directly or indirectly choosing which patients to see and treat through location, specialty and job choices and by deciding how to interact with these patients and what treatments to recommend physicians can influence inequalities of access directly or indirectly. The aim of this chapter is to summarise evidence on three main types of physician decisions that directly influence inequalities in access to healthcare: physician decisions on geographic location, working in the private sector and clinical decisions. For each type of decision, we first review existing evidence on the link between physician's choices and inequalities in access and then summarise the evidence on the effectiveness of policies to reduce inequalities for each type of decision.

2. REDUCING INEQUALITIES THROUGH INFLUENCING PHYSICIAN'S LOCATION CHOICES AND THEIR GEOGRAPHIC DISTRIBUTION

A first decision made by physicians that can impact inequalities of access to care is where they decide to work. The lack of health professionals in rural areas has been a key policy issue for many years across many countries. Depending on market conditions, physicians in most countries can choose to practice in any geographic location. Because different types of patients live in different locations, where physicians choose to work influences access to care for certain population groups. The decision of the geographic location in which to work is complex. When they choose a place to work, physicians indirectly choose which types of patients to treat (e.g. in urban or rural areas and low or high socio-economic status areas) and trade this off against other job and location characteristics (Mandeville et al., 2014; Scott et al., 2013). It may take more altruistic values to accept a job in an isolated area, where providers might become the main point of access to care but at the expense of personal or professional costs (Lagarde & Blaauw, 2014).

There is evidence from many countries that doctors are more concentrated in affluent geographic areas and that this is persistent over time (Atalay et al., 2023; McIsaac et al., 2015; Munga & Maestad, 2009; Sousa et al., 2012; Wiseman et al., 2017; Xue et al., 2019). Part of this reflects an urban–rural difference because of the historical distribution and location of large teaching hospitals in major capital cities, where doctors train and work. But even within major cities, doctors tend to locate in more affluent areas. Primary care physicians are usually more evenly distributed across geography relative to physicians in other hospital-based specialties though this is not always the case in low- and middle-income countries. It can be efficient for specialists to concentrate in hospitals and in metropolitan areas given the high fixed costs of more specialised inpatient care, yet populations living in metropolitan areas are often more affluent and healthier than those living on the edge of large cities and in rural areas. This places higher travel and time costs on patients who may also be more in need of healthcare.

There has historically been little rigorous evaluation of the effectiveness of policies to improve medical workforce distribution (Buykx et al., 2010; Grobler et al., 2015; Koebisch et al., 2020; Russell et al., 2021). Policies generally include regulation, training and the use of incentives. Regulation can include restricting the entry of physicians to geographical markets. This reduces the physicians' choice set of potential work locations. Some countries such as Australia require international medical graduates (IMGs) to practise in rural areas up to 10 years after they first arrive in Australia, with IMGs comprising 39.6% of doctors in non-metropolitan areas in 2020. In the UK until the early 2000s, the Medical Practices Committee decided on whether general practitioners (GPs) could work in a certain area or not based on estimates of local shortages and surpluses. Other countries, such as South Africa or Senegal, require medical graduates to work for a short period of time in under-served areas or in the public sector before they can qualify as medical doctors (Reid et al., 2018). In addition, there are numerous examples of 'bonded' or 'return of service' schemes where publicly funded medical training scholarships require physicians to work in areas of need or in the public sector for a fixed time period after training or where assistance is provided with medical school debt repayment (Barnighausen & Bloom, 2009; Frehywot et al., 2010).

Other policies include increasing the proportion of time spent training in areas of need, which can be mandated, during medical school, post-graduate training or during vocational (specialty) training. This sometimes involves the funding of accredited training positions in these areas which also require adequate supervision. Medical schools may be established in non-metropolitan areas and away from major teaching hospitals (Playford et al., 2014). There are also policies that require universities to select a certain proportion of students who grew up in rural areas or areas of need or affirmative action policies that involve admission quotas of students from specific ethnic backgrounds or women (McGrail, Doyle, et al., 2023). However, there is no causal evidence for the effectiveness of these policies though associations are large. In Australia, GPs who spent more than six years growing up in a non-metropolitan area were 2.3 times more likely to end up working in a rural area (McGrail et al., 2011) with stronger associations for those of rural origin and who were trained in a rural area (McGrail et al., 2016). The length of time spent training in a rural area is also associated with staying there longer (McGrail, Gurney, et al., 2023).

Specialist outreach, where physicians travel to areas of need is a further policy commonly used (O'Sullivan et al., 2014). A key issue, where there is much less evidence, is the potential role of telehealth in rural areas to improve access to physicians who remain located in metropolitan areas. Telehealth was greatly expanded during the COVID-19 pandemic. The scope for reductions in costs (for patients and the health system) is significant though there remain doubts about the quality of care provided by telehealth compared to face to face consultations, especially where care is provided by phone rather than video (Carrillo de Albornoz et al., 2022; Snoswell et al., 2021).

A final set of policies are financial and non-financial incentives to attract and retain physicians in areas of need. In addition to cash payments and loadings on existing regular payments, this might involve the provision of subsidies for housing or schooling. Capitation payments which are risk adjusted to compensate for the higher costs of treating higher need populations can change the distribution of primary care practices towards higher need areas (Anell et al., 2018). Other studies have found less of an impact for financial incentives. In a discrete choice experiment examining preferences for rural location, for those in metropolitan areas offered jobs in rural areas between 73% and 91% (depending on the characteristics of the rural job) would prefer to stay in their current job (Scott et al., 2013). For the small proportion who were prepared to move, they would need to be compensated between 10.3% and 130% of their annual income, with 130% representing a job in a rural area with the least valued job characteristics. These results suggest that financial incentives would work for only a small proportion of GPs and would need to be much higher than currently offered to persuade them to move to rural areas with poor job characteristics. The relative ineffectiveness of financial incentives is supported other studies in Peru, Norway, Australia and the US (Brunt, 2023; Holte et al., 2015; McIsaac et al., 2019; Miranda et al., 2012).

Two studies evaluated a change to an incentive programme in Australia when the eligibility of geographic areas for incentive payments changed because of a change in the way rurality was measured. This resulted in around 750 locations, mainly outside the edges of major cities, suddenly becoming eligible for incentives and increased the incomes of GPs in these areas by an average of 3.8%. Yong et al. (2018) found no impact on entries or exits of GPs overall though there was some evidence of an increase in entries for newly qualified GPs who are more mobile than more established GPs. A second study examined the effect of this same policy change on waiting times for non-urgent GP appointments and found some evidence that the number of GPs in newly eligible practices increased, and this did not lead to lower waiting times for existing patients but did lead to weak evidence of lower waiting times for new patients (Swami & Scott, 2021).

3. PUBLIC–PRIVATE PROVISION AND INEQUALITIES

In mixed healthcare systems, doctors make another potentially consequential decision for inequalities when they choose to work in the private sector rather than the public sector or when they choose to split their time between both sectors through dual practice. These choices have indirect implications for inequalities to access because of the differences in the type of patients using the two sectors on the one hand and the potential detrimental consequences for the public sector on the other hand.

Across many countries, those who can afford private healthcare are typically socioeconomically advantaged (Fiebig et al., 2021; Pulok et al., 2022). This is because in mixed healthcare systems, private healthcare is typically not covered by a form of universal health insurance, so only the more affluent populations who can afford to pay out-of-pocket or to pay for private health insurance (Kaestner & Lubotsky, 2016) can consult private doctors. In lower income settings, qualified physicians often work in expensive private facilities which are only affordable to wealthier populations, while poorer populations who use private services will typically consult lower-skilled or informal providers (Coveney et al., 2023). If a majority of doctors prefer to opt for private sector jobs, inequalities might increase between public and private sectors in terms of the quality of care offered as well as inequalities in access. South Africa is an example of a mixed system characterised by stark inequalities in the distribution of physicians, as about 80% of them work in the private sector. Since less than 20% of the population can afford a private medical insurance, the majority of South Africans rely on free public facilities where quality of care is often lower due to a lack of doctors. Furthermore, in many settings, private facilities that employ many doctors, such as hospitals and clinics, also tend to be disproportionately located in urban areas. As a result, the private sector is disproportionally used by urban populations, leaving more limited options to rural populations (Grépin, 2017).

Another source of inequality engrained in mixed health systems comes from the fact that physicians in the private sector may have discretion over which patients to treat. This 'cream-skimming' problem is rooted in the profit incentives that typically drive the private sector, which may lead providers to select less complex, lower cost and so more profitable patients (Eggleston, 2000; Ellis, 2000). For example, in the US, physicians are able to select which patients to treat depending on their insurer and the relative size of payments they offer, and this can drive inequalities in access and utilisation if lower payments are offered by public insurance programs such as Medicare and Medicaid relative to private insurers (Brunt & Jensen, 2014). An audit study of private practices in Germany found that privately insured patients, who are more profitable, are more likely to be offered an appointment compared to publicly insured individuals (Werbeck et al., 2021). Conditional on being offered an appointment, the waiting time was twice as long for publicly insured. By contrast, in universal health insurance systems, everyone is covered and providers are remunerated according to the type of care provided, promoting equal access for equal need.

Across the world, physicians holding a public sector job often get to make another type of consequential decision: how much time they spend practicing in their public job or in private practice. Such 'dual practice' is widespread across the world. In many health systems, it is legal and regulated, but dual practice also occurs when it is illegal and unregulated (McPake et al., 2016). In the UK, where healthcare is largely delivered by a free universal public healthcare system, over 60% of hospital doctors engage in private practice alongside their NHS job (Humphrey & Russell, 2004). The literature highlights a series of reasons explaining why healthcare professionals engage in dual practice, but the pursuit of supplementary income stands out as the primary motivator (García-Prado & González, 2011; Hipgrave & Hort, 2014). Differences in hourly earnings between the sectors can influence the share of hours in the private sector (Cheng et al., 2018; Saether, 2005). In settings where salaries in the public sector are particularly low, this is sometimes seen as a necessary coping strategy for staff (Ferrinho et al., 2004). Beyond monetary considerations, physicians may seek private practice opportunities to enhance their skills or broaden their network (García-Prado & González, 2011; Hipgrave & Hort, 2014). Other considerations, such as whether their work involves being on-call, opportunities for research, or the amount of administrative burden, may also play a role (Scott et al., 2020).

Similar to their choice to take up a job in the private vs the public sector, engaging in dual practice may exacerbate inequalities in different ways. Because it creates competition for physicians' time, dual practice reduces resources available to public sector patients (moonlighting physicians' time). This compromises access to services due to greater staff absenteeism and lower availability of physicians for patients in the public sector (Chaudhury et al., 2006), as well as longer waiting times for public sector treatment if private patients are prioritised (Fun et al., 2021; Sharma et al., 2013; Walpole, 2019). In some settings, there are also concerns that dual practitioners may voluntarily decide to lower the quality of services in their public practice to divert patients to their private practice (Jan et al., 2005). Overall, this debate rests mostly on theoretical arguments supported by very limited empirical evidence. Other scholars highlight potential benefits of dual practice. When it is introduced within public sector facilities, it may facilitate retention of staff and prevent worse shortages in the public sector (García-Prado & González, 2011). By transferring less complicated cases to the private sector, dual practice can free more resources for high-risk patients who may then access better care in the public sector (Barros & Olivella, 2005).

Broadly speaking, there are two types of interventions that have been proposed to tackle problems linked to dual practice: providing financial incentives and regulation. The first category of strategies seeks to limit the willingness of providers to undertake dual practice activities by making public sector jobs more financially attractive. That is done by raising public sector salaries or providing incentives for exclusive public service (such as salary supplements or promotions). The second category of interventions aims to regulate dual practice to limit its negative effects for public patients. Putting a limit to private sector earnings, a strategy adopted by the UK and France, is one indirect way of restricting moonlighting. Paradoxically, another way to control dual practice more carefully is to allow public hospitals to keep a portion of their beds for private patients, such as in Australia. At the extreme end of regulatory approaches is the complete prohibition of dual practice. Research on the effects of dual practice and strategies to influence its prevalence is largely theoretical (Biglaiser & Albert Ma, 2007; Brekke & Sørgard, 2007; González, 2004; González & Macho-Stadler, 2013), with little to no rigorous empirical evidence (Kiwanuka et al., 2011).

Overall, when choosing to work in the public or private sector, physicians make trade-offs between different working conditions (salary, autonomy, working conditions, etc), but also between different types of patients. Due to the characteristics of the private sector, when they choose to work in the private sector, physicians often choose to treat richer and more advantaged patients who are on average in less need of healthcare. The relative size of the public and private sector, which depends on the evolution of the structure of the health system, is itself critical in determining the choices available for physicians and the associated degree of inequality in utilisation.

4. PHYSICIAN DISCRIMINATION AND INEQUALITIES IN HEALTHCARE

The last way through which providers can fuel inequalities in healthcare relate to the behaviours and decisions they adopt during clinical encounters. The doctor–patient relationship relies on effective two-way transfer of information relevant to diagnosis and treatment decisions. Unless treatment variations reflect patients' assessed need for medical care and their preferences, inequalities may emerge, or be exacerbated, if providers treat differently patients with similar health needs. This issue largely falls under what economists call discrimination, which is the differential treatment of otherwise identical individuals from different groups defined by particular characteristics (i.e. race, gender, etc.). Discrimination is traditionally categorised into two types: 'taste-based' and 'statistical' discrimination (Becker, 1957). In the healthcare context, taste-based discrimination corresponds to the notion that providers may treat patients from a certain group differently because they derive disutility from interacting with them. Meanwhile, statistical discrimination is closer to the notion of bias – implicit or explicit – whereby providers may treat certain patients differently if they rely on conditional probability assumptions about an individual's health (needs or preferences) based on group-level characteristics, such as race or gender.

Physicians are very different from the general population of patients in terms of their socio-economic status and personality (Ammi et al., 2023). Physicians are also heterogenous in the distribution of personality traits recognised as important for effective doctor–patient communication, such as empathy and conscientiousness, as well as in altruism. When assessing a patients' healthcare needs and recommending diagnosis and treatment options, differences in the characteristics between physicians and their patients should not matter.

However, there is much research which has studied physicians' implicit bias in relation to race/ethnicity and to a lesser extent gender, socio-economic status and other patient traits such as obesity (Chapman et al., 2013; FitzGerald & Hurst, 2017; Hall et al., 2015; Phelan et al., 2014; Scott et al., 1996; Zestcott et al., 2016). This literature suggests that healthcare professionals in various settings exhibit similar levels of implicit bias than the general population. In turn, there are two main pathways through which such biases can result in actual disparities in patient care: communication (biases may alter how providers communicate or behave, leading to worse experiences of care for stigmatised groups, who may distrust physicians, reduce or delay access to care) and clinical decisions (biases may affect clinical judgement, leading to recommending different treatment options to patients from different population groups, despite similar health needs).

Evidence mostly from the US suggests that white patients tend to receive better communication, more information and be more involved in decision-making than black patients (Shen et al., 2018). Similarly, several studies have found that, compared to more affluent patients, physicians communicate with patients from disadvantaged backgrounds in a more directive and less participatory style, providing significantly less information and less socio-emotional support (Willems et al., 2005). There is also evidence that communication towards obese patients is worse, with physicians show less emotional support than they do for normal weight patients (Gudzune et al., 2013). Discriminatory attitudes or communication by providers may have downstream consequences contributing to worsen health inequalities. For example, across a range of countries, such as New Zealand (Harris et al., 2012), the US (Lee et al., 2009) or Sweden (Wamala et al., 2007), researchers have documented associations between minority groups' experience of racial discrimination within the healthcare setting and lower rates of healthcare use.

Causal evidence is however hard to establish although a recent field experiment in the US showed that black patients were more likely to undertake preventive tests if they were randomly allocated to be seen by black doctors (Alsan et al., 2019). A study from Denmark exploited the closure of health clinics and found that mortality rates were lower for patients who saw physicians with a similar low socio-economic status background. No mortality differences were found for patients with a similarly high socio-economic status background to physicians (Kristiansen & Sheng, 2022). A study from Sweden examined whether there is a physician in the family, where there are no differences in socio-economic status between the physician and their patient family member and found that family members had higher health status over their lifetime (Chen et al., 2022).

Studies looking at differences in treatment provided despite similar health needs may emerge from implicit or explicit bias towards certain population groups. Many studies of discrimination in healthcare treatment have focused on the field of pain management. This emphasis arises from the inherent subjectivity of pain, which provides ample opportunities for interpretation and bias to manifest. Several studies have reported that physicians, including female ones, are at risk of under-estimating the pain reported by women, with gender stereotypes about 'brave' men and 'emotional' women permeating doctors' views of patients' reporting of symptoms (Samulowitz et al., 2018). As a result, female patients were more likely to receive less and less effective pain relief and more likely to be referred to mental healthcare (Green et al., 2003; Hirsh et al., 2013; Racine et al., 2014). Similarly, many studies in the US show that, relative to white patients, black patients (including children) are less likely to be given pain medications, and, if given any, they receive lower quantities (Cintron & Morrison, 2006; Goyal et al., 2015).

In this setting, there is a growing recognition that, together with structural racism, physicians' racial bias may partly contribute to such disparities in treatment. For example, a study found that half of white medical students and residents wrongly believed the notion, rooted in historical explicit racial bias and prejudice, that there are intrinsic biological differences between white and black people making the latter less sensitive to pain (Hoffman et al., 2016). The study then showed how such beliefs led to lower pain ratings and less appropriate treatment recommendations for black people compared to white people. Research in other clinical areas have typically used hypothetical vignettes presenting patients with randomly allocated features. Examples include studies showing discriminatory treatment against foreign nationals in Switzerland in primary care (Drewniak et al., 2016), lower rates of correct diagnosis of diabetes for ethnic minorities in the US and worse management for patients from lower socio-economic status (McKinlay et al., 2013) and lower referral of female patients for appropriate treatment for osteoarthritis (Borkhoff et al., 2008).

Whilst the role of providers' biases in clinical decision-making is not refutable, empirical studies looking at discrimination in the healthcare context have struggled to overcome several methodological challenges to measure its causal impact. Because a number of outcomes of interest (e.g. quality of care or communication provided to patients, providers' beliefs and implicit bias) are hard to observe or quantify, researchers have used approaches that may suffer from hypothetical bias (administration of hypothetical vignettes of patients' cases), self-reporting bias (patients from different population groups may have internalized biases or stereotypes in a way that influence their perceptions) or measurement error (implicit association tests). Moreover, studies looking at treatment choices can seldom disentangle physician's decisions or preferences from patients' preferences. Where patients have a choice of physician, patients may prefer physicians with similar characteristics to themselves, such as gender (Godager, 2012). Greenwood et al. (2020) found that newborn–physician racial concordance, where the newborn and physician are the same race, is associated with a significant improvement in mortality for black infants. However, this may reflect patient's choice of physician.

To overcome some of these problems, a few studies in low- and middle-income countries have used the audit study approach typically adopted in the economics literature (Bertrand & Duflo, 2017), sending incognito 'standardised' patients presenting with the same attitude and symptoms and exogenously varying a personal characteristic that may drive discrimination. Despite concerns over discriminatory behaviour by physicians, these studies found no significant differences in the treatment offered to women and men presenting with tuberculosis in India (Daniels et al., 2019), and no difference in the advice provided to women from minority ethnic groups in Peru (Planas et al., 2015).

Several strategies have been introduced to reduce physicians' biases and potential discriminatory behaviour in healthcare, including training, standardised protocols and technological tools, and interventions aiming to increase the diversity of the physician workforce. These approaches aim to address either or both individual and systemic factors that contribute to disparities in health outcomes.

To reduce individual physicians' implicit biases towards various groups, healthcare organisations and medical education institutions have been developing training programs focussing on recognising implicit biases and providing strategies to reduce how implicit biases influence behaviour or judgement. It appears desirable to integrate such training modules early on during medical training, as evidence indicates that implicit prejudice and bias may increase during medical studies (Rubineau & Kang, 2011). There is some evidence that a variety of training can reduce implicit bias, at least in the short to medium term (Devine et al., 2012; Lai et al., 2014; Stone et al., 2020), though effectiveness often seems to fade quickly (Lai et al., 2016). There is also very limited work examining whether a reduction in implicit bias observed after training translates into different attitudes or behaviours of physicians and ultimately better outcomes for stigmatised groups (Mavis et al., 2022).

Another approach to reduce the influence of physicians' biases in clinical judgement has been to develop and implement decision support tools that standardise treatment protocols, with a view to 'purge' the intuitive component in physicians' medical judgement in favour of a more normative approach. Advances in artificial intelligence in particular offer promising solutions. A recent study looking at pain management shows how algorithmic approaches based on machine learning could redress inequalities in treatment (Pierson et al., 2021). Because algorithmic predictions were based on a racially and socioeconomically diverse training set, they were better able to measure the severity of a clinical condition (osteoarthritis) than human physicians, leading to more accurate prediction of patients' experienced pain, which could potentially reduce inequalities in access to treatment. However, clinical decision support tools may also perpetuate inequalities if they are not well calibrated. A recent study identified how an algorithm predicting clinical risk based on past health costs would conclude that white patients were at higher risk than black patients with similar health profiles, leading to inequalities to referral for specialist treatment (Obermeyer et al., 2019). This echoes research that has flagged how decision-support tools and clinical protocols may have to be thoroughly reviewed for any particular adjustment based on inaccurate beliefs about physiological differences that perpetuate inequalities and bias in healthcare (Eneanya et al., 2019; Vyas et al., 2020).

Finally, many scholars have been calling for a more structural approach to reducing unequal treatment of patients from different population groups by promoting promote diversity within the medical workforce. A more diverse health workforce would improve physicians' cultural competence and communication skills and ensure that the needs of patients from different backgrounds can be heard. The field experiment implemented by Alsan et al. (2019) showed how African American male patients received by black doctors were more likely to agree to take up preventive tests due to better communication and trust. This finding suggests that increasing diversity in the American medical workforce could substantially reduce differences in cardiovascular mortality between black and white population groups. Increasing diversity in physicians can be achieved through targeted recruitment efforts, mentorship programs as well as support for underrepresented groups in healthcare professions although there is limited evidence about the impact of such interventions.

5. CONCLUSIONS

This review has focused on the role of physicians in reducing inequalities and inequity in healthcare. There is consistent evidence across many countries and settings of a pro-rich distribution of specialist healthcare but more mixed evidence for primary care physicians. Though we identify a range of potential policy interventions to influence physicians' location choices, public–private mix of work and decisions made in the doctor–patient relationship to reduce discrimination, there is currently little evidence about the impact or cost-effectiveness of these policy interventions. Although individual choices of physicians are important, in many settings, the issues we underlined are often the legacy of how health systems have evolved and are organised in terms of the extent of health insurance coverage, the role of the private sector and the type of remuneration introduced. However, even with universal coverage and a small private sector with minimal out-of-pocket costs, discrimination and unconscious bias can exist that could be addressed in physician training programs, policies promoting informed patient choice of physician as well as affirmative action to ensure a more diverse physician workforce. Finally, research measuring changes in inequalities over time is essential to gauge whether such policies are effective.

REFERENCES

Alsan, M., Garrick, O., & Graziani, G. (2019). Does diversity matter for health? Experimental evidence from Oakland. *The American Economic Review, 109*(12), 4071–4111.

Ammi, M., Fooken, J., Klein, J., & Scott, A. (2023). Does doctors' personality differ from those of patients, the highly educated and other caring professions? An observational study using two nationally representative Australian surveys. *BMJ Open, 13*(4), e069850.

Anell, A., Dackehag, M., & Dietrichson, J. (2018). Does risk-adjusted payment influence primary care providers' decision on where to set up practices? *BMC Health Services Research, 18*(1).

Atalay, K., Edwards, R., & Georgiakakis, F. (2023). Mortality inequality, spatial differences and health care access. *Health Economics*. https://doi.org/10.1002/hec.4746

Bago d'Uva, T., Jones, A. M., & van Doorslaer, E. (2009). Measurement of horizontal inequity in health care utilisation using European panel data. *Journal of Health Economics, 28*(2), 280–289.

Barnighausen, T., & Bloom, D. (2009). Financial incentives for return of service in underserved areas: A systematic review. *BMC Health Services Research, 9*, 86.

Barros, P. P., & Olivella, P. (2005). Waiting lists and patient selection. *Journal of Economics and Management Strategy, 14*(3), 623–646.

Becker, G. (1957). *The economics of discrimination*. Chicago Universty Press.

Bertrand, M., & Duflo, E. (2017). Field experiments on discrimination. In E. Duflo & A. Banerjee (Eds.), *Handbook of field experiments*. Elsevier.

Biglaiser, G., & Albert Ma, C. T. (2007). Moonlighting: Public service and private practice. *The RAND Journal of Economics, 38*(4), 1113–1133.

Borkhoff, C. M., Hawker, G. A., Kreder, H. J., Glazier, R. H., Mahomed, N. N., & Wright, J. G. (2008). The effect of patients' sex on physicians' recommendations for total knee arthroplasty. *Canadian Medical Association Journal, 178*(6), 681–687.

Brekke, K. R., & Sørgard, L. (2007). Public versus private health care in a national health service. *Health Economics, 16*(6), 579–601.

Brunt, C. (2023). *Do primary care health professional shortage area physician bonus payments improve access to care or utilization of services for Medicare beneficiaries: Empirical evidence from established providers subject to HPSA designations.* Research Gate Pre-print.

Brunt, C. S., & Jensen, G. A. (2014). Payment generosity and physician acceptance of Medicare and Medicaid patients. *International Journal of Health Care Finance and Economics, 14*(4), 289–310.

Buykx, P., Humphreys, J., Wakerman, J., & Pashen, D. (2010). Systematic review of effective retention incentives for health workers in rural and remote areas: Towards evidence-based policy. *Australian Journal of Rural Health, 18*(3), 102–109.

Carrillo de Albornoz, S., Sia, K. L., & Harris, A. (2022). The effectiveness of teleconsultations in primary care: Systematic review. *Family Practice, 39*(1), 168–182.

Carvalho, N., Petrie, D., Chen, L., Salomon, J. A., & Clarke, P. (2019). The impact of Medicare part D on income-related inequality in pharmaceutical expenditure. *International Journal for Equity in Health, 18*(1), 57.

Chapman, E. N., Kaatz, A., & Carnes, M. (2013). Physicians and implicit bias: How doctors may unwittingly perpetuate health care disparities. *Journal of General Internal Medicine, 28*(11), 1504.

Chaudhury, N., Hammer, J., Kremer, M., Muralidharan, K., & Rogers, H. (2006). Missing in action: Teacher and health worker absence in developing countries. *The Journal of Economic Perspectives, 20*(1).

Chen, Y., Persson, P., & Polyakova, M. (2022). The roots of health inequality and the value of intrafamily expertise. *American Economic Journal: Applied Economics, 14*(3), 185–223.

Cheng, T. C., Kalb, G., & Scott, A. (2018). Public, private or both? Analyzing factors influencing the labour supply of medical specialists. *Canadian Journal of Economics/Revue canadienne d'économique, 51*(2), 660–692.

Cintron, A., & Morrison, R. S. (2006). Pain and ethnicity in the United States: A systematic review. *Journal of Palliative Medicine, 9*(6), 1454–1473.

Cookson, R., Propper, C., Asaria, M., & Raine, R. (2016). Socio-economic inequalities in health care in England. *Fiscal Studies, 37*(3–4), 371–403.

Coveney, L., Musoke, D., & Russo, G. (2023). Do private health providers help achieve universal health coverage? A scoping review of the evidence from low-income countries. *Health Policy and Planning*, czad075.

Dalziel, K. M., Huang, L., Hiscock, H., & Clarke, P. M. (2018). Born equal? The distribution of government Medicare spending for children. *Social Science & Medicine, 208*, 50–54.

Daniels, B., Kwan, A., Satyanarayana, S., Subbaraman, R., Das, R. K., Das, V., Das, J., & Pai, M. (2019). Use of standardised patients to assess gender differences in quality of tuberculosis care in urban India: A two-city, cross-sectional study. *Lancet Global Health, 7*(5), e633–e643.

Davillas, A., & Jones, A. M. (2021). Unmet health care need and income – Related horizontal equity in use of health care during the COVID-19 pandemic. *Health Economics, 30*(7), 1711–1716.

Devaux, M. (2015). Income-related inequalities and inequities in health care services utilisation in 18 selected OECD countries. *The European Journal of Health Economics, 16*(1), 21–33.

Devine, P. G., Forscher, P. S., Austin, A. J., & Cox, W. T. L. (2012). Long-term reduction in implicit race bias: A prejudice habit-breaking intervention. *Journal of Experimental Social Psychology, 48*(6), 1267–1278.

Dillender, M. (2022). How do Medicaid expansions affect the demand for health care workers? Evidence from vacancy postings. *Journal of Human Resources, 57*(4).

Drewniak, D., Krones, T., Sauer, C., & Wild, V. (2016). The influence of patients' immigration background and residence permit status on treatment decisions in health care. Results of a factorial survey among general practitioners in Switzerland. *Social Science & Medicine, 161*, 64–73.

Eggleston, K. (2000). Risk selection and optimal health insurance-provider payment systems. *Journal of Risk & Insurance, 67*(2), 173–196.

Ellis, R. P. (2000). Risk adjustment in competitive health plan markets. *Handbook of Health Economics, 1*, 755–845.

Eneanya, N. D., Yang, W., & Reese, P. P. (2019). Reconsidering the consequences of using race to estimate kidney function. *JAMA, 322*(2), 113–114.

Ferrinho, P., Van Lerberghe, W., Fronteira, I., Hipólito, F., & Biscaia, A. (2004). Dual practice in the health sector: Review of the evidence. *Human Resources for Health, 2*(1), 1–17.

Fiebig, D. G., van Gool, K., Hall, J., & Mu, C. (2021). Health care use in response to health shocks: Does socio-economic status matter? *Health Economics, 30*(12), 3032–3050.

FitzGerald, C., & Hurst, S. (2017). Implicit bias in healthcare professionals: A systematic review. *BMC Medical Ethics, 18*(1), 19.

Fooken, J., & Jeet, V. (2022). Using Australian panel data to account for unobserved factors in measuring inequities for different channels of healthcare utilization. *The European Journal of Health Economics, 23*(4), 717–728.

Frehywot, S., Mullan, F., Payne, P. W., & Ross, H. (2010). Compulsory service programmes for recruiting health workers in remote and rural areas: Do they work? *Bulletin of the World Health Organization, 88*(5), 364–370.

Fun, W. H., Tan, E. H., Sararaks, S., Sharif, S. M., Rahim, I. A., Jawahir, S., Eow, V. H. Y., Sibert, R. M. Y., Fadzil, M. M., & Mahmud, S. H. (2021). Implications of dual practice on cataract surgery waiting time and rescheduling: The case of Malaysia. *Healthcare (Basel), 9*(6), 653.

García-Prado, A., & González, P. (2011). Whom do physicians work for? An analysis of dual practice in the health sector. *Journal of Health Politics Policy and Law, 36*(2), 265–294.

Godager, G. (2012). Birds of a feather flock together: A study of doctor–patient matching. *Journal of Health Economics, 31*(1), 296–305.

González, P. (2004). Should physicians' dual practice be limited? An incentive approach. *Health Economics, 13*(6), 505–524.

González, P., & Macho-Stadler, I. (2013). A theoretical approach to dual practice regulations in the health sector. *Journal of Health Economics, 32*(1), 66–87.

Goyal, M. K., Kuppermann, N., Cleary, S. D., Teach, S. J., & Chamberlain, J. M. (2015). Racial disparities in pain management of children with appendicitis in emergency departments. *JAMA Pediatrics, 169*(11), 996.

Green, C. R., Wheeler, J. R. C., & LaPorte, F. (2003). Clinical decision making in pain management: Contributions of physician and patient characteristics to variations in practice. *The Journal of Pain, 4*(1), 29–39.

Greenwood, B. N., Hardeman, R. R., Huang, L., & Sojourner, A. (2020). Physician-patient racial concordance and disparities in birthing mortality for newborns. *Proceedings of the National Academy of Sciences of the U S A, 117*(35), 21194–21200.

Grépin, K. A. (2017). Private sector an important but not dominant provider of key health services in low-and middle-income countries. *Health Affairs.* https://doi.org/10.1377/hlthaff.2015.0862

Grobler, L., Marais, B. J., & Mabunda, S. (2015). Interventions for increasing the proportion of health professionals practising in rural and other underserved areas. *Cochrane Database of Systematic Reviews,* (6). https://doi.org/10.1002/14651858.CD005314.pub3

Gudzune, K. A., Beach, M. C., Roter, D. L., & Cooper, L. A. (2013). Physicians build less rapport with obese patients. *Obesity (Silver Spring, Md.), 21*(10), 2146.

Hall, W. J., Chapman, M. V., Lee, K. M., Merino, Y. M., Thomas, T. W., Payne, B. K., Eng, E., Day, S. H., & Coyne-Beasley, T. (2015). Implicit racial/ethnic bias among health care professionals and its influence on health care outcomes: A systematic review. *American Journal of Public Health, 105*(12), e60–e76.

Halldórsson, M., Kunst, A., Köhler, L., & Mackenbach, J. (2002). Socioeconomic differences in children's use of physician services in the Nordic countries. *Journal of Epidemiology and Community Health, 56,* 200–204.

Harris, R., Cormack, D., Tobias, M., Yeh, L.-C., Talamaivao, N., Minster, J., & Timutimu, R. (2012). Self-reported experience of racial discrimination and health care use in New Zealand: Results from the 2006/07 New Zealand health survey. *American Journal of Public Health, 102*(5), 1012–1019.

Hipgrave, D. B., & Hort, K. (2014). Dual practice by doctors working in South and East Asia: A review of its origins, scope and impact, and the options for regulation. *Health Policy and Planning, 29*(6), 703–716.

Hirsh, A. T., Hollingshead, N. A., Bair, M. J., Matthias, M. S., Wu, J., & Kroenke, K. (2013). The influence of patient's sex, race and depression on clinician pain treatment decisions. *European Journal of Pain, 17*(10), 1569–1579.

Hoffman, K. M., Trawalter, S., Axt, J. R., & Oliver, M. N. (2016). Racial bias in pain assessment and treatment recommendations, and false beliefs about biological differences between blacks and whites. *Proceedings of the National Academy of Sciences of the United States of America, 113*(16), 4296.

Holte, J. H., Kjaer, T., Abelsen, B., & Olsen, J. A. (2015). The impact of pecuniary and non-pecuniary incentives for attracting young doctors to rural general practice. *Social Science & Medicine, 128,* 1–9.

Humphrey, C., & Russell, J. (2004). Motivation and values of hospital consultants in south-east England who work in the national health service and do private practice. *Social Science & Medicine, 59*(6), 1241–1250.

Jan, S., Bian, Y., Jumpa, M., Meng, Q., Nyazema, N., Prakongsai, P., & Mills, A. (2005). Dual job holding by public sector health professionals in highly resource-constrained settings: Problem or solution? *Bulletin of the World Health Organization, 83*(10), 771–776.

Kaarboe, O., & Siciliani, L. (2023). Contracts for primary and secondary care physicians and equity-efficiency trade-offs. *Journal of Health Economics, 87,* 102715.

Kaestner, R., & Lubotsky, D. (2016). Health insurance and income inequality. *The Journal of Economic Perspectives, 30*(2), 53–78.

Kiwanuka, S. N., Rutebemberwa, E., Nalwadda, C., Okui, O., Ssengooba, F., Kinengyere, A. A., & Pariyo, G. W. (2011). Interventions to manage dual practice among health workers. *Cochrane Database of Systematic Reviews, 2011*(7), CD008405.

Koebisch, S. H., Rix, J., & Holmes, M. M. (2020). Recruitment and retention of healthcare professionals in rural Canada: A systematic review. *Canadian Journal of Rural Medicine, 25*(2).

Kristiansen, I., & Sheng, Y. (2022). *Doctor who? The effect of physician-patient match on the SES-health gradient.* CEBI Working Paper Series, No. 05/22. Universtiy of Copenhagen.

Lagarde, M., & Blaauw, D. (2014). Pro-social preferences and self-selection into jobs: Evidence from South African nurses. *Journal of Economic Behavior & Organization, 107*(Part A), 136–152.

Lai, C. K., Marini, M., Lehr, S. A., Cerruti, C., Shin, J.-E. L., Joy-Gaba, J. A., Ho, A. K., Teachman, B. A., Wojcik, S. P., Koleva, S. P., Frazier, R. S., Heiphetz, L., Chen, E. E., Turner, R. N., Haidt, J., Kesebir, S., Hawkins, C. B., Schaefer, H. S., Rubichi, S., . . . Nosek, B. A. (2014). Reducing implicit racial preferences: I. A comparative investigation of 17 interventions. *Journal of Experimental Psychology: General, 143*(4), 1765–1785.

Lai, C. K., Skinner, A. L., Cooley, E., Murrar, S., Brauer, M., Devos, T., Calanchini, J., Xiao, Y. J., Pedram, C., Marshburn, C. K., Simon, S., Blanchar, J. C., Joy-Gaba, J. A., Conway, J., Redford, L., Klein, R. A., Roussos, G., Schellhaas, F. M. H., Burns, M., . . . Nosek, B. A. (2016). Reducing implicit racial preferences: II. Intervention effectiveness across time. *Journal of Experimental Psychology: General, 145*(8), 1001–1016.

Lee, C., Ayers, S. L., & Kronenfeld, J. J. (2009, Summer). The association between perceived provider discrimination, healthcare utilization and health status in racial and ethnic minorities. *Ethnicity & Disease, 19*(3), 330–337.

Levesque, J.-F., Harris, M. F., & Russell, G. (2013). Patient-centred access to health care: Conceptualising access at the interface of health systems and populations. *International Journal for Equity in Health, 12*(1), 18.

Lueckmann, S. L., Hoebel, J., Roick, J., Markert, J., Spallek, J., von dem Knesebeck, O., & Richter, M. (2021). Socioeconomic inequalities in primary-care and specialist physician visits: A systematic review. *International Journal for Equity in Health, 20*(1), 58.

Mavis, S. C., Caruso, C. G., Dyess, N. F., Carr, C. B., Gerberi, D., & Dadiz, R. (2022). Implicit bias training in health professions education: A scoping review. *Medical Science Educator, 32*(6), 1541–1552.

Mandeville, K. L., Lagarde, M., & Hanson, K. (2014). The use of discrete choice experiments to inform health workforce policy: A systematic review. *BMC Health Services Research, 14*(1), 367.

McGrail, M. R., Doyle, Z., Fuller, L., Gupta, T. S., Shires, L., & Walters, L. (2023). The pathway to more rural doctors: The role of universities. *Medical Journal of Australia, 219*(Suppl. 3), S8–S13.

McGrail, M. R., Gurney, T., Fox, J., Martin, P., Eley, D., Nasir, B., & Kondalsamy-Chennakesavan, S. (2023). Rural medical workforce pathways: Exploring the importance of postgraduation rural training time. *Human Resources for Health, 21*(1).

McGrail, M., Humphreys, J., & Joyce, C. (2011). Nature of association between rural background and practice location: A comparison of general practitioners and specialists. *BMC Health Services Research, 11*, 63.

McGrail, M., Russell, D., & Campbell, D. (2016). Vocational training of general practitioners in rural locations is critical for the Australian rural medical workforce. *Medical Journal of Australia, 205*(5), 216–221.

McIsaac, M., Scott, A., & Kalb, G. (2015). The supply of general practitioners across local areas: Accounting for spatial heterogeneity. *BMC Health Services Research, 15*(1).

McIsaac, M., Scott, A., & Kalb, G. (2019). The role of financial factors in the mobility and location choices of general practitioners in Australia. *Human Resources for Health, 17*(1).

McKinlay, J., Piccolo, R., & Marceau, L. (2013). An additional cause of health care disparities: The variable clinical decisions of primary care doctors. *Journal of Evaluation in Clinical Practice, 19*(4), 664–673.

McPake, B., Russo, G., Hipgrave, D., Hort, K., & Campbell, J. (2016). Implications of dual practice for universal health coverage. *Bulletin of the World Health Organization, 94*(2), 142–146.

Miranda, J. J., Diez-Canseco, F., Lema, C., Lescano, A. G., Lagarde, M., Blaauw, D., & Huicho, L. (2012). Stated preferences of doctors for choosing a job in rural areas of Peru: A discrete choice experiment. *PLoS One, 7*(12), e50567.

Munga, M. A., & Maestad, O. (2009). Measuring inequalities in the distribution of health workers: The case of Tanzania. *Human Resources for Health, 7*, 4.

Obermeyer, Z., Powers, B., Vogeli, C., & Mullainathan, S. (2019). Dissecting racial bias in an algorithm used to manage the health of populations. *Science, 366*(6464), 447–453.

O'Sullivan, B. G., Joyce, C. M., & McGrail, M. R. (2014). Rural outreach by specialist doctors in Australia: A national cross-sectional study of supply and distribution. *Human Resources for Health, 12*(1), 50.

Phelan, S. M., Dovidio, J. F., Puhl, R. M., Burgess, D. J., Nelson, D. B., Yeazel, M. W., Hardeman, R., Perry, S., & van Ryn, M. (2014). Implicit and explicit weight bias in a national sample of 4732 medical students: The medical student changes study. *Obesity (Silver Spring, Md.), 22*(4), 1201.

Pierson, E., Cutler, D. M., Leskovec, J., Mullainathan, S., & Obermeyer, Z. (2021). An algorithmic approach to reducing unexplained pain disparities in underserved populations. *Nature Medicine, 27*(1), 136–140.

Planas, M.-E., García, P. J., Bustelo, M., Carcamo, C. P., Martinez, S., Nopo, H., Rodriguez, J., Merino, M.-F., & Morrison, A. (2015). Effects of ethnic attributes on the quality of family planning services in Lima, Peru: A randomized crossover trial. *PLoS One, 10*(2), e0115274.

Playford, D. E., Evans, S., Atkinson, D. N., Auret, K. A., & Riley, G. J. (2014). Impact of the rural clinical school of Western Australia on work location of medical graduates. *Medical Journal of Australia, 200*, 104–107.

Pulok, M., & Hajizadeh, M. (2022). Equity in the use of physician services in Canada's universal health system: A longitudinal analysis of older adults. *Social Science & Medicine, 307*, 115186.

Pulok, M., van Gool, K., & Hall, J. (2020). Inequity in physician visits: The case of the unregulated fee market in Australia. *Social Science and Medicine, 255*, 113004.

Pulok, M., van Gool, K., & Hall, J. (2022). The link between out-of-pocket costs and inequality in specialist care in Australia. *Australian Health Review, 46*(6), 652–659.

Racine, M., Dion, D., Dupuis, G., Guerriere, D. N., Zagorski, B., Choinière, M., Banner, R., Barton, P. M., Boulanger, A., Clark, A. J., Gordon, A., Guertin, M.-C., Intrater, H. M., LeFort, S. M., Lynch, M. E., Moulin, D. E., Ong-Lam, M., Peng, P., Rashiq, S., . . . Canadian STOP-PAIN Research Group by alphabetical order. (2014). The Canadian STOP-PAIN project: The burden of chronic pain—Does sex really matter? *The Clinical Journal of Pain, 30*(5), 443.

Reid, S. J., Peacocke, J., Kornik, S., & Wolvaardt, G. (2018). Compulsory community service for doctors in South Africa: A 15-year review. *South African Medical Journal, 108*(9), 741–747.

Rubineau, B., & Kang, Y. (2011). Bias in white: A longitudinal natural experiment measuring changes in discrimination. *Management Science.* https://doi.org/10.1287/mnsc.1110.1439

Russell, D., Mathew, S., Fitts, M., Liddle, Z., Murakami-Gold, L., Campbell, N., Ramjan, M., Zhao, Y., Hines, S., Humphreys, J. S., & Wakerman, J. (2021). Interventions for health workforce retention in rural and remote areas: A systematic review. *Human Resources for Health, 19*(1).

Saether, E. (2005). Physicians' labour supply: The wage impact on hours and practice combinations. *Labour, 19*(4), 673–703.

Samulowitz, A., Gremyr, I., Eriksson, E., & Hensing, G. (2018). "Brave men" and "emotional women": A theory-guided literature review on gender bias in health care and gendered norms towards patients with chronic pain. *Pain Research and Management, 2018.*

Scott, A., Holte, J. H., & Witt, J. (2020). Preferences of physicians for public and private sector work. *Human Resources for Health, 18*(1), 59.

Scott, A., Shiell, A., & King, M. (1996). Is general practitioner decision making associated with patient socio-economic status? *Social Science & Medicine, 42*(1), 35–46.

Scott, A., Witt, J., Humphreys, J., Joyce, C., Kalb, G., Jeon, S., & McGrail, M. (2013). Getting doctors into the bush: General practitioners' preferences for rural location. *Social Science & Medicine, 96*, 33–44.

Sharma, A., Siciliani, L., & Harris, A. (2013). Waiting times and socioeconomic status: Does sample selection matter? *Economic Modelling, 33*, 659–667.

Shen, M. J., Peterson, E. B., Costas-Muñiz, R., Hernandez, M. H., Jewell, S. T., Matsoukas, K., & Bylund, C. L. (2018). The effects of race and racial concordance on patient-physician communication: A systematic review of the literature. *Journal of Racial and Ethnic Health Disparities, 5*, 117–140.

Snoswell, C. L., Chelberg, G., De Guzman, K. R., Haydon, H. H., Thomas, E. E., Caffery, L. J., & Smith, A. C. (2021). The clinical effectiveness of telehealth: A systematic review of meta-analyses from 2010 to 2019. *Journal of Telemedicine and Telecare*. https://doi.org/10.1177/1357633X211022907

Sousa, A., Dal Poz, M. R., & Carvalho, C. L. (2012). Monitoring inequalities in the health workforce: The case study of Brazil 1991–2005. *PLoS One*, *7*(3), e33399.

Stone, J., Moskowitz, G. B., Zestcott, C. A., & Wolsiefer, K. J. (2020). Testing active learning workshops for reducing implicit stereotyping of Hispanics by majority and minority group medical students. *Stigma Health*, *5*(1), 94–103.

Swami, M., & Scott, A. (2021). Impact of rural workforce incentives on access to GP services in underserved areas: Evidence from a natural experiment. *Social Science & Medicine*, *281*, 114045.

van Doorslaer, E., Koolman, X., & Jones, A. M. (2004). Explaining income-related inequalities in doctor utilisation in Europe. *Health Economics*, *13*(7), 629–647.

van Doorslaer, E., Masseria, C., Koolman, X., & Group, O. H. E. R. (2006). Inequalities in access to medical care by income in developed countries. *Canadian Medical Association Journal*, *174*(2), 177–183.

van Doorslaer, E., Wagstaff, A., van der Burg, H., Christiansen, T., De Graeve, D., Duchesne, I., Gerdtham, U.-G., Gerfin, M., Geurts, J., Gross, L., Häkkinen, U., John, J., Klavus, J., Leu, R. E., Nolan, B., O'Donnell, O., Propper, C., Puffer, F., Schellhorn, M., Sundberg, G., & Winkelhake, O. (2000). Equity in the delivery of health care in Europe and the US. *Journal of Health Economics*, *19*(5), 553–583.

Vyas, D. A., Eisenstein, L. G., & Jones, D. S. (2020). Hidden in plain sight – Reconsidering the use of race correction in clinical algorithms. *New England Journal of Medicine*, *383*(9), 874–882.

Walpole, S. C. (2019). Health professionals' insights into the impacts of privately funded care within a national health service: A qualitative interview study. *Healthcare Policy*, *15*(2), 56–71.

Wamala, S., Merlo, J., Boström, G., & Hogstedt, C. (2007). Perceived discrimination, socioeconomic disadvantage and refraining from seeking medical treatment in Sweden. *Journal of Epidemiology & Community Health*, *61*(5), 409–415.

Werbeck, A., Wübker, A., & Ziebarth, N. R. (2021). Cream skimming by health care providers and inequality in health care access: Evidence from a randomized field experiment. *Journal of Economic Behavior & Organization*, *188*, 1325–1350.

Willems, S., De Maesschalck, S., Deveugele, M., Derese, A., & De Maeseneer, J. (2005). Socio-economic status of the patient and doctor–patient communication: Does it make a difference? *Patient Education and Counseling*, *56*(2), 139–146.

Wiseman, V., Lagarde, M., Batura, N., Lin, S., Irava, W., & Roberts, G. (2017). Measuring inequalities in the distribution of the Fiji health workforce. *International Journal for Equity in Health*, *16*(1), 115.

Wouterse, B., Geisler, J., Bar, M., & van Doorslaer, E. (2023). Has COVID-19 increased inequality in mortality by income in The Netherlands? *Journal of Epidemiology & Community Health*, *77*(4), 244–251.

Xue, Y., Smith, J. A., & Spetz, J. (2019). Primary care nurse practitioners and physicians in low-income and rural areas, 2010–2016. *JAMA*, *321*(1), 102–105.

Yong, J., Scott, A., Gravelle, H., Sivey, P., & McGrail, M. (2018). Do rural incentives payments affect entries and exits of general practitioners? *Social Science & Medicine*, *214*, 197–205.

Zestcott, C. A., Blair, I. V., & Stone, J. (2016). Examining the presence, consequences, and reduction of implicit bias in health care: A narrative review. *Group Processes & Intergroup Relations*, *19*(4), 528–542.

PERFORMANCE COMPARISON AND SOCIO-ECONOMIC INEQUALITIES IN UNMET NEED FOR MEDICAL TREATMENT AND DENTAL CARE IN THE EUROPEAN UNION

Andrea Riganti[a], Valerie Moran[b,c] and Luigi Siciliani[d]

[a]*University of Insubria, Italy*
[b]*Luxembourg Institute of Socio-Economic Research, Luxembourg*
[c]*Luxembourg Institute of Health, Luxembourg*
[d]*University of York, UK*

ABSTRACT

Ensuring adequate access to healthcare services is a priority across European countries. The EU has developed performance indicators to compare access using self-reported unmet need. Cross-country comparisons require adjustment for factors outside the health systems' control. We address two research questions to improve the comparability of unmet need for medical and dental care across the EU and the comparability of socio-economic inequalities in unmet need across the EU. First, we explore the role of risk adjustment for demographic and socio-economic factors, which are outside health systems' control, for both overall unmet need and unmet need due to affordability, waiting lists and distance. Second, we compare differences in unmet need by socio-economic status, and investigate whether different forms of risk adjustment affect such comparison. We show that adjusting for age, gender and chronic conditions reduces dispersion of unmet need for medical care across the EU. Controlling for income further reduces the dispersion, mostly due to affordability. When comparing socio-economic inequalities across countries, risk adjustment for age, gender and chronic conditions play a limited role. Socio-economic inequalities by income and education vary by reason of unmet need: the income gradient, even controlling for education, is mostly due to

---

Recent Developments in Health Econometrics
Contributions to Economic Analysis, Volume 297, 55–83
Copyright © 2024 Andrea Riganti, Valerie Moran and Luigi Siciliani
Published under exclusive licence by Emerald Publishing Limited
ISSN: 0573-8555/doi:10.1108/S0573-855520240000297004

affordability rather than waiting list or distance. For dental care, the main reason for unmet need is affordability. Risk adjustment for age, gender, chronic conditions and education plays a limited role. The income and education gradients are more pronounced for dental than medical care.

Keywords: Unmet need; access; affordability; waiting lists; distance; risk adjustment; EU-SILC; health system performance

1. INTRODUCTION

Ensuring adequate access to healthcare is a ubiquitous policy objective across European countries. Access is a multifaceted concept often evaluated using utilisation because realised access is easier to measure than potential access (Levesque et al., 2013). However, utilisation does not always provide insights into the barriers that individuals face when seeking care (Gulliford et al., 2002). To address this, access can be measured by unmet need, whereby patients are asked directly whether they needed a treatment but did not receive it.

European countries aim to improve the design and accessibility of health services, and to reduce inequalities in health and healthcare utilisation. European institutions can contribute to these objectives by developing performance indicators that compare access in the EU. Performance comparison can identify best practice and settings that require improvement. The European Pillar of Social Rights established a 'social scoreboard' in 2017 to monitor performance in access. Key indicators include self-reported unmet need for medical and dental care collected in the European Union Statistics on Income and Living Conditions (EU-SILC).

Risk-adjustment methods can make cross-country comparisons more meaningful for health system performance assessment by controlling for factors that influence outcomes but are outside health systems' control (Iezzoni, 2009; Moger & Peltola, 2014; Papanicolas & Smith, 2013). Risk-adjustment variables include clinical, demographic, health behaviour and socio-economic factors (Iezzoni, 2009; Juhnke et al., 2016). Age and gender are common variables (OECD, 2019). Socio-economic variables can also be included to reflect their association with morbidity (Juhnke et al., 2016). Currently, EU-SILC data on unmet need for medical care are used to compare health system performance but is not adjusted for individual-level risk factors.

In this study, we address two research questions to improve the comparison of unmet need for medical and dental care and socio-economic inequalities in unmet need across the EU. First, we explore the role of risk adjustment in comparing unmet need for medical treatment across 27 EU countries. In particular, we quantify the extent to which differences in unmet need across EU countries change after adjusting for demographic and socio-economic factors. Given that such factors are outside the control of the health system, we argue that risk-adjusted unmet need provides a better comparison of access when assessing performance across EU countries. After analysing overall unmet need, we also analyse the subset of individuals who report unmet need due to affordability (too expensive), waiting lists and distance. We focus on these three sources of unmet need because they relate to features of health systems. Countries differ in (1) financial coverage of healthcare (and out-of-pocket payments), (2) the extent to which waiting times for health services are an important policy issue or priority and (3) the geographical location of healthcare providers and transportation policies. We compare overall unadjusted and adjusted unmet need across the EU and unmet need due to affordability, waiting lists and distance separately.

Second, we compare differences in unmet need by Socio-Economic Status (SES) across the EU. Reducing socio-economic inequalities in health and healthcare utilisation is a ubiquitous policy objective in European countries. It is therefore useful to compare not only the level of unmet need but also inequalities in unmet need to mirror policymakers' desire to reduce health inequalities. Low-income individuals may have higher need and experience more barriers to access healthcare, resulting in higher unmet need. In line with the first research question, we explore the role of risk adjustment using demographic characteristics in comparing the socio-economic gradient in unmet need across the EU. Income and education are both proxies of SES but can be strongly correlated. We therefore investigate whether socio-economic inequalities in unmet need are due mostly to income or to education. We also investigate the socio-economic gradient in unmet need separately by sources of unmet need (affordability, waiting lists and distance to provider). For example, we expect the income gradient to be more pronounced if unmet need is due to affordability. Inequalities by SES can also arise when unmet need is due to long waiting lists. Individuals with higher SES may live closer or be able to travel to providers that are better endowed with shorter waiting times, or less likely to miss appointments and more likely to engage with health system processes.

We also conduct a separate analysis for unmet need for *dental* care. European countries have universal or close-to-universal coverage, with a strong public insurance component for medical care. Publicly funded dental care is more limited across EU countries with higher cost sharing and restricted eligibility and benefit packages (OECD/European Union, 2020). The extent of coverage in terms of both services and out-of-pocket payments differs significantly. We therefore expect a more pronounced socio-economic gradient in unmet need for dental care.

1.1 Related Literature

Numerous studies have used EU-SILC to investigate self-reported unmet medical need across countries (Chaupain-Guillot & Guillot, 2015; Detollenaere et al., 2017; Elstad, 2016; Fiorillo, 2019; Israel, 2016; Madureira-Lima et al., 2018; Reeves et al., 2017). Most undertook individual-level analyses while two studies (Detollenaere et al., 2017; Reeves et al., 2017) used country-level analyses. In general, women (Elstad, 2016; Fiorillo, 2019; Israel, 2016) and respondents in poorer health (Chaupain-Guillot & Guillot, 2015; Israel, 2016; Madureira-Lima et al., 2018) were associated with higher unmet need. Three studies found a negative association with education and unemployment (Elstad, 2016; Israel, 2016; Madureira-Lima et al., 2018). One study (Fiorillo, 2019) found that tertiary education was associated with lower unmet need due to care being too expensive or too far but another found it was associated with higher unmet need possibly due to respondents having less time to seek care (Chaupain-Guillot & Guillot, 2015). There were conflicting results regarding age with older age being associated with both lower (Chaupain-Guillot & Guillot, 2015) and higher (Madureira-Lima et al., 2018) unmet need. There was evidence of a negative association between unmet need and income (Chaupain-Guillot & Guillot, 2015; Israel, 2016; Madureira-Lima et al., 2018) due to care being too expensive (Fiorillo, 2019).

In contrast to these studies on the association of individual-level covariates on unmet need, one study (Moran et al., 2021) investigated whether risk adjustment affected cross-country comparisons of unmet need for medical care. The study shows that controlling for demographic, health, education, at-risk-of- poverty and unemployment variables leads to a small reduction in differences in unmet need for medical care. However, controlling for income results in a larger reduction in differences in unmet need across countries.

Two studies investigate unmet need for dental care. One found that in 2009, unmet need was higher in countries with a higher share of out-of-pocket payments (Chaupain-Guillot & Guillot, 2015), while the other examined income-related inequality in unmet need for dental care in Spain in 2007–2017 and found that the Great Recession resulted in higher inequality in access to dental care (Urbanos-Garrido, 2020).

Our study differs from Moran et al. (2021) in several respects. First, Moran et al. (2021), only focuses on unmet need for medical care in 2018. We use more recent 2019 data to examine risk adjustment for unmet need. Second, we also investigate unmet need by reason (affordability, waiting lists and distance to provider). Third, we examine unmet need for dental care. Fourth, we investigate socio-economic inequalities.

Last, we highlight that our focus is *not* on factors associated with unmet need, which has been the typical focus in previous literature. It is rather to explore whether adjusting for individual characteristics affects the international comparison of health system performance measures of unmet need across European countries, or the comparison of socio-economic inequalities in unmet need across countries.

2. DATA

We use EU-SILC data in 2019. We measure unmet need for medical examination or treatment during the previous 12 months (*ph040*), alongside the main reason for unmet need (*ph050*). Data are available for all household members who are at least 16 years old.

Unmet need for medical care is a dichotomous variable equal to one if the respondent selects 'Yes, there was at least one occasion when the person really needed an examination or treatment but did not receive it', and equal to zero if the respondent selects 'No, there was no occasion when the person really needed an examination or treatment but did not receive it'. The *main reason for unmet need* is a follow-up variable related to affordability of care, waiting lists, distance to the provider or other reasons. It is phrased as follows: 'What was the main reason for not having a medical examination or treatment?' Possible answers are: (1) could not afford to (too expensive); (2) waiting lists; (3) could not take time because of work, care for children or for others; (4) too far to travel/no means of transportation; (5) fear of doctor/hospitals/examination/treatment; (6) wanted to wait and see if problem got better on its own; (7) didn't know any good doctor or specialist and (8) other reasons.

We focus only on (1), (2) and (4) as these refer to features of the health systems that relate to financial barriers including the presence of co-payments or out-of-pocket payments that make care unaffordable (1), the presence of long waiting times and waiting lists (2) and the configuration and geographical location of providers that determine patient distance to the provider and accessibility (4), as opposed to factors related to patient preferences, their time availability to seek care or other reasons (3), (5–8).

In addition to unmet need for medical care, we also investigate unmet need for dental care, using similar definitions. We include covariates related to need: age, gender and chronic (long-standing) illness or condition. We measure SES with education (low, intermediate and high) and annual disposable household income (Appendix A for details).

The original sample included 484,103 adults. From the initial sample, 12.4% was excluded due to missing values or county-specific selection rules, leaving a final sample of 424,118 observations (details on data construction and observations exclusion are in Appendix A).

3. METHODS

Our regression model to compare unmet need for medical or dental care across the EU is:

$$y_{ij} = \alpha_j + X'_{ij}\beta + \epsilon_{ij} \tag{1}$$

where y_{ij} is a dummy variable equal to one when individual i in country j reports unmet need for medical (or dental) care (with $j = 1,\ldots,27$), α_j is a vector of country-specific fixed effects, X_{ij} is a vector of need variables (i.e. age, gender, chronic conditions). We include age as linear, quadratic and cubic functions to allow for non-linearities between unmet need and age, and for the same reason, we also include age and gender interactions. We estimate Levesque et al. (2013) as a logit model.

To obtain risk-adjusted unmet need in country j, after controlling for need factors, we compute the predicted probability $\widehat{y}_j$ of unmet need in country j evaluated at the EU sample mean, $\overline{X}$:

$$\widehat{y}_j = \widehat{\alpha}_j + \overline{X}'\widehat{\beta}$$

To compare unmet need across the EU after controlling for differences in SES, we run the following augmented model:

$$y_{ij} = \alpha_j + X'_{ij}\beta + \text{SES}'_{ij}\gamma + \epsilon_{ij} \tag{2}$$

where SES_{ij} includes education and income. The predicted probability of reporting unmet need in country j is: $\widehat{y}_j = \widehat{\alpha}_j + \overline{X}'\widehat{\beta} + \overline{SES}'\widehat{\gamma}$. We also estimate separate logit models (Gulliford et al., 2002; Levesque et al., 2013) for each of the three main reasons for unmet need related to affordability, waiting lists and distance.

Finally, we compare the socio-economic gradient in unmet need across the EU by estimating for each country j the following model (we remove j to avoid notation clutter):

$$y_i = \alpha + X'_i\beta + \text{SES}'_i\gamma + \epsilon_i \tag{3}$$

where y_i is unmet need for individual i in each country. We measure income in deciles and use the lowest decile and low education as reference groups. We can rewrite the model as:

$$y_i = \alpha + X'_i\beta + \sum_{k=1,\dots,9}\gamma_k \text{ income\_decile}_k + \lambda_1 \text{ medium\_edu} + \lambda_2 \text{ high\_edu} + \epsilon_i \tag{4}$$

The income gradient in a given country is given by γ_9, the difference in unmet need between the richest (highest income decile) and poorest individuals (first decile). Similarly, the education gradient is given by λ_2, the difference in unmet need between individuals with high and low education. We run this model for each country and compare the income and education gradient, as captured by γ_9 and λ_2 across the EU. In every specification, we use personal cross-sectional weights (UDB variable RB050) to ensure representativeness of population composition. All the models are estimated with robust standard errors.

4. RESULTS

Unmet need varied considerably across the EU (Table B1): less than 1% in Spain (0.34%), Malta (0.39%), Austria (0.67%), Germany (0.72%) and Luxembourg (0.9%). Unmet need was more than double the EU-27 mean of 3% in Estonia (17.58%), Greece (9.28%), Poland (8.51%), Denmark (8.50%), Latvia (7.93%), Romania (6.92%) and Hungary (6.46%).

Across the EU-27, unmet need for any reason was 3%, 0.94% for affordability, 0.64% for waiting lists and only 0.09% for distance (1.33% for other reasons). Over 1% reported affordability as the reason for unmet need in Greece, Romania, Portugal, Belgium, Bulgaria, Italy, Latvia and Cyprus. Unmet need due to waiting lists was greater than 1% in Estonia, Finland, Denmark, Ireland, Latvia, Lithuania, Poland, Slovakia and Slovenia. In contrast, unmet need due to distance was less than 1% in all countries.

Individuals who reported unmet need were older relative to the full sample (53 versus 49 years), more likely to be women (55.2% vs. 52.2%), have a chronic condition (56.5% vs. 33%), be in the lowest income decile (24.2% vs. 10%) and less likely to have high education (19.9% vs. 27.4%). Differences in income were pronounced for unmet need due to affordability (38.7% in the lowest income decile and 0.67% in the highest decile) and distance (42.5% vs. 0.37%) but less pronounced due to waiting lists (15.1% in the lowest income decile and 4.2% in the highest) (Table B2).

4.1 Regression Results. The Role of Risk Adjustment

Fig. 1a compares unmet need across the EU when controlling for different variables (as Table C1). Controlling for need (age, gender and chronic conditions) reduced unmet need for some countries, such as Estonia, Poland, Latvia, Hungary, Finland, Sweden, Croatia. Adjusted unmet need was statistically significantly different from unadjusted unmet need at the 5% level only in Estonia (3.2 percentage point (pp) reduction), Poland (1.5 pp), Latvia (1.6 pp) and Finland (1.6 pp). Controlling further for education did not generally alter the comparison. On the contrary, controlling for income reduced the difference between adjusted and unadjusted unmet need in several countries and reduced dispersion in unmet need across the EU. Unmet need adjusted for income was smaller than unmet need adjusted for need and education at the 5% level of statistical significance in Estonia (2.4 pp), Greece (2.5 pp), Poland (1.7 pp), Latvia (1.9 pp), Romania (2.6 pp), Hungary (1.7 pp), Slovakia (1.4 pp), Croatia (1 pp) and Bulgaria (0.8 pp).

Figs. 1b–1d replicate the analysis by main reason for unmet need due to affordability, waiting lists and distance. Controlling for age, gender and chronic conditions reduced unmet need due to *affordability* only in Greece (0.8 pp), Poland (0.4 pp) and Latvia (0.1 pp) (Table C2), due to *waiting lists* in Estonia (3.1 pp), Finland (1.6 pp) and Poland (0.7 pp) (Table C3) and due to *distance* in Estonia (0.4 pp), Croatia (0.4 pp) and Latvia (0.3 pp) (Table C4). Further controlling for income, in addition to need and education, significantly reduced (both in statistical and quantitative terms) unmet need due to affordability in Greece (3.6 pp), Romania (2.2 pp), Latvia (1.3 pp), Portugal (0.3 pp), Bulgaria (0.6 pp) and Poland (0.4 pp). In contrast, further controlling for income did not alter the comparison of unmet need due to waiting lists and distance.

4.2 Socio-Economic Gradient

Based on Equation (4), Fig. 2 plots the difference in unmet need between the richest (10th income decile) and the poorest (first decile). Panel (2a) provides the income

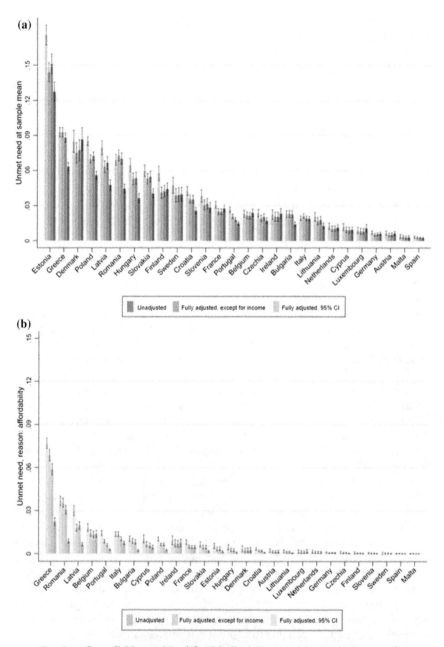

Fig. 1. Overall Unmet Need for Medical Care and by Main Reason for Unmet Need, Unadjusted and Adjusted for Covariates.

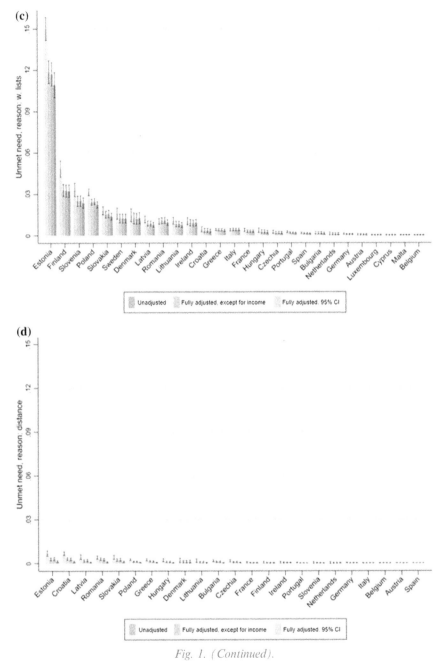

Fig. 1. (Continued).

Note: Panel (a) indicates unmet need for any reason, (b) refers to unmet need due to affordability, (c) to waiting lists and (d) to distance. In panel (a), sample size is equal to 424,118, while in panels (b–d), due to exclusion of unmet need for other categories rather than the specific one that is considered, sample sizes are equal to 411,695, 410,197 and 406,131, respectively. In all panels, unmet need is evaluated at covariates sample mean. In all specifications, age is also included with quadratic and cubic functions and interacted with gender. Income: annual equivalised disposable income, adjusted for purchasing power standard categorised in deciles according to EU distribution. Confidence intervals are set at 95%. *Source:* Our estimation using EU-SILC data.

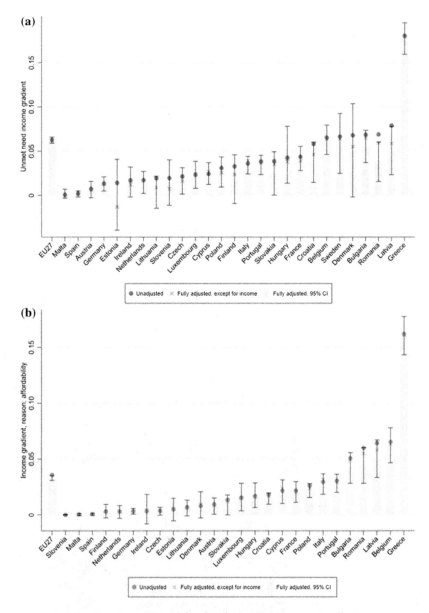

Fig. 2. Unmet Need for Medical Care Income Gradients.

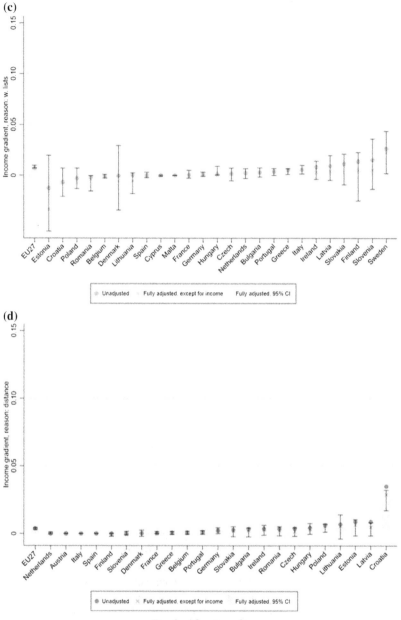

Fig. 2. (Continued).

Note: Income Gradient is the difference between whether the individual reports unmet need in or not in highest and lowest income decile. Panel (a) indicates income gradient for any reason, (b) refers to gradient due to affordability, (c) to waiting lists and (d) to distance. Unadjusted estimates are country-specific raw differences, while in adjusted specification, we include gender, age with quadratic and cubic functions, and these interacted with gender, chronic conditions. In panel (a) sample size is equal to 424,118, while in panels (b–d), due to exclusion of unmet need for other categories rather than the specific one that is considered, sample sizes are equal to 411,695, 410,197 and 406,131, respectively. Confidence intervals are set at 95%. *Source:* Our estimation using EU-SILC data.

gradient for unmet need, while panels (2b–2d) show the income gradients for each main reason (affordability, waiting lists and distance).

Panel (a) suggests that after controlling for need and education, the income gradient was highest in Greece (18 pp). The income gradient was greater than 5 pp and statistically significant in Bulgaria, Sweden and Belgium, less than 5 pp and statistically significant in Romania, Croatia, France, Hungary, Portugal, Italy and Poland, and less than 2.5 pp and statistically significant in Cyprus, Luxembourg, Czech Republic, Netherlands and Germany. Panel (a) also suggests that adjusting for need reduced the income gradient in some countries, but the impact was relatively small.

Panel (2b) shows that the income gradient in unmet need was mostly due to affordability, while demographic adjustment played a minor role. Panel (2c) shows that the income gradient in unmet need due to waiting lists was statistically significant at the 5% level only in Sweden, Greece, Italy and Hungary, while only Sweden had a gradient higher than 1 pp (2.2 pp). Panel (2d) shows that the income gradient in unmet need due to distance was generally close to zero, except for Croatia, Poland and Germany.

In Fig. D1 in the Appendix, we report the education gradient for unmet need for medical care. Panel (a) suggests that the unadjusted education gradient was mostly due to the correlation between education and income and to some extent education and need. Panels (b–d) suggest that the adjusted education gradient was mostly due to affordability but also due to waiting lists and distance in some countries.

4.3 Unmet Need for Dental Care

Table B3 shows that unmet need for dental care was higher than for medical care across the EU (4% versus 3%). Unmet need due to affordability was higher for dental care (2.6% vs 0.94%) and lower for waiting lists (0.21% vs 0.64%). Unmet need for dental care due to waiting lists was higher than medical care in Finland (5.3%) and Slovenia (3.47%). Unmet need due to distance was comparable between dental and medical care (0.04% vs. 0.09%). Latvia and Portugal reported the highest levels of unmet need for dental care, 13%. Countries with relatively high unmet need for dental care, between 5% and 10%, were Belgium, Denmark, Estonia, Finland, Greece, Romania and Spain. Countries with low levels (less than 2%) included Austria, Germany, Malta, Luxembourg and Netherlands. Given the relatively small role of waiting lists and distance as sources of unmet need, we focus on overall unmet need and unmet need due to affordability.

Fig. 3a suggests that adjusting for need and education played a relatively small role when comparing unmet need for dental care across the EU. Controlling for income played a more important role. For example, the adjusted unmet need for dental care reduced from 13.5% to 8.1% in Latvia and 13%–7.1% in Portugal. There were also marked reductions in Greece, Romania, Spain and Estonia, while reductions were lower in Slovenia, Slovakia, Lithuania, Poland, Hungary, Bulgaria, Croatia and Czechia (Table C5).

Fig. 3b focuses on affordability. The results were very similar. Adjusting for need did not tend to alter the comparison, while adjusting for income greatly reduced the dispersion of unmet need across the EU. Adjusting for education (but not income) in addition to need also reduced to some extent the dispersion of unmet need across the EU.

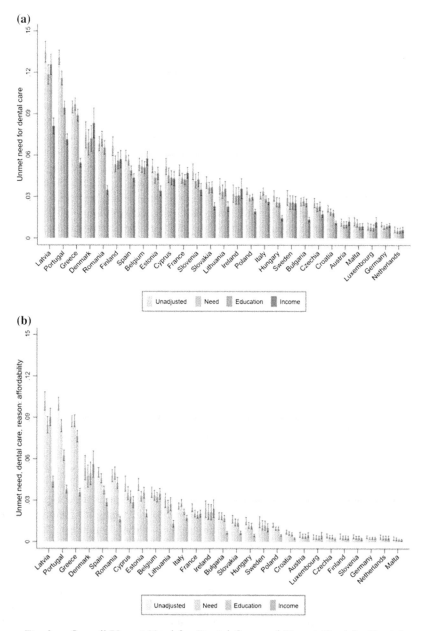

Fig. 3. Overall Unmet Need for Dental Care and Unmet Need for Dental Care due to Affordability, Unadjusted and Adjusted for Covariates.

Note: Panel (a) indicates unmet need for dental care for any reason, while (b) refers to unmet need for dental care due to affordability. In panel (a), sample size is equal to 423,719, while in panel (b), due to exclusion of unmet need for dental care for other categories rather than affordability, sample sizes is equal to 416,745. In all panels, unmet need for dental care is evaluated at covariates sample mean. In all specifications, age is also included with quadratic and cubic functions and interacted with gender. Income: annual equivalised disposable income, adjusted for purchasing power standard categorised in deciles according to EU distribution. Confidence intervals are set at 95%. *Source:* Our estimation using EU-SILC data.

Panel (a) of Fig. 4 shows the estimates of the income gradient for dental care in each country. The income gradient was more than 15 pp in Latvia (18 pp) and Portugal (17.9 pp); between 10 and 15 pp in Spain, Greece, Denmark and Belgium; and between 5 and 10 pp in Romania, France, Cyprus, Lithuania, Sweden, Ireland, Italy and Finland. Therefore, the income gradient was much more pronounced than for medical care. Panel (a) of Fig. 4 also shows that adjusting for need only played a very minor role. Panel (b) confirms that affordability was the main source of unmet need.

Fig. D2 in the Appendix displays the education gradient in unmet need for dental care. Panel (a) suggests that the education gradient, after controlling for need and income, was above 5 pp in Latvia and Romania and between 3 and 5 pp in Portugal, Spain, Denmark and Cyprus. The education gradient for dental care was again more pronounced compared to medical care. Controlling for need played a relatively small role, while controlling for income generally reduced the education gradient. Panel (b) confirms that the education gradient was mostly present when unmet need was due to affordability.

5. DISCUSSION

Our results show that for some countries with high unmet need, adjusting for age, gender and chronic conditions reduced the dispersion of unmet need across the EU. Further controlling for education did not alter the comparison, while controlling for disposable income further reduced its dispersion. These results suggest that risk adjustment can improve the comparability of unmet need across the EU by eliminating some differences that are unrelated to the health system.

Individuals experience unmet need for a variety of reasons related to health system design. Our results confirm that risk adjustment on age, gender and chronic conditions also played a role in improving the comparison of unmet need due to affordability, waiting lists and distance, while education did not.

Interestingly, we find that controlling for income does not alter the comparison of unmet need due to waiting lists or distance. Instead, controlling for income significantly reduced unmet need due to affordability in several countries. Given that countries differ in income to a great extent across the EU, controlling for income allows to isolate differences in unmet need across countries that are due to ability to pay.

In relation to our second research question on the comparison of socio-economic inequalities across countries, we show that risk adjustment for age, gender and chronic conditions plays a very limited role. Instead, socio-economic inequalities by income and education are very different depending on the reason for unmet need. The income gradient in unmet need, even after controlling for education, is mostly due to affordability and less to waiting lists.

Higher income allows individuals to afford co-payments within publicly funded systems or to purchase care in the private sector. Income should play a less prominent role in unmet need due to waiting lists, as patients' waiting time should be based on need, and not ability to pay, in many publicly funded health systems. However, long waiting lists may induce individuals with higher income to pay out of pocket in the private sector or to purchase private health insurance. Some

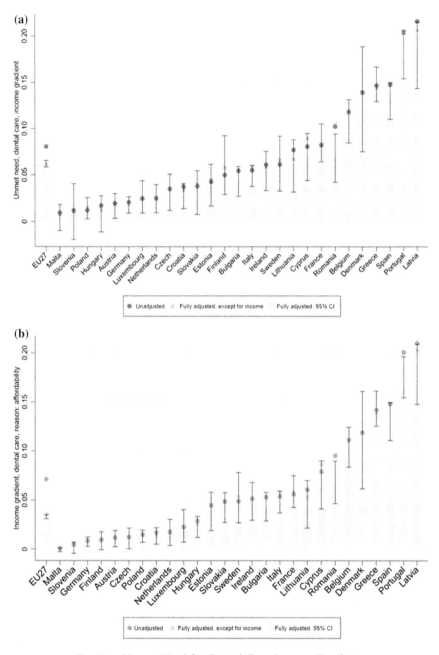

Fig. 4. Unmet Need for Dental Care Income Gradients.
Note: Income Gradient is the difference between whether the individual reports unmet need for dental care or not in highest and lowest income decile. Panel (a) indicates income gradient for any reason, (b) refers to gradient due to affordability. Unadjusted estimates are country-specific raw differences, while in adjusted specification, we include gender, age with quadratic and cubic functions and these interacted with gender, chronic conditions. In panel (a), sample size is equal to 423,719, while in panel (b), due to exclusion of unmet need for dental care for other categories rather than affordability, sample size is equal to 416,745. Confidence intervals are set at 95%.
Source: Our estimation using EU-SILC data.

evidence (Siciliani, 2016) suggests that individuals with higher SES tend to wait less even within publicly funded systems if they live closer to providers with shorter waiting times, are less likely to miss appointments and are more likely to engage with health system processes (Ellis et al., 2017). Our results suggest these mechanisms are likely to play a limited role in explaining inequalities in unmet need for medical care due to waiting lists.

We also show that there is an education gradient in unmet need, even after controlling for income. The adjusted education gradient is mostly related to affordability but not exclusively as we detect an education gradient in unmet need due to waiting lists for some countries. These findings are in line with more educated individuals being better able to navigate the health system to obtain an appointment or visit, have better social networks to ask for advice. More educated individuals are also less likely to live in remote or rural areas (Booi & Boterman, 2020) so distance may be less of a barrier to access.

We also compared the results between medical treatment and dental care. For dental care, we find that the main reason for unmet need is affordability, and to a lesser extent waiting lists or distance with few exceptions (Finland and Slovenia). This is consistent with a higher likelihood of dental care being provided in the private sector, which has shorter waiting times but where demand is rationed by prices and co-payments.

Controlling for income plays a more significant role in reducing the dispersion of unmet need for dental care across EU countries. Given that the income distribution is mostly outside the health-system influence, controlling for income can improve the comparison of unmet need across EU countries. Countries with high unmet need for dental care could expand the health basket to include routine dental care with no or limited co-payments to reduce unmet need due to affordability.

The education gradient for dental care is more pronounced even after controlling for income. This suggests that more educated individuals are better able to address affordability issues, perhaps by identifying lower cost options or undertaking regular check-ups whereby problems are identified early and require less (costly) treatment. A previous study also found that higher unmet need for dental care due to financial difficulties was associated with lower income and education levels (Kim et al., 2017).

Our study has limitations. First, we were only able to control for a limited number of need indicators contained in EU-SILC. Second, we were not able to observe whether the patient received healthcare within the public or private sector, which could explain some of the inequalities in unmet need.

6. CONCLUSION

Our analysis shows that there is scope to risk adjust unmet need to improve the comparability of this indicator across the EU by controlling for some factors that are unrelated to the health system. Controlling for income seems particularly important when unmet need is due to affordability and for dental care where affordability issues are more prominent. Risk adjustment plays a more limited role when comparing socio-economic inequalities across countries. We also show that socio-economic inequalities in unmet need by income are mostly driven by affordability, while inequalities are smaller when unmet need is due to waiting lists, suggesting that there is scope for policy interventions that limit out-of-pocket expenses.

REFERENCES

Booi, H., & Boterman, W. R. (2020). Changing patterns in residential preferences for urban or suburban living of city dwellers. *Journal of Housing and the Built Environment, 35*(1), 93–123.

Börsch-Supan, A., Hank, K., Jürges, H. (2005, December 2). A new comprehensive and international view on ageing: Introducing the 'Survey of Health, Ageing and Retirement in Europe'. *European Journal of Ageing, 2*(4), 245–253. https://doi.org/10.1007/s10433-005-0014-9. PMID: 28794739; PMCID: PMC5546288.

Chaupain-Guillot, S., & Guillot, O. (2015). Health system characteristics and unmet care needs in Europe: An analysis based on EU-SILC data. *The European Journal of Health Economics: HEPAC: Health Economics in Prevention and Care, 16*(7), 781–796.

Detollenaere, J., Hanssens, L., Vyncke, V., De Maeseneer, J., & Willems, S. (2017). Do we reap what we sow? Exploring the association between the strength of European primary healthcare systems and inequity in unmet need. *PLoS One, 12*(1), e0169274.

Di, M. E., Dupré, D., & Grundiza, S. (2021). Investing in statistics: EU-SILC. In A. G. Guio, E. Marlier, & B. Nolan (Eds.), *Improving the understanding of poverty and social exclusion in Europe 2021 Edition.* Publications Office of the European Union.

Ellis, D. A., McQueenie, R., McConnachie, A., Wilson, P., & Williamson, A. E. (2017). Demographic and practice factors predicting repeated non-attendance in primary care: A national retrospective cohort analysis. *The Lancet Public Health, 2*(12), e551–e559.

Elstad, J. I. (2016). Income inequality and foregone medical care in Europe during The Great Recession: Multilevel analyses of EU-SILC surveys 2008-2013. *International Journal for Equity in Health, 15*(1), 101.

Fiorillo, D. (2020). Reasons for unmet needs for health care: The role of social capital and social support in some western EU countries. *International Journal of Health Economics and Management, 20*, 79–98. https://doi.org/10.1007/s10754-019-09271-0

Gulliford, M., Figueroa-Munoz, J., Morgan, M., Hughes, D., Gibson, B., Beech, R., & Hudson, M. (2002). What does "access to health care" mean? *Journal of Health Services Research & Policy, 7*(3), 186–188.

Iezzoni, I. (2009). Risk adjustment for performance measurement. In P. C. Smith, E. Mossialos, I. Papanicolas, & S. Leatherman (Eds.), *Performance measurement for health system improvement.* Cambridge University Press.

Israel, S. (2016). How social policies can improve financial accessibility of healthcare: A multi-level analysis of unmet medical need in European countries. *International Journal for Equity in Health, 15*, 41.

Juhnke, C., Bethge, S., & Muhlbacher, A. C. (2016). A review on methods of risk adjustment and their use in integrated healthcare systems. *International Journal of Integrated Care, 16*(4), 4.

Kim, N., Kim, C. Y., & Shin, H. (2017). Inequality in unmet dental care needs among South Korean adults. *BMC Oral Health, 17*(1), 80.

Levesque, J. F., Harris, M. F., & Russell, G. (2013). Patient-centred access to health care: Conceptualising access at the interface of health systems and populations. *International Journal for Equity in Health, 12*, 18.

Madureira-Lima, J., Reeves, A., Clair, A., & Stuckler, D. (2018). The great recession and inequalities in access to health care: A study of unemployment and unmet medical need in Europe in the economic crisis. *International Journal of Epidemiology, 47*(1), 58–68.

Moger, T. A., & Peltola, M. (2014). Risk adjustment of health-care performance measures in a multinational register-based study: A pragmatic approach to a complicated topic. *SAGE Open Medicine, 2*. https://doi.org/10.1177/2050312114526589

Moran, V., Riganti, A., Siciliani, L., & Jones, A. (2021). Comparing unmet need for medical care across EU countries: Does risk adjustment matter? In A. G. Guio, E. Marlier, & B. Nolan (Eds.), *Improving the understanding of povery and social exclusion in Europe 2021 edition.* Publications Office of the European Union.

OECD. (2019). *Health care quality indicators: OECD. stat.* https://stats.oecd.org/Index.aspx?
    QueryId=51879
OECD/European Union. (2020). *Health at a Glance: Europe 2020: State of health in the EU cycle.*
    OECD Publishing.
Papanicolas, I., & Smith, P. C.. (2013) International comparisons of health systems. In I. Papanicolas & P.
    C. Smith (Eds.), *Health system performance comparison an agenda for policy, information and
    research.* European Observatory on Health Systems and Policies Series. Open University Press.
Reeves, A., McKee, M., Mackenbach, J., Whitehead, M., & Stuckler, D. (2017). Public pensions and
    unmet medical need among older people: Cross-national analysis of 16 European countries,
    2004–2010. *Journal of Epidemiology & Community Health, 71*(2), 174–180.
Siciliani, L. (2016). Waiting times: Evidence of social inequalities in access for care. In B. Sobolev, A.
    Levy, & S. Goring (Eds.), *Data and measures in health services research* (pp. 1–17). Springer US.
Urbanos-Garrido, R. M. (2020). Income-related inequalities in unmet dental care needs in Spain:
    Traces left by the Great Recession. *International Journal for Equity in Health, 19*(1), 207.

APPENDIX A: DATA CONSTRUCTION

For *education*, we follow the ISCED 2011 classification (UNESCO and UNESCO Institute for Statistics, 2012). In line with previous work (Börsch-Supan et al., 2005), we classify education as *Low* if the respondent had no education (level 0), primary education (level 1) or lower secondary education (level 2); as *Intermediate* if the respondent had upper secondary education (level 3) or post-secondary, non-tertiary education (level 4); and as *High* if the respondent had tertiary education (including short-cycle tertiary education, level 5 and up to Doctoral studies or equivalent, level 8).

Total *annual disposable household income* is computed in euros as the gross household income net of regular taxes on wealth, regular inter-household cash transfer and taxes on income and social insurance contributions in the previous income reference year. For countries that do not belong to the euro area (Bulgaria, Croatia, Czechia, Denmark, Hungary, Poland, Romania, Sweden), we use the conversion factor provided by Eurostat in the EU-SILC. To adjust for household size, we normalise income using the modified OECD scale provided in the EU-SILC dataset. The modified OECD scale gives a value of 1 to the first adult (above 14 years old), followed by 0.5 for each additional household member above 14 years and 0.3 for each household member under 14 years. Moreover, we use the Eurostat deflator to adjust income for Purchasing Power Standard (PPS). We categorise annual equivalised disposable income (expressed in PPS) into deciles based on the income distribution across the whole EU sample.

We exclude 15,109 observations (3.1%) due to missing values on unmet need. In *register* countries (Denmark, Finland, Netherlands, Slovenia, Sweden), most components of income and some demographic information are provided by administrative registers. Data on other personal variables are collected by interviewing only one member of a household in a representative sample of persons (the *selected respondent model*) (Di et al., 2021). This meant we excluded 42,981 (8.9%) observations who were not the interviewed household member in the *register* countries. Moreover, we excluded 46 observations (0.01%) who did not report the reason for unmet need and 1,849 observations (0.38%) with missing data on covariates (education: $n = 816$, chronic conditions: $n = 972$) and extreme or negative annual equivalised disposable income (under $-€20,000$ PPS: $n = 48$, over €600,000 PPS: $n = 13$).

APPENDIX B: UNMET NEED IN EU POPULATION AND MAIN REASON FOR UNMET NEED

Table B1. Unmet Need for Medical Care and Reason for Unmet Need by Country.

	Unmet Need in Adult Population for Any Reason (%)	Reason for Unmet Need: Affordability (%)	Reason for Unmet Need: Waiting Lists (%)	Reason for Unmet Need: Distance (%)	Reason for Unmet Need: Other (%)
Austria	0.67	0.21	0.06	>0.01	0.39
Belgium	2.32	1.81	0.01	0.01	0.50
Bulgaria	2.29	1.02	0.17	0.16	0.94
Croatia	4.25	0.33	0.43	0.66	2.83
Cyprus	1.19	1.03	0.02	–	0.14
Czech	2.36	0.09	0.25	0.15	1.87
Denmark	8.50	0.32	1.37	0.18	6.63
Estonia	17.58	0.45	14.56	0.57	2.00
Finland	5.74	0.06	4.80	0.06	0.83
France	3.07	0.77	0.39	0.06	1.85
Germany	0.72	0.10	0.10	0.02	0.49
Greece	9.28	7.55	0.39	0.23	1.11
Hungary	6.46	0.42	0.34	0.20	5.49
Ireland	2.25	0.92	1.02	0.06	0.25
Italy	1.95	1.34	0.40	0.01	0.20
Latvia	7.93	2.84	1.08	0.40	3.61
Lithuania	2.05	0.17	1.05	0.17	0.66
Luxembourg	0.90	0.16	0.02	–	0.71
Malta	0.39	0.02	0.02	–	0.36
Netherlands	1.25	0.17	0.11	0.03	0.94
Poland	8.51	0.94	2.99	0.23	4.34
Portugal	2.67	1.40	0.25	0.04	0.97
Romania	6.92	3.55	0.96	0.38	2.02
Slovakia	5.99	0.61	1.72	0.39	3.27
Slovenia	3.84	0.05	3.30	0.03	0.45
Spain	0.34	0.03	0.17	>0.01	0.14
Sweden	4.74	0.04	1.54	–	3.16
EU-27	3.00	0.94	0.64	0.09	1.33

Source: Our calculation using SILC 2019 data. Sample size: 424,118.

Table B2. Descriptive Statistics for Adult Population and Those Reporting Unmet Need for Medical Care, EU-27.

	EU Adult Population	Among Those Reporting Unmet Need for Any Reason	Among Those Reporting Unmet Need Due to Affordability	Among Those Reporting Unmet Need Due to Waiting Lists	Among Those Reporting Unmet Need Due to Distance
Age, mean and standard	49.33	52.95	56.67	54.59	64.39
Deviation	18.04	17.33	16.48	17.04	16.97
Gender: Female (%)	52.19	55.24	60.77	59.08	62.61
Reporting chronic cond. (%)	33.04	56.45	61.65	61.34	79.19
Higher education (%)	27.41	19.93	9.58	27.52	12.13
Intermediate education (%)	44.26	44.72	35.33	46.11	32.20
Low education (%)	28.33	35.35	55.10	26.36	55.67
Income: 1st decile (%)	10.00	24.20	38.72	15.06	42.48
Income: 2nd decile (%)	10.00	17.14	21.46	15.25	22.91
Income: 3rd decile (%)	10.00	12.44	12.42	12.93	11.14
Income: 4th decile (%)	10.00	11.04	9.11	12.70	7.79
Income: 5th decile (%)	10.00	10.24	7.52	12.49	6.78
Income: 6th decile (%)	10.00	7.30	4.66	9.23	2.28
Income: 7th decile (%)	10.00	5.85	2.43	6.91	4.36
Income: 8th decile (%)	10.00	4.81	2.00	6.83	0.93
Income: 9th decile (%)	10.00	3.66	1.01	4.41	0.97
Income: 10th decile (%)	10.00	3.31	0.67	4.20	0.37

Source: Our calculation using SILC 2019 data. Income: annual equivalised disposable income adjusted for purchasing power standard categorised in deciles according to EU distribution. Sample size: 424,118.

Table B3. Unmet Need for Dental Care and Reason for Unmet Need by Country.

	Unmet Need in Adult Population for Any Reason (%)	Reason for Unmet Need: Affordability (%)	Reason for Unmet Need: Waiting Lists (%)	Reason for Unmet Need: Distance (%)	Reason for Unmet Need: Other (%)
Austria	1.16	0.52	0.06	0.02	0.55
Belgium	5.35	3.52	0.07	0.06	1.70
Bulgaria	2.63	1.86	0.13	0.11	0.53
Croatia	2.15	0.72	0.07	0.19	1.18
Cyprus	5.19	4.16	0.01	0.01	1.00
Czech	2.57	0.45	0.30	0.09	1.73
Denmark	7.48	5.22	0.10	0.08	2.06
Estonia	5.23	4.09	0.65	0.05	0.44
Finland	6.65	0.39	5.30	0.01	0.95
France	4.93	2.40	0.30	0.06	2.17
Germany	1.01	0.36	0.01	0.00	0.64
Greece	9.51	8.64	0.10	0.03	0.73
Hungary	3.08	1.49	0.02	0.08	1.50
Ireland	3.23	2.34	0.08	0.01	0.80
Italy	3.10	2.58	0.11	0.01	0.40
Latvia	13.49	9.80	0.52	0.19	2.98
Lithuania	3.76	2.97	0.43	0.03	0.33
Luxembourg	0.87	0.36	0.03	0.00	0.48
Malta	1.22	0.25	0.08	0.01	0.88
Netherlands	0.64	0.36	0.01	0.00	0.27
Poland	3.41	1.19	0.63	0.04	1.55
Portugal	13.09	9.64	0.10	0.07	3.27
Romania	6.84	4.69	0.18	0.11	1.86
Slovakia	4.04	1.61	0.42	0.07	1.95
Slovenia	4.82	0.38	3.47	0.06	0.92
Spain	5.98	4.96	0.01	0.01	0.99
Sweden	2.92	1.40	0.40	0.00	1.12
EU-27	4.00	2.58	0.21	0.04	1.18

Source: Our calculation using SILC 2019 data. Countries are listed in alphabetical order.

APPENDIX C: RISK-ADJUSTED UNMET NEED

Table C1. Unmet Need, Unadjusted and Adjusted for Covariates.

	I	II	III	IV
Need factors		Yes	Yes	Yes
Education			Yes	Yes
Income				Yes
Estonia	0.17578	0.14407	0.15100	0.12739
Greece	0.09276	0.09271	0.08811	0.06330
Poland	0.08506	0.06987	0.07238	0.05588
Denmark	0.08503	0.07519	0.07742	0.08661
Latvia	0.07935	0.06320	0.06660	0.04763
Romania	0.06915	0.07293	0.07033	0.04459
Hungary	0.06456	0.05267	0.05345	0.03645
Slovakia	0.05988	0.05293	0.05476	0.04037
Finland	0.05742	0.04110	0.04225	0.04418
Sweden	0.04738	0.03878	0.03934	0.03974
Croatia	0.04251	0.03563	0.03536	0.02574
Slovenia	0.03838	0.03065	0.03160	0.02848
France	0.03070	0.02501	0.02476	0.02767
Portugal	0.02666	0.02104	0.01815	0.01488
Czechia	0.02365	0.01937	0.02052	0.01726
Belgium	0.02320	0.02174	0.02150	0.02401
Bulgaria	0.02288	0.02298	0.02277	0.01431
Ireland	0.02247	0.02070	0.02058	0.02333
Lithuania	0.02049	0.01692	0.01780	0.01291
Italy	0.01951	0.02127	0.01926	0.01898
Netherlands	0.01251	0.01050	0.01062	0.01147
Cyprus	0.01188	0.00957	0.00933	0.00956
Luxembourg	0.00896	0.00833	0.00810	0.01089
Germany	0.00718	0.00540	0.00581	0.00627
Austria	0.00668	0.00539	0.00550	0.00646
Malta	0.00395	0.00344	0.00295	0.00312
Spain	0.00342	0.00304	0.00274	0.00258

Source: Our calculation using SILC 2019 data. Sample size: 424,118.

Note: Dependent variable is whether the individual reports unmet need or not. Age is also included with quadratic and cubic functions, and these are interacted with gender. Income: annual equivalised disposable income adjusted for purchasing power standard categorised in deciles according to EU distribution. Countries are listed in descending order according to unadjusted unmet need.

Table C2. Unmet Need for Co-payment, Unadjusted and Adjusted for Covariates.

	I	II	III	IV
Need factors		Yes	Yes	Yes
Education			Yes	Yes
Income				Yes
Greece	0.07683	0.06861	0.05867	0.02218
Romania	0.03676	0.03555	0.03062	0.00869
Latvia	0.02991	0.01793	0.01938	0.00636
Belgium	0.01815	0.01432	0.01335	0.01374
Portugal	0.01422	0.00849	0.00596	0.00283
Italy	0.01346	0.01344	0.01030	0.00748
Bulgaria	0.01033	0.00886	0.00822	0.00228
Cyprus	0.01029	0.00646	0.00571	0.00452
Poland	0.01020	0.00627	0.00635	0.00249
Ireland	0.00932	0.00722	0.00682	0.00735
France	0.00787	0.00489	0.00453	0.00475
Slovakia	0.00646	0.00452	0.00454	0.00170
Estonia	0.00538	0.00323	0.00349	0.00147
Hungary	0.00447	0.00268	0.00257	0.00081
Denmark	0.00351	0.00245	0.00253	0.00275
Croatia	0.00341	0.00218	0.00198	0.00070
Austria	0.00216	0.00136	0.00134	0.00153
Lithuania	0.00172	0.00110	0.00118	0.00041
Netherlands	0.00168	0.00110	0.00108	0.00104
Luxembourg	0.00158	0.00124	0.00110	0.00169
Germany	0.00101	0.00056	0.00063	0.00055
Czechia	0.00094	0.00058	0.00061	0.00029
Finland	0.00063	0.00032	0.00033	0.00028
Slovenia	0.00055	0.00033	0.00033	0.00019
Sweden	0.00039	0.00025	0.00025	0.00019
Spain	0.00026	0.00018	0.00014	0.00009
Malta	0.00021	0.00015	0.00010	0.00008

Source: Our calculation using SILC 2019 data.

Note: Dependent variable is whether the individual reports unmet need due to co-payment, or not. Age is also included with quadratic and cubic functions, and these are interacted with gender. Income: annual equivalised disposable income adjusted for purchasing power standard categorised in deciles according to EU distribution. Countries are listed in descending order according to unadjusted unmet need.

Table C3. Unmet Need for Waiting Time, Unadjusted and Adjusted for Covariates.

	I	II	III	IV
Need factors		Yes	Yes	Yes
Education			Yes	Yes
Income				Yes
Estonia	0.15011	0.11883	0.11717	0.10932
Finland	0.04846	0.03292	0.03248	0.03241
Slovenia	0.03318	0.02502	0.02511	0.02360
Poland	0.03160	0.02431	0.02470	0.02229
Slovakia	0.01801	0.01525	0.01567	0.01385
Sweden	0.01596	0.01247	0.01237	0.01233
Denmark	0.01471	0.01235	0.01213	0.01258
Latvia	0.01161	0.00865	0.00867	0.00770
Lithuania	0.01058	0.00829	0.00831	0.00748
Ireland	0.01031	0.00921	0.00889	0.00925
Romania	0.01017	0.01067	0.01092	0.00944
Croatia	0.00449	0.00355	0.00360	0.00321
Greece	0.00426	0.00412	0.00409	0.00363
Italy	0.00408	0.00424	0.00425	0.00425
France	0.00397	0.00305	0.00303	0.00313
Hungary	0.00366	0.00279	0.00282	0.00247
Czechia	0.00259	0.00197	0.00203	0.00187
Portugal	0.00258	0.00192	0.00189	0.00177
Spain	0.00173	0.00146	0.00143	0.0014
Bulgaria	0.00171	0.00164	0.00165	0.00143
Netherlands	0.00115	0.00092	0.00090	0.00091
Germany	0.00102	0.00074	0.00073	0.00075
Austria	0.00058	0.00045	0.00045	0.00048
Luxembourg	0.00024	0.00022	0.00021	0.00025
Cyprus	0.00018	0.00014	0.00014	0.00014
Malta	0.00016	0.00013	0.00013	0.00013
Belgium	0.00011	0.00010	0.00010	0.00010

Source: Our calculation using SILC 2019 data.

Note: Dependent variable is whether the individual reports unmet need due to waiting time, or not. Age is also included with quadratic and cubic functions, and these are interacted with gender. Income: annual equivalised disposable income adjusted for purchasing power standard categorised in deciles according to EU distribution. Countries are listed in descending order according to unadjusted unmet need.

ANDREA RIGANTI ET AL.

Table C4. Unmet Need for Distance, Unadjusted and Adjusted for Covariates.

	I	II	III	IV
Need Factors		Yes	Yes	Yes
Education			Yes	Yes
Income				Yes
Estonia	0.00687	0.00284	0.00311	0.0013
Croatia	0.00682	0.00306	0.00287	0.00109
Latvia	0.00437	0.00175	0.00203	0.00067
Romania	0.00411	0.00295	0.00265	0.00082
Slovakia	0.00410	0.00229	0.00252	0.00104
Poland	0.00254	0.00116	0.00124	0.00054
Greece	0.00248	0.00144	0.00118	0.00051
Hungary	0.00212	0.00096	0.00099	0.00035
Denmark	0.00198	0.00103	0.00107	0.00112
Lithuania	0.00172	0.00072	0.00078	0.00029
Bulgaria	0.00167	0.00101	0.00099	0.00029
Czechia	0.00158	0.00071	0.00086	0.00042
France	0.00063	0.00028	0.00025	0.00027
Finland	0.00060	0.00021	0.0002	0.00017
Ireland	0.00058	0.00035	0.00032	0.00033
Portugal	0.00036	0.00015	0.00011	0.00006
Slovenia	0.00036	0.00015	0.00016	0.00009
Netherlands	0.00031	0.00016	0.00015	0.00014
Germany	0.00023	0.00012	0.00014	0.00012
Italy	0.00013	0.00009	0.00007	0.00005
Belgium	0.00007	0.00004	0.00004	0.00004
Austria	0.00005	0.00002	0.00002	0.00003
Spain	0.00003	0.00001	0.00001	0.00001

Source: Our calculation using SILC 2019 data.

Note: Dependent variable is whether the individual reports unmet need due to distance, or not. Age is also included with quadratic and cubic functions, and these are interacted with gender. Income: annual equivalised disposable income adjusted for purchasing power standard categorised in deciles according to EU distribution. Countries are listed in descending order according to unadjusted unmet need.

Table C5. Unmet Need for Dental Care, Unadjusted and Adjusted for Covariates.

	I	II	III	IV
Need Factors		Yes	Yes	Yes
Education			Yes	Yes
Income				Yes
Latvia	0.13490	0.11847	0.12586	0.08117
Portugal	0.13087	0.11593	0.09455	0.07147
Greece	0.09510	0.09702	0.08900	0.05457
Denmark	0.07500	0.06957	0.07239	0.08369
Romania	0.06838	0.07190	0.06571	0.03491
Finland	0.06652	0.05378	0.05619	0.05725
Spain	0.05987	0.05659	0.04915	0.04384
Belgium	0.05351	0.05191	0.05116	0.05781
Estonia	0.05232	0.04390	0.04699	0.03442
Cyprus	0.05187	0.04556	0.04386	0.04324
France	0.04935	0.04348	0.04250	0.04742
Slovenia	0.04819	0.04153	0.04265	0.03528
Slovakia	0.04062	0.03683	0.03723	0.02323
Lithuania	0.03761	0.03372	0.03592	0.02285
Poland	0.03415	0.02912	0.02984	0.01944
Ireland	0.03230	0.03067	0.03088	0.03593
Italy	0.03103	0.03397	0.02853	0.02645
Hungary	0.03080	0.02612	0.02585	0.01458
Sweden	0.02920	0.02591	0.02603	0.02537
Bulgaria	0.02627	0.02677	0.02559	0.01358
Czechia	0.02565	0.02229	0.02322	0.01745
Croatia	0.02153	0.01908	0.01827	0.01136
Malta	0.01217	0.01099	0.00857	0.00878
Austria	0.01171	0.01007	0.01018	0.01244
Germany	0.01013	0.00804	0.00885	0.00952
Luxembourg	0.00889	0.00835	0.00790	0.01207
Netherlands	0.00712	0.00636	0.00645	0.00701

Source: Our calculation using SILC 2019 data.

Note: Dependent variable is whether the individual reports unmet need for dental care or not. Age is also included with quadratic and cubic functions, and these are interacted with gender. Income: annual equivalised disposable income adjusted for purchasing power standard categorised in deciles according to EU distribution. Countries are listed in descending order according to unadjusted unmet need for dental care.

APPENDIX D: EDUCATION GRADIENTS

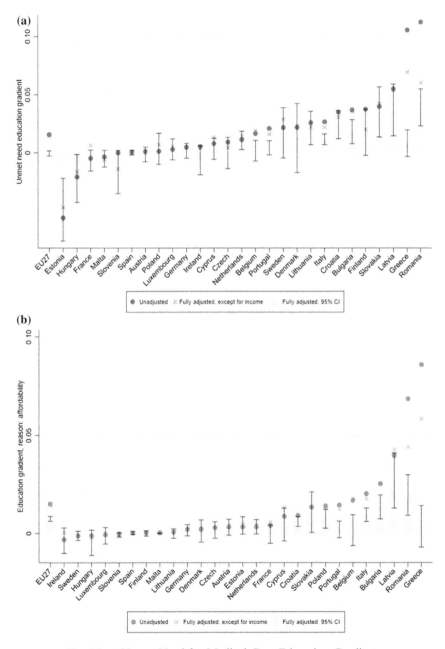

Fig. D1. Unmet Need for Medical Care Education Gradients.

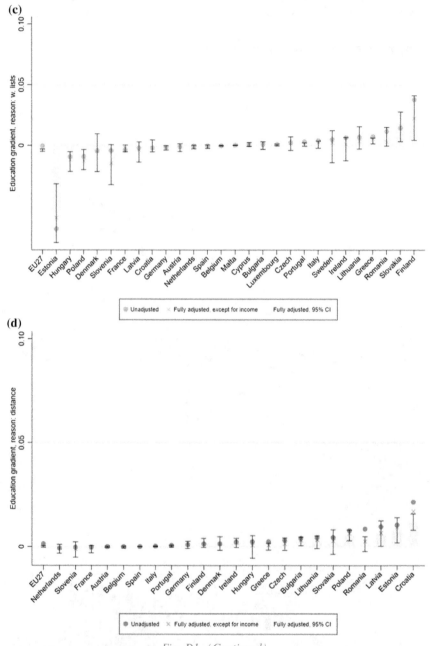

Fig. D1. *(Continued)*.

Note: Education Gradient is the difference between whether the individual reports unmet need in or not in highest and lowest educational attainment group. Panel (a) indicates education gradient for any reason, (b) refers to gradient due to affordability, (c) to waiting lists and (d) to distance. Unadjusted estimates are country-specific raw differences, while in adjusted specification we include gender, age with quadratic and cubic functions, and these interacted with gender, chronic conditions. In panel (a), sample size is equal to 424,118, while in panels (b–d), due to exclusion of unmet need for other categories rather than the specific one that is considered, sample sizes are equal to 411,695, 410,197 and 406,131, respectively. *Source:* Our calculation using SILC 2019 data.

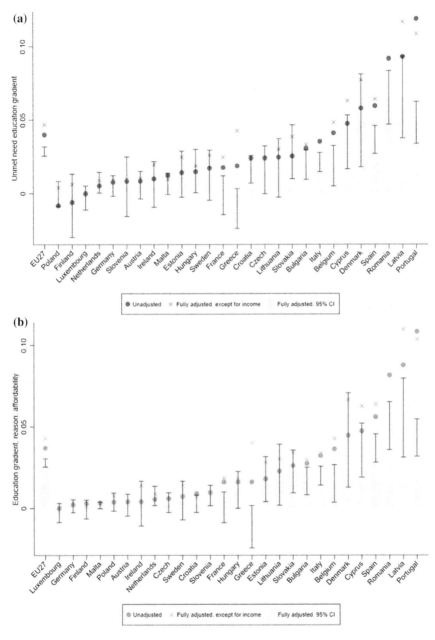

Fig. D2. Unmet Need for Dental Care Education Gradients.
Note: Education gradient is the difference between whether the individual reports unmet need for dental care or not in highest and lowest income decile. Panel (a) indicates income gradient for any reason, (b) refers to gradient due to affordability. Unadjusted estimates are country-specific raw differences, while in adjusted specification, we include gender, age with quadratic and cubic functions and these interacted with gender, chronic conditions. In panel (a), sample size is equal to 423,719, while in panel (b), due to exclusion of unmet need for dental care for other categories rather than affordability, sample size is equal to 416,745.
Source: Our calculation using SILC 2019 data.

'BEYOND THE MEAN' IN BIOMARKERS MODELLING FOR ECONOMIC EVALUATIONS: A CASE STUDY IN GESTATIONAL DIABETES MELLITUS

Georgios F. Nikolaidis, Ana Duarte, Susan Griffin and James Lomas

University of York, UK

ABSTRACT

Economic evaluations often utilise individual-patient data (IPD) to calculate probabilities of events based on observed proportions. However, this approach is limited when interest is in the likelihood of extreme biomarker values that vary by observable characteristics such as blood glucose in gestational diabetes mellitus (GDM). Here, instead of directly calculating probabilities using the IPD, we utilised flexible parametric models that estimate the full conditional distribution, capturing the non-normal characteristics of biomarkers and enabling the derivation of tail probabilities for specific populations. In the case study, we used data from the Born in Bradford study (N = 10,353) to model two non-normally distributed GDM biomarkers (2-hours post-load and fasting glucose). First, we applied fully parametric maximum likelihood to estimate alternative flexible models and information criteria for model selection. We then integrated the chosen distributions in a probabilistic decision model that estimates the cost-effective diagnostic thresholds and the expected costs and quality-adjusted life years (QALYs) of the alternative strategies ('Testing and Treating', 'Treat all', 'Do Nothing'). The model adopts the 'payer' perspective and expresses results in net monetary benefits (NMB). The log-logistic and Singh-Maddala distributions offered the optimal fit for the 2-hours post-load and fasting glucose biomarkers, respectively. At £13,000 per

---

Recent Developments in Health Econometrics

Contributions to Economic Analysis, Volume 297, 85–110

Copyright © 2024 Georgios F. Nikolaidis, Ana Duarte, Susan Griffin and James Lomas

Published under exclusive licence by Emerald Publishing Limited

ISSN: 0573-8555/doi:10.1108/S0573-855520240000297005

QALY, maximum NMB with 'Test and Treat' ($-£330$) was achieved for a diagnostic threshold of fasting glucose >6.6 mmol/L, 2-hours post-load glucose >9 mmol/L, identifying 2.9% of women as GDM positive. The case study demonstrated that fully parametric approaches can be implemented in healthcare modelling when interest lies in extreme biomarker values.

Keywords: Health technology assessment; gestational diabetes mellitus; beyond the mean; fully parametric modelling; diagnostic testing

LIST OF ABBREVIATIONS

BiB—Born in Bradford
BMI—Body mass index
CEAC—Cost-effectiveness acceptability curve
CEAF—Cost-effectiveness acceptability frontier
EEE—Extended estimation equations
EVPI—Expected value of perfect information
EVPPI—Expected value of perfect parameter information
FMM—Finite mixture model
GDM—Gestational diabetes mellitus
GLM—Generalised linear models
HTA—Health technology assessment
IPD—Individual-patient data
LEF—Linear exponential family
LL—Log-likelihood
NMB—Net monetary benefit
OGTT—Oral glucose tolerance test
OLS—Ordinary least squares
$P(T+)$—Probability of being tested positive
PSA—Probabilistic sensitivity analysis
QALY—Quality-adjusted life year
T2DM—Type 2 diabetes mellitus
VoI—Value of information

1. INTRODUCTION

Economic evaluation seeks to establish the value for money of a specific intervention. In the context of health technology assessment (HTA), interventions (or technologies) that are typically considered include new pharmaceuticals, medical devices or diagnostic strategies. Economic evaluation is a key component of HTA and is more often than not founded on cost-effectiveness analysis (CEA) where the health effects of a new intervention are considered relative to the implications of financing it from healthcare resources. As CEA is motivated by the objective of maximising health for a given budget, the resulting decision rules are implicitly risk neutral. For this reason, consideration of mean costs and effects has been the focus rather than the full distribution in most cases.

While the focus on outputs from a cost-effectiveness model is on the means due to normative reasons, it does not follow that only the mean of the distributions of model inputs needs to be estimated. In this chapter, the biomarker underlying a diagnostic test is considered, but this principle applies more broadly even in the case of an economic evaluation based on a cohort decision model. Despite this, we believe that our study is one of the first to explore this issue.

In contrast, econometric modelling of the full distribution of a variable has received considerable attention in economics (Bitler et al., 2006). In health economics, there is a large literature on the use of econometric methods, such as fully parametric approaches based on flexible size distributions, to analyse healthcare costs (Jones et al., 2015). Parametric approaches to analysis require making an assumption about the data generating process, specifically the probability distribution, that underpins a variable. If the assumption is valid, then there are gains in terms of efficiency over approaches (semi- or non-parametric) that remain somewhat agnostic on these matters. In addition, some form of parameterisation can be vital to extrapolating beyond the given sample of data. Flexible size distributions include the Pareto distribution that was initially developed to fit distributions of wealth in Italy and has since been applied to a wide range of contexts (Kleiber & Kotz, 2003). Notably, researchers have applied the same methods to analyse clinical biomarkers (including glucose levels (Davillas & Jones, 2018)).

Within HTA, it is common to undertake survival analysis in the context of an economic evaluation by specifying a fully parametric regression model. One approach is to estimate a flexible model in order to choose among nested and limiting cases (Cox, 2008). In this chapter, following Davillas and Jones (2018), we apply flexible parametric models based on size distributions to the analysis of a biomarker (glucose levels). The distribution of glucose levels shares many statistical characteristics with cost and survival data, including exhibiting right-hand skewness and heavy tails.

It is the extreme values of this biomarker that are concerning from a clinical perspective in the case of gestational diabetes mellitus (GDM), which means that modelling of the right-hand tail is particularly important for informing a decision model. The results from our models can be used to inform a cohort decision model. In particular, for a given combination of observable characteristics, a proportion testing positive can be obtained for a range of diagnostic thresholds. This enables the exploration of heterogeneity and the ability to optimise the operation of the diagnostic procedures according to cost-effectiveness.

The structure of this chapter is as follows. We first set out the clinical background and motivating case study of GDM. Then we set out the methods used, both in terms of statistical modelling of glucose level and the case study decision model about testing and treatment strategies for GDM. Results are presented along with discussion before some concluding remarks.

2. MOTIVATING CASE STUDY

2.1 Disease Context

GDM is a type 2 diabetes mellitus (T2DM) condition characterised by glucose intolerance with onset, or first detection, during pregnancy (American College of

Obstetricians and Gynecologists, 2013; American Diabetes Association, 2004). It is evidenced by chronic hyperglycaemia resulting from pancreatic β-cell dysfunction usually on a background of chronic insulin resistance. The pathophysiology of GDM is complex, involving various factors such as genetic predisposition, metabolic changes and hormonal imbalances (Plows et al., 2018). Briefly, increased levels of oestrogens, prolactin, cortisol and progesterone during pregnancy aim to provide adequate glucose and lipids supply to the mother and the growing foetus (Homko et al., 1999). However, utilisation of glucose requires its transfer from the bloodstream into the cells by insulin. Therefore, increased production of insulin is required to properly utilise the increased glucose levels (American Diabetes Association, 2004). Consequently, the pancreas produces and releases around twice as much insulin either by proliferating or increasing the per cell insulin production [ref]. The increased need for insulin stresses the pancreatic β-cells, and women with borderline pancreatic function may experience insulin insufficiency (Carr & Gabbe, 1998) which results in elevated blood glucose and ultimately GDM.

GDM can lead to various complications during pregnancy, including excessive birth weight (macrosomia) and dangerously low blood sugar (hypoglycaemia). Additionally, GDM increases the risk of high blood pressure, preeclampsia, the need for a caesarean section and developing T2DM later in life (HAPO Study Cooperative Research Group et al., 2008; Shou et al., 2019). Therefore, early detection and management of GDM are essential to prevent adverse outcomes for both the mother and the baby.

Treatment of GDM aims to maintain blood glucose levels within the normal range to minimise foetal and maternal complications. According to National Institute for Health and Care Excellence (NICE), first-line treatment includes lifestyle modification including healthier eating plans and mild exercise. In some cases, oral antidiabetic agents such as metformin or insulin can be prescribed (National Institute for Health and Care Excellence, 2020).

Diagnosis of GDM is commonly based on oral glucose tolerance tests (OGTT) (Pippitt et al., 2016), such as fasting and 2 hours post-load glucose, but diagnostic criteria differ across institutions (Farrar et al., 2016). To date, there is no standard single test established as the main diagnostic criterion, and different criteria are recommended by institutions such as the American Diabetes Association (ADA), the World Health Organization (WHO) and the International Association of Diabetes in Pregnancy Study Group (IADPSG) (Alberti & Zimmet, 1998; American Diabetes Association, 2011; International Association of Diabetes and Pregnancy Study Groups Consensus Panel et al., 2010). Since the diagnostic criteria determine the number of patients who would be treated with the various strategies, in this work, we incorporate the diagnostic threshold considerations in the decision-analytic process and estimate the optimal combination of diagnostic criteria in the economic model.

2.2 Data

2.2.1 Overview

The prospective birth cohort, Born in Bradford (BiB), is comprised of 13,773 women who delivered a singleton baby in Bradford Royal Infirmary, Bradford, UK. However, women were excluded if they did not complete the OGTT, had missing data for ethnic origin or ended in stillbirth. Our final sample is made up by 10,353 observations. Ethics approval was obtained from the Bradford Research Ethics Committee (07/H1302/112), and all participants provided informed written consent.

All participants received an OGTT after an overnight fast between 26 and 28 weeks gestation. Blood samples were taken, and glucose levels were measured with the glucose oxidase method. Then, the same women consumed, within 5 minutes, a solution of 75 gr of anhydrous glucose, a new blood sample was obtained after 2 hours and the glucose levels were measured again. The results from the first assessment correspond to the fasting glucose levels and from the second to the 2-hours post-load glucose.

The database contains, apart from the OGTT measurements, data on established clinical complications of gestational diabetes (International Association of Diabetes and Pregnancy Study Groups Consensus Panel et al., 2010). The primary outcomes include large for gestational age (LGA) i.e., macrosomia (defined as birthweight greater than the 90th percentile for gestational age), infant adiposity and caesarean section. Secondary outcomes included pre-eclampsia, preterm delivery, birthing complications (shoulder dystocia, instrumental vaginal delivery) and admission to the neonatal unit.

2.2.2 Dependent Variables

Table 1 provides the main statistical attributes of the glucose biomarkers. Mean fasting glucose is 4.52 mmol/L (median = 4.4 mmol/L) with a minimum of 3 mmol/L and maximum of 13.3 mmol/L and a. The standard deviation is 0.55, and the distribution is heavily right-hand skewed. Skewness is 3.32, and kurtosis is 31.6 (in comparison to 0 and around 3 respectively for normally distributed data). Mean 2-hours post-load glucose is 5.68 mmol/L (median = 5.5 mmol/L) with a minimum of 1.6 mmol/L and a maximum of 27.7 mmol/L, yielding a standard deviation of 1.51. The distribution is again positively skewed with skewness 1.98 and kurtosis 15.37.

2.2.3 Independent Variables

The independent variables included parity, mother's body mass index (BMI), mother's age, maternal smoking status (never smoked, smoked in the past, smokes during pregnancy), whether the mother has family history of diabetes, whether a mother's previous offspring had macrosomia, whether a mother was diagnosed with GDM in a previous pregnancy, whether the mother developed pre-eclampsia in the gestation in question, and finally whether the mother underwent caesarean delivery in the gestation in question (Table 2).

Table 1. Main Statistical Characteristics of Independent Variables (Fasting and Post-load Glucose Markers).

Variable	Mean	SD	Median	Min	Max	Skewness	Kurtosis
Fasting glucose (mmol/L)	4.52	0.55	4.4	3	13.3	3.32	31.6
Post-load glucose (mmol/L)	5.68	1.51	5.5	1.6	27.7	1.98	15.37

Abbreviations: mmol, millimole; L, litre; SD, standard deviation.

90   'Beyond the Mean'

Table 2. Main Statistical Characteristics of Independent Variables.

Variable	Mean	SD	Min	Max	Proportion
Age at delivery	27.6	5.6	15	49	–
Weeks of gestation	26.3	1.9	0	39	–
BMI	26.1	5.7	12.9	57.0	–
Parity					
No previous children	–	–	–	–	40.9
One previous child	–	–	–	–	29.1
Two or more previous children	–	–	–	–	30.0
Ethnicity					
White	–	–	–	–	39.5
South Asian	–	–	–	–	52.2
Other	–	–	–	–	8.3
Smoking					
Never	–	–	–	–	69.7
In the past	–	–	–	–	14.0
During pregnancy	–	–	–	–	16.4
Family history of diabetes	–	–	–	–	25.5
Previous macrosomia	–	–	–	–	4.9
Previous GDM	–	–	–	–	1.1

Abbreviations: SD, standard deviation.

2.2.4 Distributional Characteristics of the Dependent Variables

The right-hand skewness and the high kurtosis levels of our dependent variables are comparable to those of healthcare costs. Consequently, it is unlikely that our data will adequately fit or satisfy the assumptions of econometric approaches based on a normal distribution. In Fig. 1, we illustrate the skewness and kurtosis spaces that are supported by the fully parametric distributions, that have been used in the literature to adequately model healthcare costs, along with our variables' skewness and kurtosis levels.

In Fig. 2, it is apparent that middle range values are not the main source of non-normality (In P-P plots, data do not extensively deviate from the line). The Q-Q plots that are sensitive to tail non-normality reveal that specifically the right tail (i.e. the women with very high blood glucose levels) drives data to non-normality.

3. METHODS

3.1 Statistical Methods

Generalised linear models (GLMs) may seem like an appropriate modelling framework for these data because they can generally accommodate non-linearities between the conditional mean and observed covariates and allow for heteroskedasticity (Blough et al., 1999). However, they do not perform well with heavy-tailed data (Manning & Mullahy, 2001) and implicitly impose

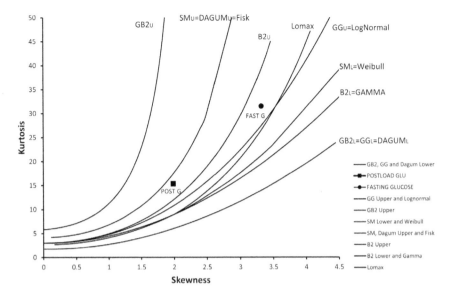

Fig. 1. Skewness-Kurtosis Spaces for the Various Fully Parametric Models. 'U' subscript denotes upper bound and 'L' lower bound. The South-West (North-East) dot represents the post-load (fasting) glucose levels.

restrictions on the entire distribution (e.g. skewness is directly proportional to the coefficient of variation, and kurtosis is linearly related to the square of the coefficient of variation) (Holly et al., 2011). More importantly, despite that GLMs can estimate the conditional mean, $E(y|x)$, and conditional variance, $Var(y|X)$, they cannot estimate the conditional distribution, $F(y|X)$, or estimate high-end parameters such as the tail probability of an OGTT exceeding a specific threshold k conditional on specific patient characteristics, i.e. $P(y > k|X)$.

Instead, where interest lies with conditional moments 'beyond the mean', fully parametric models offer a potentially valuable alternative to GLMs. Fully parametric models offer greater flexibility than GLMs and can not only model highly skewed and/or kurtotic data but also estimate both the full conditional distribution and tail probabilities (Jones et al., 2014). The fully parametric models considered here include two categories, namely duration models and beta-type models.

Duration models include Weibull, exponential, log-normal, gamma and generalised gamma and are typically applied to duration data to estimate parametric hazard models. However, duration models can also be used with count data regressions to model healthcare costs. Manning et al. (2005) proposed using the generalised gamma for non-normal healthcare cost data.The probability density function of the generalised gamma is:

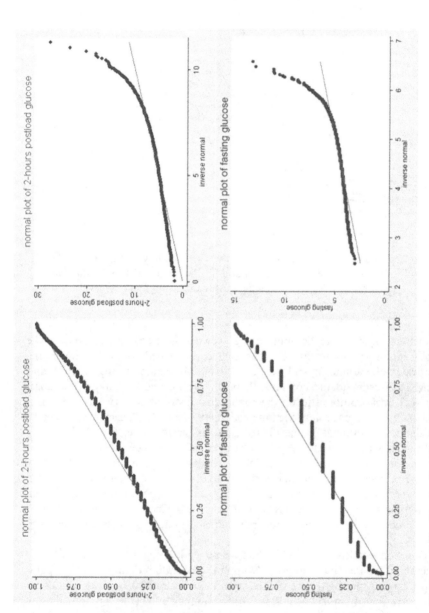

Fig. 2. On the Left, the Standardised Probability (P-P) Plots for 2-Hours Post-load Glucose (Up) and Fasting Glucose (Down). On the Right, the (Q-Q) Plots of the 2-Hours Post-load Glucose (Up) and Fasting Glucose (Down) Against the Quantiles of the Normal Distribution.

$$f(y_i; \kappa, \beta, \sigma) = \frac{\gamma^\gamma}{\sigma y_i \sqrt{\gamma} \Gamma(\gamma)} \, \exp\left(z_i \sqrt{\gamma} - u_i\right)$$

where $\gamma = |\kappa|^{-2}$, $z_i = \text{sign}(\kappa)\{\ln(y_i) - \mu_i\}$,

$$u_i = \gamma \, \exp\left(|\kappa| z_i\right)$$

$$\mu_i = x_i' \beta$$

All the remaining duration models arising as special cases, i.e. gamma ($\kappa = \sigma$), Weibull ($\kappa = 1$), exponential ($\kappa = 1$, $\sigma = 1$) and log-normal ($\kappa = 0$).

Beta-type models, introduced by Jones et al. (2014), include the generalised beta of the second kind and its nested distributions (GB2, Signh-Maddala, Dagum, B2, Lomax, Fisk). The probability density function of GB2 is:

$$f(y) = \frac{a y^{ap-1}}{b^{ap} B(p,q) \left[1 + \left(\frac{y}{b}\right)^a\right]^{(p+q)}}$$

where $B(u,v) = \Gamma(u)\Gamma(v)/\Gamma(u+v)$ is the beta function, and $\Gamma(.)$ is the gamma function.

Fig. 3 depicts the relationships across all fully parametric models. In the top, the GB2 distribution is described by four parameters (a, b, p, q) with b being the scale parameter and a, p, and q affecting the shape. Parameters p and q primarily control the skewness, while a controls the tail, with lower values producing thicker tails (Kleiber & Kotz, 2003). Despite that GB2 is the most flexible model and therefore able to handle a wider range of skewed/kurtotic data, under specific circumstances, even single parameter models could fit better than GB2, primarily on parsimony grounds (Cummins et al., 1990).

Among distributional options, the Singh-Maddala (produced from GB2 once p is set to 1) and the Fisk (produced from the Singh-Maddala once q is set to 1), demonstrate particular interest to our data and healthcare modelling more generally. This is because, unlike the GB2, their cumulative distribution function (cdf) is available in closed form (Kleiber & Kotz, 2003), and therefore, their quantile functions (qf) are tractable; hence, they can be easily mathematically specified in any modelling software (e.g. Microsoft Excel) and used to obtain predictions. Equations (1)–(3) describe the probability density functions pdf, cdf and qf of the Singh-Maddala distribution, respectively. Setting $q = 1$ directly results in the corresponding functions for the Fisk. Fig. 4 illustrates the range of shapes that the pdf of the Singh-Maddala and the Fisk can accommodate by varying parameters $q, a,$ and b.

$$f(x) = \frac{a q x^{a-1}}{b^a \left[1 + \left(\frac{x}{b}\right)^a\right]^{1+q}}, \, f \text{ or } x > 0 \tag{1}$$

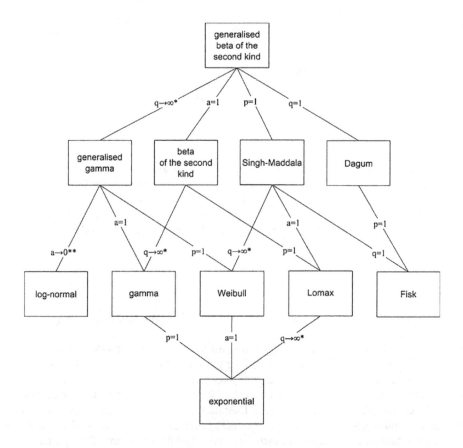

*with $b = \beta q^{1/a}$
**with $b = (\sigma^2 a^2)^{1/a}$, $p = (a\mu + 1)/\sigma^2 a^2$

Fig. 3. Relationships Among GB2 and Nested Fully Parametric Models.
Source: Adopted from Jones et al. (2014).

$$F(x) = 1 - \left[1 + \left(\frac{x}{b}\right)^a\right]^{-q}, \text{ for } x > 0 \qquad (2)$$

$$F^{-1}(u) = b\left[(1-u)^{-\frac{1}{q}} - 1\right]^{1/a}, \text{ for } 0 < u < 1 \qquad (3)$$

Importantly, all models considered here allow only the scale parameter, b, to vary with the independent variables. Although, in principle, more parameters could vary with covariates, previous attempts to model healthcare costs did not yield satisfactory results (Jones et al., 2014) and, as such, we did not consider such models.

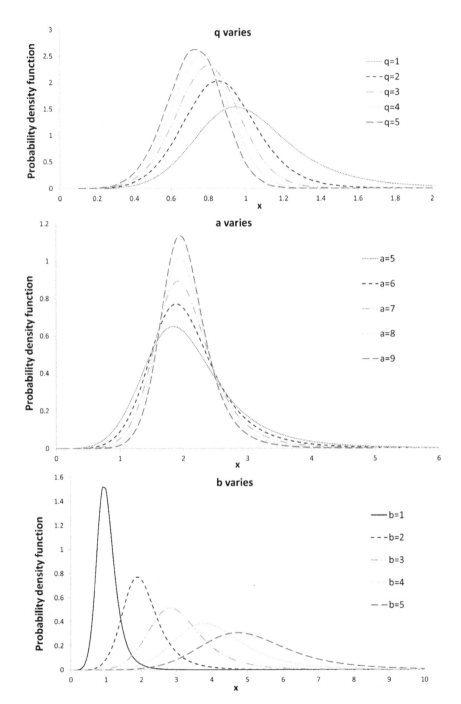

Fig. 4. Impact of Varying Shape Parameters on Probability Density Functions of the Singh-Maddala and Fisk Distributions.

96   *'Beyond the Mean'*

Finally, we estimated two finite mixture models (FMMs) with a fixed number of two gamma-distributed components. FMMs estimate the $F(y|X)$ as a weighted sum of conditional distributional components $F_j(y|X)$ and in that way allow for heterogeneity in response to observed covariates and in terms of unobserved latent classes (Deb & Trivedi, 1997). Each individual patient is assigned only to one class (the one with the highest posterior probability) and individuals are assumed to homogeneous within each class but heterogeneous across classes (Jones, 2010).

3.1.1 Estimation and Model Selection

All models were independently applied to both glucose biomarkers and estimated using maximum likelihood. Convergence difficulties were addressed, where possible, by modifying the initial values. We used four goodness-of-fit criteria that targeted either the full distribution or only its tails. For the full distribution the log-likelihood (LL), the Akaike information criterion (AIC) and the Bayesian information criterion (BIC) were calculated. Priority was given to BIC because it penalises model complexity more than AIC, while LL does not penalise model complexity at all. Differences in AIC/BIC of 5 or more units were considered important. We also calculated the tail probability prediction accuracy. The latter allows us to go 'beyond the mean' (Jones et al., 2015) and inform model choice based on high-end parameters of particular importance in our context. Two alternative approaches were used to assess the tail probability prediction accuracy. The first involved calculating the ratio of the proportion of patients who exceeded a critical diagnostic threshold over the actual proportion who exceeded that threshold based on our dataset. It follows that the closer the ratio is to 1, the more accurate the tail probability prediction. The second approach involved the use of chi-squared goodness-of-fit tests for binned data (Andrews, 1988). Two custom bins were used for the chi-squared test to align with the underlying data categorisation: one bin below the diagnostic threshold used by Farrar in their base-case (Farrar et al., 2016) and another one above.

The use of fully parametric model reasonably raises potential overfitting considerations. Here, we employ a recent development by Bilger and Manning (2015) which distinguishes between the shrinkage caused by misspecification that generates in-sample bias and shrinkage attributed to overfitting. As a result, this measure is not affected by in-sample bias.

On the top the Singh-Maddala in which $a = 6$, $b = 1$, and q varies between 1 and 5. In the middle the Singh-Maddala where $b = 2$, $q = 1$ (therefore it is Fisk as well), and a varies between 5 and 9. At the bottom the Singh-Maddala in which $a = 6$, $q = 1$ (therefore it is Fisk as well), and b varies between 1 and 5.

3.2 Economic Modelling Methods

3.2.1 Decision Model Structure and Strategies

A previously developed decision tree was used to evaluate the cost-effectiveness of alternative strategies for screening, testing and treating hyperglycaemia in women on the third pregnancy trimester was simplified, as this work focuses on the implementation of the econometric models to predict glucose measurements in a decision model.

As illustrated in Fig. 5, in the model, an initial decision is made on whether or not to test all women for hyperglycaemia at 26–28 weeks' gestation with a 75 g OGTT. This test includes a fasting measure and a post-load measure of glycaemia 2 hours after ingestion of the glucose load. If testing is undertaken, the cohort is divided into those who test positive (T+) and those who test negative (T−). Treatment following a positive test consists of dietary and lifestyle interventions, followed after two weeks by insulin or metformin for women whose hyperglycaemia remains uncontrolled. Women who test negative are not offered further intervention. For those women who are not tested, clinical management depends on the strategy.

The full set of alternative strategies under comparison in the CEA can be categorised into three types:

(1) Treat without prior test: All women receive dietary and lifestyle advice but not an active pharmaceutical treatment (i.e. metformin or insulin).
(2) Do nothing: No testing and no treatment for GDM.
(3) Test all: Offer all women 75 g OGTT at 26–28 weeks' gestation. In women who meet the diagnostic criteria (T+), provide dietary and lifestyle modification supplemented after 2 weeks with pharmacological treatment as required.

For the 'test all' strategy, the model evaluates 969 alternative dual glycaemic thresholds by varying the two measures with the range between 5.0 and 11.1

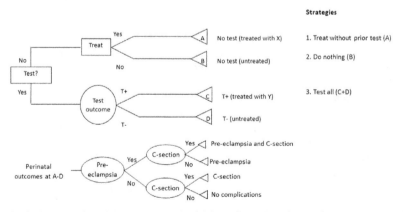

Fig. 5. Decision Tree Diagram.

mmol/L for fasting glucose and between 5.5 and 11.1 mmol/L for post-load glucose (a positive test diagnoses GDM and is defined as any glucose measurement above either cut-off of the dual threshold). The model cohort is divided into those who test positive (T+) and those who test negative (T−), for each set of dual thresholds.

The model then captures the occurrence of adverse perinatal outcomes, namely pre-eclampsia and caesarean section (C-section), with the probability of C-section condition on pre-eclampsia. Costs and health-related quality of life (HRQoL) pay-offs are attached to each of the four potential perinatal outcomes (no complications, C-section only, pre-eclampsia only and pre-eclampsia and C-section). A scenario analysis considers development of T2DM as a maternal adverse outcome.

3.2.1.1 Costs and Health-Related Quality of Life. Health of the mother and offspring is expressed in quality-adjusted life-years (QALYs), integrating mortality and HRQoL. Costs from an England and Wales National Health Service (NHS) perspective are expressed as 2013/2014 pounds sterling (£). The time horizon of the base-case analysis is limited to the third month of pregnancy, but in a scenario including maternal future costs and QALYs, an annual discount rate of 3.5% is applied to both these outcomes (National Institute for Health and Care Excellence, 2013). The adverse perinatal outcomes are assumed to result in QALY loss. The resource use and QALY impact of prevention of maternal type 2 diabetes were included in scenario analysis. Costs in the model refer to the cost of testing, treatment (including additional antenatal care) and managing adverse perinatal outcomes. HRQoL, resource use and unit cost sources are detailed elsewhere (Farrar et al., 2016).

3.2.1.2 Implementation of the Distributions Predicting Glucose Levels in the Decision Tree. The probability that either measurement of glucose in the 75 g OGTT test is positive cannot be directly estimated from each glucose (fasting or post-load) distribution. Instead, the probability that either glucose measurement is positive is calculated as 1- probability that both are negative. This imposes an assumption that the two glucose measurements are independently distributed.

3.2.1.3 Predicting the Adverse Outcomes. The probability of developing pre-eclampsia is predicted in the model conditional on test outcome and treatment received, while the probability of undergoing C-section is conditional on pre-eclampsia presentation, the test outcome and treatment received. Logistic regressions models are used to estimate these probabilities. The first covariate is the fasting glucose level, and the second post-load glucose level, and a cumulative factor 'lambda' that includes all the rest of the parameters (for the C-section regression pre-eclampsia is included in the 'lambda'). For the test only strategy, the glucose levels vary between groups by test outcome (T+ or T−), while on the remaining strategies, the glucose levels correspond to the cohort mean values. Treatment effects were modelled as relative risks, which modified the adverse outcome probabilities.

3.2.1.4 Cost-Effectiveness Analysis. Healthcare resources devoted to detecting and managing GDM could otherwise be used to provide interventions for other patients. The cost-effective strategy is the one that generates the highest net monetary benefit (NMB) expressed as the expected monetary value of the total generated health benefits (TE × k) minus the health benefits forgone as a result of the costs that strategy imposes on the health system (TC) (see Eq. 4). The monetary value of expected health benefits was estimated assuming health is generated at a rate (k, the cost-effectiveness threshold) of one QALY per £13,000 invested into the healthcare system (Claxton et al., 2015).

$$NMB = TE \times k - TC \tag{4}$$

The cost-effectiveness of the strategies is evaluated in three steps:

(1) The optimal combination of glucose thresholds is calculated by backwards induction. The NMB of all 969 combinations of dual glycaemic thresholds is estimated. The optimal combination is the one that yields the maximum NMB across all the alternative combinations in the model.
(2) The alternative strategies are evaluated under the optimal glucose threshold combination definition of GDM (step 1).
(3) Of the three alternative strategies, the one yielding the highest NMB is identified as optimal.

More effective strategies reduce QALY losses from adverse perinatal outcomes and increase QALY gains from treatment of GDM and treatment or avoidance of T2DM. Negative QALYs and/or NMB for a strategy do not suggest that it is harmful, only that treatment cannot offset all adverse perinatal outcomes.

3.2.1.5 Parameter Uncertainty Analysis. Probabilistic sensitivity analysis (PSA) was undertaken to assess the implications of the joint uncertainty in all input parameters. The results of the PSA are used to inform cost-effectiveness acceptability distribution frontier (CEAF), which illustrates the probability of cost-effectiveness for the cost-effective strategy at a range of cost-effectiveness thresholds (Briggs et al., 2006). Value of information (VoI) analysis was performed; expected value of perfect information (EVPI) was calculated to estimate the health gains that could be achieved if uncertainty could be eliminated (i.e. the value of conducting further research). We also calculated the population expected value of parameter information (EVPPI) for model parameters to indicate where additional research would be most valuable. EVPPI calculations assume an annual population of 700,000 pregnancies in England and Wales (Statistics OfN, 2014).

3.2.1.6 Scenario Analysis. Scenario analyses show how results vary with alternative assumptions to those in the base-case analysis ones. Scenario 1 includes costs and QALY gains from early detection of maternal T2DM at post-partum follow-up and prevention of T2DM later in maternal life through intensive life-style interventions to women treated for GDM. In scenario 2, we assumed a

100   *'Beyond the Mean'*

reduction in treatment costs (due to a lower proportion of women receiving insulin and some antenatal care being delivered in groups). Finally, we combine the assumptions of scenarios 1 and 2 in a third scenario.

4. RESULTS

4.1 Fully Parametric Models

All duration, beta-type and FMM models were applied to both glucose variables, independently. Despite efforts to tailor initial values, some models (B2, FMM with log-link, FMM with sqrt-link) did not converge for fasting glucose. Table 3 shows the goodness-of-fit measures pertaining to the whole distribution (LL, AIC, and BIC) across models for both biomarkers. Overall, beta-type models performed better than duration models. For the 2-hours post-load glucose, the Fisk distribution offers the best fit in terms of BIC, while its AIC is not meaningfully different from other distributions that provide numerically lower values. For the fasting glucose, the Singh-Maddala fits best across all measures, with BIC being the only measure meaningfully lower than other models.

Interestingly, despite that the Lomax model converged, its results were quite different from the remaining models indicating problems with convergence. This is due to the additional parameter constraint ($a = 1$) that the Lomax model imposes on Singh-Maddala which is quite unrealistic for the shape of our data distribution. Indicatively, when the Singh-Maddala freely estimates both a, q, the resulting estimates are $a = 8$, $q = 0.93$. Additional explorations revealed that when a is constrained to low values, q soars in an attempt to maintain the shape of the distribution, with values of $a < 2.7$, resulting in $q > 350$ and, therefore, lack of convergence.

As illustrated in Table 3, the same distributions that fit best according to BIC also provide the most accurate tail probability predictions based on the WHO 1999 thresholds which were also prioritised by Farrar et al. (2016). However, it should be noted that the differences are quite small across some models indicating that other distributions could also accurately predict tail probabilities.

Overfitting checks using the Bilger and Manning test (Bilger & Manning, 2015) suggested that neither model overfits; hence, both models could in fact be even further expanded to include more covariates. Overall, the histograms of both glucose biomarkers are overlaid by the estimated best-fitting distributions in Fig. 6. In both cases, the BiB data are accurately modelled across all the parts of the distribution, with particular emphasis on the tails. Finally, estimated coefficients of both best-fitting models are provided in Table 4.

4.2 Cost-Effectiveness

4.2.1 Optimization of Dual Glycaemic Threshold for the 'Test All' Strategy
At a cost-effectiveness threshold of £13,000 per additional QALY, our results suggest that the optimal diagnostic threshold is 6.6 mmol/L and 9.0 mmol/L for fasting and post-load glucose, respectively (Fig. 7). When the cost-effectiveness

Table 3. Goodness-Of-Fit Measures Based for All Models Applied to Both Glucose Biomarkers.

Distribution/measure	2-Hours Post-Load Glucose				Fasting Glucose			
	LL	AIC	BIC	Tail prediction accuracy¥	LL	AIC	BIC	Tail prediction accuracy¥
Duration Models								
Weibull	−15.455	30.941	31.047	1.489	−8.526	17.083	17.189	2.662
Exponential	−23.160	46.348	46.447	5.643	−21237	42.502	42.601	3.856
Log-normal	−14.104	28.238	28.343	1.000	−5.110	10.250	10.355	1.365
Gamma	−14.207	28.445	28.550	0.926	−5.329	10.688	10.794	1.440
Generalised gamma	−14.097	28.227	28.340	1.039	−4.596	9.225	9.338	1.244
Beta-Type Models								
GB2, log-link	−13.989	28.012	28.132	1.011	−4.419	8.872	8.991	1.159
GB2, sqrt-link	−13.992	28.019	28.139	1.008	−4.420	8.875	8.995	1.158
Singh-Maddala	−13.990	28.013	28.126	1.019	−4.419	8.870	8.983	1.159
Dagum	−13.989	28.011	28.124	1.024	−4.445	8.922	9.035	1.136
B2	−14.087	28.207	28.320	1.026			Did not converge	
Lomax	−23.160	46.350	46.456	5.643	−21237	42.504	42.610	3.856
Fisk	−13.992	28.014	28.119	0.979	−4.600	9.231	9.337	0.986
Finite Mixture Models								
2-Component gamma, log-link	−13.951	27.965	28.184	0.984			Did not converge	
2-Component gamma, sqrt-link	−14.083	28.226	28.437	0.844			Did not converge	

Abbreviations: AIC, Akaike information criterion; BIC, Bayesian information criterion; LL, Log-likelihood.
¥ Tail prediction accuracy was calculated as the ratio of the predicted over the true proportion of patients over the WHO 2013 threshold which was 8.5 mmol/L for 2-hours post-load glucose and 5.1 mmol/L for fasting glucose.

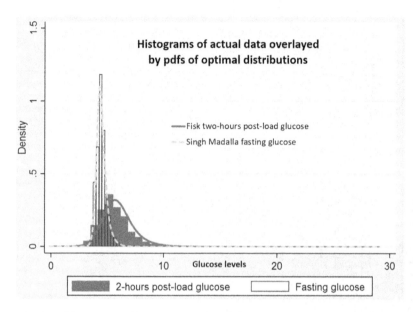

Fig. 6. Histograms of 2-Hours Post-load Glucose and Fasting Glucose in the BiB Dataset Overlaid by the Best Fitting Estimated Fully Parametric Models.

Table 4. Maximum Likelihood Estimation Results Best-Fitting Models for Each Glucose Biomarker.

	2-Hours Post-load Glucose		Fasting Glucose	
Covariates	Coefficient (SE)	p Value	Coefficient (SE)	p Value
Mother's age	00,076 (00,005)	0,000	0.0022 (000,019)	0,000
Weeks of gestation	00,038 (00,013)	0,004	0.0012 (000,051)	0,02
Mother's BMI	00,199 (0,003)	0,000	00,080 (000,115)	0,000
Mother BMI squared	−0,00,023 (000,005)	0,000	−0,0001 (000,002)	0,000
1 previous kid	−0,0455 (00,061)	0,000	−0,0066 (00,023)	0,005
2 or more previous kids	−0,0413 (00,069)	0,000	−0,0093 (00,026)	0,000
South Asian ethnicity	00,445 (00,063)	0,000	00,329 (00,024)	0,000
Other (non-white, non-SA) ethnicity	−0,0022 (00,092)	0,808	00,017 (00,034)	0,613
Smoked in the past	−0,1814 (00,076)	0,017	00,007 (00,028)	0,796
Smokes during pregnancy	−0,0348 (00,075)	0,000	−0,0024 (00,028)	0,386
Family history of diabetes	00,230 (00,058)	0,000	00,075 (00,022)	0,001

Table 4. *(Continued)*

	2-Hours Post-load Glucose		Fasting Glucose	
Covariates	Coefficient (SE)	p Value	Coefficient (SE)	p Value
Previous macrosomia	00,453	0,000	00,157	0,001
	(00,075)		(00,047)	
Previous GDM	02,400	0,000	00,570	0,000
	(0,025)		(00,099)	
Constant	1,034	0,000	11,896	0,000
	(00,559)		(00,212)	

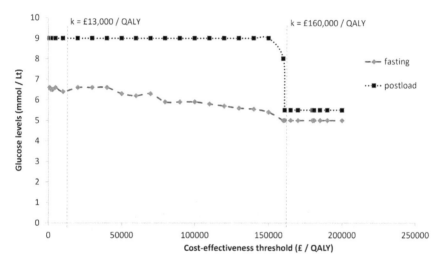

Fig. 7. Optimal Glucose Threshold for Each Glucose Measurement at a Cost-Effectiveness Threshold Range.

threshold is varied across a range of values, the optimal combination of glycaemic thresholds remains stable until £160,000 per additional QALY, where it shifts to 5.0 mmol/L and 5.5 mmol/L for fasting and post-load glucose, respectively. This is the cost-effectiveness threshold, where the cost-effective strategy shifts from 'Do nothing' to 'Treat without prior test' (Fig. 8).

4.2.2 Base-Case Analysis

Our base-case analysis suggests that it is not cost-effective to test and treat women diagnosed with GDM regardless of the diagnostic threshold for this condition. For the base-case, the optimal dual glycaemic theshold was 6.6 mmol/L and 9.0 mmol/L for fasting and post-load glucose, respectively. At £13,000 per additional QALY, the cost-effective strategy appears to be 'Do nothing'. When GDM is

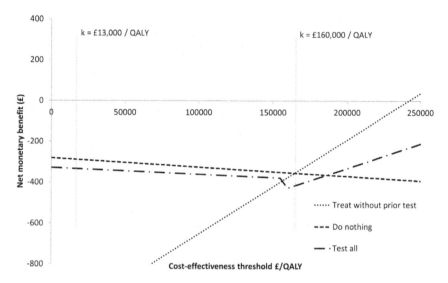

Fig. 8.   Net Monetary Benefit for Each Strategy at a Range of Cost-Effectiveness Thresholds.

defined as having fasting glucose higher than 6.6 mmol/L and post-load glucose higher than 9.0 mmol/L, 2.9% of tested women would be diagnosed with GDM with the 'Test all' strategy. This yields on average a total cost of £333 and 0.0003 QALY loss per pregnant woman, resulting in a NMB of −£294. In contrast, the 'Do nothing' strategy accrues on average £280 and 0.00045 QALY loss per pregnant woman, with a NMB of −£274.

NMB results for each strategy are illustrated over a range of thresholds in Fig. 8. This graph suggests that the 'Treat without prior test' strategy only becomes cost-effective at cost-effective thresholds above £160,000 per additional QALY.

4.2.3 Parameter Uncertainty Analysis
The PSA suggests that the 'Treat without prior test' has the highest probability of being cost-effective for cost-effectiveness thresholds of £155,000 per additional QALY. However, as illustrated in the CEAF (Fig. 9), it is only beyond £ 165,000 per additional QALY that this strategy becomes cost-effective. This is due to the skewed distribution of NMB values for each strategy estimated by the PSA.

The VoI analysis shows that further research is unlikely to be worthwhile for cost-effectiveness thresholds lower than £50,000 per QALY (Fig. 10), given the low EVPI values. The EVPI rises with the cost-effectiveness threshold value, reaching approximately £700 per pregnant woman £250,000 per QALY. The EVPPI for all uncertain parameters at £13,000 per QALY was close to zero.

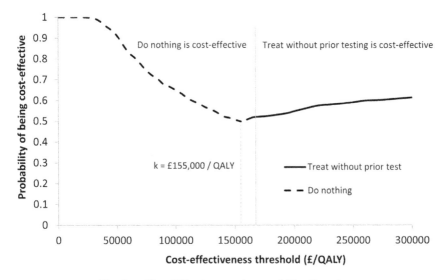

Fig. 9. Cost-Effectiveness Acceptability Frontier.

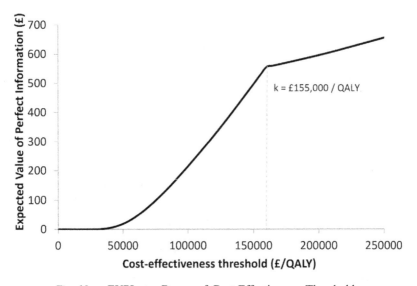

Fig. 10. EVPI at a Range of Cost-Effectiveness Thresholds.

4.2.4 Scenario Analysis

When the average lifetime costs and benefits from early T2DM diagnosis are included in scenario 1 (£558 and 0.05 QALYs per pregnant woman), the optimal diagnostic threshold becomes 5.0 mmol/L and 5.5 mmol/L for fasting and post-load glucose, respectively. At this diagnostic threshold, 75 g OGTT diagnoses 53% of women with GDM, with the 'Test all' strategy incurring on average a cost of £1077 and a QALY gain of 0.023 QALY per pregnant woman. This suggests a NMB of −£778, which remains lower than the NMB for 'Do nothing'. For this scenario, EVPI is the highest at £30,000 per QALY and is £180 per woman. The most uncertain parameter is the cost of early T2DM diagnosis with a population EVPPI of £95 million.

When lowering the costs of managing GDM in scenario 2, the optimal diagnostic threshold becomes 5.9 mmol/L and 9.0 mmol/L for fasting and post-load glucose, respectively. This suggests a slightly lower fasting glucose threshold compared to base-case analysis (5.9 vs. 6.6 mmol/L), but the cost-effective strategy remains 'Do nothing'.

For the combined scenario 3 (inclusion of longer term outcomes and reduced costs of managing GDM), the optimal diagnostic threshold is the same as for scenario 1. The NMB of the strategy 'Test only' are higher than for scenario 1 (-£449 vs -£778), due to the lower total costs with this strategy under scenario 3 assumptions. However, the cost-effective strategy remains 'Do nothing'.

5. DISCUSSION

This is one of the first studies of which we are aware that performs statistical analysis using fully parametric econometric techniques on a continuous, right-hand skewed and leptokurtic diagnostic marker in the context of an economic evaluation for HTA. A decision analytic model was parameterised using this approach in order to evaluate the cost-effectiveness of the alternative strategies for testing and treating in GDM.

In the base-case, the decision analytic model indicates the best performing diagnostic glucose threshold combination, in terms of cost-effectiveness, to be Fasting: 6.6 mmol/L, 2-hours post-load: 9.0 mmol/L. As a result, 2.9% of the pregnant women originating from Bradford are predicted to exceed the glucose threshold of either of the two OGTT measurements and consequently will be diagnosed with GDM. However, the cost-effective strategy was the 'Do Nothing' (No Test; No Treat) incurring a cost of £280 and QALY loss of 0.00045 per pregnant woman. The testing strategy was consistently extendedly dominated by the No Test; Treat every woman strategy, which produced much higher average costs and QALYs. Even though the mechanism of the higher costs is easy to understand since now treatment is offered to every woman instead of the positively diagnosed 3%, the mechanism of the higher QALYs is less straightforward. The answer lies in the fact that treatment effects on the development of adverse outcomes are similar for those who are positively diagnosed after being first offered an OGTT and those who, untested, get straight into treatment without prior OGTT. In other words, first-line treatment, i.e. lifestyle modifications, however expensive, achieves in significantly preventing adverse outcomes in the cohort of women that would not be positively diagnosed by the OGTT.

One of the most important limitations is that we did not consider the screening option in the purpose of keeping the model to a reasonably complex level. Also, we only took into account pre-eclampsia and caesarean section as adverse outcomes. The inclusion of more adverse outcomes would augment the cost-effectiveness of the treating strategies since treatment would reduce the probability of adverse events, thus expanding the health benefits of treatment.

Furthermore, even though we tried to build dependency between the fasting and the 2-hours post-load glucose variables, the resulting models did not perform well, so we moved on to assume independence between the aforementioned variables. While most of our model selection is driven by in-sample measures of goodness of fit, we were able to test for overfitting for a subset of the models that were estimated (Bilger & Manning, 2015). According to its results, our models do not suffer from overfitting but instead could be further enhanced by increasing the number of variables in our econometric specification.

Future research should focus on further enabling the incorporation of complex econometric distributions in healthcare modelling by finding ways for distributions without closed form cdf and quantile function (e.g. GB2) to be incorporated in the decision analytic process. Moreover, allowing for correlated variables to be jointly distributed, thus not assuming independence, could significantly increase the efficiency of the estimates and reduce uncertainty. To that direction, either a Bayesian approach or even copulas (Roncally, 2001) can be adopted. The latter are even more complex econometric frameworks that use maximum-likelihood estimation and are employed in Finance for risk management of multi-asset options and credit derivatives to model multivariate probability distributions.

Regarding GDM, the availability of estimates of long-term benefits can significantly affect the cost-effectiveness of the alternative strategies. Allowing for benefits to accrue for a lifetime horizon instead of the 3-month period of the third trimester of pregnancy can have considerable health benefits. Those health benefits, for the mother, could take the form of early identification of T2DM, while for the offspring prevention of obesity and cardio-metabolic conditions. However, evidence linking short and longer terms of treating GDM is sparse.

Our results indicate that current practice is not cost-effective unless considerable long-term benefits are realised. In fact, even under an exorbitant monetary threshold and a cost-effective glucose threshold combination, testing for GDM and treating only the positively diagnosed women would not be preferred since it is extendedly dominated by the (No Test; Treat every woman) strategy. Based on 700,000 births per year in the United Kingdom, a change in current practice to the cost-effective 'Do nothing' strategy could potentially save around £33 million with the cost of only 80 QALYs, while a change to the 'No Test; treat every woman' strategy would incur further £550 million of costs for an amount of additional 3,200 QALYs.

The conclusions of our study are consistent with those of the HTA by Farrar. Both studies suggest 'Do Nothing' strategy as cost-effective, underline the fact that conclusions are sensitive to the inclusion of long-term benefits and identify a cluster of cost-effective glucose threshold combinations instead of a single combination. However, our model is much less complex because it neglects the effect of a number of complications. Potential adaptation of the fully parametric models that we found to optimally characterise the glucose variables by the original model used for the HTA could lead to a fully fledged, methodologically

108   *'Beyond the Mean'*

coherent and innovative model, that not only provides the most possible accurate estimates of the cost-effectiveness of the alternative strategies for GDM but also paves the way for the implementation of the aforementioned techniques to achieve more generalisable results in HTAs. Indeed, interest in outcomes 'beyond the mean' may follow from recent developments in modelling approaches relevant to HTA that capture outcome variability (Caro et al., 2010) combined with an increased interest in the risk preferences of decision-makers in HTA (Lakdawalla & Phelps, 2021; Sendi et al., 2021).

6. CONCLUSIONS

Fully parametric econometric models, previously used to model healthcare costs, can also be used to model highly skewed and leptokurtic biomarkers. Such models can eliminate the reliance on observed quantities through the IPD, accurately predict tail probabilities (thus going 'beyond the mean') and be easily incorporated in decision-analytic models to facilitate HTA.

ACKNOWLEDGEMENTS

Born in Bradford (BiB) is only possible because of the enthusiasm and commitment of the children and parents in BiB. We are grateful to all the participants, health professionals, schools and researchers who have made Born in Bradford happen.

REFERENCES

Alberti, K. G., & Zimmet, P. Z. (1998). Definition, diagnosis and classification of diabetes mellitus and its complications. Part 1: Diagnosis and classification of diabetes mellitus provisional report of a WHO consultation. *Diabetic Medicine, 15*(7), 539–553.

American College of Obstetricians and Gynecologists. (2013). Practice Bulletin No. 137: Gestational diabetes mellitus. *Obstetrics & Gynecology, 122*(2 Pt 1), 406–416.

American Diabetes Association. (2004). Diagnosis and classification of diabetes mellitus. *Diabetes Care, 27*(Suppl. 1), S5–S10.

American Diabetes Association. (2011). Standards of medical care in diabetes-2011. *Diabetes Care, 34*(Suppl. 1), S11–S61.

Andrews, D. (1988). Chi-Square diagnostic tests for econometric models: Theory. *Econometrica, 56*(6), 1419–1453.

Bilger, M., & Manning, W. G. (2015). Measuring overfitting in nonlinear models: A new method and an application to health expenditures. *Health Economics, 24*(1), 75–85.

Bitler, M. P., Gelbach, J. B., & Hoynes, H. W. (2006). What mean impacts miss: Distributional effects of welfare reform experiments. *The American Economic Review, 96*(4), 988–1012.

Blough, D. K., Madden, C. W., & Hornbrook, M. C. (1999). Modeling risk using generalized linear models. *Journal of Health Economics, 18*(2), 153–171.

Briggs, A., Sculpher, M., & Claxton, K. (2006). *Decision modelling for health economic evaluation.* Oxford University Press.

Caro, J. J., Möller, J., & Getsios, D. (2010). Discrete event simulation: The preferred technique for health economic evaluations? *Value in Health, 13*(8), 1056–1060.

Carr, D., & Gabbe, S. (1998). Gestational diabetes: Detection, management, and implications. *Clinical Diabetes, 16*(1), 4–11.

GEORGIOS F. NIKOLAIDIS ET AL.

Claxton, K., Martin, S., Soares, M., Rice, N., Spackman, E., Hinde, S., Devlin, N., Smith, P. C., & Sculpher, M. (2015, February). Methods for the estimation of the National Institute for health and care excellence cost-effectiveness threshold. *Health Technology Assessment, 19*(14), 1–503, v–vi. https://doi.org/10.3310/hta19140. PMID: 25692211; PMCID: PMC4781395.

Cox, C. (2008). The generalized F distribution: An umbrella for parametric survival analysis. *Statistics in Medicine, 27*(21), 4301–4312.

Cummins, J., Dionne, G., McDonald, J., & Pritchett, B. M. (1990). Applications of the GB2 family of distributions in modeling insurance loss processes. *Insurance: Mathematics and Economics, 9*(4), 257–272.

Davillas, A., & Jones, A. M. (2018). Parametric models for biomarkers based on flexible size distributions. *Health Economics, 27*(10), 1617–1624.

Deb, P., & Trivedi, P. (1997). Demand for medical care by the elderly: A finite mixture approach. *Journal of Applied Econometrics, 12*(3), 313–336.

Farrar, D., Simmonds, M., Griffin, S., Duarte, A., Lawlor, D. A., Sculpher, M., Fairley, L., Golder, S., Tuffnell, D., Bland, M., Dunne, F., Whitelaw, D., Wright, J., & Sheldon, T. A. (2016, November). The identification and treatment of women with hyperglycaemia in pregnancy: An analysis of individual participant data, systematic reviews, meta-analyses and an economic evaluation. *Health Technology Assessment, 20*(86), 1–348. https://doi.org/10.3310/hta20860. PMID: 27917777; PMCID: PMC5165282.

HAPO Study Cooperative Research Group, Metzger, B. E., Lowe, L. P., Dyer, A. R., Trimble, E. R., Chaovarindr, U., Coustan, D. R., Hadden, D. R., McCance, D. R., Hod, M., McIntyre, H. D., Oats, J. J., Persson, B., Rogers, M. S., & Sacks, D. A. (2008, May 8). Hyperglycemia and adverse pregnancy outcomes. *The New England Journal of Medicine, 358*(19), 1991–2002. https://doi.org/10.1056/NEJMoa0707943. PMID: 18463375.

Holly, A., Monfort, A., & Rockinger, M. (2011). Fourth order pseudo maximum likelihood methods. *Journal of Econometrics, 162*(2), 278–293.

Homko, C. J., Sivan, E., Reece, E. A., & Boden, G. (1999). Fuel metabolism during pregnancy. *Seminars in Reproductive Endocrinology, 17*(2), 119–125.

International Association of Diabetes and Pregnancy Study Groups Consensus Panel, Metzger, B. E., Gabbe, S. G., Persson, B., Buchanan, T. A., Catalano, P. A., Damm, P., Dyer, A. R., Leiva, Ad., Hod, M., Kitzmiler, J. L., Lowe, L. P., McIntyre, H. D., Oats, J. J., Omori, Y., & Schmidt, M. I. (2010 March). International association of diabetes and pregnancy study groups recommendations on the diagnosis and classification of hyperglycemia in pregnancy. *Diabetes Care, 33*(3), 676–682. https://doi.org/10.2337/dc09-1848. PMID: 20190296; PMCID: PMC2 827530.

Jones, A. (2010). *Models for health care*. HEDG, c/o Department of Economics, University of York.

Jones, A. M., Lomas, J., & Rice, N. (2014). Applying beta-type size distributions to healthcare cost regressions. *Journal of Applied Econometrics, 29*(4), 649–670.

Jones, A. M., Lomas, J., & Rice, N. (2015). Healthcare cost regressions: Going beyond the mean to estimate the full distribution. *Health Economics, 24*(9), 1192–1212.

Kleiber, C., & Kotz, S. (2003). *Statistical size distributions in economics and actuarial sciences*. John Wiley & Sons, Inc.

Lakdawalla, D. N., & Phelps, C. E. (2021). Health technology assessment with diminishing returns to health: The generalized risk-adjusted cost-effectiveness (GRACE) approach. *Value in Health, 24*(2), 244–249.

Manning, W. G., Basu, A., & Mullahy, J. (2005). Generalized modeling approaches to risk adjustment of skewed outcomes data. *Journal of Health Economics, 24*(3), 465–488.

Manning, W. G., & Mullahy, J. (2001). Estimating log models: To transform or not to transform? *Journal of Health Economics, 20*(4), 461–494.

National Institute for Health and Care Excellence. (2013). *Guide to the methods of technology appraisal 2013*.

National Institute for Health and Care Excellence (NICE). (2020, December 16). *Diabetes in pregnancy: Management from preconception to the postnatal period*. National Institute for Health and Care Excellence (NICE). (NICE Guideline, No. 3.). https://www.ncbi.nlm.nih.gov/books/NBK555331/

Pippitt, K., Li, M., & Gurgle, E. H. (2016). *Diabetes mellitus: Screening and diagnosis*. American Family Physician.

Plows, J. F., Stanley, J. L., Baker, P. N., Reynolds, C. M., & Vickers, M. H. (2018). The pathophysiology of gestational diabetes mellitus. *International Journal of Molecular Sciences, 19*(11), 3342.

Roncally, T. (2001). *Modelling dependence in finance using copulas*. Groupe de Recherche Opérationnelle Crédit Lyonnais.

Sendi, P., Matter-Walstra, K., & Schwenkglenks, M. (2021). Handling uncertainty in cost-effectiveness analysis: Budget impact and risk aversion. *Healthcare (Basel), 9*(11), 1419.

Shou, C., Wei, Y.-M., Wang, C., & Yang, H.-X. (2019). Updates in long-term maternal and fetal adverse effects of gestational diabetes mellitus. *Maternal-Fetal Medicine, 1*(2), 91–94.

Statistics OfN. (2014). *Births in England and Wales*.

EMPIRICAL HEALTH ECONOMICS FOR EVIDENCE-BASED POLICIES: SOME LESSONS FROM ITALY

Vincenzo Carrieri[a,b] and Francesco Principe[c]

[a]*Department of Political and Social Sciences, University of Calabria, Italy*
[b]*RWI and IZA, Germany*
[c]*University of Bergamo, Italy*

ABSTRACT

This chapter pays tribute to Andrew Jones' research in health programme evaluation, health-risky behaviour and income-related health inequalities by reviewing policy-relevant empirical studies in these domains using Italian data. In the first section, We discuss the impact of reimbursement systems on healthcare behaviour, particularly the transition from incurred-cost-based to prospective systems in hospitals. We explore incentive-driven practices like up-coding and cream skimming, while also considering the potential advantages of primary care incentives and the mixed outcomes associated with cost-sharing schemes. The second section delves into health-risk behaviours in Italy, encompassing substance use, preventive healthcare and responses to health information. The last section presents some evidence on socioeconomic status (SES)-related health disparities and discusses the necessity of accounting for these factors in the Italian National Health Service (NHS)'s resource allocation formula in line with British NHS experience.

Keywords: Health programme evaluation; risky behaviours; income-related health inequalities; evidence-based policy; incentives in healthcare

1. INTRODUCTION

Over the past three decades, there has been a significant increase in economists' interest in health and healthcare. This can be attributed to the growth in both public and private healthcare spending, which has highlighted the need to address

---

Recent Developments in Health Econometrics
Contributions to Economic Analysis, Volume 297, 111–125
Copyright © 2024 Vincenzo Carrieri and Francesco Principe
Published under exclusive licence by Emerald Publishing Limited
ISSN: 0573-8555/doi:10.1108/S0573-855520240000297006

the fundamental economic concept of resource scarcity within the healthcare sector. Following the recent advancements in applied economics, often referred to as the 'credibility revolution' (Angrist & Pischke, 2010), health economics has embraced counterfactual empirical evaluations. Additionally, it has benefited from the wealth of medical and genetic data, which is unparalleled in other branches of applied economics. The availability of increasingly granular data, combined with new programme evaluation methods, has facilitated the examination of various issues concerning the economics of health, healthcare and health-risky behaviours. Simultaneously, interdisciplinary research on the causes and consequences of socioeconomic inequalities in health and healthcare has experienced significant growth. This research has also benefited from new tools for measuring and decomposing inequalities and the availability of objective health measures, such as biomarkers.

Andrew Jones' extensive research agenda focuses on these three areas: program evaluation in health and healthcare, the economics of health-risky behaviors and income-related inequalities in health and healthcare. In this chapter, we aim to honour Andrew's work by providing a critical and selective review of empirical papers relevant to policy, specifically focusing on Italian data. Our objective is to summarise the main findings from this literature and derive implications for evidence-based policies, primarily in Italy but with broader applicability to other developed countries. Italy serves as an interesting case study for several reasons. First, health economics is a relatively newer field compared to other branches of applied economics, such as labor economics and education economics. Consequently, it arrived in Italy later than these other fields. This delay can also be attributed to early health economics studies being conducted by scholars with management backgrounds, who often favoured case study methodologies over counterfactual evaluation techniques. The second significant reason, and perhaps the most prominent one, is the limited availability of Italian data. As is well-known, counterfactual empirical analyses and normative analyses of income-related health and healthcare inequalities require microdata, such as individual or hospital-level data, as well as administrative data. This needs to dispose of socioeconomic variables, health outcomes, healthcare utilisation and, when examining health-risky behaviors, information on alcohol consumption, tobacco use, eating habits, physical activity and other relevant factors. Finding such information simultaneously within the currently available microdata in Italy is challenging.

Indeed, there are mainly three surveys currently available in Italy. The 'Health Conditions and Use of Health Services' of the Italian Institute of Statistics (ISTAT) is a cross-sectional survey repeated every 4–5 years on a very large and representative sample of the Italian population, about 60,000 individuals interviewed in each wave.

The survey contains fairly detailed information on health conditions and use of services. However, it has two very important limitations. The first is that both pieces of information (on health and use of services) are self-reported by individuals. This is a quite large limitation, for example for the analysis of health inequalities where there is a known problem of reporting bias related to socioeconomic conditions. The second limitation, and perhaps the most important one, is the absence of information regarding the income of individuals. This hampers counterfactual analyses aiming to assess the impact of health or health-relevant reforms (e.g. redistributive policies and urban planning policies) on the socioeconomic outcomes of individuals.

The second and third available surveys are the 'Survey on Income and Living Conditions' (IT-SILC) and the 'Survey on Household Income and Wealth' (SHIW), respectively. The former is a cross-sectional ISTAT survey falling under the multi-country EU statistics on income and living conditions (EU-SILC) system, with detailed information on the socio-economic conditions of individuals and households. The latter is a longitudinal-type survey by the Bank of Italy on a representative sample of the Italian population with rich information also on household wealth and savings.

The major limitation of both surveys is that there is only little information on health outcomes, which are only self-reported and very general: perceived health, limitation in daily activities due to health problems and presence of chronic diseases. In Italy, for example, there is a lack of a longitudinal dataset similar to Understanding Society in the United Kingdom (UK), which provides comprehensive information on socio-economic conditions alongside data on biomarkers and genetic characteristics for a subsample of the interviewed individuals. This includes individual-level data on blood test values (such as cholesterol and blood glucose levels), anthropometric measurements, and saliva analysis (e.g. for detecting cotinine, which enables accurate measurement of active and passive smoking habits). The absence of such detailed datasets has clearly penalised research in Italy on these issues. Even when taking into account administrative data, a significant gap is evident in Italy: the absence of a unified database comprising digitised medical records for the entire country. Currently, these records are only accessible for research purposes in specific regions, as per agreements between research units and data owners. As a result, their utilisation for research, particularly in southern regions, has been greatly restricted due to the complexity of these agreements.

Before proceeding with the analysis, it is important to briefly recall the study selection criteria employed. First, we prioritised studies addressing broad themes of general interest and relevance to the ongoing debate in Italy, even at the expense of methodologically robust studies focusing on more niche or less relevant topics. Second, the study's editorial placement was not a primary factor in our selection. We only analysed studies published in refereed scientific journals indexed in major scientific databases, as well as working papers from recognised series. Lastly, we structured the discussion around three areas related to Andrew's work as follows: The first section focuses on counterfactual studies in healthcare, the second section examines the impact of health policies and/or public regulations on health-risky behaviours and the third section presents the key empirical findings related to measuring and decomposing socio-economic status (SES)-related inequalities in health and healthcare. Additionally, it explores implications for healthcare financing in Italy and the allocation of healthcare funds among Italian regions.

2. COUNTERFACTUAL STUDIES IN HEALTH AND HEALTH CARE

A highly debated topic in healthcare, particularly during the recent COVID-19 emergency, is the reimbursement systems and their impact on the behaviour of market agents. The underlying theme of this debate revolves around the sustainability of the public healthcare system and the containment of inappropriate healthcare spending. This issue is complex and requires careful examination. While incentives are undoubtedly useful in reducing inappropriate spending, there is concern that they may lead to strategic behaviour among operators, potentially worsening the overall health conditions of the population.

In the context of hospitals, one extensively discussed issue is the effects of the recent healthcare policy trend, which involves transitioning from incurred-cost-based reimbursement schemes to prospective systems. The former reimburses hospitals based on actual costs incurred, providing no strong incentive for cost containment but also no risk of strategic resource utilisation. On the other hand, with prospective systems, hospitals receive a fixed price per treated case, which varies based on the assigned diagnostic category (known as diagnosis-related groups or DRGs) for each patient. This scheme offers high cost-containment incentives but may encourage strategic behaviour among different DRG categories.

Empirical evidence from Italy provides interesting insights into the effects of this change. For example, Verzulli et al. (2017) studied the effects of a reform implemented in Emilia-Romagna in 2007 that modified reimbursement prices for a specific DRG category while keeping other DRGs unchanged. The authors employed a policy-induced quasi-experimental design, naturally creating treated groups (DRGs subject to price change) and a control group (DRGs unaffected by the change). The study's most relevant finding indicates that the reform incentivised hospitals to selectively increase the number of higher-paying treatments at the expense of lower-paying ones. Specifically, a 1% increase in the price of surgical DRGs resulted in a 1.7% increase in the short term and a 4% increase in the medium term of patients treated within this category. This effect was observed to a greater extent in hospitals with a lower proportion of occupied beds prior to the policy, suggesting greater opportunities to strategically select the most financially rewarding admissions.

This finding is significant as it suggests that public management, despite having different objectives than private management, is also influenced by reimbursement arrangements and the need for expenditure restraint. Institutional factors, including the ability of public facilities to reinvest profits and the reduction in public subsidies, further reinforce the incentives for spending control. However, the potential risk this poses to public health remains a topic of extensive debate. Insufficient research on this subject exists, partly due to a lack of data that could provide insights into this dilemma.

The issue of incentive effects in healthcare becomes even more relevant when considering opportunistic practices such as upcoding (i.e. classifying a patient into a more lucrative DRG opportunistically) and cream skimming (selecting the most profitable patients). These practices appear to be strongly incentivised by prospective payment systems, leading to negative impacts on hospital efficiency, particularly in private hospitals, as demonstrated by Berta et al. (2010).

Also, in the context of primary care, different reactions are observed concerning performance-related incentives. For instance, Iezzi et al. (2014) examined the impact of pay-for-performance financial incentive schemes on improving diabetic patient care in Emilia-Romagna between 2003 and 2005. They perform a panel data analysis using fixed-effects models and assess the effect of funding disbursement on diabetes hospitalizations as an indicator of primary care quality. The results are significant, showing a 1% reduction in hospitalizations per 100 euros increase in incentives per physician. This suggests that well-designed performance incentive schemes can be effective in healthcare. Currently, the evidence primarily pertains to primary care medicine, as there are no established pay-for-performance mechanisms in the hospital setting. It could be a potential health policy proposal to evaluate the effects of such schemes in a controlled experimental setting before implementing them in hospitals.

Another area where empirical evidence in Italy offers valuable policy insights is the use of health co-payments, also known as cost sharing. The utilisation of co-payments has been increasing, especially in regions facing significant health deficits, as a means to reduce those deficits. However, the evidence suggests that while co-payments can effectively control demand, they do not exclusively reduce inappropriate demand and provide limited revenue. Furthermore, they contribute to increase inequity in financing, as the burden disproportionately affects the poor compared to the richer patients. Ponzo and Scoppa (2016) study the effects of age exemption thresholds on health demand using a quasi-experimental fuzzy regression discontinuity design. They found that the sudden increase in the probability of not paying co-payments at the age of 65 led to a significant rise in specialist visits, diagnostic tests and drug consumption. Interestingly, no deterioration in general health conditions or hospitalizations was observed, indicating potential moral hazard by patients. These findings are in line with finding from the Rand Health Insurance Experiment also showing small effects on health outcomes (Manning et al., 1987). However, it is important to note that the Rand experiment revealed a significant worsening of health outcomes for vulnerable groups, particularly low-income individuals and those at higher risk. The impact on public health remains highly controversial, and further research is needed to gain important insights, which are currently lacking in Italy. Additionally, co-payments have regressive effects and fail to generate significant revenue due to the concentration of health spending among groups typically exempt from co-payment requirements (Carrieri & Granaglia, 2008). The ongoing discussion on co-payments in Italy seems to be disconnected from the evidence presented here, emphasising the need for evidence-based policies.

Decentralisation in healthcare is another crucial topic that holds considerable interest in today's debate, particularly in light of the recent pandemic crisis and the challenges associated with coordinating regional health policies. Decentralisation is viewed as an institutional approach to address regional-specific needs and enhance regional responsibility in controlling healthcare spending. However, it also highlights the risk, especially for financially burdened regions, of reducing healthcare provision and exposing the population to significant public health risks. Porcelli (2014), for instance, look at the effects of the 1995 majority-based regional electoral reform and the 1998 reform, which increased fiscal autonomy for regions by introducing local taxes and reducing state transfers for healthcare. By utilising a differences-in-differences approach, the paper assessed the impact of the 1995 reform on the efficiency of regional health production, measured through infant mortality rates and regional spending. The findings indicated that the 1995 reform improved the efficiency of the health sector. Additionally, Cavalieri and Ferrante (2016), using longitudinal regional data from 1996 to 2012, show positive effects of decentralisation, measured by the proportion of local taxes and dependence on state transfers, on health outcomes, specifically infant mortality. Moreover, the study highlighted that poor regions benefited more from decentralisation. However, regarding the trade-off between decentralisation and public health risks, there is worrying empirical evidence. This issue is closely linked to the effects of recovery plans, which were introduced by the 2005 Budget Law to restore the economic and financial balance of regions with healthcare spending deficits. These plans involved tightening hospital and pharmaceutical co-payments for users. Recent studies show negative effects associated with these measures, such as increased hospitalizations and mortality (Depalo, 2019). Similarly, Arcà et al. (2020), using the recovery plans as an instrumental variable, revealed that the austerity measures resulted in a 3% increase in 'avoidable mortality', a reduction in hospital capacity and an increase in health migration from the South to the North of the country. While the reform achieved its fiscal goals, it came at a considerable cost in terms of lives saved and potential health inequalities between regions.

The evidence on decentralisation should be interpreted cautiously due to the challenges in implementing robust quasi-experimental designs. However, it does suggest the existence of a trade-off, imposing difficult policy choices. The management of the COVID-19 crisis has further highlighted the limitations of decentralisation in public health, especially in situations like communicable diseases, where meeting health needs has spillover effects on other regional health systems.

3. RISKY BEHAVIOURS AND POLICIES

The second research field on Italian data that we analyse in this work concerns health-risk behaviours, including preventive healthcare, the use of legal and illegal substances, smoking and eating habits. This field of research would greatly benefit from longitudinal microdata that collects information on individual lifestyles and health conditions. However, due to the lack of such data, most studies in Italy have relied on unique self-collected datasets, field experiments or cross-sectional data.

For instance, in the context of illegal substances, a significant change occurred in the market for cannabinoid substances in Italy in May 2017 with the Law 242/2016 that aimed to promote the cultivation of industrial hemp but allow unintentionally to produce and sell 'light cannabis', i.e. a cannabis with very low levels of Tetrahydrocannabinol (THC). This unintentional liberalisation created a thriving grey market for light cannabis and provided a unique opportunity for researchers to evaluate the effects of liberalisation in a quasi-experimental setting. Carrieri et al. (2020) look at the impact of light cannabis availability on the consumption of certain prescription drugs, such as anxiolytics, sedatives, anti-psychotics and anti-depressants. The study found that the availability and easy access to light cannabis led some patients to substitute these drugs with light cannabis for self-medication. The study emphasises the need for regulation of this new product in Italy, particularly considering its therapeutic use by patients.

Health information and its influence on preventive health behaviours have recently gained attention among economists in Italy. One relevant topic is the response rates to screening program invitations, often sent in the form of invitation letters to individuals by regional health units. Carrieri and Wuebker (2016) find that such invitations increased program adherence by approximately 24%. However, not all regions were able to reach 100% of the population due to organizational delays in sending the letters. The study also highlighted the role of individuals' education and cognitive abilities in correctly processing the information in the invitation letters. Similarly, in a randomised field experiment conducted in the province of Messina, Bertoni et al. (2020) study whether manipulating the information content of invitation letters had an effect on the response to the prevention program. The experiment involved sending letters with different levels of information presented with either positive or negative framing. The results show an increase in participation rates for women who received detailed information presented with negative framing. This study suggests that participation in screening programs can be increased at no cost by manipulating the information content to highlight the risk of non-participation.

Health warnings issued by health authorities are another important aspect of health information. Carrieri and Principe (2022) look at the effect of a warning from the World Health Organization (WHO) regarding excessive consumption of red meat and its association with certain types of cancer. The study shows a decline in meat consumption in the first month after the warning, but the effect was mixed in the long run and varied among different educational levels. Only the most educated individuals reduced their consumption of processed red meat, which is considered more harmful to health by the WHO. This study emphasises the importance and risks associated with health information dissemination through mass media and suggests the need for tailored information based on the cognitive abilities of different population segments.

Another interesting paper suggesting the importance of the counterfactual method in identifying robust causal links in health research is the one by Del Bono and Vuri (2018). They look at the smoking ban in public places introduced in Italy in 2005 and its effect on cigarette consumption. While previous studies based on before–after assessments find a positive deterrent effect on cigarette consumption, Del Bono and Vuri (2018) show that when accounting for seasonality in cigarette consumption, the smoking ban had no overall effect on smoking and only marginal effects on certain population subgroups. However, the ban did have positive effects on the well-being of non-smokers due to reduced exposure to second-hand smoke. This study suggests the need for counterfactual studies to provide accurate policy implications in healthcare.

4. INEQUALITIES IN HEALTH AND ALLOCATION OF NHS FUNDS

In Italy, despite the presence of the National Health Service (NHS)(Servizio Sanitario Nazionale) ensuring universal healthcare coverage, significant SES-related health inequalities persist. According to the data from the ISTAT, in the 2010s, men with a university degree had a life expectancy that was 3.1 years longer than those with only primary education or less. For women, the advantage in life expectancy at birth was 1.5 years, half of that for men.

A unique aspect of the Italian situation, in addition to SES-related inequalities, is the existence of a strong health gradient between the wealthier central-northern area and the less economically developed southern regions. Regions in the south and the islands have generally shorter life expectancy due to a higher proportion of individuals with low SES. However, even when controlling for SES, living in certain southern regions increases the risk of premature mortality. For example, even a graduate in the south may, on average, die one year earlier than a graduate in the central-northern region (ISTAT, 2021).

In line with this, van Doorslaer and Koolman (2004) show that regional differences in Italy contribute the most among European countries to explaining income-related health inequalities. Similarly, according to the latest data from ISTAT (2021), women's life expectancy at birth is three years higher in Trentino than in Campania (85.89 vs 82.87), and differences in healthy life expectancy amount to as much as 11 years between Trentino and Calabria (66.6 vs 55.14).

To understand the sources of these regional inequalities, the concentration index can be decomposed into two main factors: compositional effects (higher concentration of poverty in certain areas) and elasticity effects (variations in the health-income relationship slope), as well-explained by van Doorslaer and Koolman (2004). This difference is significant from a policy perspective. Addressing differences in effects would require health policies, while compositional differences would ask more for redistributive policies. In Italy, evidence exists for both effects, including a compositional effect (Costa et al., 2014) and a higher elasticity of health to socioeconomic status in the southern part of the country (Marinacci et al., 2004).

However, there is still limited explicit recognition of health risks related to socioeconomic conditions in Italian health and economic policies. Only in 2022 it was decided to include the index of socioeconomic deprivation of areas, which takes into account individual relative poverty, level of education and unemployment rate, in the methodology for distributing the national health fund (Fondo Sanitario Nazionale). The introduction of this criterion in the allocation in Italy is late and still insufficient for various reasons. Indeed, many healthcare systems with characteristics similar to the Italian system, which guarantees universality of access and uniformity of services throughout the country, face challenges in allocating funds equitably among citizens (Rice & Smith, 2001). Equity, in this context, means the principle of horizontal equity – equal treatment of individuals with the same characteristics – applied from a territorial perspective. The allocation of available funds is guided by the principle that individuals with the same healthcare needs should have equal access to healthcare services, regardless of their location (Gravelle et al., 2003). Implementing this principle practically is more complex than simply stating it because the public decision-maker often lacks the necessary information to accurately measure health needs. Therefore, most national fund allocation criteria are based on econometric models of healthcare utilisation. These models estimate the determinants of health service utilisation, identify population characteristics – primarily demographic – that are most associated with consumption and use them to determine the parameters for national fund allocation. For example, the UK's healthcare system, which closely resembles the Italian system in terms of care universality and performance uniformity, has been using such an approach to health consumption since 1995 (Carr-Hill et al., 1994), and the current allocation formula used in Italy is also based on health consumption patterns.

Simultaneously, the literature on the determinants of health consumption has identified various variables suggesting that consumption models based solely on demographic indicators need updating (Gravelle et al., 2003). It has been empirically observed in numerous studies that the socioeconomic structure of the population has a significant impact on health consumption (Carr-Hill et al., 1996). Grossman's (1972) pioneering model of health demand and demand for health services recognised the influence of income and education on health consumption. More educated individuals can make more efficient choices regarding healthcare inputs because they are more aware of health risks (allocative efficiency) and better able to follow treatment protocols (technical efficiency). Similarly, income provides a greater incentive to invest in healthy activities since it enhances the value of days spent in perfect health. Micro-level studies have consistently shown positive associations between these determinants and greater utilization of healthcare services in various forms (e.g. Carr-Hill et al., 1994; Culica et al., 2002; Hjortsberg, 2003). Additionally, literature also reveals a specific vulnerability in terms of psychophysical health among unemployed individuals, regardless of their level of education and the presence of income support instruments (Theodossiou, 1998). Socioeconomic conditions, therefore, appear to be a significant and easily measurable indicator of health needs, as they are present in most regional databases. While estimating the causal effects of these variables on healthcare service utilisation is complex, they are however strongly correlated with healthcare service utilisation, directly or indirectly (through their impact on health conditions). Moreover, adopting health-risk lifestyles such as smoking, obesity and alcohol consumption significantly influence health outcomes but are also strongly related to SES status. Whether these lifestyles serve as a *comfort foods* for disadvantaged individuals or result from market failures due to the absence of risk information, there is substantial evidence that such lifestyles are concentrated among the most disadvantaged segments of society and tend to be contagious, amplified by their concentration among disadvantaged individuals living in the same areas (see, e.g. Bilger & Carrieri, 2013). Consequently, incorporating weighting for lifestyles at the aggregate level could be another potential approach to allocating health funds more closely aligned with the health needs of the population.

The funding allocation method for clinical commissioning groups (CCGs) in England, and in the future integrated care boards (ICBs) subject to the passage of the Health and Care Bill, might serve as an important example for the Italian national health system to follow. Since 1999, the UK government has introduced a new objective for resource allocation in the NHS in England, aiming to reduce avoidable health inequalities. To achieve this, more resources are targeted at deprived areas. The actual allocation scheme (relative to 2002–2023 allocations) explicitly follows the principle of ensuring equal access opportunities based on need and reducing inequalities between patients in terms of their ability to access services and the outcomes they achieve. The target formula is based on an assessment of factors such as demography, morbidity, deprivation and the unavoidable cost of providing services in different areas. The core of the formula involves the weighted population for each ICB, considering the size of each ICB's registered population; a weight or adjustment per head for healthcare service needs related to age and sex (all else being equal, areas with older populations typically have a higher per capita need) and for needs beyond those attributable to age (all else being equal, areas with poorer health have a higher per capita need); a weight or adjustment per head for unmet needs and health inequalities; a weight or adjustment per head for unavoidably higher costs of delivering healthcare due to location alone, known as the farket forces Factor (reflecting higher unit staff, land and building input costs in some parts of the country, particularly London) and adjustments in the core ICB formula for higher costs of providing emergency ambulance services in sparsely populated areas, higher costs of unavoidably small hospitals with 24-hour accident and emergency services in remote areas and unavoidable costs associated with the Private Finance Initiative (PFI).

The different components and adjustments are summarised in the Fig. 1.

Barr et al. (2014) calculated that the allocation of NHS resources increased in real terms in the most deprived areas: by £865 (€1,053; $1,465)/head, from £1,074/head in 2001 to £1,938/head in 2011, representing an 81% increase. In more affluent areas, allocations still increased but to a lesser extent: by £621/head, from £881/head in 2001 to £1,502/head in 2011, representing an increase of 70%. They also calculate that this increase of resources to deprived areas lead to a reduction in the gap between deprived and affluent areas in male mortality amenable to healthcare of 35 deaths per 100,000 population and female mortality of 16 deaths per 100,000.

Until the last year, a measure of area deprivation in terms of education, employment, housing and/or family conditions has never been included among the criteria for the distribution of the Fondo Sanitario Nazionale (FSN) in Italy. From 1978 (the year the FSN was established) to the present, the total amount to

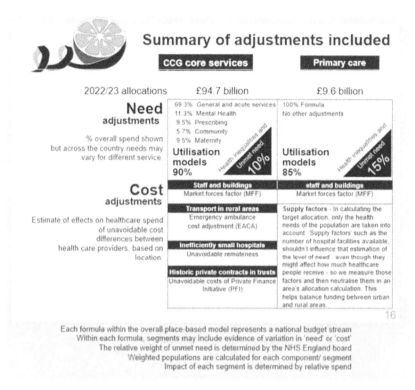

Fig. 1. NHS Allocation Formula. *Source:* Technical guide of NHS, available here: https://www.england.nhs.uk/wpcontent/uploads/2022/04/technical-guide-to-integrated-care-board-allocations-22-23-to-24-25.pdf

be allocated to the Fund has been determined on the basis of budgetary choices, starting from the previous year's spending and increasing it according to available resources. The current scheme introduced in 2011 only considers, for the determination of per capita expenditure, the demographic composition of the population. The direct consequence of this is that the southern regions, which have a younger average population structure than the central north, have actually been penalised in the allocation. For example, Fig. 2 shows per capita public health spending from 2000 to 2020 in northern and southern regions including Calabria, which is the poorest region in Italy, according to gross domestic product (GDP) per capita.

As shown in Fig. 2, per capita spending in the southern regions has been systematically lower than in the northern regions. This further penalised Calabria, which had even lower per capita spending than the average of the other southern regions.

The situation has not improved when looking at the last available year of data (2021). Fig. 3 clearly shows the existence of a gradient in per capita public spending between the North, Centre and South. On the one hand, regions such as

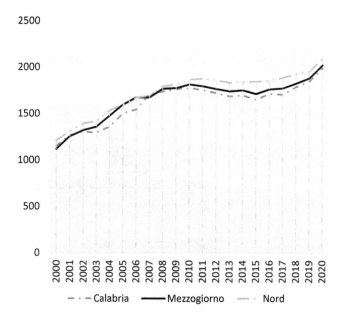

Fig. 2. Public Health Expenditure per Capita - 2000–2020. *Source:* ISTAT Health for all data and authors' calculation.

Liguria and Val d'Aosta have much higher per capita spending predominantly due to a very elderly population structure, having nearly 2,500 euros per capita spending. Southern regions, on the other hand, have about 2,000 euros per capita.

The great austerity strategy adopted in 2001 greatly contributed to the actual difference. Indeed, in 2001, the Italian constitutional reform led to the decentralisation and federalisation of the healthcare system, granting almost complete administrative and financial autonomy to each of the 21 regions and autonomous provinces. Since then, healthcare funding targets are fixed by the Ministry of Health and modulated at the regional level in accordance with regional planning targets. However, relatively soon after the federalisation, 10 out of 21 regions – due to weak managerial capacity, lower health service performance and also to the penalising NHS allocation formula – failed to reach the set goals, and the regional health budgets quickly ran into severe deficits. Therefore, recent history of healthcare expenditure is marked by attempts to place stricter control over regions' health spending.

Since 2006, a process of recentralisation has been underway. In particular, the central government has prompted the defaulting regions to adopt financial recovery plans Piano di Rientro (PdR) in the form of agreements between the region and the central government. Such agreements constitute a formal commitment from the regions with budget deficit towards the Ministry of Health and the Ministry of Finance to design and implement consolidation path.

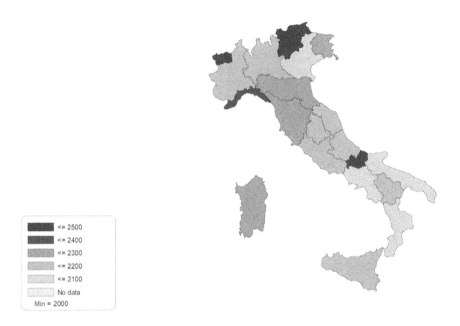

Fig. 3. Per Capita Public Health Expenditure per Capita - 2021. *Source:* ISTAT Health for all data and authors' calculation.

Arcà et al., 2020 find that – on average – PdR led to annual spending cuts of 3.8%, which in turn resulted again in a 3% rise in average avoidable deaths among both men and women. Cause-specific estimates suggest that most of these deaths were cancer-related. These harmful effects on mortality appear to have been mediated by substantial capacity cuts in hospital beds (−6.5%) and health workforce employment (−4%) which, in turn, have led to reductions in the rate of hospitalisation (−8.5%), as well as a rise in hospital care seeking in non-PdR regions, mainly in the north of the country.

Depalo (2019) uses regional data to estimate effect bounds of PdR on total (not amenable) mortality and hospitalisation rates. He relies on milder nonparametric assumptions than the common trend assumption required for difference-in-differences (DID) to identify the treatment effect bounds. The estimates suggest negative consequences on health indicators, namely hospitalisation rates and total mortality rates but only in some regions.

Another issue related to the cost-containment strategy adopted is the automatic mechanism of increasing co-payments, which are regressive by their nature. This has meant financing part of the deficits by taking more – as a proportion of income – from the least affluent and often sickest individuals (net of exemptions on the poorest), as discussed in Carrieri (2010).

In conclusion, comparing the experiences of health fund allocation in England and Italy highlights the importance of considering the relationship between socioeconomic conditions and health in order to achieve a fair distribution of resources in Italy. Failing to account for this relationship may result in underfunded regions with poorly measured health needs, which can lead to inefficient utilisation of public resources. The utilisation of modern empirical tools such as the measurement and decomposition of inequality indices and econometric modelling of healthcare utilisation and costs – areas in which Andrew's work has been particularly valuable – can provide valuable insights to policymakers in ensuring equitable and efficient resource allocation.

ACKNOWLEDGEMENT

Both authors are indebted to Andrew. Working alongside him has enriched us professionally and personally. Vincenzo Carrieri acknowledges PRIN-Next Generation EU grant P202223J4J 'The Economic Returns and Distributional Effects of Hospital Public Spending for Technological Progress in Health Care'.

REFERENCES

Angrist, J., & Pischke, J. S. (2010). The credibility revolution in empirical economics: How better research design is taking the con out of econometrics. *Journal of Economic Perspectives*, *24*(2), 3–30.

Arcà, E., Principe, F., & Van Doorslaer, E. (2020). Death by austerity? The impact of cost containment on avoidable mortality in Italy. *Health Economics*, *29*(12), 1500–1516.

Barr, B., Bambra, C., & Whitehead, M. (2014). The impact of NHS resource allocation policy on health inequalities in England 2001–11: Longitudinal ecological study. *BMJ*. https://doi.org/10.1136/bmj.g3231

Berta, P., Callea, G., Martini, G., & Vittadini, G. (2010). The effects of upcoding, cream skimming and readmissions on the Italian hospitals efficiency: A population-based investigation. *Economic Modelling*, *27*, 812–821.

Bertoni, M., Corazzini, L., & Robone, S. (2020). The good outcomes of bad news. A randomized field experiment on formatting breast cancer screening invitations. *American Journal of Health Economics*, *6*(3), 372–409.

Bilger, M., & Carrieri, V. (2013). Health in the cities: When the neighbourhood matters more than income. *Journal of Health Economics*, *32*, 1–11.

Carr-Hill, R., Rice, N., & Roland, M. (1996). Socioeconomic determinants of rates of consultation in general practice based on fourth national morbidity survey of general practices. *British Medical Journal*, *312*, 1008–1012.

Carr-Hill, R., Sheldon, T. A., Smith, P. C., Martin, S., Peacock, S., & Hardman, G. (1994). Allocating resources to health authorities: Development of methods for small area analysis of use of inpatient services. *British Medical Journal*, *309*, 1046–1049.

Carrieri, V. (2010). The effects of cost-sharing in health care: What do we know from empirical evidence? *Economia Politica*, *27*(2), 351–374.

Carrieri, V., & Granaglia, E. (2008). Searching for new ways to finance national health services: A note on the role of cost sharing. *Journal of Public Finance and Public Choice*, *2–3*, 109–122.

Carrieri, V., Madio, L., & Principe, F. (2020). Do-it-yourself medicine? The impact of light cannabis liberalization on prescription drugs. *Journal of Health Economics*, *74*, 102371.

Carrieri, V., & Principe, F. (2022). WHO and for how long? An empirical analysis of the consumers' response to red meat warning. *Food Policy*, *108*, 102231.

Carrieri, V., & Wuebker, A. (2016). Quasi-experimental evidence on the effects of health information on preventive behaviour in Europe. *Oxford Bulletin of Economics & Statistics, 78*, 765–791.

Cavalieri, M., & Ferrante, L. (2016). Does fiscal decentralization improve health outcomes? Evidence from infant mortality in Italy. *Social Science and Medicine, 164*, 74–88.

Costa, G., Bassi, M., Censini, G. F., Marra, M., Nicelli, A. L., & Zengarini, N. (a cura di). (2014). *L'equità in salute in Italia. Secondo rapporto sulle disuguaglianze sociali in sanità.* Edito da Fondazione Smith Kline. presso Franco Angeli Editore.

Culica, D., Rohrer, J., Ward, M., Hilsenrath, P., & Pomrehn, P. (2002). Medical checkups: Who does not get them? *American Journal of Public Health, 92*, 88–91.

Del Bono, E., & Vuri, D. (2018). Smoking behaviour and individual well-being: A fresh look at the effects of the 2005 public smoking ban in Italy. *Oxford Economic Papers, 70*(3), 741–762.

Depalo, D. (2019). The side effects on health of a recovery plan in Italy: A nonparametric bounding approach. *Regional Science and Urban Economics, 78*, 103466.

Gravelle, H., Sutton, M., Morris, S., Windmeijer, F., Leyland, A., Dibben, C., & Muirhead, M. (2003). Modelling supply and demand influences on the use of health care: Implications for deriving a needs-based capitation formula. *Health Economics, 12*(12), 985–1004.

Grossman, M. (1972). On the concept of health capital and the demand for health. *Journal of Political Economy, 80*, 223–255.

Hjortsberg, C. (2003). Why do the sick not utilize healthcare? The case of Zambia. *Health Economics, 12*, 755–770.

Iezzi, E., Lippi Bruni, M., & Ugolini, C. (2014). The role of GP's compensation schemes in diabetes care: Evidence from panel data. *Journal of Health Economics, 34*, 104–120.

ISTAT. (2021). *Disuguaglianze nella mortalità per causa in Italia secondo caratteristiche demografiche, sociali e territoriali - anno 2020.* https://www.istat.it/it/archivio/286642

Manning, G., Newhouse, P., Duan, N., Keeler, B., & Leibowitz, A. (1987). Health insurance and the demand for medical care: Evidence from a randomized experiment. *American Economic Review*, 251–277.

Marinacci, C., Spadea, T., Buggeri, A., Demaria, M., Caiazzo, A., & Costa, G. (2004). The role of individual and contextual socio-economic circumstances on mortality: Analysis of time variations in a city of Northwest Italy. *Journal of Epidemiology & Community Health, 58*(3), 199–207.

Ponzo, M., & Scoppa, V. (2016). *Cost-sharing and use of health services in Italy: Evidence from a fuzzy regression discontinuity design.* IZA Discussion Paper N. 9772.

Porcelli, F. (2014). Electoral accountability and local government efficiency: Quasi-experimental evidence from the Italian health care sector reforms. *Economics of Governance, 15*, 221–251.

Rice, N., & Smith, P. C. (2001). Capitation and risk adjustment in health care financing: An international progress report. *Milbank Qualterly, 79*, 81–113.

Theodossiou, I. (1998). The effects of low-pay and unemployment on psychological well-being: A logistic regression approach. *Journal of Health Economics, 17*(1), 85–104.

van Doorslaer, E., & Koolman, X. (2004). Explaining the differences in income-related health inequalities across European countries. *Health Economics, 13*(7), 609–628.

Verzulli, R., Fiorentini, G., Lippi Bruni, M., & Ugolini, C. (2017). Price changes in regulated healthcare markets: Do public hospitals respond and how? *Health Economics, 26*(11), 1429–1446.

TYPES OF INACTIVITY AND DEPRESSION AMONG OLDER INDIVIDUALS

Anwar S. Adem[a], Bruce Hollingsworth[b] and Eugenio Zucchelli[c]

[a]*University of Warwick, UK*
[b]*Lancaster University, UK*
[c]*Universidad Autónoma de Madrid, Spain*

ABSTRACT

Depression imposes substantial individual and societal economic costs, including lower productivity and higher healthcare use. However, while the relationship between employment and mental health has been explored, less is known about the potentially countervailing effects of different types of economic inactivity on depression among older individuals. The authors employ a series of models, including fixed effects panel data models and matching on rich data from the English Longitudinal Study of Ageing (ELSA) to investigate whether different types of inactivity might have heterogenous effects on depression. The authors find that whereas transitions to involuntary inactivity (unemployment) do not appear to have a perceivable effect on depression, transitions to voluntary inactivity (retirement) seem to decrease it.

Keywords: Depression; unemployment; retirement; matching; ELSA

1. INTRODUCTION

Depression is a widespread mental health disorder affecting more than 250 million people worldwide and one of the leading causes of the global burden of disease (GBD) (e.g. James et al., 2015; Vigo et al., 2016). Evidence suggests that depression imposes substantial health-related and economic costs on individuals and the broader society, including increased risks of chronic physical conditions and early mortality (Kessler, 2012); major productivity losses due to work

---

Recent Developments in Health Econometrics
Contributions to Economic Analysis, Volume 297, 127–145
Copyright © 2024 Anwar S. Adem, Bruce Hollingsworth and Eugenio Zucchelli
Published under exclusive licence by Emerald Publishing Limited
ISSN: 0573-8555/doi:10.1108/S0573-855520240000297007

absences and reduced work performance (e.g. Gotlib & Hammen, 2008). Importantly, recent studies show that mental disorders appear to be increasingly concentrated among older adults with around 20% of individuals 60 years old or older suffering from neurological conditions (WHO, 2017). Depression is the most prevalent among such conditions, affecting around 7% of the world's older population.[1] Despite its relevance, the causes of depression within this age group are often overlooked within the economics literature.

A large body of research within both the economics and epidemiology literature has analysed the effects of voluntary inactivity (retirement) on mental health. Overall, previous studies based mostly on statistical correlations find mixed results and discuss potential issues related to selection and reverse causality (e.g. Jokela et al., 2010; Lindeboom et al., 2002; Mein et al., 2003; Mosca & Barrett, 2016). Other contributions attempt to identify the causal impact of retirement on mental ill-health exploiting eligibility retirement ages as instruments via instrumental variable(IV) or (fuzzy) regression discontinuity design (RDD) approaches as well as quasi-experiments using the variation brought by pension reforms (e.g. Behncke, 2012; Charles & DeCicca, 2008; Coe & Zamarro, 2011; Eibich, 2015). In general, these contributions tend to find either limited or positive effects of retirement on mental health. However, further works examining potential differences between short- vs long-term causal effects find that retirement could have either no impact (Fé & Hollingsworth, 2016) or a large negative long-term impact on mental health (Heller-Sahlgren, 2017). While such variation in results might be due to differences in both methods and definitions of mental ill-health used in each study, both the magnitude and direction of the effect of voluntary inactivity on mental health remain largely unexplored.

We build upon the previous literature and explore the effects of both voluntary (retirement) and involuntary (unemployment) economic inactivity on depression among older individuals. We exploit rich individual-level data from the English Longitudinal Study of Ageing (ELSA) and define depression using the Centre for Epidemiology Depression Scale (CES-D), a psycho-metrically validated tool.[2] Our empirical strategy relies on a series of fixed-effects models to establish standard correlations while accounting for time-invariant unobserved heterogeneity and flexible semi-parametric matching methods to more precisely identify the effects of different types of inactivity on depression.

We find that whereas transitions to involuntary inactivity (unemployment) seem to have no statistically significant effects on depression, transitions to voluntary inactivity (retirement) appear to decrease the likelihood of becoming depressed. Importantly, this appears to be in line with previous studies finding similar results by looking at unemployment and retirement separately.

---

[1]This is likely to be an underestimation as depression is often under-diagnosed among older individuals due to the social stigma attached to it, thus making patients reluctant to describe symptoms and difficulties surrounding its diagnosis (as often co-occurring with other conditions typical of old age) (WHO, 2017).

[2]We restricted our sample to those above the age of 50; however, the data include information on the household members as well.

This chapter contributes to the large and growing literature on the health effects of employment among older individuals by looking at the potential heterogenous effects of different types of economic inactivity using rich data from ELSA. This could shed some further light on whether planned vs unplanned changes to one's employment status, especially at the end of an individual's career, might affect mental health. In addition, the evidence produced by our empirical analysis might be relevant to policymakers, informing more targeted policies to improve mental health among older individuals.

The rest the chapter is organised as follows: in Section 2, we describe the data used for this study. Section 3 presents the empirical approach; section 4 presents the main results while the last section concludes and discusses potential implications of key findings.

2. DATA

We employ data drawn from the first seven waves (2002–2014) of the English Longitudinal Study of Ageing (ELSA). ELSA is a rich source of information on older individuals that has been specifically designed to study substantive issues around population ageing. The survey includes a representative sample of the English population aged 50 years old or above and unique information on a wide range of relevant dimensions of physical and mental health as well as employment and socioeconomic status including wealth, earnings and pensions (Steptoe, Breeze, et al., 2013). ELSA started being collected biennially in 2002, and its first wave included a total of sample of 12,099 individuals followed through biannual interviews until wave 8 (2016–2017).[3]

Our main outcome of interest is depression as measured by the CES-D; a psycho-metrically validated screening tool commonly used to identify the presence of clinical depression. More specifically, ELSA includes individuals' answers to the short version of the 20 CES-D measure of depression as developed by Radloff (1977). The structure and psychometric properties of these questions have been validated among older adults by Karim et al. (2015). This 8-item version asks individuals to report whether they agree with a series of statements about symptoms and feelings experienced during the past week.[4] A depression score can be built using the binary (yes/no) response to each item, ranging from 0 (no symptoms) to 8 (all eight symptoms). We follow the literature and employ a binary measure of clinical depression based on the standard cut-off of four items

---

[3]More specifically, the wave 1's total sample of 12,099 consisted of 11,391 core members; 636 partners aged < 50 years and 72 new partners aged ≥ 50 years (Cable et al., 2017; Steptoe, Shankar, et al., 2013).

[4]The eight-item questions are as follows: 'have you feel depression'; 'have you feel that everything you did was an effort'; 'was your sleep restless'; 'were you happy'; 'have you feel lonely'; 'have you enjoyed life'; 'have you feel sad' and 'could you not get going'.

or above over the total of eight items provided by the CES-D scale (e.g. Cable et al., 2017; Courtin et al., 2015; Han, 2002; Turvey et al., 1999).[5] We also use a more stringent cut-off point of six items in our robustness checks.

Since we focus on the effects of different types of economic inactivity on depression, we distinguish between voluntary inactivity, i.e., retirement, and involuntary inactivity, i.e., unemployment. To reduce simultaneity and endogeneity concerns, we look at the effects of between waves transitions to inactivity (retirement or unemployment) on depression. Specifically, we look at the effects of transitions between employment at time $t-1$ into inactivity (retirement or unemployment) at time t on depression. In our matching models, control groups include individuals who remain employed between consecutive waves. All models include a rich set of controls. Following previous studies, these controls include individual and household-level demographic (age, gender and marital status), socioeconomic characteristics (education and head of household) and as well as health behaviours (smoking status and alcohol consumption) and other controls concerning wealth and financial conditions (pension membership, wealth and number of people in household) (e.g. Behncke, 2012; Lemieux, 2006). Table 1 provides basic descriptive statistics for the variables used in the analysis.

Table 1. Descriptive Statistics of Variables of Interest for All and by Gender.

	Count	All Mean	Sd	Count	Female Mean	Sd	Count	Male Mean	Sd
Depression	70,744	0.18	0.39	38,908	0.2	0.4	31,836	0.15	0.36
Born in the UK	70,545	0.92	0.27	38,821	0.92	0.27	31,724	0.92	0.27
Age	70,743	66.27	10	38,907	66.35	10.3	31,836	66.17	9.61
Gender	70,744	0.45	0.5	38,908	0	0	31,836	1	0
Ethnicity	70,721	0.97	0.17	38,898	0.97	0.17	31,823	0.97	0.18
Part-time	23,731	0.43	0.5	11,815	0.61	0.49	11,916	0.25	0.43
Hours of work	70,744	11.77	19.65	38,908	9.09	16.72	31,836	15.05	22.29
Pension plan	70,744	0.68	0.46	38,908	0.57	0.5	31,836	0.83	0.38
Smoking	70,061	0.14	0.35	38,569	0.14	0.35	31,492	0.14	0.35
Alcohol	70,744	0.29	0.46	38,908	0.23	0.42	31,836	0.37	0.48
Mean income (in logs)	34,004	6.41	1.97	17,599	6.26	2	16,405	6.58	1.92
Mean wealth (in logs)	65,524	10.71	1.87	35,857	10.63	1.92	29,667	10.81	1.8
Unemployed	70,744	0.008	0.091	38,908	0.005	0.071	31,836	0.012	0.11
Retired	70,744	0.516	0.499	38,908	0.514	0.499	31,836	0.517	0.499
Becoming unemployed	70,744	0.003	0.054	38,908	0.002	0.041	31,836	0.004	0.066
Becoming retired	70,744	0.039	0.194	38,908	0.035	0.184	31,836	0.044	0.206
Observations	70,744			38,908			31,836		

Notes: Estimates displayed in this table were obtained by the authors using data drawn from ELSA.

---

[5]To indicate depression from Centre for Epidemiological Studies-Depression Scale (CES-D), a cut-off of four is commonly used (see. Cable et al., 2017; Irwin et al., 1999).

3. EMPIRICAL APPROACH

First, we estimate a series of linear pooled and fixed effects models to explore standard correlations between depression and transitions into economic inactivity. After that, we employ more flexible semi-parametric propensity score matching (PSM) methods to identify treatment effects more precisely. In this case, the advantage of PSM is that it produces more reliable estimates by exploiting the wealth of data included in ELSA while building treatment and control groups as similar as possible to each other based on pre-treatment observable characteristics, with the only difference being the treatment (i.e., transitions to inactivity).

Our initial linear probability model (LPM) specification is as follows:

$$\text{Depression}_{it} = \beta_0 + \beta_1 \text{inactivity}_{it} + \beta_2 X_{it} + \delta_i + \eta_t + \varepsilon_{it} \tag{1}$$

where our outcome of interest is Depression_{it} defined using a binary variable which takes value 1 if individual i's CES-D measure is above the cut-off of 4 items at time t; inactivity_{it} is a binary indicator defining (between consecutive waves) transitions to economic inactivity (retirement or unemployment, alternatively) conditional on being previously employed; X_{it} is a vector including relevant individual- and household-level characteristics such as age, gender, marital status, education, being the household head, financial status, smoking status and frequency of alcohol use. δ_i represents individual fixed effects, accounting for any time-invariant individual-level unobserved heterogeneity, while η_t are wave fixed effects and ε_{it} is the idiosyncratic error term. We estimate model (1) using pooled and fixed effects specifications. In our PSM model, the group of 'treated' individuals includes those who transition towards either retirement or unemployment between consecutive waves whereas the control group comprises those who do not change employment status (i.e. remain employed). We estimate the average treatment effect on the treated (ATET) which is given by:

$$\text{ATET} = E[Y^1 - Y^0 | Z = 1] = E[Y^1 | Z = 1] - E[Y^0 | Z = 1] \tag{2}$$

To identify the counterfactual $E[Y^0 | Z = 1]$ and estimate ATET, we rely on Propensity score matching (PSM) (Rosenbaum & Rubin, 1983). The propensity score (PS) can be defined as the probability of treatment assignment conditional on observable characteristics:

$$P_{it}(x) = \text{Pr}(Z_{it} = 1 | X_{it} = x) \tag{3}$$

where Z_{it} is an indicator function which takes value 1 if an individual i is treated at time t, that is if an individual becomes inactive between consecutive waves; X_{it} stands for any individual- and household-level observable characteristics which may affect the probability of our treatment.

We use a probit model to estimate Eq. (3). Furthermore, to properly account for the panel dimension of our data, we follow Wooldridge (2005) and estimate our PS for both the pooled sample and each wave separately. We match individuals using the PS to obtain the counterfactual (using the estimated PS values for each individual in treatment and control groups). Conditioning on PS implies $E[Y^0|Z = 1, P(x)] = E[Y^0|Z = 0, P(x)]$ and allows building a counterfactual and thus comparable treated and control groups. The ATET can be rewritten as follows:

$$\text{ATET} = E[Y^1|Z = 1, P(x)] - E[Y^0|Z = 0, P(x)] \tag{4}$$

Here, we first use a conservative 1:1 nearest neighbour matching to match treated and control groups.[6] However, the estimation results are robust to alternative matching techniques such as kernel matching and also to the different number of nearest neighbours used in matching.

It is worth noting that all matching methods, and more specifically the identification of the corresponding treatment effects, are based on the fundamental assumptions of common support and conditional independence. According to the first assumption, individuals with the same pre-treatment observed characteristics have a positive probability of be-coming inactive between consecutive waves. This assumption can be met by dropping off-support observations from the analysis. The latter implies that selection into treatment (i.e., becoming inactive whether voluntarily or involuntarily) is based only on observable characteristics. Hence, conditional on a set of pre-treatment observable characteristics, our potential outcomes (inactive vs not inactive) are independent of assignment to treatment. The tables in Appendix A i.e., Tables A1 and A2, provide standard diagnostics about these assumptions.

4. RESULTS

We first present estimates on the relationship between unemployment and depression followed by those between retirement and depression. Here, estimates are obtained using both pooled and fixed effects linear probability models (LPMs). Second, we use PSM to further explore these relationships.

Results are shown in columns 1 and 2 of Table 2 for pooled LPM and fixed effect LPM, respectively. In both specifications, the effect of becoming unemployed on the likelihood of being depressed is positive but not statistically significant. We also find that depression has a positive and statistically significant association with age as well as with being single; divorced; separated and being a current smoker. Here, smoking has a negative effect in the pooled specification while it switches sign in the FE specification. This could be a negative effect at the general population level, whereas, if one individual

---

[6]One-to-one matching involves identifying a single individual rather than using a weighted average of several individuals within a specific proximity (neighbourhood). While finding a one-to-one match can be challenging, it provides a strong and suitable match. Nonetheless, our findings remain consistent and reliable even when using different numbers of neighbourhood matches.

Table 2. Models Under Different Approaches: Regression on the Whole Sample.

	(1) OLS	(2) FE
Become unemployed	0.0161	0.0213
	(0.027)	(0.025)
Age	−0.0209***	−0.0426***
	(0.002)	(0.004)
Age square	0.000150***	0.000248***
	(0.000)	(0.000)
Male	−0.00286	0
	(0.004)	(.)
White	−0.0813***	0
	(0.010)	(.)
Born in the UK	−0.0252***	0
	(0.006)	(.)
Cohabiting	0.00889	0.00858
	(0.007)	(0.016)
Single, never married	0.0370***	0.0609**
	(0.007)	(0.031)
Widowed	0.0775***	0.112***
	(0.006)	(0.011)
Divorced	0.0447***	0.0648***
	(0.007)	(0.017)
Separated	0.0748***	0.105***
	(0.013)	(0.020)
Higher ed below degree	0.00951*	0.00870
	(0.005)	(0.015)
NVQ3/GCE A level equiv	0.00244	−0.00964
	(0.006)	(0.016)
NVQ2/GCE O level equiv.	0.00172	0.0000844
	(0.005)	(0.015)
NVQ1/CSE other grade equiv.	0.0181**	0.00121
	(0.008)	(0.021)
Foreign/other	0.00102	0.00293
	(0.006)	(0.013)
No qualification	0.0349***	−0.000745
	(0.005)	(0.016)
Pension member	−0.116***	−0.166***
	(0.003)	(0.006)
Head of household	0.00630	0.0198*
	(0.005)	(0.010)
Number of people	−0.00295	−0.00212
	(0.002)	(0.003)
Log of mean wealth	−0.0137***	−0.00274
	(0.001)	(0.002)
Smoker	0.0388***	−0.0256***
	(0.004)	(0.009)
Alcohol	−0.0499***	−0.0423***
	(0.003)	(0.005)

(Continued)

134 Types of Inactivity and Depression

Table 2. (Continued)

	(1) OLS	(2) FE
R^2	0.0702	0.0252
N	64,216	64,216

Notes: Standard errors in parentheses. Wave fixed effects are included. Estimates displayed in this table were obtained by the authors using pooled ordinary least squares and fixed effect models and data drawn from ELSA. $*p < 0.10$, $**p < 0.05$ and $***p < 0.01$.

is smoking, the 'within' individual, smoking seems to be positively associated with mental ill-health.

On the contrary, depression seems to have a negatively and statistically significant correlation with ethnicity (being white); being born in the UK; (low) levels of education (although the corresponding estimated coefficient is only statistically significant in the pooled LPM model); being married; being a member of a private pension scheme as well as alcohol consumption. Here, alcohol consumption could potentially proxy socialisation whose positive effect on mental health is well documented (e.g. Holdsworth et al., 2016). It is also worth noting that all specifications include wave fixed effects to capture any wave-specific shock.

Table 3 reports findings from the same pooled LPM and fixed effect LPM models exploring the effect of voluntary inactivity (retirement) on depression. While both specifications present a negative association between retirement and depression, the corresponding coefficient is only statistically significant in the pooled LPM case. This might imply that despite a (potential) positive role of retirement in improving mental health, the strength of this statistical correlation is not confirmed once individual-level time-variant observables are accounted for. The coefficient estimates for the remaining covariates appear to have similar sign and levels of statistical significance as the ones presented in the model with unemployment.

Table 4 presents results from the PSM models. As the average treatment effect on the treated (ATET) result in the first column shows, transitions to unemployment appear to have a positive and statistically significant effect on depression in our PSM model including all waves. This implies that becoming unemployed appears to increase the risk of clinical depression by 6.85 percentage points (pp). This result is in line with previous studies which find a negative effect of unemployment on mental health (see. Paul & Moser, 2009).

To further explore this relationship, results presented in columns 2–7 of Table 4 show the ATET computed using data in each wave separately. Interestingly, the only statistically significant ATET is the one identified by the model estimated using only individuals in wave 5 and corresponding to the years

ANWAR S. ADEM ET AL.

Table 3. Models Under Different Approaches: Regression on the Whole Sample.

	(1) OLS	(2) FE
Become retired	−0.0174**	0.00188
	(0.007)	(0.006)
Age	−0.0204***	−0.0427***
	(0.002)	(0.004)
Age square	0.000147***	0.000248***
	(0.000)	(0.000)
Male	−0.00275	0
	(0.004)	(.)
White	−0.0813***	0
	(0.010)	(.)
Born in the UK	−0.0251***	0
	(0.006)	(.)
Cohabiting	0.00905	0.00874
	(0.007)	(0.016)
Single, never married	0.0368***	0.0609**
	(0.007)	(0.031)
Widowed	0.0774***	0.112***
	(0.006)	(0.011)
Divorced	0.0447***	0.0648***
	(0.007)	(0.017)
Separated	0.0747***	0.105***
	(0.013)	(0.020)
Higher ed below degree	0.00936*	0.00864
	(0.005)	(0.015)
NVQ3/GCE A level equiv	0.00235	−0.00961
	(0.006)	(0.016)
NVQ2/GCE O level equiv	0.00151	0.000126
	(0.005)	(0.015)
NVQ1/CSE other grade equiv	0.0178**	0.00128
	(0.008)	(0.021)
Foreign/other	0.000877	0.00296
	(0.006)	(0.013)
No qualification	0.0346***	−0.000726
	(0.005)	(0.016)
Pension member	−0.116***	−0.166***
	(0.003)	(0.006)
Head of household	0.00628	0.0197*
	(0.005)	(0.010)
Number of people	−0.00308	−0.00212
	(0.002)	(0.003)
Log of mean wealth	−0.0136***	−0.00275
	(0.001)	(0.002)
Smoker	0.0388***	−0.0255***
	(0.004)	(0.009)
Alcohol	−0.0498***	−0.0423***
	(0.003)	(0.005)

(Continued)

136   *Types of Inactivity and Depression*

Table 3. *(Continued)*

	(1) OLS	(2) FE
R^2	0.0703	0.0252
N	64,216	64,216

Notes: Standard errors in parentheses. Wave fixed effects are included. Estimates displayed in this table were obtained by the authors using pooled ordinary least squares (OLS) and fixed effect (FE) models and data drawn from ELSA. $*p < 0.10$, $**p < 0.05$ and $***p < 0.01$.

Table 4. Regression for Becoming Unemployed on the Whole Sample and for Each Wave.

Waves	(1) All	(2) Wave 2	(3) Wave 3	(4) Wave 4	(5) Wave 5	(6) Wave 6	(7) Wave 7
ATET	0.0685***	0.00451	0.0170	0.0784	0.119**	0.118	0.0859
	(0.025)	(0.056)	(0.069)	(0.051)	(0.048)	(0.076)	(0.090)
Cons	0.114***	0.0989***	0.0941***	0.0981***	0.109***	0.132***	0.128***
	(0.002)	(0.006)	(0.005)	(0.005)	(0.006)	(0.006)	(0.007)
R^2	0.000310	0.00000237	0.0000201	0.000663	0.00206	0.000754	0.000395
Observations	23,569	2,758	3,015	3,500	3,014	3,174	2,311

Notes: Standard errors in parentheses. Estimates displayed in this table were obtained by the authors using matching model and data drawn from ELSA. $*p < 0.10$, $**p < 0.05$ and $***p < 0.01$.

2010–2011, the year following the Great Recession in England.[7] The effect is sizeable (nearly 12pp) and, overall, appears to drive the ATET results produced by the PSM model for all waves. Also, this lagged effect of becoming unemployed on mental health is in line with the literature (Tefft, 2011) and may suggest the presence of a delayed effect of unemployment on mental health (Drydakis, 2015).

Table 5 includes ATET computed by PSM models on the effects of retirement on depression. In this case, the ATET in the first column (PSM model including data from all waves) appears to be negative and statistically significantly different from zero. This implies that retiring decreases the risk of depression by around 3.5 pp. Notably, ATET reported in columns 2–7 show negative and statistically significant effects on depression for models computed using information in waves

---

[7]The Great Recession in the UK happened between the second quarter of 2008 and the second quarter of 2009, that is, between 1st of April 2008 to 31st of June 2009. The data in wave 4, which covers the period May 2008–July 2009, was entirely collected during the Great Recession. That is also implies the observations in wave 5 are not contaminated by the Great Recession, and our significant effect in wave 5 (collected between June 2010 and July 2011) seems a genuine lag effect.

ANWAR S. ADEM ET AL.

Table 5. Regression for Becoming Retired on the Whole Sample and for Each Wave.

Waves	(1) All	(2) Wave 2	(3) Wave 3	(4) Wave 4	(5) Wave 5	(6) Wave 6	(7) Wave 7
ATET	−0.0351***	−0.0178	−0.00203	−0.0404	−0.0619***	−0.0557**	−0.0368
	(0.010)	(0.024)	(0.030)	(0.031)	(0.022)	(0.023)	(0.024)
Cons	0.152***	0.149***	0.144***	0.146***	0.154***	0.165***	0.170***
	(0.002)	(0.005)	(0.005)	(0.004)	(0.005)	(0.005)	(0.005)
R^2	0.000268	0.0000926	0.000000768	0.000249	0.00124	0.000886	0.00043
Observations	45,199	5,962	6,021	6,902	6,287	6,562	5,625

Notes: Standard errors in parentheses. Estimates displayed in this table were obtained by the authors using Matching model and data drawn from ELSA. $*p < 0.10, **p < 0.05$ and $***p < 0.01$.

5 and 6. Once again, the effects of transitions into inactivity appear to be relevant up to four years following the Great Recession.

Overall, our findings imply countervailing effects of transitions to retirement and unemployment on depression only after at least one year and up until four years, following the Great Recession. This may also suggest that further investigation into delayed (un)employment effects on mental health might be needed.

In Table 6, we report the probit regression result for the PSestimation.[8]

Table 6. Probit Regression on Becoming Unemployed and Retired.

	(1) Become Unemployed	(2) Become Retired
Age	1.166***	0.530***
	(0.169)	(0.036)
Age square	−0.00986***	−0.00400***
	(0.001)	(0.000)
Male	0.353***	0.0652*
	(0.080)	(0.036)
White	−0.0997	−0.0104
	(0.155)	(0.075)
Born in the UK	−0.0918	0.00832
	(0.107)	(0.046)
Cohabiting	0.131	0.0579
	(0.095)	(0.046)
Single, never married	0.345***	−0.105*
	(0.099)	(0.062)

(Continued)

---

[8]The common support assumptions are visualised in Figs. A1 and A2 in the Appendix.

Table 6. *(Continued)*

	(1) Become Unemployed	(2) Become Retired
Widowed	−0.304	−0.241***
	(0.220)	(0.055)
Divorced	−0.0195	−0.0453
	(0.116)	(0.052)
Separated	0.0998	−0.105
	(0.173)	(0.097)
Higher ed below degree	0.0764	−0.0952**
	(0.102)	(0.038)
NVQ3/GCE A level equiv	0.0937	−0.0826*
	(0.110)	(0.046)
NVQ2/GCE O level equiv	0.127	−0.116***
	(0.093)	(0.036)
NVQ1/CSE other grade equiv	0.306**	−0.090
	(0.133)	(0.057)
Foreign/other	0.278***	−0.111***
	(0.101)	(0.042)
No qualification	0.182*	−0.164***
	(0.095)	(0.037)
Pension member	−0.0919	0.113***
	(0.069)	(0.029)
Head of household	−0.178**	−0.0878**
	(0.086)	(0.039)
Number of people	−0.0828**	−0.0873***
	(0.039)	(0.019)
Log of mean wealth	−0.0635***	0.0240***
	(0.014)	(0.008)
Smoker	0.208***	−0.0475
	(0.063)	(0.033)
Alcohol	−0.0386	0.0316
	(0.059)	(0.024)
N	19,613	37,433

Notes: Standard errors in parentheses. Wave fixed effects are included. Estimates displayed in this table were obtained by the authors using Probit model and data drawn from ELSA. $*p < 0.10$, $**p < 0.05$ and $***p < 0.01$.

The probability of becoming unemployed and becoming retired increases with age, and pension membership decreases the probability of the former but increases the latter.

4.1 Robustness Checks

In order to check the validity and further investigate our main results, we also performed a series of robustness checks. First, we employed a different and stricter cut-off to identify clinical depression, that is, instead of four, we use six yes answers as a cut-off. This more conservative measure of depression does not appear to change our key results. Over all waves, the results show that becoming retired and unemployed are associated with a 1.6 pp. decrease and a 4.8 pp. increase in the incidence of clinical depression, respectively (see Tables B5 and B6 in the Appendix B).

Second, since the literature appears to suggest that gender may play a role in the relationship between employment and mental health (DHSC, 2018), we re-estimated all our models for men and women separately. Overall, results show that for men becoming unemployed has a large and significant negative effect, whereas for women, the gain from retirement is large and significant. For men, over all waves, retiring has no significant effect. However, becoming unemployed is associated with an increase of 9.39 pp in the incidence of clinical depression. On the other hand, for women, retiring is associated with a 4.73 pp. decrease in incidence of clinical depression, whereas becoming unemployed has no statistically significant effect. Corresponding results can be found in Tables B1–B4 in the Appendix. These results from the baseline regression are robust to those changes and are in line with the literature.

We also re-estimated our PSM models using different matching methods. These include varying the number of nearest neighbours used in constricting the controls to alternative matching techniques such as kernel matching. The full set of results is available upon request.

5. CONCLUSIONS AND DISCUSSION

We examine the heterogenous effects of different types of economic inactivity on depression among older individuals on rich longitudinal data from ELSA. Overall, our findings provide evidence suggesting that different types of inactivity might be associated with contrasting effects on depression. While unemployment (involuntary inactivity) appears to increase the incidence of clinical depression, retirement seems to decrease it. Findings from matching indicate that these effects tend to increase in magnitude and significance in the years after the Great Recession, potentially suggesting a delayed effect of inactivity on mental health. Furthermore, gender also appears to play a role since becoming unemployed has a stronger effect on men, while retirement presents a larger effect on women. It should be kept in mind that, although similar, results from linear fixed effects models, accounting time-invariant individual-level unobservables, exhibit reduced statistical significance. Importantly, the main results are robust to alternative (and more stringent) measures of depression.

This chapter provides new evidence to the growing literature on the mental health effects of labour market outcomes by disentangling the effect of different types of economic inactivity (see. Belloni et al., 2016). More generally, our analysis helps shed further light on the relationship between employment and (mental) health among older individuals. This may be relevant to policymakers when devising unemployment benefits and retirement programs targeted at specific groups of older workers, as well as incentives to either encourage pension scheme involvement or insuring against unemployment, especially in the light of future cycles of recessions. As people are living longer and remaining economically active well into older ages, the impact of recessions on the mental health of older populations who may feel 'left behind' will continue to grow as an emerging concern.

140   *Types of Inactivity and Depression*

It should be noted that these results are exploratory and further research might help identify causal effects. In addition, external validation of the findings may present challenges due to the presence of relatively generous unemployment benefits in the UK, which might alleviate both the financial and psychological strain associated with being jobless. Thus, it could be interesting to see the effect of retirement and unemployment at a later age in places where unemployment insurance is less generous or absent.

REFERENCES

Behncke, S. (2012). Does retirement trigger ill health? *Health Economics, 21*, 282–300.

Belloni, M., Meschi, E., & Pasini, G. (2016). The effect on mental health of retiring during the economic crisis. *Health Economics, 25*, 126–140.

Cable, N., Chandola, T., Aida, J., Sekine, M., & Netuveli, G. (2017). Can sleep disturbance influence changes in mental health status? Longitudinal research evidence from ageing studies in England and Japan. *Sleep Medicine, 30*, 216–221.

Charles, K. K., & DeCicca, P. (2008). Local labor market fluctuations and health: Is there a connection and for whom? *Journal of Health Economics, 27*, 1532–1550.

Coe, N. B., & Zamarro, G. (2011). Retirement effects on health in Europe. *Journal of Health Economics, 30*, 77–86.

Courtin, E., Knapp, M., Grundy, E., & Avendano-Pabon, M. (2015). Are different measures of depressive symptoms in old age comparable? An analysis of the CES-D and Euro-D scales in 13 countries. *International Journal of Methods in Psychiatric Research, 24*, 287–304.

DHSC. (2018). *The women's mental health taskforce. Final report.* Department of Health and Social Care, UK.

Drydakis, N. (2015). The effect of unemployment on self-reported health and mental health in Greece from 2008 to 2013: A longitudinal study before and during the financial crisis. *Social Science & Medicine, 128*, 43–51.

Eibich, P. (2015). Understanding the effect of retirement on health: Mechanisms and heterogeneity. *Journal of Health Economics, 43*, 1–12.

Fé, E., & Hollingsworth, B. (2016). Short-and long-run estimates of the local effects of retirement on health. *Journal of the Royal Statistical Society – Series A: Statistics in Society, 179*, 1051–1067.

Gotlib, I. H., & Hammen, C. L. (2008). *Handbook of depression.* Guilford Press.

Han, B. (2002). Depressive symptoms and self-rated health in community-dwelling older adults: A longitudinal study. *Journal of the American Geriatrics Society, 50*, 1549–1556.

Heller-Sahlgren, G. (2017). Retirement blues. *Journal of Health Economics, 54*, 66–78.

Holdsworth, C., Mendonça, M., Pikhart, H., Frisher, M., de Oliveira, C., & Shelton, N. (2016). Is regular drinking in later life an indicator of good health? Evidence from the English longitudinal study of ageing. *Journal of Epidemiology & Community Health, 70*, 764–770.

Irwin, M., Artin, K. H., & Oxman, M. N. (1999). Screening for depression in the older adult: Criterion validity of the 10-item center for epidemiological studies depression scale (CES-D). *Archives of Internal Medicine, 159*, 1701–1704.

James, P., Banay, R. F., Hart, J. E., & Laden, F. (2015). A review of the health benefits of greenness. *Current Epidemiology Reports, 2*, 131–142.

Jokela, M., Ferrie, J. E., Gimeno, D., Chandola, T., Shipley, M. J., Head, J., Vahtera, J., Westerlund, H., Marmot, M. G., & Kivimäki, M. (2010). From midlife to early old age: Health trajectories associated with retirement. *Epidemiology (Cambridge, Mass.), 21*, 284.

Karim, J., Weisz, R., Bibi, Z., & ur Rehman, S. (2015). Validation of the eight-item center for epidemiologic studies depression scale (CES-D) among older adults. *Current Psychology, 34*, 681–692.

Kessler, R. C. (2012). The costs of depression. *Psychiatria Clinica, 35*, 1–14.

Lemieux, T. (2006). The "mincer equation" thirty years after schooling, experience, and earnings. In *Jacob Mincer a pioneer of modern labor economics* (pp. 127–145). Springer.

Lindeboom, M., Portrait, F., & Van den Berg, G. J. (2002). An econometric analysis of the mental-health effects of major events in the life of older individuals. *Health Economics, 11*, 505–520.

Mein, G., Martikainen, P., Hemingway, H., Stansfeld, S., & Marmot, M. (2003). Is retirement good or bad for mental and physical health functioning? Whitehall II longitudinal study of civil servants. *Journal of Epidemiology & Community Health, 57,* 46–49.

Mosca, I., & Barrett, A. (2016). The impact of adult child emigration on the mental health of older parents. *Journal of Population Economics, 29,* 687–719.

Paul, K. I., & Moser, K. (2009). Unemployment impairs mental health: Meta-analyses. *Journal of Vocational Behavior, 74,* 264–282.

Radloff, L. S. (1977). The CES-D scale: A self-report depression scale for research in the general population. *Applied Psychological Measurement, 1,* 385–401.

Rosenbaum, P. R., & Rubin, D. B. (1983). The central role of the propensity score in observational studies for causal effects. *Biometrika, 70,* 41–55.

Steptoe, A., Breeze, E., Banks, J., & Nazroo, J. (2013). Cohort profile: The English longitudinal study of ageing. *International Journal of Epidemiology, 42,* 1640–1648.

Steptoe, A., Shankar, A., Demakakos, P., & Wardle, J. (2013). Social isolation, loneliness, and all-cause mortality in older men and women. *Proceedings of the National Academy of Sciences, 110,* 5797–5801.

Tefft, N. (2011). Insights on unemployment, unemployment insurance, and mental health. *Journal of Health Economics, 30,* 258–264.

Turvey, C. L., Wallace, R. B., & Herzog, R. (1999). A revised CES-D measure of depressive symptoms and a DSM-based measure of major depressive episodes in the elderly. *International Psychogeriatrics, 11,* 139–148.

Vigo, D., Thornicroft, G., & Atun, R. (2016). Estimating the true global burden of mental illness. *The Lancet Psychiatry, 3,* 171–178.

WHO. (2017). *Fact sheet, mental health of older adults.* Online report. https://www.who.int/news-room/fact-sheets/detail/mental-health-of-older-adults. Accessed on January 8, 2020.

Wooldridge, J. M. (2005). Violating ignorability of treatment by controlling for too many factors. *Econometric Theory, 21,* 1026–1028.

APPENDIX A: BALANCENESS CHECKS

Table A1. *t*-test for Becoming Unemployment.

| Variable | Unmatched | Mean | | %reduct | | %reduct | | |
	Matched	Treated	Control	%bias	bias	T	$p > t$	V(T)/V(C)
Age	U	58.478	58.457	0.5		0.05	0.963	0.34*
	M	58.478	58.421	1.2	−172.8	0.16	0.876	1.08
Age Squared	U	3,430.5	3,448.8	−3.3		−0.33	0.738	0.32*
	M	3,430.5	3,423.1	1.3	59.7	0.17	0.863	1.09
White	U	0.950	0.964	−6.9		−0.94	0.346	1.38*
	M	0.950	0.931	9.3	−34.3	0.71	0.479	0.74
Born in the UK	U	0.887	0.910	−7.5		−1	0.318	1.23
	M	0.887	0.868	6.2	17.3	0.51	0.609	0.88
Marital status	U	1.868	1.666	14.7		1.89	0.058	1.09
	M	1.868	1.943	−5.5	62.7	−0.47	0.638	0.92
Educ. Qual	U	4.239	3.667	26.7		3.34	0.001	0.98
	M	4.239	4.107	6.2	76.9	0.55	0.58	1.01
Pension member	U	0.767	0.823	−13.7		−1.82	0.069	.
	M	0.767	0.698	17.1	−25.1	1.39	0.164	.
Head of household	U	0.679	0.616	13.3		1.64	0.102	.
	M	0.679	0.648	6.6	50.3	0.59	0.554	.

(Continued)

142

Types of Inactivity and Depression

Table A1. *(Continued)*

Variable	Unmatched Matched	Mean Treated	Control	%reduct %bias	bias	%reduct T	$p > t$	V(T)/V(C)
# people	U	2.113	2.353	−25.2		−3.16	0.002	0.99
	M	2.113	2.113	0	100	0	1	1.16
log(Wealth)	U	10.295	11.032	−38.5		−6.26	0	2.37*
	M	10.295	10.071	11.7	69.5	0.8	0.425	0.69*
Smoker	U	0.296	0.151	35.1		5.05	0	.
	M	0.296	0.264	7.6	78.2	0.62	0.534	.
Alcohol	U	0.308	0.348	−8.5		−1.05	0.292	.
	M	0.308	0.289	4	52.7	0.37	0.714	.

Notes: Estimates displayed in this table were obtained by the authors using data drawn from ELSA. *$p < 0.10$, **$p < 0.05$ and ***$p < 0.01$.

Table A2. *t*-test for Becoming Retired.

Variable	Unmatched Matched	Mean Treated	Control	%reduct %bias	bias	*t*-test T	$p > t$	V(T)/V(C)
Age	U	64.212	65.301	−13.2	−3.89	0	0.35*	
	M	64.212	64.572	−4.4	67	−1.53	0.125	0.97
Age squared	U	4,158.4	4,365.3	−18.4	−5.41	0	0.34*	
	M	4,158.4	4,205.9	−4.2	77	−1.52	0.129	1.01
White	U	0.97237	0.97052	1.1	0.39	0.697	0.94	
	M	0.97237	0.97237	0	100	0	1	1
Born in the UK	U	0.91711	0.91819	−0.4	−0.14	0.889	1.01	
	M	0.91711	0.91558	0.6	−42.3	0.14	0.888	0.98
Marital status	U	1.6539	1.9133	−18.7	−6.34	0	0.82*	
	M	1.6539	1.6623	−0.6	96.7	−0.16	0.871	0.98
Educ. Qual	U	3.7606	4.2821	−23.1	−8.17	0		0.97
	M	3.7606	3.68	3.6	84.5	0.92	0.357	1.01
Pension member	U	0.81274	0.73111	19.5	6.57	0	.	
	M	0.81274	0.80814	1.1	94.4	0.3	0.764	.
Head of household	U	0.60706	0.64275	−7.4	−2.65	0.008	.	
	M	0.60706	0.62087	−2.9	61.3	−0.72	0.469	.
# people	U	2.0445	2.0818	−4.8	−1.5	0.134	0.54*	
	M	2.0445	2.013	4	15.6	1.23	0.22	0.99
log(Wealth)	U	11.255	10.733	31.3	10.36	0	0.72*	
	M	11.255	11.347	−5.5	82.3	−1.63	0.103	1.26*
Smoker	U	0.10898	0.13703	−8.5	−2.91	0.004	.	
	M	0.10898	0.10591	0.9	89.1	0.25	0.8	.
Alcohol	U	0.37989	0.31133	14.5	5.26	0	.	
	M	0.37989	0.39064	−2.3	84.3	−0.56	0.573	.

Notes: Estimates displayed in this table were obtained by the authors using data drawn from ELSA. *$p < 0.10$, **$p < 0.05$ and ***$p < 0.01$.

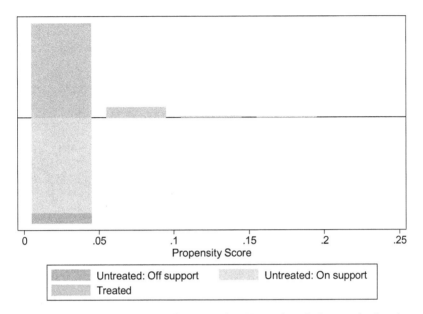

Fig. A1. Common Support for Becoming Unemployed. *Source:* Authors' computation.

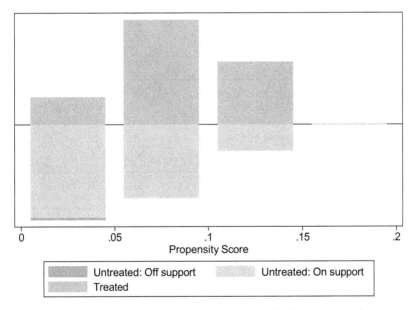

Fig. A2. Common Support for Becoming Retired. *Source:* Authors' computation.

APPENDIX B: ROBUSTNESS CHECKS

Table B1. Main ATET Becoming Retired for Men.

Waves	(1) All	(2) Wave 2	(3) Wave 3	(4) Wave 4	(5) Wave 5	(6) Wave 6	(7) Wave 7
ATET	−0.0194	−0.0173	−0.00208	−0.0372	−0.0483	−0.0350	−0.0189
	(0.013)	(0.030)	(0.038)	(0.039)	(0.030)	(0.030)	(0.032)
Cons	0.127***	0.114***	0.113***	0.113***	0.132***	0.157***	0.158***
	(0.002)	(0.006)	(0.006)	(0.006)	(0.006)	(0.007)	(0.007)
R^2	0.000104	0.000115	0.00000106	0.000278	0.000906	0.000433	0.000139
Observations	21,283	2,838	2,855	3,234	2,875	3,046	2,511

Notes: Standard errors in parentheses. Estimates displayed in this table were obtained by the authors using matching model and data drawn from ELSA. $*p < 0.10, **p < 0.05$ and $***p < 0.01$.

Table B2. Main ATET Becoming Retired for Women.

Waves	(1) All	(2) Wave 2	(3) Wave 3	(4) Wave 4	(5) Wave 5	(6) Wave 6	(7) Wave 7
ATET	−0.0473***	−0.0152	0.00690	−0.0401	−0.0724**	−0.0784**	−0.0530
	(0.015)	(0.037)	(0.045)	(0.047)	(0.032)	(0.035)	(0.035)
Cons	0.175***	0.180***	0.167***	0.174***	0.172***	0.172***	0.181***
	(0.002)	(0.007)	(0.007)	(0.006)	(0.007)	(0.006)	(0.007)
R^2	0.000402	0.0000558	0.00000774	0.000201	0.00146	0.00142	0.000742
Observations	23,916	3,124	2,979	3,668	3,412	3,516	3,087

Notes: Standard errors in parentheses. Estimates displayed in this table were obtained by the authors using matching model and data drawn from ELSA. $*p < 0.10, **p < 0.05$ and $***p < 0.01$.

Table B3. Main ATET Becoming Unemployed for Men.

Waves	(1) All	(2) Wave 2	(3) Wave 3	(4) Wave 4	(5) Wave 5	(6) Wave 6	(7) Wave 7
ATET	0.0939***	0.0811	0.0106	0.119*	0.129***	0.146	0.0159
	(0.029)	(0.062)	(0.091)	(0.062)	(0.050)	(0.101)	(0.111)
Cons	0.0984***	0.0768***	0.0894***	0.0809***	0.0927***	0.127***	0.109***
	(0.003)	(0.007)	(0.009)	(0.006)	(0.008)	(0.009)	(0.013)
R^2	0.000842	0.00121	0.0000126	0.00202	0.00435	0.00164	0.0000341
N	12,089	1,426	1,084	1837	1,567	1,262	604

Notes: Standard errors in parentheses. Estimates displayed in this table were obtained by the authors using Matching model and data drawn from ELSA. $*p < 0.10, **p < 0.05$ and $***p < 0.01$.

Table B4. Main ATET Becoming Unemployed for Women.

Waves	(1) All	(2) Wave 2	(3) Wave 4	(4) Wave 5
ATET	0.0391	−0.108	0.0261	0.121
	(0.045)	(0.098)	(0.086)	(0.119)
Cons	0.125***	0.108***	0.117***	0.129***
	(0.003)	(0.010)	(0.009)	(0.012)
R^2	0.0000705	0.00132	0.0000638	0.00125
Observations	10,862	923	1,436	824

Notes: Standard errors in parentheses. Estimates displayed in this table were obtained by the authors using Matching model and data drawn from ELSA. $*p < 0.10, **p < 0.05$ and $***p < 0.01$.

Table B5. Main ATET Becoming Retired With Cut-off of 6.

Waves	(1) All	(2) Wave 2	(3) Wave 3	(4) Wave 4	(5) Wave 5	(6) Wave 6	(7) Wave 7
ATET	−0.0165**	−0.0160	−0.0155	0.000156	−0.0449***	−0.0344*	−0.0108
	(0.007)	(0.017)	(0.022)	(0.022)	(0.016)	(0.019)	(0.019)
Cons	0.0771***	0.0684***	0.0723***	0.0675***	0.0780***	0.0983***	0.102***
	(0.001)	(0.003)	(0.003)	(0.003)	(0.003)	(0.004)	(0.004)
R^2	0.000108	0.000149	0.0000828	7.26e-09	0.00119	0.000526	0.0000562
Observations	45,199	5,962	6,021	6,902	6,287	6,562	5,625

Notes: Standard errors in parentheses. Estimates displayed in this table were obtained by the authors using Matching model and data drawn from ELSA. $*p < 0.10, **p < 0.05$ and $***p < 0.01$.

Table B6. Main ATET Becoming Unemployed With Cut-off of 6.

Waves	(1) All	(2) Wave 2	(3) Wave 3	(4) Wave 4	(5) Wave 5	(6) Wave 6	(7) Wave 7
ATET	0.0481**	0.0602	−0.0427	0.0121	0.104***	0.0172	0.130*
	(0.019)	(0.038)	(0.048)	(0.036)	(0.035)	(0.062)	(0.075)
Cons	0.0588***	0.0432***	0.0427***	0.0467***	0.0549***	0.0828***	0.0845***
	(0.002)	(0.004)	(0.004)	(0.004)	(0.004)	(0.005)	(0.006)
R^2	0.000279	0.000899	0.000266	0.0000315	0.00294	0.0000245	0.00130
Observations	23,569	2,758	3,015	3,500	3,014	3,174	2,311

Notes: Standard errors in parentheses. Estimates displayed in this table were obtained by the authors using matching model and data drawn from ELSA. $*p < 0.10, **p < 0.05$ and $***p < 0.01$.

MENTAL HEALTH, LIFESTYLE AND RETIREMENT

Silvia Balia[a] and Erica Delugas[b]

[a]University of Cagliari, Italy
[b]CRENoS, Italy

ABSTRACT

This chapter presents a mediation model that aims to disentangle the indirect from the direct effects of retirement on health, considering the mediating role of lifestyles. The model is applied to the risk of depression, and physical inactivity is assumed to potentially mediate the effect of retirement. The results indicate that there is a significant indirect effect via the mediator, albeit relatively small in comparison to the direct effect. The analysis highlights the importance of further exploring the influence of lifestyle factors in the relationship between retirement and health, in order to gain a better understanding of the potential pathways through which retirement impacts health.

Keywords: Retirement; risky behaviour; depression; mediating effect; instrumental variables

1. INTRODUCTION

The ageing of the working population raises concerns about the health and well-being of workers before and after retirement. In many developed countries, this also brings up worries about the sustainability of the health and welfare system. The growing number of early retirees further pressures the welfare systems, as many countries have encouraged workers to opt for early retirement.

This chapter provides a brief overview of the literature concerning how retirement impacts individual health, with a focus on the potential role of changes in risky health behaviors induced by retirement as the underlying mechanism. Empirical evidence suggests that the effect of retirement on health varies depending on the health outcome chosen by researchers. Many studies have found that general health improves in retirement. However, other studies

---

Recent Developments in Health Econometrics
Contributions to Economic Analysis, Volume 297, 147–166
Copyright © 2024 Silvia Balia and Erica Delugas
Published under exclusive licence by Emerald Publishing Limited
ISSN: 0573-8555/doi:10.1108/S0573-855520240000297008

focussing on measures that better describe the health status of the ageing population, such as cognitive functioning indicators, have suggested that retirement has a detrimental effect on health. The heterogeneity of findings may also be due to differences in the definition of retirement, the sample selection criteria and the identification strategy adopted.

A few studies have tried to analyse the impact of retirement on risky behaviours and lifestyle, namely smoking, alcohol consumption, diet, physical activity, sleep and participation in social activities (Celidoni & Rebba, 2017; Eibich, 2015). Many others have mentioned changes in health-related behaviours and lifestyles in general, as a channel through which retirement might affect health without providing supporting evidence (see, e.g. Behncke, 2012; Insler, 2014). Therefore, more research is needed to unravel the role of risky behaviours and lifestyles in the relationship between retirement and health.

We propose a mediation analysis to unpack the causal pathway from retirement to health. Using four waves of the Survey of Health, Ageing and Retirement in Europe (SHARE), we examine a simple model where mental well-being (approximated by a validated scale that measures the risk of depression) is the health outcome, and retirement, which is defined as an absorbing state, is described by either the current occupational status or the time already spent into retirement at the time of the interview. In this analysis, physical inactivity is the risky behaviour, among others potentially influencing depression, that might mediate the health effect of retirement. The inclusion of a mediator allows for separating the total causal effect into an indirect effect and a direct effect of retirement on depression. The direct effect refers to any causal mechanism that does not operate through the mediator. We demonstrate that these effects can be easily estimated with instrumental variables for identification using a fixed-effects two-stage least square estimator (see Huber, 2020). In the absence of instrumental variables for the mediator, we address the endogeneity issue that may arise from the inclusion of physical activity in the regression equation for depression by using Oster (2019)'s approach. Our empirical exercise shows that retirement has a protective effect on the risk of depression, which is still present even when considering time spent in retirement. The effects are mainly due to causal pathways that do not involve changes in physical activity. However, we find that the indirect effect of retirement is statistically significant and explains approximately 4% of the total causal effect.

The chapter is structured as follows: Section 2 briefly reviews the relevant literature. Section 3 describes the data and presents summary statistics for the sample used in the econometric model. In Section 4, we outline the mediation model, describe the estimation procedure and detail the identification strategy. The empirical results are presented in Section 5. Finally, Section 6 concludes the chapter.

2. RELATED LITERATURE

Scholars have long studied the relationship between health and labour market exits, particularly retirement (e.g. García-Gómez et al., 2010). Evidence suggests that individual health status significantly influences retirement choices and early exit from the labour market (Bound et al., 1999; Disney et al., 2006; Giustinelli & Shapiro, 2019; Jones et al., 2010; Roberts et al., 2010). As interest in the aging working population grows, researchers are increasingly focusing on understanding the causal effect of retirement on health and well-being. Upon retirement, individuals might have a lower demand for health as they no longer need to be healthy and productive workers. In turn, and in the presence of a reduced disposable income, this might increase the cost opportunity associated with investing in health.

However, whether retirement influences health, to what extent, and through which mechanisms remains an open question. An up-to-date review of the literature can be found in the study of Garrouste and Perdrix (2022) and van Ours (2022).

The existing findings have revealed a non-univocal effect of retirement on individual health, with studies showing improvements in general health (e.g. Apouey et al., 2019; Atalay & Barrett, 2014; Bertoni, Maggi, et al., 2018; Coe & Zamarro, 2011; Leimer & Van Ewijk, 2022), deterioration in cognitive functioning (e.g. Atalay et al., 2019; Celidoni et al., 2017; Clouston & Denier, 2017; Mazzonna & Peracchi, 2012, 2017; Schmitz & Westphal, 2021) and enhancement in mental health and subjective well-being (e.g. Belloni et al., 2016; Gorry & Slavov, 2021; Jimenez et al., 2021; Kettlewell & Lam, 2020).

The mixed evidence may depend on the data used, the different empirical approaches, and the various definitions of retirement used.[1] Retirement is typically treated as an absorbing status in most studies. Some studies compare workers to individuals who keep working while receiving a pension benefit or individuals in a different occupational status (e.g. unemployed and permanently sick) who might respond to pension system incentives (e.g. Heller-Sahlgren, 2017). Others compare current workers' health to that of workers who have left the labour market and will never return to work (e.g. Behncke, 2012). Furthermore, some studies have investigated the immediate effect of the transition out of the labour market (e.g. Leimer & Van Ewijk, 2022) or the effect of its duration (e.g., Coe et al., 2012). Other studies have analysed the health impacts of different types of retirement, such as voluntary or involuntary (Dave et al., 2008).

2.1 The Role of Risky Health Behaviours

The heterogeneity in the existing evidence on the effect of retirement on health suggests that further investigation is needed to unravel the pathways that link them. One key channel through which retirement affects health is likely represented by

---

[1]In terms of methods, most of the studies adopt instrumental variable approaches by exploiting the exogenous variation in retirement eligibility ages across and within countries (e.g. Apouey et al., 2019; Belloni et al., 2016; Bertoni, Brunello, et al., 2018; Celidoni et al., 2017; Gorry & Slavov, 2021; Kettlewell & Lam, 2020; Leimer & Van Ewijk, 2022) or retirement expectation Insler (2014). Other studies use DID(e.g. Barschkett et al., 2022; Carrino et al., 2020; Jimenez et al., 2021; Shai, 2018) and regression discontinuity approaches (e.g. Barschkett et al., 2022; Clouston & Denier, 2017).

individuals' risky health behaviours, which might change at retirement.[2] Research suggests that retirement can lead to changes in exercise and social interaction, with implications for physical health (Dave et al., 2008). Consistently, Behncke (2012) found that retirement is associated with an increased risk of cardiovascular disease, which is linked to higher body mass index (BMI), cholesterol and blood pressure levels, as well as reduced engagement in physical activity.

A few works have focused on the direct link between retirement and lifestyle, overlooking the effects on health outcomes. For instance, Celidoni and Rebba (2017) show that retirement induces an improvement in practising physical activity, particularly for higher-educated individuals. Similarly, Kesavayuth et al. (2018) show a reduction in smoking, an increase in exercise and an increase in alcohol consumption after retirement.

Other studies have explored the mechanisms behind the retirement effect on health using a comprehensive set of outcomes that include lifestyle and health indicators. For the United States (US), Insler (2014) shows that retirement improves general health, thanks to additional leisure time that is supposed to induce healthier behaviours, such as increased physical exercise and smoking cessation. For Germany, Eibich (2015) finds that retirement improves self-assessed health, mental health and healthy habits. Similarly for Australia, Atalay et al. (2019) find a negative effect of retirement on cognitive functioning for men but not for women. They argue that retirement is associated with improved social activities for women and with a decrease in a mental exercise for men. More recently, Rose (2020) documents an immediate improvement in self-assess health after retirement, a reduction in the probability of health problems, and a decrease in men's depression score, albeit only after some time spent in retirement, an increase in sleep and leisure time and a decrease in stress.

Lifestyle factors, particularly exercise, are commonly cited as important when considering mental health. The clinical and epidemiological evidence shed light on how and why conducting a (un)healthy life is associated with (poorer) better mental health. For instance, regular physical activity can enhance mental well-being primarily through improved mood and self-perception. Exercising regularly is found to be effective in treating clinical depression and anxiety, and it works well as a tool for prevention (Fox, 1999; Nyström et al., 2015; Paluska & Schwenk, 2000). Contrarily, alcohol consumption and smoking are associated with greater risks of developing depression, anxiety and other mental disorders, as well as worsen them (An & Xiang, 2015; Boden & Fergusson, 2011; Driessen et al., 2001; Saunders et al., 1991; Sullivan et al., 2005), especially in the elderly.

Psychological well-being may be threatened when workers are exposed to adverse working conditions, such as rotation shifts, excess overtime hours, lack of job satisfaction, job worries and lack of support from colleagues (Cottini & Ghinetti, 2017;

---

[2]Also, past occupations are associated with heterogeneity in health changes after retirement. Psychosocially demanding jobs might decelerate the process of cognitive decline (Mazzonna & Peracchi, 2017; Rohwedder & Willis, 2010; Salthouse, 2006), thus suggesting a potential protective effect of working for cognitive functioning and that retirement causes a beneficial variation in physical health for those who had a physically demanding job (Mazzonna & Peracchi, 2017).

Cottini & Lucifora, 2013; Robone et al., 2011). Retirement is not always a *panacea*: for many, it can be a highly stressful event that completely changes one's life. On the one hand, leaving behind work-related stress and having more leisure time can stimulate people to practice healthier habits than before when they conflicted with the little time left over from work. On the other hand, retirement can fuel feelings of isolation, hopelessness and lack of purpose in life. Retirement can diminish interest in daily activities and exercise, prompting people to reduce their health investments. Heller-Sahlgren (2017), for example, reports a negative long-term effect of retirement on depression. However, the study does not provide evidence of the mechanisms through which this effect operates.

While most empirical evidence suggests that retirement has a protective effect on mental well-being, the extent to which risky behaviours mediate this effect remains unclear. This chapter aims to identify the indirect effect of retirement on depression, which is channelled through physical activity, and the direct effect of retirement itself.

3. DATA AND VARIABLES

For our empirical exercise, we use data from the first (2004–2005), second (2006–2007), fourth (2011–2012) and fifth (2013) wave of the SHARE, which is designed in accordance with the approaches of the Health and Retirement Study (HRS) and the English Longitudinal Study of Ageing (ELSA).[3] The SHARE data provide a rich set of information on health, labour market participation and risky health behaviours and have been largely used in empirical research on the economics of health and risky behaviours. We use data collected in 10 countries that entered the panel in the first wave: Denmark, Sweden, the Netherlands, Switzerland, Austria, Belgium, Germany, France, Italy and Spain.[4]

For the analysis, we have restricted the sample to individuals aged between 50 and 75 years old at the time of the first interview, who have answered the questions on depression symptoms that occurred no longer than the last month, according to the EURO-D standardized scale measure of depression and on physical activity and for whom we have complete information on demographics, socioeconomic characteristics, job situation and year of retirement and risky health behaviours.[5]

---

[3]We do not use more recent waves because the Netherlands is not included. The third wave (2008–2009) uses a retrospective questionnaire that does not collect information on the variables of interest in this study and for this reason is not used.

[4]We exclude Greece because of well-known sample selection issues at wave 1 and because it is the only country that did not participate at waves 4 and 5.

[5]The EURO-D, developed by Prince et al. (1999), is a short standardised scale, which consist of 12 items (feelings of depression or sadness, pessimism, death wish, guilt, sleep, interest, irritability, appetite, fatigue, concentration, enjoyment and tearfulness). It identifies the most common symptoms of depression and is typically used in large population surveys to measure the risk of depression. For each item, each specific questions refer either to the recent time, as for interest or irritability, or to the present time, as for concentration, or to the last month as in the case of sadness, fatigue or death wish, for example.

152   *Mental Health, Lifestyle and Retirement*

We keep records on individuals who declare to be retired, employed and self-employed and who are observed at least in two consecutive waves. This selection avoids confounding effects due to the comparison with permanent sick, home-maker who never entered the labour market and unemployed individuals for whom the retirement effect might have a similar impact as unemployment on health. We also drop from the sample all those respondents who declared to have moved from retirement back to employment, because in our setting, retirement is an absorbing status. Our final sample is composed of 18,529 individuals (46,250 observations) who stayed in the survey for at least two and up to four waves.

Table 1 reports summary statistics of the variables included in the analysis. Retired individuals (56% of the sample) are individuals who self-reported to be retired at the time of the interview and have been in the labour force at age 50 (so to exclude those who retired before the age of 50 probably because of health issues). On

Table 1. Summary Statistics by Employment Status.

	All Respondents	Retired	Employed
Depression symptoms	1.873	1.951	1.773
	(1.915)	(1.992)	(1.810)
More than 1 depression symptom	0.717	0.726	0.706
	(0.451)	(0.446)	(0.456)
More than 4 depression symptoms	0.180	0.192	0.165
	(0.384)	(0.394)	(0.371)
Retired	0.557	–	–
	(0.497)	–	–
Years into retirement	4.325	7.765	–
	(5.377)	(5.020)	–
Physically inactivity	0.564	0.631	0.480
	(0.496)	(0.482)	(0.500)
Male	0.535	0.551	0.514
	(0.499)	(0.497)	(0.500)
Age	62.686	67.275	56.916
	(6.670)	(4.366)	(4.087)
Married	0.762	0.758	0.768
	(0.426)	(0.428)	(0.422)
Household size	2.201	1.996	2.458
	(0.924)	(0.738)	(1.061)
Living alone	0.064	0.074	0.052
	(0.245)	(0.262)	(0.221)
Number of children	2.122	2.147	2.091
	(1.295)	(1.328)	(1.252)
Number of grandchildren	2.075	2.806	1.156
	(2.588)	(2.819)	(1.901)
Wealth quartile – 1	0.184	0.199	0.166
	(0.388)	(0.399)	(0.372)
Wealth quartile – 2	0.247	0.255	0.238
	(0.432)	(0.436)	(0.426)

SILVIA BALIA AND ERICA DELUGAS

Table 1. *(Continued)*

	All Respondents	Retired	Employed
Wealth quartile – 3	0.274	0.278	0.270
	(0.446)	(0.448)	(0.444)
Wealth quartile – 4	0.294	0.268	0.326
	(0.456)	(0.443)	(0.469)
Individuals	18,529	11,476	9,460
Observations	46,250	25,763	20,487

average, they have spent 7.8 years into retirement, considering also those respondents who entered the panel as workers and retired at some point between waves of the survey. Transition into retirement during the observation period concerns a non-negligible share of workers in the sample (approximately 18%), suggesting that the analysis of the long-term effect of retirement need to be focused on respondents who are retired in all waves. Retirees exhibit higher depression scores, with approximately 73% reporting at least one depressive symptom and 19% reporting four or more depressive symptoms. In comparison, among employed individuals, these figures are slightly lower, with approximately 71% reporting at least one depressive symptom and 16.5% reporting four or more. They also have a more sedentary life as documented by the indicator of physical inactivity (63% of retirees report doing no regular vigorous activity, while this number is 48% in the subsample of workers). We adopt a broad definition of physical inactivity, so that the binary indicator used in the analysis takes the value 1 if the respondent practices sports or activities that are vigorous less than twice a week.[6] On average, retirees are older than workers, less often married, have smaller households, live more often alone and have more children and grandchildren.

4. MEDIATION MODEL

As discussed in Section 2, the existing literature has provided some evidence about a possible lifestyle channel through which leaving the labour force due to retirement influences health, yet it lacks clear and solid evidence on the direction and relevance of such channel. In this chapter, we detail the econometric method employed to unpack the causal pathway by which retirement affects the risk of depression, as measured by the EURO-D depression score, and decompose its impact into a direct and an indirect effect. The latter is mediated by physical activity, chosen among all the potentially risky behaviours associated with depression.

Mediation analysis is a familiar concept in economic literature. Traditional approach assumes exogeneity of the mediator and the treatment variables. Causal

---

[6]Possible answers to the question of vigorous activity are 'more than once a week', 'once a week', 'once to three times a month', 'hardly ever or never'. Definitions that are more restrictive than ours could be adopted.

mediation analysis is commonly employed to investigate the causal mechanisms behind the effect of a treatment on the outcome of interest, by unravelling the role of intermediate outcomes (mediators). The remaining portion of the total causal effect is left to any other potential channel. Recent studies have revisited mediation analysis within the counterfactual/potential outcomes framework (see, e.g. Celli, 2022; Huber, 2014; Imai et al., 2010, 2011). Typically, sequential conditional independence is assumed (see Bijwaard and Jones (2019) and Huber (2020) for a review). However, when the randomness of the treatment and the mediator are non-met conditions (because they are not plausible), researchers typically use alternative (quasi-experimental) sources of identification that accommodate treatment and mediator endogeneity, which cannot be tackled by observed covariates alone: instrumental variables, difference-in-differences (DID), synthetic control and regression discontinuity design. In particular, while some studies use separate instruments for the treatment and the mediator to unpack the causal chain (for an overview, see e.g. Frölich and Huber (2017)), others use a single instrument approach. Recently proposed methods utilise 'omitted variable concerns' to identify the effect of the mediator, employing the same instrumental variable available for the treatment (Dippel, Ferrara, et al., 2020; Dippel, Gold, et al., 2020).[7]

Our mediation model is described by the following linear equations for the health outcome H, the mediator (a risky health behaviour) B and retirement status R:

$$H = \beta_R R + \gamma_B B + v \tag{1}$$

$$B = \delta_R R + e \tag{2}$$

$$R = \alpha Z + u \tag{3}$$

where the mediator is assumed to be exogenous and retirement is potentially endogenous both in the health and the mediator equations. The β_R, γ_B and δ_R are the parameters of interest. Once instrumental variables Z are used in the first-stage linear regression for Eq. (3) to estimate the fitted values of $\widehat{R}$ that will replace R in the second-stage regressions for Eqs. (1)–(2), the direct effect (DE) of retirement on health is measured by (β_R), and its indirect effect (IE) is calculated as the product $(\gamma_B \delta_R)$.[8]

---

[7]They assume that confounders affecting the relationship between the treatment and the mediator are statistically independent of those that jointly cause the mediator and the final outcome of interest. Hence, the endogeneity of the treatment on the final outcome would be only explained by confounders that affect the final outcome through the mediator.

[8]This is equivalent to substituting B in Eq. (1) with the right-hand side of Eq. (2), which yields to $H = \phi R + \gamma \widehat{e} + v$, where R is replaced by the fitted values obtained from the first-stage regression for Eq. (3), $\widehat{e}$ are the 2SLS residuals from Eq. (2), and $\phi = (\beta_R + \gamma_B \delta_R)$ is the total effect of retirement on health. This approach based on residual substitution is used in Tubeuf et al. (2012) and Bubonya and Cobb-Clark (2021) among others.

This is a special case of a more general model, where both retirement and the mediator are endogenous in the health equation because of the presence of unobserved factors. This double endogeneity typically occurs when experimental randomisation is not an option for the researcher. In the absence of feasible instrumental variables for the mediator and in the hypothesis that unobserved confounders are not absorbed by fixed effects, the single instrumental variable approach by Dippel, Ferrara, et al. (2020) could be used.[9] Furthermore, we rely on the Oster (2019)'s method to deal with unobservable selection and show that the endogeneity of the mediator is not necessarily a concern for the identification of the parameters of interest in our setting.

4.1 Estimation Procedure

The instrumental variable approach is adopted to estimate Eqs. (1)–(3). To identify the effect of retirement on the outcome and the mediator, we exploit the exogenous within and between-country variation in eligibility to early and normal retirement, which is due to the numerous reforms of the pension systems that have characterised European countries in the last decades. Instruments based on eligibility indicators have been shown to be valid in consumption, wealth and health models (see, e.g. Angelini et al., 2009; Coe & Zamarro, 2011; Mazzonna & Peracchi, 2012). We construct two binary indicators, for early (ER) and normal retirement (NR), taking value 1 if the difference between the age at the interview and the respective eligibility age is larger or equal to zero. Age at pension eligibility is calculated using official information on the statutory ages for both early and normal retirement in each European country in the sample and self-reported year of retirement.[10]

First, a linear model for retirement is estimated:

$$R_{it} = Z_{it}\theta + X_{it}\beta_x + \alpha_i + \delta_t + u_{it} \qquad (4)$$

where the exogenous covariates in X are the logarithm of age, the indicator of being married, living alone, household size, number of children and grandchildren and the wealth quartile; Z indicates the instrumental variables ER and NR; α_i are individual fixed-effects (FE) and δ_t are interview year dummies that account for any possible time-varying shock to retirement.

Fitted values from Eq. (4) are then used to estimate the following second-stage linear equations:

---

[9]In Section 5, we briefly document the (unsuccessful) application of this approach to our empirical application.

[10]We mostly follow the approach described in the study of Angelini et al. (2009) that uses country-specific and gender-specific pension eligibility ages. For respondents who are already retired, we consider the eligibility rules in effect at the time they retired; for respondents who still work, we consider current rules. When available, we also include information on the occupation type and the number of potential years of pension contributions.

$$B_{it} = \beta_R^{\text{Med1}} \widehat{R}_{it} + X_{it}\beta + \alpha_i + \delta_t + e_{it} \tag{5}$$

$$H_{it} = \beta_R^{\text{Dir}} \widehat{R}_{it} + \beta_B^{\text{Med2}} B_{it} + X_{it}\beta + \alpha_i + \delta_t + v_{it} \tag{6}$$

where B is physical inactivity, the intermediate outcome on which is influenced by retirement and H is depression. The DE of retirement on depression is β_R^{Dir}, and the IE is the product $(\beta_R^{\text{Med1}}\beta_B^{\text{Med2}})$. The total effect is calculated as the sum of DE and IE.

5. RESULTS

We begin by investigating the extent to which unobservable selection is an issue in our model for depression or whether the inclusion of FE leaves us with an unbiased estimate of the effect of the mediator (physical inactivity). The potential endogeneity of risky health behaviours in models for health might be related to the presence of unobserved factors that might influence both the individual health status and the behaviour and reverse causality (because individual health itself might influence the observed lifestyle). One way to limit reverse causality bias is to use the (one period) lagged value of the endogenous variable. This would impede, however, the estimation of the immediate effect of physical inactivity on the contemporaneous depression score, which is key in our setting. Nonetheless, we suspect that reverse causality is not a big issue here because the number of depressive symptoms that have occurred recently (i.e. no more than the last month) may have only limited influence on the choices about the amount of vigorous physical activity, which generally requires earlier engagement.

We use the Oster (2019)'s approach and show that observables and unobservables are equally important and affect the coefficient of interest in the same direction. We estimate a 'controlled' regression model using the EURO-D depression score as the dependent variable and including physical inactivity and the observed covariates (including a dummy for being retired) described in Section 3, and an 'uncontrolled' regression that includes only physical inactivity and the interview year dummies which capture any time-varying shock that can be correlated with retirement.[11] Table 2 presents a comparison of the coefficient of physical inactivity in the controlled model under two scenarios: when $\delta = 0$, indicating that unobservable factors have minimal influence relative to observable factors on physical inactivity, and when $\delta = 1$, indicating that observable and unobservable factors are equally influential and affect the coefficient in the same direction. When $\delta = 0$, the coefficient of interest is 0.116 (0.119 in the uncontrolled model) and represents an upper bound estimate. The corresponding values when $\delta = 1$ represent lower bound estimates as they range between 0.115 (when the theoretical R-squared is 1.3 times that of the controlled model) and

---

[11]Following Bryan et al. (2022), we transform the data using within-individual means in order to use the Stata routine developed by (Oster, 2016).

SILVIA BALIA AND ERICA DELUGAS

Table 2. Estimated Coefficients for Physical Inactivity in the Controlled Model Using the Oster's Method.

	$\delta = 0$		$\delta = 1$			
		Rsq.^{max} = 1.3Rsq.	Rsq.^{max} = 1.5Rsq.	Rsq.^{max} = 1.8Rsq.	Rsq.^{max} = 2Rsq.	Rsq.^{max} = 2.2Rsq.
Controlled	0.116	0.115	0.114	0.112	0.111	0.110
SE	(0.021)	(0.016)	(0.016)	(0.016)	(0.016)	(0.016)
95% CI	[0.076; 0.156]					

Notes: The model is estimated by adopting demeaned OLS estimator. Sample size is 46,250. Uncontrolled estimated coefficient for physical inactivity is 0.119 (SE: 0.021).

0.110 (when the theoretical R-squared is 2.2 times higher) and lie in the confidence interval of the $\delta = 0$ estimate.[12] These results are comforting about the absence of omitted variable bias using our FE estimator and leave us quite confident estimating the mediation model without instrumenting the mediator.

5.1 Direct and Indirect Effects

Here, we present results from the causal mediation model described by Eqs. (4)–(6). We use a Fixed Effects – Two Stages Least Squares (FE-2SLS) approach to estimate two different specifications which use alternative retirement variables: *Retired*, for the retirement status at the time of the interview, and the percentile score of *Years into retirement*. When using the latter variable, we carry out the analysis on the sub-sample of respondents who are retired in all waves (21,836 individuals).[13] We compare coefficient estimates from three models, which estimate different local average treatment effects of the retirement variable. The first model uses ER and NR as instruments, thus identifying the effect on all compliers to pension eligibility rules.[14] The second and third models use only ER and NR as instruments, thus separately identifying the effects of retirement on the early pension eligibility rules compliers and the normal pension eligibility rules

---

[12]Results are confirmed when observed retirement status is replaced by the fitted values obtained from a regression of retirement on exogenous covariates and the instrumental variables ER and NR.

[13]The restriction of the sample avoids over-representing short periods in retirement. We use the percentile scores of observed *Years into retirement* because the variable is asymmetric and does not represent well individuals with the longest spells into retirement.

[14]Following the study of Dippel, Ferrara, et al. (2020), we have used one instrumental variable for retirement at a time (ER or NR) to instrument the mediator in the depression equation conditioning on exogenous retirement. Estimations allow us to recover the same total effect estimated by our mediation model, but its decomposition is different as Dippel, Ferrara, et al.'s (2020) approach clearly gives a heavier weight to the IE. It must be noted that there is no economic support for using pension age eligibility as an instrumental variable for physical inactivity and that the F test is far below the reasonable value, thus suggesting a weak instrument issue. Results are available upon request.

compliers. In the latter case, the instrumental variables are continuous indicators that measure the percentile score of the distance between the respondent's age at the interview and the (early or normal retirement) eligibility age.

Table 3 shows the decomposition of the total effect of retirement on the depression score in all models and specifications. More precisely, the table reports estimation results for the three parameters of interest $(\beta_R^{\text{Dir}}, \beta_R^{\text{Med1}}, \beta_B^{\text{Med2}})$ and the total effect calculated as the sum of the direct and indirect effects. It also displays the Wald F and the Hansen J-statistics, which confirm that our instrumental variables have power and that over-identification is not an issue in the models where two instruments are used for one endogenous regressor.[15]

Results reported in the first panel of Table 3 provide evidence that being retired lowers the depression score (by 0.217) and that this result is mainly driven by the effect on the ER compliers (which indicates a larger reduction, of about 0.315, for early retirees). The table also shows that physical inactivity increases the depression score (about 0.12 in all models), while being retired negatively influences the probability of having a sedentary life, suggesting a protective effect of retirement on lifestyle. The total and direct effects of *Retired* are very close, suggesting a small mediating effect.

The second panel of Table 3 shows a significant beneficial total effect of time in retirement, suggesting that a long period in retirement is not associated with a worse outcome as in the case of cognitive ability (Celidoni et al., 2017). The depression score decreases with Years into retirement by 0.023, and this effect coincides with the direct effect, meaning that in the long run changes in risky behaviour do not contribute to explaining the effect of retirement. This result is driven by the NR compliers, for whom we estimate a decrease of 0.026 in the depression score. Time in retirement does not affect the probability of being physically inactive, while physical inactivity again is responsible for higher depression scores.

We have investigated the heterogeneity of the effect by gender to account for potential differences in retirement choices and behaviours. Table 4 shows that the total effect of *Retired* is significant only for men, and it is larger than the direct effect.[16] Being a male retiree lowers the depression score of 0.305. However, these estimates need to be interpreted with caution because the Hansen *J*-statistics suggests that the model for EURO-D is overidentified. The second panel of the table shows that the long-run effect of retirement is significant only in the sub-sample of women. The total and direct effects coincide: the depression score decreases by 0.03 for female retirees.

Fig. 1 plots the direct and indirect effects, calculated as $(\beta_R^{\text{Med1}} \beta_B^{\text{Med2}})$, of being retired (top panel) and time in retirement (bottom panel) and their robust confidence intervals at 95% level for all estimated models. The direct effect of being retired is always negative and significant except for the NR compliers and the sub-sample of women, while the indirect effect is negative and significant only for

---

[15]Coefficient estimates from the first stage estimation of Eq. (4) are not reported for the sake of brevity.

[16]This result is line with Belloni et al. (2016), who find that retirement improves only men mental health, especially for those who have been hit by the economic crisis.

Table 3. Components of the Total Effects of Retirement on Depression.

	ER and NR		ER		NR	
	(1) EURO-D	(2) Physical Inactive	(3) EURO-D	(4) Physical Inactive	(5) EURO-D	(6) Physical Inactive
Retired	-0.209**	-0.072**	-0.306**	-0.082**	-0.097	-0.062
	(0.103)	(0.030)	(0.130)	(0.040)	(0.136)	(0.041)
Physical inactive	0.115***		0.115***		0.116***	
	(0.021)		(0.021)		(0.021)	
Total effect of retired	-0.217**		-0.315**		-0.105	
	(0.103)		(0.130)		(0.137)	
Kleibergen-Paap rk Wald F statistic	998.789		994.358		917.552	
Hansen J statistic	1.505	0.144				
Chi-sq(1) p value	0.220	0.704				
Observations	46,250	46,250	46,250	46,250	46,250	46,250
Years into retirement	-0.023**	0.001	-0.020	0.002	-0.026**	0.002
	(0.010)	(0.003)	(0.012)	(0.003)	(0.012)	(0.003)
Physical inactive	0.163***		0.163***		0.163***	
	(0.031)		(0.031)		(0.031)	
Total effect of years into retirement	-0.023**		-0.020		-0.026**	
	(0.010)		(0.012)		(0.012)	
Kleibergen-Paap rk Wald F-statistic	206.363		315.217		315.217	
Hansen J statistic	0.230	1.450				
Chi-sq(1) p value	0.632	0.228				
Observations	21,836	21,836	21,836	21,836	21,836	21,836

Notes: This table reports the total effect of being retired in the top panel and the total effect of time spent into retirement and the decomposition according to the models presented in Eqs. (5) and (6). Columns 1–2 report the local average treatment effect of retirement on compliers to early and normal retirement rules, columns 3–4 and 5–6 report, respectively, the local average treatment effect of retirement on compliers to early retirement and to normal retirement rules. In the bottom panel, we use a sub-sample of respondents who have always been retired in the observation period. All regression models are estimated using a FE-2SLS estimator and include the logarithm of age, living alone, married, household size, number of children, number of grandchildren, wealth quartiles and interview year fixed effect. Bootstrapped standard errors in parentheses (500 replications). * $p < 0.10$, ** $p < 0.05$ and *** $p < 0.01$.

Table 4. Gender Heterogenety in the Components of the Total Effects of Retirement on Depression.

	Men		Women	
	(1) EURO-D	(2) Physical inactive	(3) EURO-D	(4) Physical inactive
Retired	−0.286**	−0.124**	−0.164	−0.023
	(0.141)	(0.045)	(0.148)	(0.040)
Physical inactive	0.147***		0.081**	
	(0.027)		(0.032)	
Total effect of retired	−0.305**		−0.166	
	(0.142)		(0.148)	
Kleibergen-Paap rk Wald F statistic	444.637		577.198	
Hansen J statistic	5.345	0.019	0.481	0.195
Chi-sq(1) p value	0.021	0.891	0.488	0.659
Observations	24,728	24,728	21,522	21,522
Years into retirement	−0.007	0.003	−0.030**	−0.001
	(0.017)	(0.005)	(0.012)	(0.003)
Physical inactive	0.205***		0.112**	
	(0.031)		(0.012)	
Total effect of years into retirement	−0.023**		−0.020	
	(0.010)		(0.012)	
Kleibergen-Paap rk Wald F statistic	60.677		200.548	
Hansen J statistic	0.329	0.490	0.001	2.134
Chi-sq(1) p value	0.566	0.484	0.972	0.144
Observations	11,955	11,955	9,881	9,881

Notes: This table reports the effect of being retired in the top panel and the effect of time spent into retirement. All columns report the local average treatment effect of retirement on compliers to early and normal retirement rules. In the bottom panel, we use sub-sample of male and female respondents who have always been retired in the observation period. All regression models are estimated using a FE-2SLS estimator and include the logarithm of age, living alone, married, household size, number of children, number of grandchildren, wealth quartiles and interview year fixed effect. Bootstrapped standard errors in parentheses (500 replications). *$p < 0.10$, **$p < 0.05$ and ***$p < 0.01$.

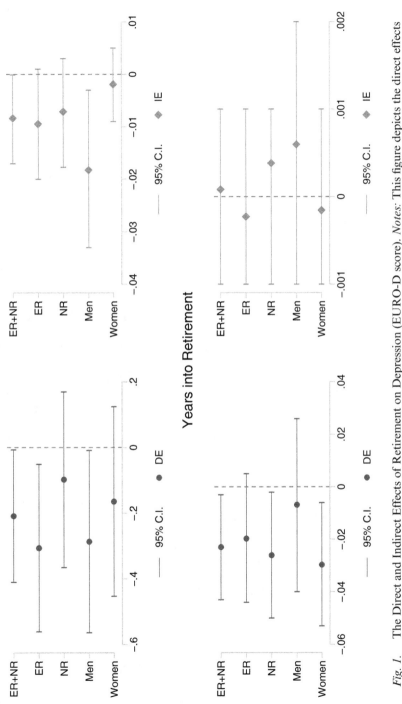

Fig. 1. The Direct and Indirect Effects of Retirement on Depression (EURO-D score). *Notes*: This figure depicts the direct effects (DE) and indirect effects (IE) of being retired (top panel) and time in retirement (second panel) and their bootstrapped 95% confidence intervals. Regressions are estimated using FE-2SLS and the parameters of interests are also reported in Tables 3 and 4.

all compliers and for men. In the case of time in retirement, the direct effect is smaller in size but still negative and significant for all compliers, NR compliers and women, while the indirect effect is never significant.

The share of the total effect that can be attributed to physical inactivity, which is calculated as $\frac{IE}{(DE + IE)}$, indicates that the physical inactivity channel explains approximately 4% of the total effect of retirement for all compliers, 3% for early retirees and 6% for men retirees.

6. CONCLUSIONS

In this chapter, we aim to investigate the causal effect of retirement on health by using a mediation model that addresses the endogeneity of retirement. We use the SHARE data to estimate a model for the risk of depression. We adopt an IV approach relying on the exogenous country- and gender-specific variation in eligibility ages to early and normal retirement. To remove any bias that might arise from unobserved time-invariant factors influencing both depression and retirement choice and from time-varying macro-shocks, we exploit the longitudinal nature of the data and use an FE estimator.

We test the hypothesis that physical activity mediates the effect of retirement. However, other risky behaviours, such as smoking and drinking, could also be used as mediators. The model provides estimates of the direct and indirect effects of retirement, distinguishing between a mechanism that operates specifically through changes in sedentary life and all other mechanisms behind the changes in depression risk for retirees. Our analysis shows a significant but relatively small indirect effect mediated by physical activity. Therefore, further investigation is necessary to explore the role of lifestyle and to provide insights into the potential pathways through which retirement affects health.

However, our analysis is limited by the use of a single indicator for lifestyles and the relatively short time span considered. Therefore, a sensitivity analysis could be carried out using alternative measures for mental health, including binary indicators that use different cut-off scores to identify the most severe cases of depression. Additionally, alternative health outcomes could be used to capture health deterioration in the elderly population, such as measures of cognitive impairment or functional limitations in daily activities. Finally, further research is needed to analyse the heterogeneity of the direct and indirect effects in different occupations, working conditions and psychological burdens of the job. This will provide a better understanding of the mechanisms behind the relationship between retirement and health in different subgroups of the population.

ACKNOWLEDGEMENTS

The authors are grateful to Viola Angelini, Luca Stella and Coen van de Kraats for sharing material on pension eligibility in European countries. The authors also thank Emanuela Marrocu, Irene Mammi and Cristina Orso for suggestions and comments. The authors use data from SHARE Waves 1, 2, 4, 5 (DOIs: 10.6103/ SHARE.w1.800, 10.6103/SHARE.w2.800, 10.6103/SHARE.w4.800, 10.6103/ SHARE.w5.800). See Börsch-Supan et al. (2013) for methodological details. The SHARE data collection has been funded by the European Commission, DG RTD through FP5 (QLK6-CT-2001–00360), FP6 (SHARE-I3: RII-CT-2006–062193, COMPARE: CIT5-CT2005-028857, SHARELIFE: CIT4-CT-2006–028812), FP7 (SHARE-PREP: GA N°211909, SHARE-LEAP: GA N°227822, SHARE M4: GA N°261982, DASISH: GA N°283646) and Horizon 2020 (SHARE-DEV3: GA N°676536, SHARE-COHESION: GA N°870628, SERISS: GA N°654221, SSHOC: GA N°823782, SHARECOVID19: GA N°101015924) and by DG Employment, Social Affairs & Inclusion through VS 2015/0195, VS 2016/0135, VS 2018/0285, VS 2019/0332 and VS 2020/0313. Additional funding from the German Ministry of Education and Research, the Max Planck Society for the Advancement of Science, the US National Institute on Aging (U01 AG09740-13S2, P01 AG005842, P01 AG08291, P30 AG12815, R21 AG025169, Y1AG-4553–01, IAG_BSR06-11, OGHA 04–064, HHSN271201300071C and RAG052527A) and from various national funding sources is gratefully acknowledged (see www.share-project.org).

REFERENCES

An, R., & Xiang, X. (2015). Smoking, heavy drinking, and depression among US middle-aged and older adults. *Preventive Medicine*, *81*, 295–302.

Angelini, V., Brugiavini, A., & Weber, G. (2009). Ageing and unused capacity in Europe: Is there an early retirement trap? *Economic Policy*, *24*(59), 463–508.

Apouey, B. H., Guven, C., & Senik, C. (2019). Retirement and unexpected health shocks. *Economics and Human Biology*, *33*, 116–123.

Atalay, K., & Barrett, G. F. (2014). The causal effect of retirement on health: New evidence from Australian pension reform. *Economics Letters*, *125*(3), 392–395.

Atalay, K., Barrett, G. F., & Staneva, A. (2019). The effect of retirement on elderly cognitive functioning. *Journal of Health Economics*, *66*, 37–53.

Barschkett, M., Geyer, J., Haan, P., & Hammerschmid, A. (2022). The effects of an increase in the retirement age on health—Evidence from administrative data. *The Journal of the Economics of Ageing*, *23*, 100403.

Behncke, S. (2012). Does retirement trigger ill health? *Health Economics*, *21*(3), 282–300.

Belloni, M., Meschi, E., & Pasini, G. (2016). The effect on mental health of retiring during the economic crisis. *Health Economics*, *25*, 126–140.

Bertoni, M., Brunello, G., & Mazzarella, G. (2018). Does postponing minimum retirement age improve healthy behaviors before retirement? Evidence from middle-aged Italian workers. *Journal of Health Economics*, *58*, 215–227.

Bertoni, M., Maggi, S., & Weber, G. (2018). Work, retirement, and muscle strength loss in old age. *Health Economics*, *27*(1), 115–128.

Bijwaard, G. E., & Jones, A. M. (2019). An IPW estimator for mediation effects in hazard models: With an application to schooling, cognitive ability and mortality. *Empirical Economics*, *57*(1), 129–175.

Boden, J. M., & Fergusson, D. M. (2011). Alcohol and depression. *Addiction*, *106*(5), 906–914.

Börsch-Supan, A., Brandt, M., Hunkler, C., Kneip, T., Korbmacher, J., Malter, F., Schaan, B., Stuck, S., & Zuber, S. (2013). Data resource profile: The survey of health, ageing and retirement in Europe (SHARE). *International Journal of Epidemiology*, *42*(4), 992–1001.

Bound, J., Schoenbaum, M., Stinebrickner, T. R., & Waidmann, T. (1999). The dynamic effects of health on the labor force transitions of older workers. *Labour Economics*, *6*(2), 179–202.

Bryan, M. L., Rice, N., Roberts, J., & Sechel, C. (2022). Mental health and employment: A bounding approach using panel data. *Oxford Bulletin of Economics & Statistics, 84*(5), 1018–1051.

Bubonya, M., & Cobb-Clark, D. A. (2021). Pathways of disadvantage: Unpacking the intergenerational correlation in welfare. *Economics of Education Review, 80*, p.102066.

Carrino, L., Glaser, K., & Avendano, M. (2020). Later retirement, job strain, and health: Evidence from the new state pension age in the United Kingdom. *Health Economics, 29*(8), 891–912.

Celidoni, M., Dal Bianco, C., & Weber, G. (2017). Retirement and cognitive decline. A longitudinal analysis using SHARE data. *Journal of Health Economics, 56*, 113–125.

Celidoni, M., & Rebba, V. (2017). Healthier lifestyles after retirement in Europe? Evidence from SHARE. *The European Journal of Health Economics, 18*(7), 805–830.

Celli, V. (2022). Causal mediation analysis in economics: Objectives, assumptions, models. *Journal of Economic Surveys, 36*(1), 214–234.

Clouston, S. A. P., & Denier, N. (2017). Mental retirement and health selection: Analyses from the US health and retirement study. *Social Science & Medicine, 178*, 78–86.

Coe, N. B., von Gaudecker, H. M., Lindeboom, M., & Maurer, J. (2012). The effect of retirement on cognitive functioning. *Health Economics, 21*(8), 913–927.

Coe, N. B., & Zamarro, G. (2011). Retirement effects on health in Europe. *Journal of Health Economics, 30*(1), 77–86.

Cottini, E., & Ghinetti, P. (2017). Is it the way you live or the job you have? Health effects of lifestyles and working conditions. *The B.E. Journal of Economic Analysis & Policy, 17*(3).

Cottini, E., & Lucifora, C. (2013). Mental health and working conditions in Europe. *ILR Review, 66*(4), 958–988.

Dave, D., Rashad, I., & Spasojevic, J. (2008). The effects of retirement on physical and mental health outcomes. *Southern Economic Journal, 75*(2), 497–524.

Dippel, C., Ferrara, A., & Heblich, S. (2020). Causal mediation analysis in instrumental-variables regressions. *STATA Journal, 20*(3), 613–626.

Dippel, C., Gold, R., Heblich, S., & Pinto, R. (2020). *Mediation analysis in IV settings with a single instrument*. Unpublished manuscript.

Disney, R., Emmerson, C., & Wakefield, M. (2006). Ill health and retirement in Britain: A panel data-based analysis. *Journal of Health Economics, 25*(4), 621–649.

Driessen, M., Meier, S., Hill, A., Wetterling, T., Lange, W., & Junghanns, K. (2001). The course of anxiety, depression and drinking behaviours after completed detoxification in alcoholics with and without comorbid anxiety and depressive disorders. *Alcohol and Alcoholism, 36*(3), 249–255.

Eibich, P. (2015). Understanding the effect of retirement on health: Mechanisms and heterogeneity. *Journal of Health Economics, 43*, 1–12.

Fox, K. R. (1999). The influence of physical activity on mental well-being. *Public Health Nutrition, 2*(3a), 411–418.

Frölich, M., & Huber, M. (2017). Direct and indirect treatment effects–causal chains and mediation analysis with instrumental variables. *Journal of the Royal Statistical Society: Series B, 79*(5), 1645–1666.

García-Gómez, P., Jones, A. M., & Rice, N. (2010). Health effects on labour market exits and entries. *Labour Economics, 17*(1), 62–76.

Garrouste, C., & Perdrix, E. (2022). Is there a consensus on the health consequences of retirement? A literature review. *Journal of Economic Surveys, 36*(4), 841–879.

Giustinelli, P., & Shapiro, M. D. (2019). *SeaTE: Subjective ex ante treatment effect of health on retirement*. Technical Report. National Bureau of Economic Research.

Gorry, D., & Slavov, S. N. (2021). The effect of retirement on health biomarkers. *Economics and Human Biology, 40*, 100949.

Heller-Sahlgren, G. (2017). Retirement blues. *Journal of Health Economics, 54*, 66–78.

Huber, M. (2014). Identifying causal mechanisms (primarily) based on inverse probability weighting. *Journal of Applied Econometrics, 29*(6), 920–943.

Huber, M. (2020). Mediation analysis. In *Handbook of labor, human resources and population economics* (pp. 1–38). Springer International Publishing.

Imai, K., Keele, L., Tingley, D., & Yamamoto, T. (2011). Unpacking the black box of causality: Learning about causal mechanisms from experimental and observational studies. *American Political Science Review, 105*(4), 765–789.

Imai, K., Keele, L., & Yamamoto, T. (2010). Identification, inference and sensitivity analysis for causal mediation effects. *Statistical Science, 25*(1), 51–71.

Insler, M. (2014). The health consequences of retirement. *Journal of Human Resources, 49*(1), 195–233.

Jimenez, M. M., Hollingsworth, B., & Zucchelli, E. (2021). Health, retirement and economic shocks. IZA Discussion Paper No. 14574. https://www.iza.org/publications/dp/14574/health-retirement-and-economic-shocks

Jones, A. M., Rice, N., & Roberts, J. (2010). Sick of work or too sick to work? Evidence on self-reported health shocks and early retirement from the BHPS. *Economic Modelling, 27*(4), 866–880.

Kesavayuth, D., Rosenman, R. E., & Zikos, V. (2018). Retirement and health behaviour. *Applied Economics, 50*(54), 5859–5876.

Kettlewell, N., & Lam, J. (2020). Retirement, social support and mental well-being: A couple-level analysis. *The European Journal of Health Economics*, 1–25.

Leimer, B., & Van Ewijk, R. (2022). No "Honeymoon Phase": Whose health benefits from retirement and when. *Economics and Human Biology, 47*, 101171.

Mazzonna, F., & Peracchi, F. (2012). Ageing, cognitive abilities and retirement. *European Economic Review, 56*(4), 691–710.

Mazzonna, F., & Peracchi, F. (2017). Unhealthy retirement? *Journal of Human Resources, 52*(1), 128–151.

Nyström, M. B. T., Neely, G., Hassmén, P., & Carlbring, P. (2015). Treating major depression with physical activity: A systematic overview with recommendations. *Cognitive Behaviour Therapy, 44*(4), 341–352.

Oster, E. (2016). *PSACALC: Stata module to calculate treatment effects and relative degree of selection under proportional selection of observables and unobservables.* https://EconPapers.repec.org/RePEc:boc:bocode:s457677

Oster, E. (2019). Unobservable selection and coefficient stability: Theory and evidence. *Journal of Business & Economic Statistics, 37*(2), 187–204.

Paluska, S. A., & Schwenk, T. L. (2000). Physical activity and mental health: Current concepts. *Sports Medicine, 29*, 167–180.

Prince, M. J., Reischies, F., Beekman, A. T. F., Fuhrer, R., Jonker, C., Kivela, S.-L., Lawlor, B. A., Lobo, A., Magnusson, H., Fichter, M., van Oyen, H., Roelands, M., Skoog, I., Turrina, C., & Copeland, J. R. (1999). Development of the EURO–D scale – A European Union initiative to compare symptoms of depression in 14 European centres. *The British Journal of Psychiatry, 174*(4), 330–338.

Roberts, J., Rice, N., & Jones, A. M. (2010). Early retirement among men in Britain and Germany: How important is health? *The Geneva Papers on Risk and Insurance – Issues and Practice, 35*(4), 644–667.

Robone, S., Jones, A. M., & Rice, N. (2011). Contractual conditions, working conditions and their impact on health and well-being. *The European Journal of Health Economics, 12*(5), 429–444.

Rohwedder, S., & Willis, R. J. (2010). Mental retirement. *The Journal of Economic Perspectives, 24*(1), 119–138.

Rose, L. (2020). Retirement and health: Evidence from England. *Journal of Health Economics, 73*, 102352.

Salthouse, T. A. (2006). Mental exercise and mental aging: Evaluating the validity of the "use it or lose it" hypothesis. *Perspectives on Psychological Science, 1*(1), 68–87.

Saunders, P. A., Copeland, J. R. M., Dewey, M. E., Davidson, I. A., Mcwilliam, C., Sharma, V., & Sullivan, C. (1991). Heavy drinking as a risk factor for depression and dementia in elderly men: Findings from the liverpool longitudinal community study. *The British Journal of Psychiatry, 159*(2), 213–216.

Schmitz, H., & Westphal, M. (2021). *The dynamic and heterogeneous effects of retirement on cognitive decline* Ruhr Economic Papers, No. 918. RWI - Leibniz-Institut für Wirtschaftsforschung, Essen. https://doi.org/10.4419/96973064. ISBN 978-3-96973-064-5.

Shai, O. (2018). Is retirement good for men's health? Evidence using a change in the retirement age in Israel. *Journal of Health Economics, 57*, 15–30.

Sullivan, L. E., Fiellin, D. A., & O'Connor, P. G. (2005). The prevalence and impact of alcohol problems in major depression: A systematic review. *The American Journal of Medicine, 118*(4), 330–341.

Tubeuf, S., Jusot, F., & Bricard, D. (2012). Mediating role of education and lifestyles in the relationship between early-life conditions and health: Evidence from the 1958 British cohort. *Health Economics, 21*, 129–150.

van Ours, J. C. (2022). How retirement affects mental health, cognitive skills and mortality; an overview of recent empirical evidence. *De Economist, 170*(3), 375–400.

THE ASSOCIATION BETWEEN MEDICAL CANNABIS LAWS AND FLOWS OF OPIOIDS BY DOSAGE STRENGTH TO US PHARMACIES – EVIDENCE FROM DETAILED ARCOS DATA, 2006–2014

Shelby R. Steuart[a] and W. David Bradford[b]

[a]The University of Chicago, USA
[b]University of Georgia, USA

ABSTRACT

A growing body of research finds a consistently negative relationship between medical cannabis access and aggregate measures of opioid use. Nothing is currently known about the types of opioids that are being most impacted by cannabis access. Using the Callaway and Sant'Anna (2021) difference-in-differences (DID) estimator for the main analysis and data on all opioid shipments to every United States (US) pharmacy from 2006 to 2014, the authors found no evidence of overall change in the total number of morphine milligram equivalent (MME) units of opioids shipped to pharmacies, following the opening of medical cannabis dispensaries. However, across all opioids, the authors found a reduction in the highest MME dosage strengths (8.8% decrease in 50–89 MME doses and 11.3% decrease in 90+ MME doses). This decrease appears to be driven predominantly by commonly diverted opioids, where the authors found a reduction in the highest MME dosage strengths (12.2% in 50–89 MME doses and 13.8% in 90+ MME doses). Further, the authors see a 6.0% increase in low-to-moderate dose opioids (0–49 MMEs). This is consistent with patients using cannabis concomitantly with opioids in order to achieve a lower opioids dose.

Recent Developments in Health Econometrics
Contributions to Economic Analysis, Volume 297, 167–200
Copyright © 2024 Shelby R. Steuart and W. David Bradford
Published under exclusive licence by Emerald Publishing Limited
ISSN: 0573-8555/doi:10.1108/S0573-855520240000297009

Keywords: Opioids; medical cannabis; cannabis policy; prescription drug use; difference-in-differences

1. INTRODUCTION

In the past 20 years, there has been a well-documented and substantial increase in the rate of opioid use and mortality in the United States (US). While the underlying causes are complex, one common view is that the roots lie in the rapid proliferation of opioid pain medications that were prescribed by physicians and distributed by local pharmacies in the early 2000s to treat both chronic and acute pain (Institute of Medicine et al., 2011; Jones et al., 2018). As one example, OxyContin prescriptions alone increased by almost an order of magnitude from about 670,000 in 1997 to about 6.2 million in 2002 (US GAO, 2015). Overall, prescriptions for self-administered opioids rose throughout the first decade and a half in the US, peaking in 2012 at more than 255 million prescriptions before falling to just over 142 million prescriptions by 2020 (Centers for Disease Control and Prevention [CDC], 2022). As opioid prescriptions have increased so has opioid mortality, rising from just over 21,000 opioid-associated overdose deaths in 2010 to 47,600 opioid deaths in 2017 (and rising again during the pandemic to 68,630 opioid deaths by 2020). Given the strongly correlated trends with opioid prescribing, particularly prior to 2013, the persistent increase in opioid-associated mortality is often attributed at least in part to prescription opioid dispensing by pharmacies (CDC, 2022; Powell et al., 2020).

A growing body of research suggests that patients substitute away from opioids when they have access to medical cannabis via state legalisation. In 2017, the National Academies of Sciences, Engineering and Medicine determined that there is 'conclusive evidence', supporting the treatment of chronic pain with cannabis, after a thorough review of clinical peer-reviewed research (NASEM, 2017). In addition to clinical evidence, studies using insurance claim data show mounting evidence of substitution away from opioids in states that allow medical consumption of cannabis. Several papers found significant changes in general prescribing patterns and spending in Medicare Part D once cannabis became medically available (Bradford & Bradford, 2017; Bradford et al., 2018). Other studies show similar results in Medicaid fee-for-service claims (Bradford & Bradford, 2017). Evidence shows medical cannabis laws are also specifically associated with decreased opioid prescribing in the Medicare Part D population (Bradford et al., 2018), in Medicaid (Bradford et al., 2018; Wen & Hockenberry, 2018) and among commercially insured individuals (Lozano-Rojas et al., 2022; Shah et al., 2018). To date, this literature has often been taken to suggest that in addition to providing other avenues for pain relief to patients, state legalisation of medical or recreational cannabis may contribute to the decreased use of opioid medications and ultimately may hold promise to decrease the number of deaths from opioid overdoses (Bachhuber et al., 2014; Powell et al., 2018) though more recent work has called that latter conclusion into question (Mathur & Ruhm, 2023).

However, it is worth noting that the studies cited above which all find decreases in opioid usage as a result of medical cannabis legalisation are focused on insured populations. This paper uses a unique dataset which captures all shipments of opioids to retail pharmacies irrespective of who ultimately pays for the prescriptions; thus, we explore the net effect of medical cannabis policy on all patients – both insured and cash-paying. The analysis in this paper is for the study period 2006–2014, a time before the wide adoption of mandatory prescription drug monitoring programs (PDMPs), which have been seen as an important tool to decrease opioid diversion through 'doctor shopping'. This is also a period of time when the Drug Enforcement Administration (DEA) was involved with numerous investigations of 'pill mills' or rogue pain management clinics that aided in the diversion and non-medical use of prescription opioids for profit (DEA, 2015). To our knowledge, this is the first paper to analyse how medical cannabis legalisation impacted the supply of opioids, including diverted opioids purchased through cash transactions.

Additionally, nothing is currently known about the relative substitutability of opioids by strength or formulation. Clinical literature indicates cannabis is effective for managing chronic pain (Hill et al., 2017; Russo, 2019). Chronic pain is often treated with higher dose extended-release opioid formulations, which can lead to a greater potential of opioid dependence (Kraft et al., 2008; Wallace et al., 2007); misuse and dependence potential of opioids is much greater for high-strength doses than for lower strength doses. Cannabis has also been showed to improve the efficacy of opioids and reduce the opioid dose in the treatment of chronic non-cancer pain (Lynch & Clark, 2003). For this reason, there is some hope that cannabis can be used concomitantly with opioids, which would also differentially implicate opioids by dosage strength. This paper investigates the relationship between prescribing patterns for opioids distributed to pharmacies and statewide legal access to medical cannabis, controlling for factors such as mandatory access PDMPs.

2. DATA

We utilise data from the Automated Reports and Consolidated Ordering System (ARCOS). ARCOS is an automated drug reporting system which tracks every unit of substances controlled by the DEA at all points along their commercial distribution channels. The raw ARCOS data includes details of drug shipment packaging, dosage strength, quantity, point of sale/distribution information on hospitals, retail pharmacies, practitioners, mid-level practitioners and teaching institutions and is usually held confidential by the DEA. This paper focuses specifically on the impact of access to medical cannabis in states with active cannabis dispensaries on shipments of opioids to pharmacies. Cannabis access through dispensaries is most analogous to prescription drug access via pharmacies, so we opt for that signal of easy medical cannabis access rather than the potentially less impactful legalisation date used in some past research.

The raw version of ARCOS we use was publicly released by the US federal court in the Northern District of Ohio as part of a large multi-district litigation (MDL) legal action against nearly all opioid manufacturers and the major drug wholesalers (e.g. McKessen, AmeriSourceBergen and Cardinal) and includes seller name, seller major business activity, address, buyer name, buyer major business activity, buyer address, drug identifiers (drug name and National Drug Code (NDC)), packages in shipment, units per package, grams of base controlled substance, morphine milligram equivalent (MME) conversion factors and other key data (Polster, 2018).

Data on state medical cannabis limits were gathered from state legal statutes. States were coded as allowing access to medical cannabis in each year if they had open medical cannabis dispensaries that allow for the sale of cannabis products above 0.3% Tetrahydrocannabinol (THC). Applicable data pertaining to dates of legalisation and dispensary openings in our dataset have been compared against RAND's OPTIC-Vetted Medical Marijuana Policy Data (OPTIC, 2020). Variables coding recreational cannabis laws were not included in the model because of collinearity with medical cannabis law variables and the fact that only two states had operational recreational cannabis markets prior to December 31, 2014: for 12 months in the case of Colorado (which is excluded since medical cannabis dispensaries opened before our study period begins) and for six months in the case of Washington state. Given recent developments in the difference-in-differences (DID) literature, our models were largely uncontrolled.

The one exception to omitting controls was our treatment of PDMPs. PDMPs are databases of patients' opioid prescriptions, maintained by each state (Davis et al., 2014). State laws dictating who can or must make PDMP reports and check PDMPs vary considerably, but most states have some requirements on physicians and medical providers with prescribing power to report prescriptions of opioid medications and on pharmacy or dispensing professionals at the time of opioid dispensation (PDMP TTAC, 2023b). PDMPs have changed considerably over the 20-plus years of the Opioid Epidemic. Many early PDMPs were based on carbon copies. Early electronic PDMPs were updated infrequently and used technology that is now outdated (Horwitz et al., 2018). In recent years, many states have implemented automated reporting and started using a modern electronic PDMP system that is integrated with the patient's electronic medical record (EMR) (Buchmueller & Carey, 2018). As of 2020, 41 states have integrated patient EMRs with PDMPs, allowing clinicians to see patients' prescribing histories (PDMP TTAC, 2023b).

While improving the ease of access of PDMPs has somewhat increased the number of physicians that report checking PDMPs (Deyo et al., 2015; Mastarone et al., 2019; Richwine & Everson, 2022), current research indicates provider participation in PDMPs is highest when states implement a 'must-access' provision (Haffajee et al., 2015; PDMP COE, 2014), which legally require providers to use the PDMP before prescribing or dispensing in certain situations (PDMP TTAC, 2023a). There is evidence that mandatory PDMPs have not only been successful at increasing provider interaction with PDMPs but have also decreased opioid prescribing, in some contexts (PDMP TTAC, 2023a; Strickler et al., 2019).

For this reason, we include mandatory access PDMP dates as the only control variable in our analyses.

Given the evolution of PDMPs, the knowledge that PDMPs were much harder to use and access, much less stringent and less frequently updating than today, and the more recent research on what should qualify a PDMP as 'mandatory access', we used Kim (2021) and Sacks et al. (2019)'s mandatory PDMP dates to code a PDMP control variable for our main analysis (Horwitz et al., 2018; Kim, 2021; PDMP TTAC, 2023a; Sacks et al., 2019; Strickler et al., 2019). The start dates were very similar (the dates for six states are exactly the same, the dates for five states are within six months of each other, the dates for four states are multiple years off and Sacks et al. (2019) includes three states that Kim (2021) excludes). Additionally, we found consistent results regardless of whether we use Kim (2021)'s primary must-access PDMP start date (which comes from Mallatt (2019) or Sacks et al. (2019)'s must-access PDMP start date (which Kim (2021) also uses as alternative must-access PDMP start dates). We also estimated versions of our main specification using mandatory access PDMP dates from RAND's OPTIC-vetted policy datasets (OPTIC, 2020) (Appendix B, Figs. B1–B3) as well as a version with no PDMP control (Appendix C, Figs. C1–C3).

3. METHODS

We converted grams of opioids (by NDC) to MMEs using an ARCOS-provided NDC dictionary file. We then aggregated total shipped MMEs to the county-year level and expressed MMEs on a per capita basis for analysis; our aggregations were for all opioids together, opioids in 0–49 MME dosage units, opioids in 50–89 MME dosage units and opioids in 90 MME and up dosage units. The unit of analysis was the number of MMEs in each dosage strength per capita, per county and per year of opioids shipped only to retail pharmacies (i.e. we exclude pharmacies located in and serving institutional settings like hospitals or nursing homes). We also separately analysed commonly diverted opioids (oxycodone, hydrocodone, oxymorphone and hydromorphone) and less commonly diverted opioids (buprenorphine, codeine, dihydrocodeine, fentanyl, levorphanol, meperidine, methadone, morphine, opium and tapentadol) in terms of total MMEs per capita and by MME dose range. Oxycodone and Hydrocodone were, by many accounts, the most frequently diverted (Inciardi et al., 2007; US DOJ, 2004, 2018) and prescribed opioids in the US during the past 20 years (Kenan et al., 2012; Surratt et al., 2014). The opioids classified as commonly diverted were also commonly prescribed. Descriptive statistics from our data show that hydrocodone tablets make up 19.4% of opioid tablets shipped to pharmacies during this period, and 40% of all opioid tablet shipments were of oxycodone tablets. Together oxycodone, hydrocodone, oxymorphone and hydromorphone thus comprised 62% of all opioids shipped to US pharmacies during our study period (means and standard deviations of opioid MMEs (per capita), by county, can be seen in Table 1, and Fig. 1 shows a time series descriptive graph of all shipments of opioids, by state, in relative time around medical cannabis dispensary opening).

Table 1. Means and Standard Deviations of Explanatory Variables and Opioid MMEs (Per Capita) by County.

	Mean	Standard Deviation	Count of Non-zero Observations
Treatment and Control Variables			
Medical dispensary open in state	0.14	0.34	
County is in a must-access PDMP state	0.049	0.22	
County population	107453.7	266714.4	
Opioid MMEs (Per Capita Per Year) by County			
All opioids, all MMEs	176.9	118.4	13,918
All opioids in 0–49 MME	118.1	92.8	13,916
All opioids in 50–89 MME	11.8	9.44	13,731
All opioids in 90 MME+	12.6	16.2	13,195
Commonly diverted MMEs	104.1	88.3	13,918
Commonly diverted opioids in 0–49 MME/dose	86.6	80.3	13,914
Commonly diverted opioids in 50–89 MME/dose	7.95	6.61	13,630
Commonly diverted opioids in 90 MME/dose and up	8.62	8.81	12,983
Less commonly diverted MMEs per capita	72.8	44.8	13,918
Less commonly diverted opioids in 0–49 MME/dose	31.5	24.0	13,916
Less commonly diverted opioids in 50–89 MME/dose	3.97	4.08	13,497
Less commonly diverted opioids in 90 MME/dose and up	4.37	11.7	12,509

Source: Authors calculations.

Note: Counties in states adopting MCLs prior to 2006 and between 2014–2019 are excluded from the analysis.

Buprenorphine formulations approved to treat opioid use disorder were excluded from the analysis. By definition, methadone distributed to retail pharmacies is prescribed for pain management, not opioid use disorder treatment, and so was included in the analysis. MME dose ranges were determined using the CDC's recommendations for calculating a safer opioid dosage (CDC, 2019), which designates daily doses under 50 MMEs as relatively low risk, 51–89 MMEs as high doses and 90+ MMEs as very high doses which present high risk.

We excluded 5,791 county year observations for rural counties (identified by the US Department of Agriculture's Rural–Urban Continuum Code of 8 or higher) because they were more likely to be outliers in opioid prescriptions and prescription overdoses (Eyre, 2016; Kennedy-Hendricks et al., 2016; Monnat & Rigg, 2018). We excluded 882 county-year observations for California and Colorado because they had medical cannabis dispensaries open for the entirety of our study period. We excluded 7,515 county year observations in states that opened medical cannabis dispensaries within five years of the end of our study period in order to decrease contamination in our control states from anticipation effects that might occur leading up to medical cannabis dispensaries opening.

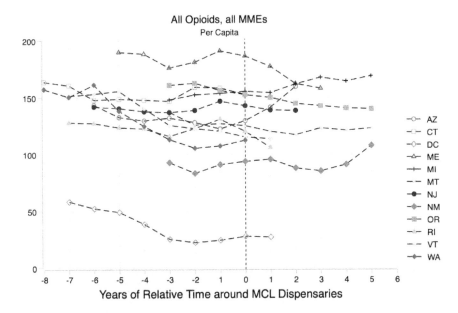

Fig. 1. All Shipments in Relative Time Around Dispensary Openings in States Treated During the Study Period, per Capita. *Note:* This descriptive graph shows the mean total opioid shipments (including all formulations and dose ranges) for all states that become treated during our study period. Total opioids are in terms of the number of MMEs per capita, per county, of opioids shipped only to pharmacies. *Source:* Authors calculations.

Some states technically had legal medical cannabis but did not have legal access to medical cannabis (because they have not yet opened dispensaries) during our study period. However, due to the sequential nature of medical cannabis legalisation, these states were the same as the states that opened dispensaries in the five years following the end of our study period. Thus, these were excluded following our previous rule. Finally, since our models were estimated with logged dependent variables, a further 166 county year observations where there were no opioid deliveries in the year were dropped. The final dataset had 13,918 county year observations available for estimating our various models. For more information about which states are included and excluded from our study, see Figs. 2–4.

We weighted all models by county population (extracted from the Area Health Resources File). Recent literature on DID methods has found that estimated treatment effects can be biased by the inclusion of time-varying unit characteristics and so increasingly recommends estimating uncontrolled versions of DID model (Callaway & Sant'Anna, 2021; de Chaisemartin & D'Haultfoeuile, 2020, 2022c).

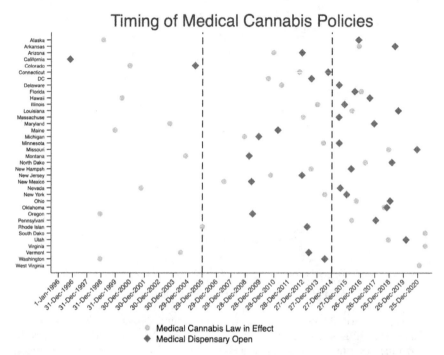

Fig. 2. Timing of Medical Cannabis Legalisation and Dispensary Openings.
Note: This figure shows when medical cannabis laws went into effect and when medical dispensaries opened, across US states. The dotted lines indicate the beginning and end of our study period. As noted in the Data and Methods sections, states that opened medical dispensaries in the time before our study period begins have been dropped. We also dropped the states that opened medical cannabis dispensaries within five years of the end of our study period and this had the consequence of also dropping states that legalised medical cannabis during our study period (but did not yet provide legal access). *Source:* Authors' calculations from review of policy data.

We conducted two types of analyses to assess the relationship between easy-access medical cannabis policies (open cannabis dispensaries) and all-payor retail pharmacy opioid prescribing. Our main analysis employed the Callaway and Sant'Anna's (2021) estimator (using the Stata 16 package csdid, henceforth referred to as 'C&S (2021)') (Callaway & Sant'Anna, 2021). We supplemented this with event study graphs showing a comparison of the results using C&S (2021) to three additional heterogeneity-robust estimators (Borusyak et al., 2024; de Chaisemartin & D'HaultfŒuille, 2018; de Chaisemartin & D'Haultfoeuille 2022a, 2022b; Sun & Abraham, 2021; Wright, 2021). We also included two canonical DIDs: one using OLS with robust fixed effects and one using Poisson pseudo-likelihood regression with robust fixed effects.

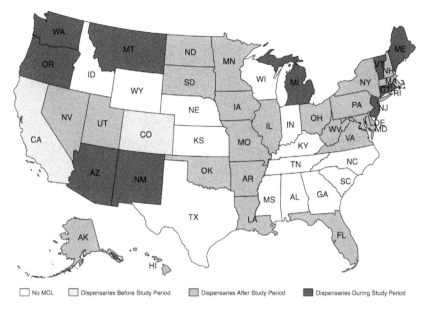

Fig. 3. Map of States With Medical Cannabis Dispensaries, Including Before and After Study Period. *Note:* Dispensary opening dates as of December 2022. CA and CO were omitted from analysis. States implementing cannabis dispensaries between 2015 and 2019 were also omitted from analysis to avoid contaminating the results with cannabis dispensary opening anticipatory effects. *Source:* Authors' calculations from review of policy data.

The C&S (2021) heterogeneity–robust estimator conducts a series of two-by-two DIDs for each treated cohort of the study then aggregates all two-by-two estimates using weights to give average causal effects by treatment time, by event, by calendar period, by group or overall. If treatment is binary and staggered, groups can be aggregated into cohorts (*g*) based on when they receive treatment (when $G = 1$).

The baseline model for each two-by-two DID cohort was specified by the following model:

$$\log\left(Y_{c,\tau}^{g}\right) = \alpha_{1}^{g,t} + \alpha_{2}^{g,t} \cdot G_{g} + \alpha_{3}^{g,t} \cdot 1\{T = t\} + \beta^{g,t} \cdot \left(G_{g} \times 1\{T = t\}\right) + \epsilon_{c,\tau}^{g,t} \quad (1)$$

Assuming that the parallel trends assumption holds and that there are not anticipatory effects, this model can be estimated on the subset of data that retains only observations at post-treatment time *t* (the post-treatment period over which the Average treatment on the treated [ATT] is being calculated) and time immediately preceding treatment, *g* − *1*. Further, *g* indexes a treated cohort, *t* indexes the (post) treatment time for which each ATT was calculated and *G* denotes the time period that a unit was first treated (and defines each treatment 'cohort'; untreated states are set as $G = \infty$). $Y_{c,\tau}^{g}$ represents the county-level MMEs shipped for each treatment

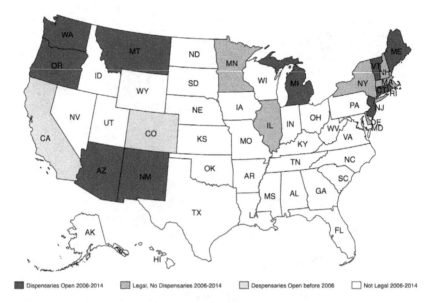

Fig. 4. Status of Medical Cannabis Laws During Study Period. *Note:* CA and CO were omitted from analysis. DE, IL, MA, MN, NH and NY opened cannabis dispensaries between 2015 and 2019 and so were omitted from analysis to avoid contaminating the results with cannabis dispensary opening anticipatory effects. This also allows us to avoid contaminating the results due to grey-market access to cannabis during the study period. *Source:* Authors' calculations from review of policy data.

cohort at calendar time τ for each type of drug and dosage strength, and $\epsilon_{c,\tau}^{g,t}$ represents the 'cohort-treatment time-county-calendar time' error. Similar to a canonical DID model, this approach provides estimated parameters for a treated group ($\alpha_2^{g,t} \cdot G_g$), a post-policy time period ($\alpha_3^{g,t} \cdot 1\{T = t\}$) and a parameter for the interaction of the treated groups during the post treatment period ($\beta^{g,t} \cdot (G_g \times 1\{T = t\})$). The main difference between the canonical DID and C&S (2021) is the added notation to specify that there is a separate DID models estimated for each treated cohort and post-treatment time period, instead of one DID for all groups. If treatment occurs at period t, to estimate ATT(g, t), C&S (2021) proposes a DID comparing $t - 1$ to $t + l$ outcome between cohort g and the never-treated groups. The two-by-two DIDs were estimated to compare $l + n$ for all n time periods.

The $\beta^{g,t}$ parameter in Eq. (1) is also referred to as the average treatment on the treated for cohort g in time t, which can be described as the expectation of the difference between the treated and untreated cohorts, in period t, after treatment:

$$\text{ATT}(g, t) = E[Y^1 - Y^0 | G_g = 1]$$

Each two-by-two DID generated a separate ATT(g, t), which was combined in different ways with other ATT(g, t) parameters, in order to summarise our findings. Tables 2–4 present the overall average ATT, which is a simple average with all ATTs weighed equally. However, for this project we also wanted to be able to evaluate the dynamic effects changing over time. For this reason, we also presented results using the event specification of C&S (2021), which aggregates ATT(g, t) using the following rule:

$$\theta_{es}^{bal}\left(e;\ e^{'}\right) = \sum_{g \in G} 1\left\{g + e^{'} \le T\right\} \cdot ATT(g, g + e) \cdot P\left(G = g \mid G + e^{'} \le T\right), \quad (2)$$

Where $\theta_{es}^{bal}(e;\ e^{'})$ is the average effect of participating in the treatment e time periods after the treatment was adopted across all groups that were ever observed to have participated in the treatment for exactly e time periods. The event time, $e = t-g$, denotes the time elapsed since cannabis dispensaries opened, up to e' (which, for this

Table 2. All Opioids, Callaway and Sant'Anna (2021) Estimator, Simple ATT.

	(1) All Doses	(2) 0–49 MMEs	(3) 50–89 MMEs	(4) 90+ MMEs
ATT	−0.0258	0.0143	−0.0878***	−0.113*
	(0.0187)	(0.0292)	(0.0179)	(0.0447)
Observations	13,918	13,916	13,731	13,195

Source: Authors' calculations.

Note: Standard errors in parentheses. All models include a control variable for whether a mandatory PDMP was in effect in the state and a population weight. Analysis was done at the county level, numbers of observations vary due to not every county receiving shipments of opioids at all dose levels, every year. The ATT is a simple average of the average causal effect across all cohort two-by-two DIDs, with each state-year observation being given equal weight, and should be interpreted as semi-elasticities. *$p < 0.05$, **$p < 0.01$ and *** $p < 0.001$.

Table 3. Commonly Diverted, Callaway and Sant'Anna (2021) Estimator and Simple ATT.

	(1) All Doses	(2) 0–49 MMEs	(3) 50–89 MMEs	(4) 90+ MMEs
ATT	−0.0114	0.0604*	−0.122***	−0.139**
	(0.0228)	(0.0304)	(0.0207)	(0.0498)
Observations	13,918	13,914	13,630	12,983

Source: Authors' calculations.

Note: Standard errors in parentheses. All models include a control variable for whether a mandatory PDMP was in effect in the state and a population weight. Analysis was done at the county level, numbers of observations vary due to not every county receiving shipments of opioids at all dose levels, every year. The ATT is a simple average of the average causal effect across all cohort two-by-two DIDs, with each state-year observation being given equal weight, and should be interpreted as semi-elasticities. *$p < 0.05$, **$p < 0.01$, ***$p < 0.001$.

Table 4. Less Commonly Diverted, Callaway and Sant'Anna (2021) Estimator and Simple ATT.

	(1) All Doses	(2) 0–49 MMEs	(3) 50–89 MMEs	(4) 90+ MMEs
ATT	−0.0323*	−0.000967	−0.0633	0.0135
	(0.0140)	(0.0181)	(0.0372)	(0.0948)
Observations	13,918	13,916	13,497	12,509

Source: Authors' calculations.

Note: Standard errors in parentheses. All models include a control variable for whether a mandatory PDMP was in effect in the state and a population weight. Analysis was done at the county level, numbers of observations vary due to not every county receiving shipments of opioids at all dose levels, every year. The ATT is a simple average of the average causal effect across all cohort two-by-two DIDs, with each state-year observation being given equal weight, and should be interpreted as semi-elasticities. $*p < 0.05$, $**p < 0.01$, $***p < 0.001$.

project, was 5 years post-policy). G denotes the time period that a unit is first treated (and defines each treatment 'cohort'; untreated states are set as $G = \infty$). T represents each time period. ATT(g, t) is group-time average treatment effect, but in this equation there is a limit to t (e), so ATT (g, t) becomes ATT(g, $g + e$). Eq. (2) is equivalent to the post-treatment period aggregated ATT. Tables 5–7 show the point estimates of the dynamic effects by event time.

C&S (2021) can be specified for a balanced or an unbalanced panel. If data are not in a panel that is balanced from $t-1$ to $t + n$, the estimator will keep whichever units are balanced in $t-1$ through $t + n$ and drop the rest. Our overall model (all opioid formulations, all dose ranges) was a balanced panel because each county had at least one opioid shipment in all years. But at deeper levels of stratification by diversion potential and dose range, there were some counties that had occasional years where they did not receive a shipment of opioids for a specific stratification. However, we saw the strongest dispensary responses occurring in the highest dose range stratifications. Thus, we included a table in the Appendix A (Tables A1–A3 and Figs. A1–A3), comparing the results with balanced and unbalanced panels, to show that results were robust to the nature of the panel.

C&S (2021) may use either never or never and not-yet-treated as controls, depending on the desired comparison. We found both ways to be consistent but used the never and not-yet-treated counties as controls in our main results because as of December 2022, 37 states provided some form of medical cannabis access, so this definition not only gave us more states to use as controls but also avoided selection bias related to states choosing not to legalise medical cannabis.

We expected that cohort distinctions existed between states that adopted cannabis policies before the Ogden memo in 2009, states that adopted cannabis between the Ogden memo and widespread recreational/adult use cannabis adoption in the late 2010s and the most recent wave of cannabis policy adopters which include predominately conservative-leaning states. This provides additional justification for our use of the C&S (2021) estimator because it allowed us to compute ATTs comparing across and between adoption cohorts and then estimate final treatment effects using results for the best comparisons.

4. RESULTS

4.1 Descriptive Statistics

Table 1 shows the means and standard deviations of explanatory and dependent variables included in our study. We found 176.9 MMEs per capita for all opioids were shipped to county pharmacies each year. This may seem high compared with published CDC opioid dispensing rates per 100 persons (CDC, 2022) but that is because published CDC rates were based on the number of prescriptions, whereas we are looking at the actual measurement of grams of raw opioids. The average MMEs per capita we observed in ARCOS combined with the CDC's opioid prescribing rate in 2010 would roughly correspond to 81.2 prescriptions of roughly 29 5mg oxycodone pills, for every 100 people in the population.[1] This is a similar strength prescription to what was frequently prescribed for a common outpatient surgery (Nooromid et al., 2018) or a month's worth of the mean daily dose of opioid MMEs for adults with chronic pain mentioned in two studies published in 2010 (Dunn et al., 2010; Saunders et al., 2010).

Low-to-moderate dose (0–49 MMEs) made up the bulk of yearly shipments (118 MME per capita per year). While moderate (50–90 MME doses) and high (90 MME and up doses) each contributed 11.83 and 12.6 MME (respectively) per capita per year to overall shipments. Of the 176.9 MMEs of all opioids per capita per year, 104.1 per capita MMEs of them were commonly diverted opioids and 72.8 per capita MME were less commonly diverted opioids.

About 14% of county-year observations had open medical cannabis dispensaries during our study period.

4.2 Main Results

Overall, when looking across all opioid formulations and all dose ranges, we found no statistically significant change in the shipments of opioids to pharmacies after the opening of medical cannabis dispensaries (Table 2). However, we did observe changes in the composition of opioids shipped to pharmacies. When looking at all formulations of opioids, having access to medical cannabis dispensaries was associated with an 8.78% decrease ($p < 0.001$) in 50–89 MME strength opioids and an 11.3% decrease ($p < 0.05$) in 90+ MME strength opioids. This would have corresponded with a decrease in about 1 MME per capita for 50–89 MME opioids and about 1.5 MMEs per capita for 90+ MME opioids. While this sounds like a small change on the individual level, with an average county population of just over 100,000, this would mean a decrease of about

---

[1]176.9 MMEs * 100 (to make it per 100 people), divided by 81.2 equals 217.86 MMEs per prescription. Oxycodone has an MME conversion rate of 1.5, so after dividing by 1.5, that equals 145.23 milligrams, divided by 5mg is 29 doses.

100,000–150,000 total MMEs per county, per year or about 670–1000 100mg oxycodone pills per year.

Similarly, when looking specifically at commonly diverted (and commonly prescribed) opioids (Table 3), we continued to see no change in the total amount across doses, but we did find a 6.04% increase in 0–49 MME per dose opioids ($p < 0.05$), and at the same time, we estimated a 12.2% and 13.9% decrease in 50–89 MME per dose ($p < 0.001$) and 90+ MME per dose opioids ($p < 0.01$), respectively. This was consistent with patients using cannabis concomitantly with opioids in order to take a lower dose of opioids while maintaining adequate analgesic effects. For an average county population of just over 100,000, this would have meant an increase of about 5.5 MMEs per capita from the lowest dosage strength opioids and decreases of about 2.2 total MMEs per capita, per year of the moderate and highest dosage strength opioids.

5. DISCUSSION

From evaluating the event studies in Figs. 5–7 and the event study point estimates in Tables 2–7, it appears that the commonly diverted opioids drove the decreases in shipments of opioids of the highest doses that we found overall. In the

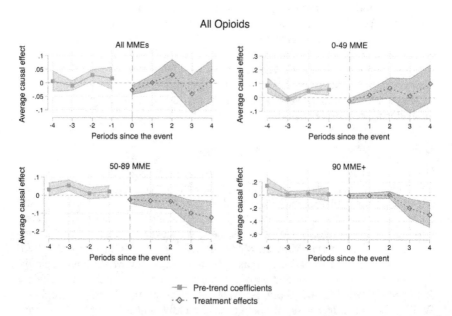

Fig. 5. All Opioids, Callaway and Sant'Anna (2021) Estimator, Event Study. *Note:* All models include a control variable for whether a mandatory PDMP was in effect in the state and a population weight. Dots indicate the coefficient on the indicator variable for years prior to and after medical cannabis dispensaries opened; shading represents the 95% confidence intervals. Average causal effect should be interpreted as semi-elasticities. *Source:* Authors' calculations.

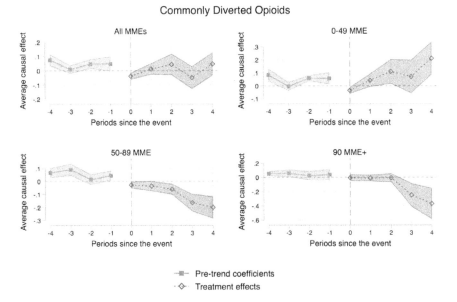

Fig. 6. Commonly Diverted, Callaway and Sant'Anna (2021) Estimator and Event Study. *Note:* All models include a control variable for whether a mandatory PDMP was in effect in the state and a population weight. Dots indicate the coefficient on the indicator variable for years prior to and after medical cannabis dispensaries opened; shading represents the 95% confidence intervals. Average causal effect should be interpreted as semi-elasticities. *Source:* Authors' calculations.

commonly diverted opioid event studies (Fig. 6), the increase in shipments in the 0–49 MME range was relatively noisy and the parallel trend assumption did not appear to be fully met. Additionally, there was evidence of a decline in shipments starting before the policy in the case of the 50–89 MME per dose formulations. The 90+ MME per dose formulation event study, however, appeared to be more precisely estimated, with a clear decline starting around two year post-policy. The parallel trends assumption was also met. Thus, our strongest finding was the negative association estimated between medical cannabis dispensaries opening and the volume of shipments of 90+ MME per dose opioid formulations.

From evaluating the regression results in Table 4, we found suggestive evidence of a decrease in the total amount of less commonly diverted opioids shipped to pharmacies when medical cannabis dispensaries opened. However, the event studies in Fig. 7 also suggest that while we did see a decrease in the post-policy period for all less diverted opioids, the parallel trends assumption may not have been met in the pre-policy period.

We also estimated event studies aggregating the results of all the currently-available heterogeneity–robust DID estimators (Figs. 8–10). While there was some variation from one model to the next in the size of the confidence intervals and the satisfaction of the parallel trend assumption, the models

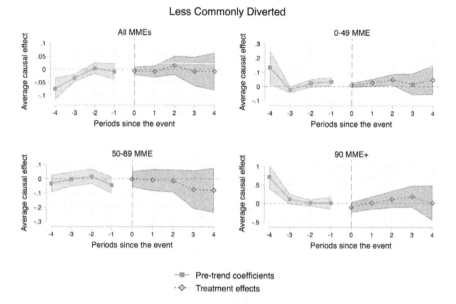

Fig. 7. Less Commonly Diverted, Callaway and Sant'Anna (2021) Estimator and Event Study. *Note:* All models include a control variable for whether a mandatory PDMP was in effect in the state and a population weight. Dots indicate the coefficient on the indicator variable for years prior to and after medical cannabis dispensaries opened; shading represents the 95% confidence intervals. Average causal effect should be interpreted as semi-elasticities. *Source:* Authors' calculations.

Table 5. All Opioids, Callaway and Sant'Anna (2021) Estimator and Event Study Point Estimates.

	(1) All Doses	(2) 0–49 MMEs	(3) 50–89 MMEs	(4) 90+ MMEs
Pre_avg	−0.00570	0.0368**	−0.00425	0.0161
	(0.00951)	(0.0121)	(0.0106)	(0.0203)
Post_avg	−0.0307	0.0208	−0.110***	−0.164**
	(0.0203)	(0.0350)	(0.0233)	(0.0529)
Tm5	−0.0174	0.0523**	−0.0846*	−0.0513
	(0.0205)	(0.0184)	(0.0330)	(0.0426)
Tm4	−0.00972	0.0702*	0.0157	0.127*
	(0.0197)	(0.0297)	(0.0198)	(0.0637)
Tm3	−0.0196*	−0.0180	0.0434**	−0.00200
	(0.00928)	(0.0114)	(0.0151)	(0.0258)
Tm2	0.0174*	0.0373***	0.000665	0.0100
	(0.00862)	(0.00863)	(0.0143)	(0.0233)
Tm1	0.000859	0.0423*	0.00354	−0.00350
	(0.0185)	(0.0203)	(0.0149)	(0.0531)
Tp0	−0.0359***	−0.0342***	−0.0349***	−0.0189
	(0.00900)	(0.00988)	(0.0103)	(0.0223)

SHELBY R. STEUART AND W. DAVID BRADFORD   183

Table 5. *(Continued)*

	(1) All Doses	(2) 0–49 MMEs	(3) 50–89 MMEs	(4) 90+ MMEs
Tp1	−0.0132	0.00506	−0.0444**	−0.0170
	(0.0176)	(0.0224)	(0.0163)	(0.0212)
Tp2	0.00513	0.0440	−0.0598***	−0.0215
	(0.0340)	(0.0420)	(0.0170)	(0.0309)
Tp3	−0.0888**	−0.0354	−0.150***	−0.252**
	(0.0284)	(0.0551)	(0.0310)	(0.0841)
Tp4	−0.0524	0.0396	−0.182***	−0.364***
	(0.0296)	(0.0571)	(0.0381)	(0.109)
Tp5	0.00123	0.106	−0.190***	−0.309***
	(0.0333)	(0.0564)	(0.0531)	(0.0837)
Observations	13,918	13,916	13,731	13,195

Source: Authors' calculations.

Note: Standard errors in parentheses. All models include a control variable for whether a mandatory PDMP was in effect in the state and a population weight. Analysis was done at the county level, numbers of observations vary due to not every county receiving shipments of opioids at all dose levels, every year. Results should be interpreted as semi-elasticities. *$p < 0.05$, **$p < 0.01$ and ***$p < 0.001$.

Table 6. Commonly Diverted, Callaway and Sant'Anna (2021) Estimator and Event Study Point Estimates.

	(1) All Doses	(2) 0–49 MMEs	(3) 50–89 MMEs	(4) 90+ MMEs
Pre_avg	0.0225*	0.0384***	0.00507	−0.00334
	(0.0114)	(0.00996)	(0.0137)	(0.0182)
Post_avg	−0.01000	0.0833*	−0.155***	−0.199***
	(0.0242)	(0.0339)	(0.0239)	(0.0585)
Tm5	−0.0158	0.0490*	−0.134*	−0.133**
	(0.0287)	(0.0202)	(0.0637)	(0.0425)
Tm4	0.0597**	0.0677**	0.0490*	0.0391*
	(0.0219)	(0.0253)	(0.0197)	(0.0180)
Tm3	−0.00116	−0.0143	0.0787***	0.0463
	(0.0145)	(0.0166)	(0.0233)	(0.0261)
Tm2	0.0372**	0.0489***	0.00583	0.0126
	(0.0141)	(0.0105)	(0.0175)	(0.0305)
Tm1	0.0325	0.0406	0.0256	0.0182
	(0.0241)	(0.0222)	(0.0186)	(0.0372)
Tp0	−0.0483***	−0.0452***	−0.0414**	−0.0163
	(0.0126)	(0.0127)	(0.0126)	(0.0249)
Tp1	−0.00279	0.0269	−0.0518**	−0.0262
	(0.0231)	(0.0284)	(0.0172)	(0.0232)
Tp2	0.0185	0.0846	−0.0878***	−0.0345
	(0.0434)	(0.0515)	(0.0230)	(0.0326)

(Continued)

Table 6. (Continued)

	(1) All Doses	(2) 0–49 MMEs	(3) 50–89 MMEs	(4) 90+ MMEs
Tp3	−0.0979**	0.0210	−0.219***	−0.302***
	(0.0343)	(0.0568)	(0.0342)	(0.0915)
Tp4	−0.0144	0.149**	−0.263***	−0.436***
	(0.0338)	(0.0512)	(0.0394)	(0.124)
Tp5	0.0850*	0.263***	−0.270***	−0.380***
	(0.0348)	(0.0451)	(0.0471)	(0.0901)
Observations	13,918	13,914	13,630	12,983

Source: Authors' calculations.

Note: Standard errors in parentheses. All models include a control variable for whether a mandatory PDMP was in effect in the state and a population weight. Analysis was done at the county level, numbers of observations vary due to not every county receiving shipments of opioids at all dose levels, every year. Results should be interpreted as semi-elasticities. *$p < 0.05$, **$p < 0.01$ and ***$p < 0.001$.

Table 7. Less Commonly Diverted, Callaway and Sant'Anna (2021) Estimator and Event Study Point Estimates.

	(1) All Doses	(2) 0–49 MMEs	(3) 50–89 MMEs	(4) 90+ MMEs
Pre_avg	−0.0368***	0.0297	−0.0232*	0.139***
	(0.00887)	(0.0159)	(0.0107)	(0.0409)
Post_avg	−0.0406*	−0.00698	−0.0830	0.0258
	(0.0167)	(0.0234)	(0.0461)	(0.117)
Tm5	−0.0187	0.0363**	0.00496	−0.0661
	(0.0139)	(0.0121)	(0.0279)	(0.0958)
Tm4	−0.0914***	0.117	−0.0505	0.679***
	(0.0219)	(0.0603)	(0.0316)	(0.162)
Tm3	−0.0426***	−0.0333**	−0.0151	0.0987
	(0.00727)	(0.0116)	(0.0263)	(0.0724)
Tm2	−0.00632	0.0111	0.00587	−0.00623
	(0.0100)	(0.0122)	(0.0259)	(0.0495)
Tm1	−0.0251	0.0173	−0.0612*	−0.00825
	(0.0141)	(0.0141)	(0.0285)	(0.0856)
Tp0	−0.0157*	−0.000507	−0.0154	−0.113
	(0.00651)	(0.00691)	(0.0270)	(0.0729)
Tp1	−0.0234*	0.0122	−0.0228	0.00752
	(0.0119)	(0.0111)	(0.0352)	(0.0888)
Tp2	−0.0101	0.0217	−0.0421	0.0807
	(0.0205)	(0.0165)	(0.0339)	(0.117)
Tp3	−0.0572**	−0.0329	−0.124	0.140
	(0.0218)	(0.0309)	(0.0639)	(0.145)
Tp4	−0.0697**	−0.0159	−0.140	−0.0411
	(0.0266)	(0.0400)	(0.0733)	(0.232)

Table 7. (Continued)

	(1) All Doses	(2) 0–49 MMEs	(3) 50–89 MMEs	(4) 90+ MMEs
Tp5	−0.0675	−0.0265	−0.154	0.0806
	(0.0349)	(0.0496)	(0.0932)	(0.313)
Observations	13,918	13,916	13,497	12,509

Source: Authors' calculations.
Note: Standard errors in parentheses. All models include a control variable for whether a mandatory PDMP was in effect in the state and a population weight. Analysis was done at the county level, numbers of observations vary due to not every county receiving shipments of opioids at all dose levels, every year. Results should be interpreted as semi-elasticities. $*p < 0.05$, $**p < 0.01$ and $***p < 0.001$.

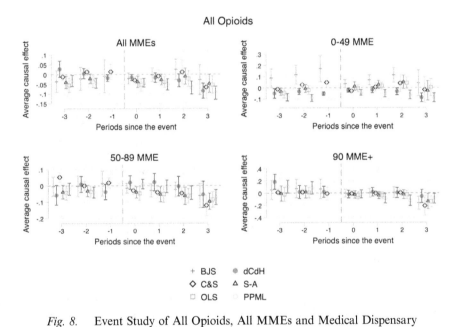

Fig. 8. Event Study of All Opioids, All MMEs and Medical Dispensary Openings. *Note:* All models include a control variable for whether a mandatory PDMP was in effect in the state and a population weight. Dots indicate the coefficient on the indicator variable for years prior to and after medical cannabis dispensaries opened; shading represents the 95% confidence intervals. Average causal effect should be interpreted as semi-elasticities. BJS = Borusyak et al. (2024) Imputation Estimator, C&S = Callaway and Sant'Anna (2021) DID Estimator, OLS = canonical difference-in-difference using OLS with two-way fixed-effects, dCdH = de Chaisemartin and D'Haultfoeuille (2022a) multi-period DID estimator, S-A = Sun and Abraham's (2021) Event Study Interaction DID estimator and PPML = canonical difference-in-difference using Poisson pseudo-likelihood regression with multiple levels of fixed effects. *Source:* Authors' calculations.

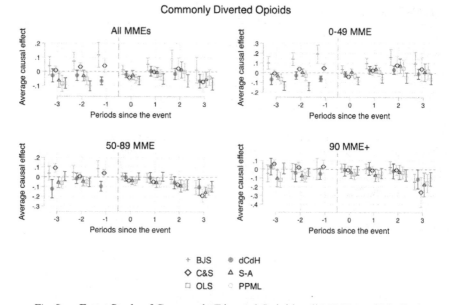

Fig. 9. Event Study of Commonly Diverted Opioids, all MMEs and Medical Dispensary Openings. *Note:* All models include a control variable for whether a mandatory PDMP was in effect in the state and a population weight. Dots indicate the coefficient on the indicator variable for years prior to and after medical cannabis dispensaries opened; shading represents the 95% confidence intervals. Average causal effect should be interpreted as semi-elasticities. BJS = Borusyak et al. (2024) Imputation Estimator, C&S = Callaway and Sant'Anna (2021) DID Estimator, OLS = canonical difference-in-difference using OLS with two-way fixed-effects, dCdH = de Chaisemartin and D'Haultfoeuille (2022a) multi-period DID estimator, S-A = Sun and Abraham's (2021) Event Study Interaction DID estimator and PPML = canonical difference-in-difference using Poisson pseudo-likelihood regression with multiple levels of fixed effects. *Source:* Authors' calculations.

consistently showed compositional changes of decreases in shipments of the highest level opioids and increases at the low-to-moderate range, with no overall net changes in the total shipments of all opioids together.

6. LIMITATIONS

This study has several limitations. We did not attempt to control for drug prices or changes in private or public insurance coverage and made no attempt to separately identify supply or demand functions (Meinhofer & Rubli, 2021). Similarly, we did not measure downstream effects of opioid shipments on prescription opioid overdose (NIDA, 2023). While there was substantial evidence oxycodone, oxymorphone, hydrocodone and hydromorphone were more

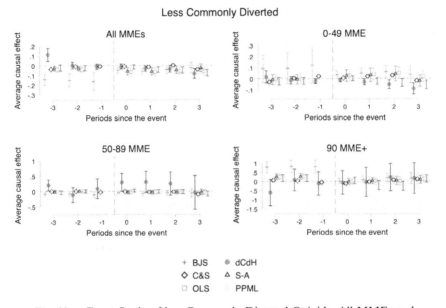

Fig. 10. Event Study of less Commonly Diverted Opioids, All MMEs and Medical Dispensary Openings. *Note:* All models include a control variable for whether a mandatory PDMP was in effect in the state and a population weight. Dots indicate the coefficient on the indicator variable for years prior to and after medical cannabis dispensaries opened; shading represents the 95% confidence intervals. Average causal effect should be interpreted as semi-elasticities. BJS = Boruysak et al. (2024) Imputation Estimator, C&S = Callaway and Sant'Anna (2021) DID Estimator, OLS = canonical difference-in-difference using OLS with two-way fixed-effects, dCdH = de Chaisemartin and D'Haultfoeuille (2022a) multi-period DID estimator, S-A = Sun and Abraham's (2021) Event Study Interaction DID estimator and PPML = canonical difference-in-difference using Poisson pseudo-likelihood regression with multiple levels of fixed effects. *Source:* Authors' calculations.

commonly diverted than other opioids, they were also the most frequently prescribed for both acute and chronic pain.

Additionally, we observed a sudden drop in shipments of 90+ MME dose range opioids of all kinds, in the fourth quarter of 2007. However, this anomaly occurred equally in both medical cannabis dispensary opening states and non-medical cannabis dispensary opening states. This drop was not significant enough to be noticeable when looking at all dose ranges together and occurred two years into our study period (whereas our results become statistically significant three-year post policy for cannabis dispensary states). Our results were stable across additional sensitivity analyses that started the study period after the sudden drop (2008–2014).

7. CONCLUSION

While we did not find an overall change in the total volume of opioids (measured in MME units per capita) being shipped to pharmacies in response to medical cannabis access, we did find a change in the composition of opioids. Total shipped MMEs of commonly diverted opioids increased while total MMEs of the less commonly diverted opioids decreased when measured across all dosage strengths aggregated together. We also found a shift away from the highest MME dosage strength pills and towards moderate MME dosage strength pills for both commonly diverted opioids and all opioids. This pattern of response at the population level was consistent with the behaviours that would be expected if pain patients used cannabis concomitant with lower dose opioids as a substitute for higher dose opioids (Wendelboe et al., 2019). Since we modelled aggregate shipment data, we cannot assume that these patterns reflect changes in individual patient behaviour. Nonetheless, our findings suggested that cannabis access had the effect of making the overall portfolio of opioids consumed somewhat safer in that lower dose formulations tended to be more prevalent with cannabis access than without. More research is warranted into how patients use cannabis and prescription medication in combination to manage pain while minimising the harmful side effects of opioid use.

REFERENCES

Bachhuber, M. A., Saloner, B., Cunningham, C. O., & Barry, C. L. (2014). Medical cannabis laws and opioid analgesic overdose mortality in the United States, 1999–2010. *JAMA Internal Medicine*, *174*(10), 1668–1673.

Borusyak, K., Jaravel, X., & Spiess, J. (2024). Revisiting event-study designs: Robust and efficient estimation. *The Review of Economic Studies*. https://doi.org/10.1093/restud/rdae007

Bradford, A. C., & Bradford, W. D. (2017). Medical marijuana laws may be associated with a decline in the number of prescriptions for medicaid enrollees. *Health Affairs*, *36*(5), 945–951.

Bradford, A. C., Bradford, W. D., Abraham, A., & Bagwell Adams, G. (2018). Association between US state medical cannabis laws and opioid prescribing in the Medicare Part D population. *JAMA Internal Medicine*, *178*(5), 667–672.

Buchmueller, T. C., & Carey, C. (2018). The effect of prescription drug monitoring programs on opioid utilization in medicare. *American Economic Journal: Economic Policy*, *10*(1), 77–112. https://doi.org/10.1257/pol.20160094

Callaway, B., & Sant'Anna, P. H. C. (2021). Difference-in-differences with multiple time periods. *Journal of Econometrics*, *225*(2), 200–230.

Centers for Disease Control. (2019). *Calculating a total daily dose of opioid medications*. https://www.cdc.gov/drugoverdose/pdf/calculating_total_daily_dose-a.pdf. https://stacks.cdc.gov/view/cdc/38481 Accessed on March 4, 2022.

Centers for Disease Control. (2022). *U.S. Opioid dispensing rate maps*. https://www.cdc.gov/drugoverdose/rxrate-maps/index.html

Davis, C. S., Pierce, M., & Dasgupta, N. (2014). Evolution and Convergence of state laws governing controlled substance prescription monitoring programs, 1998–2011. *American Journal of Public Health*, *104*(8), 1389–1395. https://doi.org/10.2105/ajph.2014.301923

de Chaisemartin, C., & D'HaultfŒuille, X. (2018). Fuzzy differences-in-differences. *The Review of Economic Studies*, *85*(2), 999–1028. https://doi.org/10.1093/restud/rdx049

de Chaisemartin, C., & D'Haultfœuille, X. (2020). Two-way fixed effects estimators with heterogeneous treatment effects. *The American Economic Review*, *110*(9), 2964–2996. https://doi.org/10.1257/aer.20181169

de Chaisemartin, C., & D'Haultfoeuille, X. (2022a). *Difference-in-differences estimators of intertemporal treatment effects* (No. 29873). National Bureau of Economic Research. https://doi.org/10.3386/w29873

de Chaisemartin, C., & D'Haultfoeuille, X. (2022b). Two-way fixed effects and differences-in-differences estimators with several treatments. https://doi.org/10.3386/w30564

de Chaisemartin, C., & D'Haultfoeuille, X. (2022c). Two-way fixed effects and differences-in-differences with heterogeneous treatment effects: A survey. https://doi.org/10.3386/w29734

DEA. (2015). *2014 National drug threat assessment.* https://www.dea.gov/documents/2014/2014-11/2014-11-01/2014-national-drug-threat-assessment. Accessed on February 22, 2023.

Deyo, R. A., Irvine, J. M., Hallvik, S. E., Hildebran, C., Beran, T., Millet, L. M., & Marino, M. (2015). Leading a horse to water: Facilitating registration and use of a prescription drug monitoring program. *The Clinical Journal of Pain, 31*(9), 782.

Dunn, K. M., Saunders, K. W., Rutter, C. M., Banta-Green, C. J., Merill, J. O., Sullivan, M. D., Weisner, C. M., Silverberg, M. J., Campbell, C. I., Psaty, B. M., & Korff, M. V. (2010). Opioid prescriptions for chronic pain and overdose: A cohort study. *Annals of Internal Medicine.* https://doi.org/10.7326/0003-4819-152-2-201001190-00006

Eyre, E. (2016, May 23). Drug firms fueled "pill mills" in rural WV. *Charleston Gazette-Mail.* https://www.wvgazettemail.com/news/cops_and_courts/drug-firms-fueled-pill-mills-in-rural-wv/article_14c8e1a5-19b1-579d-9ed5-770f09589a22.html

Haffajee, R. L., Jena, A. B., & Weiner, S. G. (2015). Mandatory use of prescription drug monitoring programs. *JAMA, 313*(9), 891. https://doi.org/10.1001/jama.2014.18514

Hill, K. P., Palastro, M. D., Johnson, B., & Ditre, J. W. (2017). Cannabis and pain: A clinical review. *Cannabis and Cannabinoid Research, 2*(1), 96–104.

Horwitz, J., Davis, C. S., McClelland, L. S., Fordon, R. S., & Meara, E. (2018). *The problem of data quality in analyses of opioid regulation: The case of prescription drug monitoring programs* (No. w24947). National Bureau of Economic Research. https://doi.org/10.3386/w24947

Inciardi, J. A., Surratt, H. L., Lugo, Y., & Cicero, T. J. (2007). The diversion of prescription opioid analgesics. *Law Enforcement Executive Forum, 7*(7), 127–141.

Institute of Medicine, Board on Health Sciences Policy, and Committee on Advancing Pain Research, Care, and Education. (2011). *Relieving pain in America: A blueprint for transforming prevention, care, education, and research.* National Academies Press.

Jones, M. R., Viswanath, O., Peck, J., Kaye, A. D., Gill, J. S., & Simopoulos, T. T. (2018). A brief history of the opioid epidemic and strategies for pain medicine. *Pain and Therapy, 7*(1), 13–21.

Kenan, K., Mack, K., & Paulozzi, L. (2012). Trends in prescriptions for oxycodone and other commonly used opioids in the United States, 2000–2010. Open medicine: A peer-reviewed, independent. *Open-Access Journal, 6*(2), e41–e47.

Kennedy-Hendricks, A., Richey, M., McGinty, E. E., Stuart, E. A., Barry, C. L., & Webster, D. W. (2016). Opioid overdose deaths and Florida's Crackdown on Pill Mills. *American Journal of Public Health, 106*(2), 291.

Kim, B. (2021). Must-access prescription drug monitoring programs and the opioid overdose epidemic: The unintended consequences. *Journal of Health Economics, 75,* 102408.

Kraft, B., Frickey, N. A., Kaufmann, R. M., Reif, M., Frey, R., Gustorff, B., & Kress, H. G. (2008). Lack of Analgesia by oral standardized cannabis extract on acute inflammatory pain and hyperalgesia in volunteers. *Anesthesiology, 109*(1), 101–110. https://doi.org/10.1097/aln.0b013e31817881e1

Lozano-Rojas, F., Abraham, A. J., Gupta, S., & David Bradford, W. (2022). The effect of cannabis laws on access to pain medications among commercially insured patients in the United States. *SSRN Electronic Journal.* https://doi.org/10.2139/ssrn.4299449

Lynch, M. E., & Clark, A. J. (2003). Cannabis reduces opioid dose in the treatment of chronic non-cancer pain. *Journal of Pain and Symptom Management, 25*(6), 496–498. https://doi.org/10.1016/s0885-3924(03)00142-8

Mallatt, J. (2019). Unintended consequences of prescription monitoring: Policy-induced substitution to illicit drugs. *SSRN Electronic Journal.* https://doi.org/10.2139/ssrn.3418615

Mastarone, G. L., Wyse, J. J., Wilbur, E. R., Morasco, B. J., Saha, S., & Carlson, K. F. (2019). Barriers to utilization of prescription drug monitoring programs among prescribing physicians and advanced practice registered nurses at veterans health administration facilities in Oregon. *Pain Medicine, 21*(4), 695–703.

Mathur, N. K., & Ruhm, C. J. (2023). Marijuana legalization and opioid deaths. *Journal of Health Economics, 88,* 102728.

Meinhofer, A., & Rubli, A. (2021). Illegal drug market responses to state recreational cannabis laws. *Addiction, 116*(12), 3433–3443. https://doi.org/10.1111/add.15517

Monnat, S. M., & Rigg, K. K. (2018). The opioid crisis in rural and small Town America. https://doi.org/10.34051/p/2020.332

Nooromid, M. J., Blay, E., Jr., Holl, J. L., Bilimoria, K. Y., Johnson, J. K., Eskandari, M. K., & Stulberg, J. J. (2018). Discharge prescription patterns of opioid and nonopioid analgesics after common surgical procedures. *Pain Reports, 3*(1). https://doi.org/10.1097/PR9.0000000000000637

National Academies of Sciences, Engineering, and Medicine, Health and Medicine Division, Board on Population Health and Public Health Practice, and Committee on the Health Effects of Marijuana: An Evidence Review and Research Agenda. (2017). *Cannabis: Prevalence of use, regulation, and current policy landscape.* National Academies Press.

National Institute on Drug Abuse. (2023, February 9). *Drug overdose death rates.* National Institute on Drug Abuse. https://nida.nih.gov/research-topics/trends-statistics/overdose-death-rates

OPTIC. (2020). *OPTIC-Vetted Policy Data Sets.* https://www.rand.org/health-care/centers/optic/resources/datasets.html. Accessed on May 20, 2022.

PDMP Center of Excellence. (2014). *Mandating PDMP participation by medical providers: Current status and experience in selected states.* https://www.ojp.gov/pdffiles1/bja/247134.pdf. Accessed on February 17, 2023.

Polster, D. A. (2018). *Protective order Re: DEA's ARCOS/DADS database* (pp. 18132–18135). https://www.ohnd.uscourts.gov/sites/ohnd/files/17-2804ARCOS.pdf

Powell, D., Pacula, R. L., & Jacobson, M. (2018). Do medical marijuana laws reduce addictions and deaths related to pain killers? *Journal of Health Economics, 58*, 29–42.

Powell, D., Pacula, R. L., & Taylor, E. (2020). How increasing medical access to opioids contributes to the opioid epidemic: Evidence from Medicare Part D. *Journal of Health Economics, 71*, 102286. https://doi.org/10.1016/j.jhealeco.2019.102286

Prescription Drug Monitoring Program Training and Technical Assistance Center. (2023a). *Prescription drug monitoring program training and technical assistance center.* Bureau of Justice Assistance (BJA). https://www.pdmpassist.org/. Accessed on February 17, 2023.

Prescription Drug Monitoring Program Teaching and Technical Assistance Center. (2023b). *PDMP policies and capabilities. Maps and Tables.* https://www.pdmpassist.org/Policies/Maps/PDMPPolicies. Accessed on October 15, 2022.

Richwine, C., & Everson, J. (2022). National estimates and physician-reported impacts of prescription drug monitoring program use. *Journal of General Internal Medicine, 1*–8.

Russo, E. B. (2019). Cannabis and pain. *Pain Medicine, 20*(11), 2083–2085.

Sacks, D., Hollingsworth, A., Nguyen, T., & Simon, K. (2019). Can policy affect initiation of addictive substance use? Evidence from opioid prescribing. https://doi.org/10.3386/w25974

Saunders, K. W., Dunn, K. M., Merrill, J. O., Sullivan, M., Weisner, C., Braden, J. B., Psaty, B. M., & Von Korff, M. (2010). Relationship of opioid use and dosage levels to fractures in older chronic pain patients. *Journal of General Internal Medicine, 25*(4), 310–315.

Shah, A. B., Hayes, C. J., Lakkad, M., & Martin, B. C. (2018). Impact of medical Marijuana legalization on opioid use, chronic opioid use and high-risk opioid use. *Value in Health, 21*, S247. https://doi.org/10.1016/j.jval.2018.04.1674

Strickler, G. K., Zhang, K., Halpin, J. F., Bohnert, A. S. B., Baldwin, G. T., & Kreiner, P. W. (2019). Effects of mandatory prescription drug monitoring program (PDMP) use laws on prescriber registration and use and on risky prescribing. *Drug and Alcohol Dependence, 199*, 1–9. https://doi.org/10.1016/j.drugalcdep.2019.02.010

Sun, L., & Abraham, S. (2021). Estimating dynamic treatment effects in event studies with heterogeneous treatment effects. *Journal of Econometrics, 225*(2), 175–199. https://doi.org/10.1016/j.jeconom.2020.09.006

Surratt, H. L., O'Grady, C., Kurtz, S. P., Stivers, Y., Cicero, T. J., Dart, R. C., & Chen, M. (2014). Reductions in prescription opioid diversion following recent legislative interventions in Florida. *Pharmacoepidemiology and Drug Safety, 23*(3), 314–320.

United States Department of Justice. (2004). *Intelligence bulletin: OxyContin diversion, availability, and abuse.* https://www.justice.gov/archive/ndic/pubs10/10550/index.htm. Accessed on February 22, 2023.

United States Department of Justice. (2018). *DEA propose significant opioid manufacturing reduction in 2019.* https://www.justice.gov/opa/pr/justice-department-dea-propose-significant-opioid-manufacturing-reduction-2019. Accessed on February 2023.

United States Government Accountability Office. (2015). *Prescription drugs: Oxycontin abuse and diversion and efforts to address the problem – Scholar's choice edition.* Scholar's Choice.

Wallace, M., Schulteis, G., Hampton Atkinson, J., Wolfson, T., Lazzaretto, D., Bentley, H., Gouaux, B., & Abramson, I. (2007). Dose-dependent effects of smoked cannabis on capsaicin-induced pain and hyperalgesia in healthy volunteers. *Anesthesiology*, *107*(5), 785–796. https://doi.org/10.1097/01.anes.0000286986.92475.b7

Wen, H., & Hockenberry, J. M. (2018). Association of medical and adult-use marijuana laws with opioid prescribing for medicaid enrollees. *JAMA Internal Medicine*, *178*(5), 673–679.

Wendelboe, A. M., Mathew, R., Chongsuwat, T., Rainwater, E., Wendelboe, M. A., Wickersham, E., & Chou, A. F. (2019). Is there less opioid abuse in States where marijuana has been decriminalized, either for medicinal or recreational use? A Clin-IQ. *Journal of Patient-Centered Research and Reviews*, *6*(4), 267–273. https://doi.org/10.17294/2330-0698.1704

Wright, T. (2021, June 13). Kirill Borusyak "revisiting event study designs: Robust and efficient estimation". Youtube. https://www.youtube.com/watch?v=rdfTxWnudt4

APPENDIX A: COMPARING BALANCED AND UNBALANCED PANELS

Table A1. All Opioids, Callaway and Sant'Anna (2021) Estimator, Simple ATT.

	Unbalanced Panel		Balanced Panel	
	50–89 MMEs	90+ MMEs	50–89 MMEs	90+ MMEs
ATT	−0.0878***	−0.113*	−0.0874***	−0.103*
	(0.0179)	(0.0447)	(0.0174)	(0.0428)
Observations	13,731	13,195	13,710	13,141

Source: Authors' calculations.

Note: Standard errors in parentheses. All models include a control variable for whether a mandatory PDMP was in effect in the state and a population weight. Analysis was done at the county level, numbers of observations vary due to not every county receiving shipments of opioids at all dose levels, every year. The ATT is a simple average of the average causal effect across all cohort two-by-two DIDs, with each state-year observation being given equal weight, and should be interpreted as semi-elasticities. $^*p < 0.05$, $^{**}p < 0.01$ and $^{***}p < 0.001$.

Table A2. Commonly Diverted, Callaway and Sant'Anna (2021) Estimator, Simple ATT.

	Unbalanced Panel		Balanced Panel	
	50–89 MMEs	90+ MMEs	50–89 MMEs	90+ MMEs
ATT	−0.122***	−0.139**	−0.121***	−0.126**
	(0.0207)	(0.0498)	(0.0202)	(0.0479)
Observations	13,630	12,983	13,596	12,919

Source: Authors calculations.

Note: Standard errors in parentheses. All models include a control variable for whether a mandatory PDMP was in effect in the state and a population weight. Analysis was done at the county level, numbers of observations vary due to not every county receiving shipments of opioids at all dose levels, every year. The ATT is a simple average of the average causal effect across all cohort two-by-two DIDs, with each state-year observation being given equal weight, and should be interpreted as semi-elasticities. $^*p < 0.05$, $^{**}p < 0.01$ and $^{***}p < 0.001$.

Table A3. Less Commonly Diverted, Callaway and Sant'Anna (2021) Estimator and Simple ATT.

	Unbalanced Panel		Balanced Panel	
	50–89 MMEs	90+ MMEs	50–89 MMEs	90+ MMEs
ATT	−0.0633	0.0135	−0.0606	−0.00897
	(0.0372)	(0.0948)	(0.0338)	(0.0909)
Observations	13,497	12,509	13,449	12,371

Source: Authors calculations.

Note: Standard errors in parentheses. All models include a control variable for whether a mandatory PDMP was in effect in the state and a population weight. Analysis was done at the county level, numbers of observations vary due to not every county receiving shipments of opioids at all dose levels, every year. The ATT is a simple average of the average causal effect across all cohort two-by-two DIDs, with each state-year observation being given equal weight, and should be interpreted as semi-elasticities. *$p < 0.05$, **$p < 0.01$ and ***$p < 0.001$.

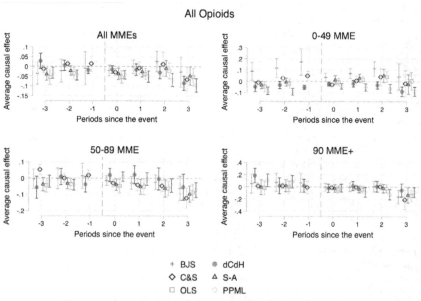

Fig. A1. Event Study of All Opioids, All MMEs and Medical Dispensary Openings (Balanced Panel). *Note:* All models include a control variable for whether a mandatory PDMP was in effect in the state and a population weight. Dots indicate the coefficient on the indicator variable for years prior to and after medical cannabis dispensaries opened; shading represents the 95% confidence intervals. Average causal effect should be interpreted as semi-elasticities. BJS = Borusyak et al. (2024) Imputation Estimator, C&S = Callaway and Sant'Anna (2021) DID Estimator, OLS = canonical difference-in-difference using OLS with two-way fixed-effects, dCdH = de Chaisemartin and D'Haultfoeuille (2022a) multi-period DID estimator, S-A = Sun and Abraham's (2021) Event Study Interaction DID estimator and PPML = canonical difference-in-difference using Poisson pseudo-likelihood regression with multiple levels of fixed effects. *Source:* Authors' calculations.

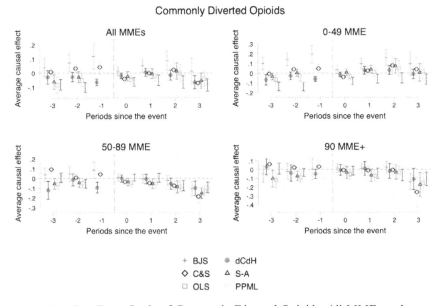

Fig A2. Event Study of Commonly Diverted Opioids, All MMEs and Medical Dispensary Openings (Balanced Panel). *Note:* All models include a control variable for whether a mandatory PDMP was in effect in the state and a population weight. Dots indicate the coefficient on the indicator variable for years prior to and after medical cannabis dispensaries opened; shading represents the 95% confidence intervals. Average causal effect should be interpreted as semi-elasticities. BJS = Borusyak et al. (2024) Imputation Estimator, C&S = Callaway and Sant'Anna (2021) DID Estimator, OLS = canonical difference-in-difference using OLS with two-way fixed-effects, dCdH = de Chaisemartin and D'Haultfoeuille (2022a) multi-period DID estimator, S-A = Sun and Abraham's (2021) Event Study Interaction DID estimator and PPML = canonical difference-in-difference using Poisson pseudo-likelihood regression with multiple levels of fixed effects. *Source:* Authors' calculations.

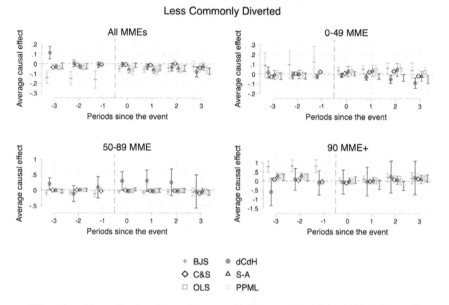

Fig. A3. Event Study of Less Commonly Diverted Opioids, All MMEs and Medical Dispensary Openings (Balanced Panel). *Note:* All models include a control variable for whether a mandatory PDMP was in effect in the state and a population weight. Dots indicate the coefficient on the indicator variable for years prior to and after medical cannabis dispensaries opened; shading represents the 95% confidence intervals. Average causal effect should be interpreted as semi-elasticities. BJS = Borusyak et al. (2024) Imputation Estimator, C&S = Callaway and Sant'Anna (2021) DID Estimator, OLS = canonical difference-in-difference using OLS with two-way fixed-effects, dCdH = de Chaisemartin and D'Haultfoeuille (2022a) multi-period DID estimator, S-A = Sun and Abrahams (2021) Event Study Interaction DID estimator and PPML = canonical difference-in-difference using Poisson pseudo-likelihood regression with multiple levels of fixed effects. *Source:* Authors' calculations.

APPENDIX B: MAIN SPECIFICATION WITH OPTIC MANDATORY PDMP DATES

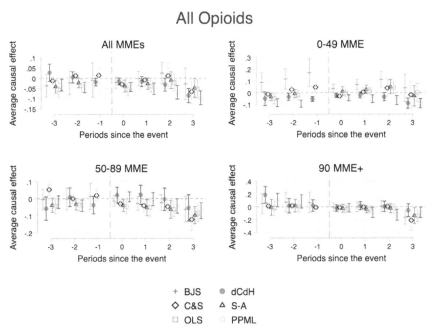

Fig. B1. Event Study of All Opioids, All MMEs, Medical Dispensary Openings. *Note:* All models include a control variable for whether a mandatory PDMP was in effect in the state and a population weight. Dots indicate the coefficient on the indicator variable for years prior to and after medical cannabis dispensaries opened; shading represents the 95% confidence intervals. Average causal effect should be interpreted as semi-elasticities. BJS = Borusyak et al. (2024) Imputation Estimator, C&S = Callaway and Sant'Anna (2021) DID Estimator, OLS = canonical difference-in-difference using OLS with two-way fixed-effects, dCdH = de Chaisemartin and D'Haultfoeuille (2022a) multi-period DID estimator, S-A = Sun and Abraham's (2021) Event Study Interaction DID estimator and PPML = canonical difference-in-difference using Poisson pseudo-likelihood regression with multiple levels of fixed effects. *Source:* Authors' calculations.

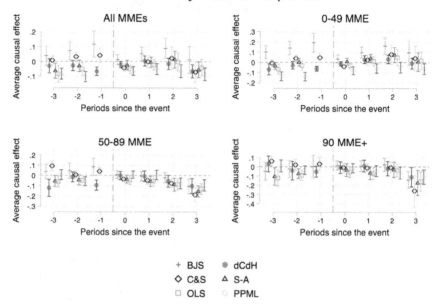

Fig. B2. Event Study of Commonly Diverted Opioids, All MMEs and Medical Dispensary Openings. *Note:* All models include a control variable for whether a mandatory PDMP was in effect in the state and a population weight. Dots indicate the coefficient on the indicator variable for years prior to and after medical cannabis dispensaries opened; shading represents the 95% confidence intervals. Average causal effect should be interpreted as semi-elasticities. BJS = Borusyak et al. (2024) Imputation Estimator, C&S = Callaway and Sant'Anna (2021) DID Estimator, OLS = canonical difference-in-difference using OLS with two-way fixed-effects, dCdH = de Chaisemartin and D'Haultfoeuille (2022a) multi-period DID estimator, S-A = Sun and Abraham's (2021) Event Study Interaction DID estimator and PPML = canonical difference-in-difference using Poisson pseudo-likelihood regression with multiple levels of fixed effects. *Source:* Authors' calculations.

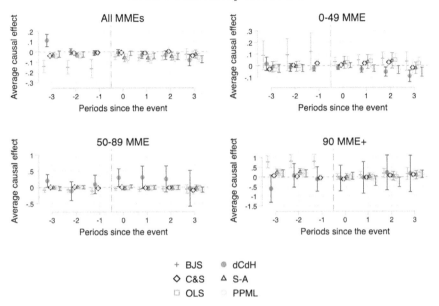

Fig. B3. Event Study of Less Commonly Diverted Opioids, All MMEs and Medical Dispensary Openings. *Note:* All models include a control variable for whether a mandatory PDMP was in effect in the state and a population weight. Dots indicate the coefficient on the indicator variable for years prior to and after medical cannabis dispensaries opened; shading represents the 95% confidence intervals. Average causal effect should be interpreted as semi-elasticities. BJS = Borusyak et al. (2024) Imputation Estimator, C&S = Callaway and Sant'Anna (2021) DID Estimator, OLS = canonical difference-in-difference using OLS with two-way fixed-effects, dCdH = de Chaisemartin and D'Haultfoeuille (2022a) multi-period DID estimator, S-A = Sun and Abraham's (2021) Event Study Interaction DID estimator and PPML = canonical difference-in-difference using Poisson pseudo-likelihood regression with multiple levels of fixed effects. *Source:* Authors' calculations.

APPENDIX C: MAIN SPECIFICATION WITHOUT MANDATORY PDMP CONTROL VARIABLE AND POPULATION WEIGHT

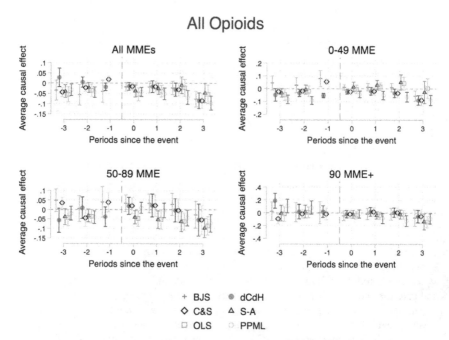

Fig. C1. Event Study of All Opioids, All MMEs and Medical Dispensary Openings (No Mandatory PDMP). *Note:* Dots indicate the coefficient on the indicator variable for years prior to and after medical cannabis dispensaries opened; shading represents the 95% confidence intervals. Average causal effect should be interpreted as semi-elasticities. BJS = Borusyak et al. (2024) Imputation Estimator, C&S = Callaway and Sant'Anna (2021) DID Estimator, OLS = canonical difference-in-difference using OLS with two-way fixed-effects, S-A = Sun and Abraham's (2021) Event Study Interaction DID estimator and PPML = canonical difference-in-difference using Poisson pseudo-likelihood regression with multiple levels of fixed effects. *Source:* Authors' calculations.

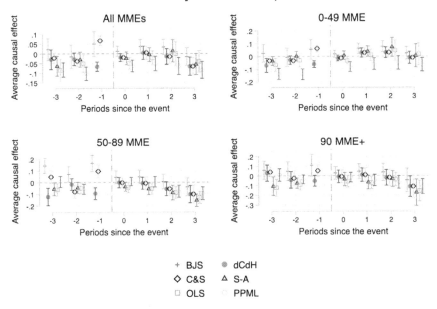

Fig. C2. Event Study of Commonly Diverted Opioids, All MMEs and Medical Dispensary Openings (No Mandatory PDMP). *Note:* Dots indicate the coefficient on the indicator variable for years prior to and after medical cannabis dispensaries opened; shading represents the 95% confidence intervals. Average causal effect should be interpreted as semi-elasticities. BJS = Borusyak et al. (2024) Imputation Estimator, C&S = Callaway and Sant'Anna (2021) DID Estimator, OLS = canonical difference-in-difference using OLS with two-way fixed-effects, S-A = Sun and Abraham's (2021) Event Study Interaction DID estimator and PPML = Canonical difference-in-difference using Poisson pseudo-likelihood regression with multiple levels of fixed effects. *Source:* Authors' calculations.

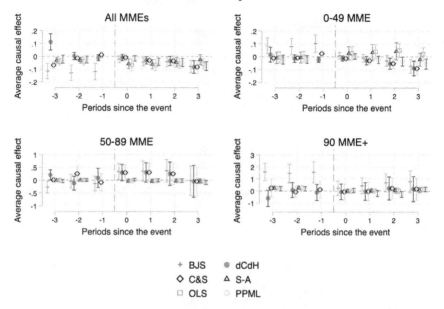

Fig. C3. Event Study of Less Commonly Diverted Opioids, All MMEs and Medical Dispensary Openings (No Mandatory PDMP). *Note:* Dots indicate the coefficient on the indicator variable for years prior to and after medical cannabis dispensaries opened; shading represents the 95% confidence intervals. Average causal effect should be interpreted as semi-elasticities. BJS = Borusyak et al. (2024) Imputation Estimator, C&S = Callaway and Sant'Anna (2021) DID Estimator, OLS = canonical difference-in-difference using OLS with two-way fixed-effects, S-A = Sun and Abraham's (2021) Event Study Interaction DID estimator and PPML = Canonical difference-in-difference using Poisson pseudo-likelihood regression with multiple levels of fixed effects. *Source:* Authors' calculations.

THE PREVALENCE, TRENDS AND HETEROGENEITY IN MATERNAL SMOKING AROUND BIRTH BETWEEN THE 1930s AND 1970s

Stephanie von Hinke[a], Jonathan James[b], Emil Sorensen[a], Hans H. Sievertsen[a] and Nicolai Vitt[a]

[a]*University of Bristol, UK*
[b]*University of Bath, UK*

ABSTRACT

This chapter shows the prevalence, trends and heterogeneity in maternal smoking around birth in the United Kingdom (UK), focussing on the war and post-war reconstruction period in which there exists surprisingly little systematic data on (maternal) smoking behaviours. Within this context, the authors highlight relevant events, the release of new information about the harms of smoking and changes in (government) policy aimed at reducing smoking prevalence. The authors show stark changes in smoking prevalence over a 30-year period, highlight the onset of the social gradient in smoking as well as genetic heterogeneities in smoking trends.

Keywords: Maternal smoking around birth; war and post-war period; social science genetics; UK Biobank; ESSGN

1. INTRODUCTION

The impacts of prenatal smoking on offspring health have been a topic of research for over a century. Animal studies from the early to mid-1900s showed a reduction in foetal growth, birth weight and red blood cell counts after prenatal exposure to tobacco smoke and nicotine, as well as an increase in prenatal and neonatal deaths (see e.g. Fleig, 1908; Guillain & Gy, 1907; Pechstein & Reynolds,

---

Recent Developments in Health Econometrics
Contributions to Economic Analysis, Volume 297, 201–227
Copyright © 2024 Stephanie von Hinke, Jonathan James, Emil Sorensen, Hans H. Sievertsen and Nicolai Vitt
Published under exclusive licence by Emerald Publishing Limited
ISSN: 0573-8555/doi:10.1108/S0573-855520240000297010

1937; Schoeneck, 1941; Willson, 1942). Others noted similar growth restrictions for tobacco exposure in early life (see e.g. Fleig, 1908; Richon & Perrin, 1908), suggesting this to be driven by nicotine-inhibiting lactation (e.g. Hatcher & Crosby, 1927) or by the secretion of nicotine into milk (e.g. Willson, 1942).

The first research papers that showed the detrimental impacts of tobacco on *human* health were published in the late 1940s and early 1950s (Doll & Hill, 1950; Kennaway & Kennaway, 1947), soon followed by research focussing on the impacts of *prenatal* smoking on offspring outcomes around birth. These studies showed that the results from animal studies extended to humans, as maternal smoking was associated with foetal growth restrictions and an increase in the likelihood of infants being premature, with stronger associations for heavier smokers (Simpson, 1957). These associations were robust to controlling for a range of confounders such as maternal age, parity and social circumstances (Lowe, 1959). Since then, many subsequent studies have shown the adverse impacts of *in utero* exposure to tobacco and cigarette smoke on outcomes around birth (e.g. birth weight; Pereira et al., 2022; Rantakallio, 1978b; Walker et al., 2009; Yang et al., 2020) but also the impacts of prenatal smoking on outcomes in the longer run (e.g. hospital admissions, childhood height, educational outcomes, child behaviour; Butler & Goldstein, 1973; Dolan et al., 2016; Rantakallio, 1978a).[1] While the harmful effects of smoking during pregnancy are well-known today and maternal smoking rates are lower than decades ago (see e.g. Fertig, 2010), we have limited evidence on how the prevalence of maternal smoking developed during the period when much of the evidence was established, as well as how maternal smoking rates varied across different groups in society.

This paper explores the prevalence, trends and heterogeneity in maternal smoking around birth in the UK. We focus on women who had children between the late 1930s and early 1970s. Between 2006 and 2010, these *children* were asked whether their mother smoked around the time of their birth, allowing us to get an interesting insight into maternal smoking during the war and post-war recon-struction period. We also highlight two types of heterogeneity in the prevalence and trends of smoking behaviour during this time: by social class and by indi-viduals' genetic variation.

Perhaps surprisingly, very little systematic individual-level data exists about the prevalence of smoking in the UK (especially, *female* or *maternal* smoking) during this period, its heterogeneity and its potential drivers. An exception is Forster and Jones (2001) who use retrospective individual-level data on smoking, or Jones (1989a), who model aggregate smoking data between 1954 and 1986. Instead, most systematic data collection on smoking focuses on the post-1970s period. This is perhaps unexpected, since there was much research on the potential impacts of smoking (e.g. lung cancer) and even some on the impact of maternal smoking on offspring (see above). These studies, however, tended to

---

[1]Given the difficulty of accounting for the endogeneity of maternal smoking, the empirical specifications used range from simple linear regressions to instrumental variable regressions to mother fixed effects and matching approaches.

STEPHANIE VON HINKE ET AL.

collect their own data using specific population subgroups (e.g. hospital patients) or small samples. This means that relatively little is known about the prevalence, trends and heterogeneity in maternal smoking during this period. For example, although Wald and Nicolaides-Bouman (1991) provide 'a comprehensive description of smoking in the United Kingdom by amalgamating the published and unpublished data from various sources', with one chapter focussing solely on smoking during pregnancy, it merely highlights the prevalence of prenatal smoking in a limited and selected number years from 1958 to 1986. It also highlights the social gradient in maternal smoking in the 1980s but focuses on a few years and does not show any statistics for the pre-1958 period.

We use the UK Biobank, a prospective cohort study that focuses on the health and well-being of over half a million individuals living in the UK. Participants are born between the late 1930s and early 1970s and the data record rich information on participants' health and economic outcomes in older age. Individuals are also asked whether their mother smoked around their birth. This is the main information that we use in this paper. We also highlight relevant events, the release of new information about the harms of smoking and changes in (government) policy around this time period that may explain the (change in) trends and gradients that we observe. Note, however, that because of the many changes in society and government policy at the time, some happening relatively close together, we do not attempt to identify the impact of these separate events. The chapter is therefore merely descriptive, showing the trends and gradients that we observe over this period.

Although this is a large UK study, it is important to note that it is not representative of the population in the UK. On average, UK Biobank participants are healthier and wealthier (Fry et al., 2017), implying that we cannot necessarily generalise our findings to the full UK population, and our descriptive statistics and trends capture variation in maternal smoking among a more select group of women in the UK. Nevertheless, it allows us to describe systematic trends in maternal prenatal smoking during the second half of the 20th century for a group of slightly wealthier and healthier individuals: something that has not been possible until now. Furthermore, merging in data on occupational socio-economic status (SES) at the local area level from the 1951 Census allows us to explore social gradients in prenatal smoking among this group as well as how this changed over time. Finally, exploiting the genetic data available in the UK Biobank allows us to explore genetic heterogeneity in these trends. This sheds further light on the variation in maternal smoking and *when* as well as *how* this changes over time.

The prevalence, trends and heterogeneity in smoking during this time period are important and interesting for multiple reasons. In addition to it shedding light on societal norms and values during this period, it allows us to better understand societal changes in smoking perceptions, and how policy may have helped shape these. Indeed, understanding trends in maternal smoking rates – and heterogeneity thereof – within the societal context of the time may help us learn more about *how* individuals respond to information and (government) policy, as well as *who* is most likely to respond. Furthermore, because the early life environment

204

can have life-long and irreversible impacts on offspring from birth to older age, a better understanding of the trends in maternal smoking during our period of observation may explain some of the variation in outcomes in adulthood and older age that we observe nowadays.[2]

Our paper speaks to the literature on the determinants of smoking, such as those identifying tax elasticities for starting and quitting smoking (see e.g. Forster & Jones, 2001, who investigate smoking in general (rather than *maternal* smoking) during this time period), studies that explore the determinants of starting and quitting (see e.g. Etilé & Jones, 2011; Jones, 1994; Yen & Jones, 1996) as well as the best ways of modelling smoking decisions (see e.g. Jones, 1989a, 1989b, 1989c, 1992; Jones & Labeaga, 2003). Our paper, however, is descriptive in nature. Rather than identifying the determinants of smoking behaviour or highlighting methodological issues that are relevant in modelling smoking behaviour, we provide a thorough description of maternal smoking across a 30-year period, highlighting relevant social, contextual and legislative changes for this generation of mothers.

The rest of this chapter is structured as follows: Section 2 provides a background to the chapter, discussing the history of smoking regulation and other (government) policy that may affect smoking take-up. The data are described in Section 3, showing the general trends in maternal smoking during this time period, with the heterogeneity analysis shown in Section 4. We conclude in Section 5.

2. BACKGROUND

Tobacco was one of the few items that was never rationed during the Second World War, since the government thought doing so would be bad for morale, and it would be in conflict with tobacco's revenue-raising function (Zweiniger-Bargielowska, 2000). However, demand far exceeded supply, leading to a well-functioning black market, where demand was subdued due to the high price, with some anecdotal evidence suggesting that tobacco was generally sold on the black market for three times its normal price.

Tobacco taxes at this time were relatively low. In April 1947, however, the then-Chancellor of the Exchequer, Hugh Dalton, dramatically increased the tobacco customs duty. He stated that he would raise this 'from tomorrow by about 50 per cent [...] The effect of this increase will be that the price of a packet of 20 cigarettes will be raised from 2s. 4d. to 3s. 4d.'[3] The rationale for the increase was not to improve health or to increase tax revenue. Rather, the concern was that the vast majority of tobacco consumed was imported from the United States and 'to satisfy this insatiable demand, we are drawing heavily and improvidently on the dollars

---

[2]Indeed, adult outcomes are shaped by the early life environment, including nutrition, alcohol, smoking, disease, mental health, economic conditions, pollution and so on (for reviews, see e.g. Almond & Currie, 2011a, 2011b; Almond et al., 2018).
[3]Hansard, 15 April 1947.

which we earn with our exports. [. . .] I regard the saving of dollars as much more important than an increase in the revenue in this connection.' Indeed, the budget was dubbed a 'save the dollars' budget.[4] The tax rise implied an overnight 43% increase in the price of a pack of 20 cigarettes.[5]

In 1948, however, health was on the minds of the Labour administration. On 5th July, the National Health Service (NHS) was established, following the 1942 Beveridge report which set out the degree to which there were social and health inequalities in the UK. The NHS had three main goals: free provision of healthcare, access based on clinical need and equalisation of access to medical services. The NHS was funded through general taxation and was free at the point of use. Before the establishment of the NHS, healthcare was mainly provided through private doctors and hospitals, and limited access to free healthcare was available through voluntary hospitals and local authority-run hospitals under the Poor Law. Local authorities were in charge of a number of public health programmes including ante-natal clinics and domiciliary midwifery. Once the NHS was introduced, hospitals were taken into public ownership, and general practitioners (GPs) became contractors that were paid a set fee per treatment. Local authorities remained in charge of family health services.

The NHS dramatically changed women's ability to access healthcare. Lührmann and Wilson (2018) document the impact that the introduction of the NHS had on health outcomes. In particular, they find a drop in infant mortality for the affected cohorts. The increase in access to both pre- and post-natal care would have been greater for those who were likely to be uninsured prior to the introduction of the NHS. Indeed, Lührmann and Wilson (2018) find larger mortality reductions in areas with lower expected levels of health insurance (proxied by the proportion of illegitimate births). While ante-natal clinics remained in the control of local authorities, women now had free access to GPs and – as part of that – maternity services.[6] This greater access to primary care may have potentially provided women with greater access to information about the dangers of smoking via their GP as that information diffused through the medical community.

It had been long thought that smoking was dangerous and deleterious to health. The first anti-smoking literature was published in 1604 by King James I of England. In his 'Counterblaste to Tobacco', he described smoking as 'a custom loathsome to the eye, hateful to the nose, harmful to the brain and dangerous to the lungs' (King, 1604). Then the RCP met in 1605 to discuss the King's pamphlet; however, they dismissed his views (ASH, n.d.). It was not until some 300 years later that the medical and academic community began to catch up with the King.

The key publication showing the adverse effects of smoking was that by Doll and Hill (1950). Using a case-control study that examined smoking habits of lung cancer

---

[4]Hugh Dalton's Budget, 1947

[5]To ease the impact on old-age pensioners, MPs urged Dalton to provide OAPs access to cheap tobacco. The government agreed and from October 1947, OAPs who could prove they were 'habitual smokers' could purchase a limited amount of tobacco each week at a reduced price (Singleton, 2023).

[6]'Your New National Health Service', 5 July 1948.

patients, they showed that those who smoked were 20 times more likely to develop lung cancer compared to non-smokers. They also found that the risk of lung cancer increased with the number of cigarettes smoked per day and the duration of smoking. Simultaneously, in the United States (US), Wynder and Graham (1950) were working on the same issue and discovered the same pattern. Ronald Fisher was very critical of this work. He was concerned that the estimates reflected correlations rather than causation and was strongly against anti-smoking publicity, which he dubbed propaganda (Fisher, 1959). Over the next decade, further work established the link between smoking and carcinoma of the lung as well as other diseases and made attempts to establish that this relationship was causal. Doll and Hill extended their work, starting 'The British Doctors Study' in 1951, where they sent a questionnaire on smoking habits to all registered British doctors. It was the first large prospective study and established a link between tobacco smoking and the risk of dying from lung cancer (Doll & Hill, 1954), as well as myocardial infarction and chronic obstructive pulmonary disease (Doll & Hill, 1956).

Evidence on the negative effects of smoking during pregnancy began to come to light towards the latter part of the 1950s and early 1960s. The evidence was pointing to smoking leading to babies being born of lower birth weight (Frazier et al., 1961; Lowe, 1959; Simpson, 1957). However, as documented by the Royal College of Physicians (RCPs), the evidence at the time did not conclude that there were greater complications surrounding births.

On 7th March 1962, the RCP published 'Smoking and Health', a report highlighting the dangers of smoking for human health. The report was written with the general public in mind as opposed to the medical profession. The RCP, for the first time, put out a press release and held a press conference. The report generated attention from the media in both the press and on television.[7] On 12th March, there was a special edition of the British Broadcasting Corporation (BBC) flagship current affairs programme, *Panorama*, discussing the report, including interviews with scientists and members of the public (Berridge, 2007).[8]

The work of Doll and Hill formed the basis of the RCP's report. Smoking was linked not only to lung cancer but also other serious conditions such as bronchitis and cardiovascular disease.[9] The publication of the report was an important point in the history of public health: it was no longer tied to just the provision of health services. Furthermore, it led to the wider dissemination of medical research to the public rather than it being discussed only within the medical community.

The RCP report covered the alternative hypotheses that had been put forward to attempt to explain the relationship between smoking and lung cancer, including omitted variables that determined both smoking and lung cancer, the

---

[7]See the archive footage from the BBC on the report.

[8]Although the relationship between parental smoking and children's birthweight was discussed, it was only afforded one paragraph in the 70-page pamphlet.

[9]Within the RCP, there was a discussion that suggested the report should also espouse the dangers and risks of air pollution. This did not happen in order to prevent the message that smoking led to lung cancer and other health problems being watered down (Berridge, 2007).

correlation between heavy smoking and heavy alcohol use, falling death rates of tuberculosis, reverse causality, that smoking determines the location of cancer but not the cancer itself and motor vehicle pollution; each of these was dismissed.

The RCP report also gained traction in the US, with the US Surgeon General publishing an equivalent report in 1964. Aizer and Stroud (2010) examine the effect of the Surgeon General's report on both maternal smoking and the health of newborns. In particular, they focus on the education-health gradient, finding that the gradient opens up after the publication of the report. This is apparent not only for smoking, but they also find differences in birth weight and foetal death. James (Forthcoming) documents what happened to the education-smoking gradient in the UK after the publication of the RCP report. Using a contemporaneous survey of the general population he finds, similar to Aizer and Stroud (2010), a widening of the education-smoking gradient after the report's publication. He also finds significant gaps in the knowledge of the dangers of smoking by education 20 years after the report was published.

The RCP report made several suggestions for ways in which the government could act to reduce smoking. There was an emphasis on education, particularly for those of school age. Other recommendations included the use of television and radio media campaigns, restricting the sale of tobacco products and smoking bans in public places, which did not come into effect in the UK until over 40 years later. The report also suggested that the government provide anti-smoking clinics to help individuals quit smoking, and it called for higher (or differential) cigarette and tobacco taxes.

Restrictions on the advertising of tobacco was another recommendation of the report. Independent Television (ITV) was set up as an alternative service to the BBC in 1954, and it was funded through advertising. Although advertising was strictly controlled (Woodhouse, 1971), cigarettes were allowed to be advertised.[10] This came to an end in 1965, when the 1964 Television Act came into effect, banning all advertising of cigarettes on television. Loose tobacco and cigars could still be advertised on television, and advertising elsewhere (such as on radio or on billboards) remained permitted.

In summary, in a relatively short time since the end of the Second World War, the public's understanding of the dangers of smoking had evolved, and towards the second half of this period, the government had acted to try to reduce the harms that it caused. Alongside greater knowledge of the dangers of smoking, people now had greater access to medical care, particularly so for women and for those of lower socio-economic status. Although the information was not targeted at pregnant women, they may have been more exposed since they have regular medical appointments, and their pregnancy may make them more responsive to information.

---

[10]Six minutes per hour were allowed, sponsorship of programmes was not permitted, and the scripts and advertisements themselves were reviewed by representatives of the 'Independent Television Authority' (ITA).

3. DATA

We use the UK Biobank data, a major resource that follows the health and well-being of approximately 500,000 individuals in the UK aged 40–69 between 2006–2010. They are born between 1938 and 1971, with the majority born in the late 1940s through to the early 1960s. Participants have provided information on their health and well-being and given blood, urine and saliva samples; all participants have also been genotyped.

An advantage of the UK Biobank is that it is a very large sample of individuals for whom we observe an extensive amount of relevant health (as well as social and economic) outcomes later in life. However, it has little information on individuals' early life environment. More specifically, the data include the location of birth, (self-reported) birth weight, an indicator for whether the participants were breastfed and an indicator for whether the participants' mothers smoked during their pregnancy.[11] Our analysis explores trends in the latter, investigating how maternal smoking during pregnancy changed from the late 1930s to the early 1970s.

We are also interested in heterogeneity in the trends of maternal prenatal smoking across two dimensions. First, we explore the social gradient of maternal prenatal smoking and how this has changed over time. Since we do not observe participants' SES at birth, we merge in external data on the SES at the local area level, proxied by residents' social class and obtained from the 1951 Census. The 1951 Census classifies individuals into five social classes based on occupation (Register Office, 1960) and records the frequencies of each class at the Local Government District (henceforth: district) level. We exploit individuals' location (i.e. eastings and northings) of birth to identify the district in which they were born and use that to define 'high social class districts' by whether the district's proportion of residents in professional and intermediate occupations is above the median of all districts in the 1951 census year. The 1951 Census also records the number of residents by groups of educational attainment. We use an above-median proportion of residents who left education aged 20 years or older as an alternative definition of high social class districts in a robustness check.

Second, we explore heterogeneity in the trends of maternal smoking by genetic 'predisposition' using the molecular genetic data in the UK Biobank. See Appendix B for more detail on the genetic data and how our genetic variables are constructed. Whilst we do observe molecular genetic information of UK Biobank participants, we do not observe the genetic variation of their *mothers*, whose smoking decisions are our main variable of interest. However, as children inherit genetic variation from their parents, we proxy the mother's genetics by those of the child, exploiting that children with high genetic predisposition for smoking would likely have had parents who are genetically predisposed to smoking. We use two variables capturing genetic variation in the form of single base pair substitutions called single-nucleotide polymorphisms (SNPs). First, we use a

---

[11]The exact question in the UK Biobank is 'Did your mother smoke regularly around the time when you were born?'

single SNP on the nicotine receptor gene CHRNA5 (RS16969968) that is well-known to correlate with how many cigarettes an individual smokes per day (see e.g. Bierut, 2010; Liu et al., 2019; The Tobacco and Genetics Consortium, 2010). For each individual, we encode the SNP by the minor allele account (taking values 0, 1 or 2), such that the number of cigarettes smoked per day increases with allele count. As an individual always receives one copy of each chromosome from their mother, two risk alleles in the child imply that the mother had at least one risk allele. Analogously, zero risk alleles imply that the mother had at most one risk allele. We exploit this to construct two subsamples to compare mothers of children with two risk alleles to those of children with zero risk alleles, thereby comparing mothers with respectively a higher and lower genetic predisposition for smoking intensity.

Second, since existing genome-wide association studies have linked many SNPs to smoking, we use two polygenic indices (PGIs) to capture the combined effect of all such SNPs and thereby increase the predictive power for smoking behaviour compared to a single SNP. We obtain our polygenic indices from the PGI repository (Becker et al., 2021), which contains pre-computed polygenic indices for common outcomes in the UK Biobank. We focus on the polygenic indices for 'ever smoked' and 'number of cigarettes per day', allowing us to look at genetic predisposition across both the extensive and intensive margins. We standardise all polygenic indices to have mean zero, standard deviation one. Due to the child inheriting their genetic make-up from their parents, the polygenic index of the child (which we observe) will be positively correlated with the polygenic index of the mother (which we do not observe). We again exploit this to construct two subsamples of mothers with respectively higher and lower genetic 'predisposition' to smoking by splitting at the median of the distribution of the child's polygenic index. Table B1 in Appendix B shows the predictive power of RS16969968 and the polygenic indices for both the child's and mother's smoking behaviour.

We refer to genetic 'predisposition' in quotation marks. This reflects the fact that their effect is not immutable and not necessarily biological. Instead, poly-genic indices can be interpreted as the best linear genetic predictor of the outcome of interest (Mills et al., 2020). In addition to potential biological effects, the association may capture gene-environment *correlation* (e.g. individuals selecting into specific environments based on their genetic variation; genetic variation invoking environmental responses). They can also capture 'genetic nurture': an environment shaped by *parental* genetic variation (see e.g. Kong et al., 2018). This means that polygenic indices can capture genetic as well as environmental components. Note, however, that because genes are fixed at conception, the environment cannot affect individuals' genetic variation; there is no reverse causality.

We make the following sample selection. First, to merge in data from the 1951 census, we drop individuals with missing birth co-ordinates or with co-ordinates that we cannot link to a district in England or Wales. We also drop 398 individuals born in two districts for which data on social classes is missing. This results in 404,711 individuals. Second, we drop the last two birth cohorts born in 1970 and 1971 as they are very small compared to earlier cohorts (118 and 1 individuals, respectively, compared to 1,949 born in 1969), leaving us with 404,592 individuals. We next drop those with missing data on maternal prenatal smoking, resulting in a final sample size of 348,188 individuals.

For the analyses using genetic data, we additionally drop genetic outliers, individuals of non-European genetic ancestry and those without a polygenic index in the PGI repository. See Appendix B for details on this procedure. This leaves us with a final sample size of 334,573 individuals for the analyses using genetic data.

Fig. 1 presents the proportion of children in our sample who indicate their mother smoked on the vertical axis by birth cohort on the horizontal axis. Maternal smoking rates increased quickly during the late 1930s and the 1940s, from approximately 18% in 1938 to 35% in 1949. In the 1950s, aggregate maternal smoking rates were initially stable at approximately 35% and then started to fall during the second half of the decade reaching 31% in 1959. This downward trend continued throughout the 1960s until the end of our study period.

The vertical lines in Fig. 1 mark a series of potentially important events for the evolution of (maternal) smoking, as described in the background section. The first line indicates the end of the Second World War, the second shows 1947 which saw a large tax increase on tobacco and next is the introduction of the NHS in 1948. The fourth line is 1950 which saw the publication of Doll and Hill (1950)'s key work that began to establish the link between smoking and cancer. The next line shows the publication of the first report by the RCP on the negative health effects of smoking in

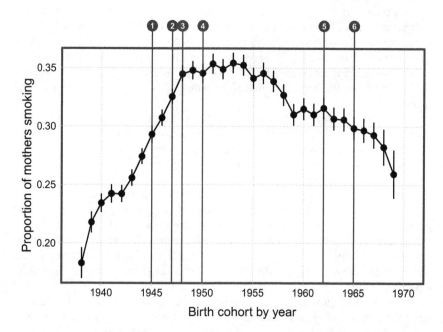

Fig. 1. Trends in Maternal Prenatal Smoking; 1938–1969. *Notes:* (1) WW2 ends, (2) tax hike, (3) introduction of NHS, (4) first paper on smoking and cancer, (5) RCP report and (6) ban on TV advertising of cigarettes. See the main text for details.

1962, and the final line shows 1965, the year when cigarette advertising was banned on television in the UK.

4. HETEROGENEITY IN SMOKING TRENDS

Building on the general trends shown in Fig. 1, we now investigate how these trends differ by the local social class shares and genetic predisposition.

4.1 By District Socioeconomic Status

Fig. 2 presents the trends in maternal prenatal smoking by the SES of one's district of birth, proxied by whether the proportion of district residents from high social classes in 1951 is above vs below the median proportion taken across all districts in that year. From 1938 to 1945, the levels and trends were almost identical across the two groups, starting at around 17–9% in 1938 and increasing to almost 30% of mothers smoking during pregnancy at the end of Second World War. After the war, a gap of around two to three percentage points opened between the two groups, with higher maternal smoking rates in low social class districts. This gap grew further after the introduction of the NHS in 1948. Following the first evidence of the harmful effects of

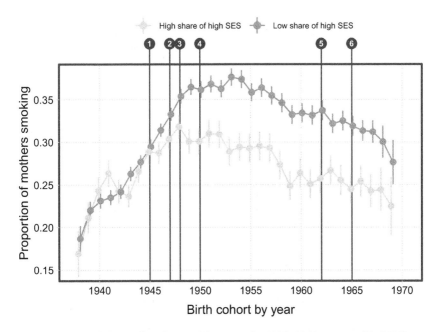

Fig. 2. Social Gradient in Smoking Trends; 1938–1969. *Notes:* (1) WW2 ends, (2) tax hike, (3) introduction of NHS, (4) first paper on smoking and cancer, (5) RCP report and (6) ban on TV advertising of cigarettes. Defines high SES as individuals born in districts with an above-median proportion of residents in professional and intermediate occupations in the 1951 Census.

smoking in the beginning of the 1950s, the gap increased to almost six percentage points. In 1953, the maternal smoking rate in low social class districts was 38% compared to 29% in high social class districts. Since the mid-1950s the gap between the groups has been stable, with some signs of narrowing in the last years of our study period, when the low social class group had a rate of 28% compared to 22% for the high social class group.[12]

4.2 By Genetic Variation

We now investigate the patterns in maternal smoking by children's genetic variation as proxies for the maternal genetic 'predisposition' for smoking. In Fig. 3, we split the sample by the individuals' minor allele counts for SNP RS16969968 which correlates with individuals' (and their mothers') smoking behaviour. In contrast to Fig. 2, the trends and levels are similar until the mid-1950s when the two lines start to diverge. As expected, we observe slightly higher maternal smoking rates for offspring with an

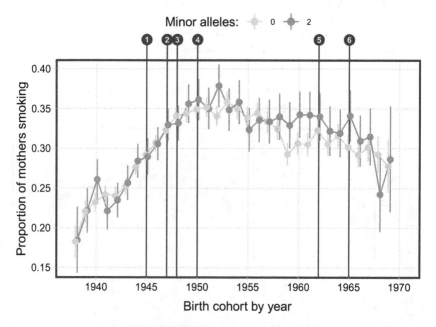

Fig. 3. Maternal Smoking by Offspring's rs16969968 Minor Allele Count; 1938–1969. *Notes:* (1) WW2 ends, (2) tax hike, (3) introduction of NHS, (4) first paper on smoking and cancer, (5) RCP report and (6) ban on TV advertising of cigarettes.

---

[12] In Fig. A1 in the Appendix, we split the sample by district shares of educational attainment. The pattern is similar to Fig. 9.2 with low education districts mimicking the low social class districts and high education districts mimicking the high social class districts.

allele count of two (whose mothers must have had at least one minor allele) compared to those with a count of zero. However, this gap only persists for about a decade; the levels are again indistinguishable across the two groups in the last years of our study period, potentially due to the smaller sample sizes towards the end of the observation window.[13]

In Fig. 4, we study heterogeneity by the median split of the individuals' polygenic index for the extensive margin of smoking (ever smoked), which correlates with the smoking statuses of their mothers (see Table B1, Appendix B). Compared to the earlier figures, the first difference is that the median split creates two groups with very different levels of maternal smoking throughout the study period. The above median group had a maternal smoking rate starting at about 21% in 1938 and increasing to more than 40% in the early 1950s, before it started to fall in the late 1950s. However, this fall is limited, and for the last cohorts, we still observe rates of about 34% in the above median group. The below median group started at a level of about six percentage points lower in 1938, and the rate

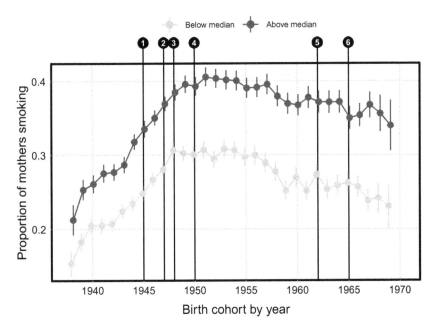

Fig. 4. Maternal Smoking by Offspring's Polygenic Index for 'Ever Smoked'; 1938–1969. *Notes:* (1) WW2 ends, (2) tax hike, (3) introduction of NHS, (4) first paper on smoking and cancer, (5) RCP report and (6) ban on TV advertising of cigarettes.

---

[13]In Fig. A2 in the Appendix, we additionally include offspring with an allele count of 1 in the analysis.

peaked a bit earlier than for the above median group at around 30% in the late 1940s. This gap persists throughout the remaining study period, and by the late 1960s, the gap is about 11 percentage points. In Fig. A3 in the Appendix, we show the patterns for the intensive margin of genetic predisposition and split the sample based on the polygenic index for 'cigarettes per day'. We observe level differences across these two groups throughout the period, except for the first 2 years. Similar to our earlier findings, the gap widens and persists after the Second World War.

In summary, we observe no social gradient in maternal smoking rates until after the Second World War. In both low and high social class districts, we observe a smoking rate increasing from around 17–19% in 1938 to about 30% at the end of the war. After the war – coinciding with the tax changes, the introduction of the NHS and the first evidence of the harmful effects of smoking – we observe a gap between the maternal smoking rates in high and low social class districts, with a higher rate in lower social class districts peaking at 38% in the early 1950s, about nine percentage points higher than for high social class districts. The gap between the groups remained throughout the period, and even for children born in the last years of our study period, 1968 and 1969, we observe a gap of about five to six percentage points.

Looking at heterogeneity by polygenic index of the offspring, we observe level differences earlier on than for social class, especially when splitting the sample by genetic predisposition for 'ever smoking'. However, also for these groups do we see a widening gap afterthe Second World War. From 1938 up until the war, the maternal smoking rates increase in both above- and below-median polygenic index individuals, but the gap widened from about six percentage points in 1938 to around nine to 10 percentage points in the early 1950s.

5. CONCLUSION

This paper presents trends in the prevalence of maternal smoking around birth in England and Wales between 1938 and 1969 and explores heterogeneities of these trends with regard to district-level social class and genetic predisposition for smoking. Maternal smoking rates increased quickly during the late 1930s and the 1940s, from approximately 18% in 1938 to 35% in 1949. Our heterogeneity analysis highlights two distinct periods during this time of substantial increase in maternal smoking. During the Second World War, when tobacco was in limited supply and expensive to purchase, mothers in high- and low-social-class districts displayed very similar smoking behaviours and even the gap in smoking rates between those with an above- and below-median genetic predisposition for smoking was relatively small. This suggests that the high price of tobacco at this time may have subdued demand, preventing mothers living in disadvantaged areas (or with a high genetic predisposition) from smoking as much as they would have liked. Following the war, when these supply constraints eased, a gap in maternal smoking opens up between districts of a high and low social class and the gap by genetic predisposition widens. The large tobacco tax increase in 1947 and the NHS introduction in 1948 fall in this immediate post-war period, but due to the short time gaps between these events, it is not possible to distinguish their (potential) impact from the effects of the post-war easing of tobacco supply constraints.

During the 1950s, aggregate maternal smoking rates were initially stable at approximately 35% and then started to fall during the second half of the decade reaching 31% in 1959. Again, this overall trend masks some heterogeneities with regards to social class. Smoking rates among mothers from high social class districts, on the one hand, followed a downwards trend throughout most of the 1950s; indeed, the highest smoking prevalence we observe for this group was in 1948. Maternal smoking in low social class districts, on the other hand, continued to increase until 1953 and only began to fall thereafter. This may suggest that information on the early evidence linking smoking with adverse health (in particular the link with cancer shown by Doll & Hill, 1950) may have spread differently in districts of high and low social class.

The downward trend in aggregate maternal smoking rates continued throughout the 1960s. As the RCP report was published and cigarettes were banned from being advertised on television, the rates for both high- and low-class areas continued to fall as seen in our heterogeneity analysis. There are some signs of narrowing between these groups in the latter part of our analysis period. Trends for those with high and low genetic predisposition for smoking were relatively similar throughout the 1950s and 1960s; furthermore, these trends did not differ as the information on the health risks of smoking diffused through the population nor when the ban on television advertising of cigarette was introduced.

These potential links between historic policy changes, prices as well as information campaigns and the (differential) trends in maternal smoking are merely descriptive. The high frequency of relevant events during the time period we consider does not allow any causal interpretations. Existing research in health economics has, however, provided extensive causal evidence on the impact of these and other factors. Higher cigarette prices (or taxes) have been found to decrease prenatal smoking (see e.g. Colman et al., 2003; Evans & Ringel, 1999; Levy & Meara, 2006; Lien & Evans, 2005) although the reported price elasticities vary substantially between studies. While early cross-sectional research suggested smoking prevalence among youths to be strongly negatively affected by price or tax increases (e.g. Chaloupka & Grossman, 1996; Lewitt et al., 1981), more recent causal evidence shows that this price sensitivity of youth smoking is quite limited (Carpenter & Cook, 2008; DeCicca et al., 2008; Hansen et al., 2017; Lillard et al., 2013; Nonnemaker & Farrelly, 2011). Similarly, price and tax sensitivity of adult smoking behaviour has been shown to be only limited (see e.g. DeCicca & McLeod, 2008; Farrelly et al., 2001; Forster & Jones, 2001; MacLean et al., 2016; Sloan & Trogdon, 2004), especially when it comes to smoking initiation. There is furthermore evidence that adults compensate for tax increases by extracting more nicotine from each cigarette (Adda & Cornaglia, 2006) and by switching to cigarettes that are higher in nicotine and tar (Farrelly et al., 2004).

Providing information on the adverse health effects of smoking is a commonly used policy instrument. There is substantial evidence that the first large-scale reports on these adverse health consequences of smoking in the UK and US lead to a reduction in smoking and a switch to filter cigarettes with a lower tobacco content (see e.g. Atkinson & Skegg, 1973; Schneider et al., 1981; Sumner, 1971; Warner, 1977). Recent evidence shows, however, that this new information mainly affected smoking behaviours among more highly educated parts of the population, thus widening the educational gap in smoking (Aizer and Stroud, 2010; de Walque, 2010; James, Forthcoming). Health messages on tobacco products have been introduced in many countries since the adverse health consequence of smoking became known. Both the introduction of early text-format warnings and later pictorial warnings have been studied, with the evidence suggesting moderate reductions in smoking after mandatory warning messages were introduced (see e.g. Abernethy & Teel, 1986; Bardsley & Olekalns, 1999; Hammond, 2011; Meier & Licari, 1997; Monárrez-Espino et al., 2014; Noar et al., 2016). Recent evidence by Kuehnle (2019) finds that pictorial warnings decreased smoking rates in Australia by encouraging smoking cessation.

Restrictions on the advertisement of tobacco products began shortly after the health consequences of smoking became widely known. Partial bans on advertisements have been shown to have limited impact on cigarette consumption in the long-run whereas comprehensive bans have been found to be more effective (see e.g. reviews by Blecher, 2008; Saffer & Chaloupka, 2000).

Smoking bans in public places have become a common policy to limit the externalities of smoking, and their causal impact on smoking behaviours have been studied e.g. by Evans et al. (1999), Carpenter (2009), Adda and Cornaglia (2010), Bitler et al. (2010), Anger et al. (2011), Carpenter et al. (2011) and Jones et al. (2015). This causal evidence is mixed and does not support a clear impact of smoking bans on smoking behaviour, but there is some evidence that the bans reduced second-hand smoke exposure. However, smoking bans have also been suggested to shift smoking to private places, thus increasing second-hand smoke exposure outside of public places (Adda & Cornaglia, 2010).

Causal evidence on genetic heterogeneities relating to smoking behaviours is sparse since this area of research is still relatively young. Pereira et al. (2022) examine whether the causal effects of maternal smoking on birth weight differ by genetic 'predisposition' for smoking, but find no evidence of such gene-environment interactions.

Beyond the descriptive nature of our analysis, the research presented in this chapter has some further limitations. First, the UK Biobank is not a representative sample of the UK population (Fry et al., 2017). Women, healthy individuals and those from less deprived areas are over-represented in the study sample.

Second, our data do not allow us to distinguish between trends in the general smoking behaviour of women and trends in the specific smoking behaviour during pregnancy. The maternal smoking variable used in our analysis captures both the overall prevalence of smoking as well as any changes in the likelihood to stop smoking during a pregnancy.

Finally, our measure of maternal smoking is based on a 40+ year recall by the children rather than a direct observation of smoking behaviour at the time of pregnancy. While this likely introduces some measurement error due to children not correctly recalling whether their mother smoked around the time of their birth, test–retest correlations in a subsample of participants which were asked the question a second time (at least two years after the first interview) are between 0.94 and 0.95 suggesting a strong consistency over time of the reported maternal smoking around birth. The unconventional measure furthermore allows us to study maternal smoking during a time for which no systematic data are available. It also allows us to link maternal smoking data during this period with genetic data and provides a much larger sample size than any historic survey data. As such, the data allow us to shed light on the stark trends in maternal smoking around pregnancy during the war and post-war reconstruction period and highlight the substantial heterogeneities in smoking behaviour during this time.

ACKNOWLEDGEMENTS

The authors would like to thank the GEIGHEI/ESSGN team for interesting discussions and comments on an earlier version of this paper. This research has been conducted using the UK Biobank Resource under Application Number 74002, as well as data provided through www.VisionofBritain.org.uk. It uses historical material which is copyright of the Great Britain Historical GIS Project and the University of Portsmouth. The authors gratefully acknowledge financial support from NORFACE DIAL (462-16-100) and the European Research Council (ERC) under the European Union's Horizon 2020 research and innovation programme (Grant agreement No. 851725). For the purpose of open access, the author(s) has applied a Creative Commons Attribution (CC BY) licence to any Author Accepted Manuscript version arising from this submission.

REFERENCES

Abernethy, A. M., & Teel, J. E. (1986). Advertising regulation's effect upon demand for cigarettes. *Journal of Advertising, 15*(4), 51–55.

Adda, J., & Cornaglia, F. (2006, August). Taxes, cigarette consumption, and smoking intensity. *The American Economic Review, 96*(4), 1013–1028. https://doi.org/10.1257/aer.96.4.1013

Adda, J., & Cornaglia, F. (2010, January). The effect of bans and taxes on passive smoking. *American Economic Journal: Applied Economics, 2*(1), 1–32. https://doi.org/10.1257/app.2.1.1

Aizer, A., & Stroud, L. (2010). *Education, knowledge and the evolution of disparities in health.* Tech. rep. NBER Working Paper No. 15840. National Bureau of Economic Research.

Almond, D., & Currie, J. (2011a). Human capital development before age 5. In *Handbook of labor economics* (pp. 1315–1486). Elsevier.

Almond, D., & Currie, J. (2011b). Killing me softly: The fetal origins hypothesis. *The Journal of Economic Perspectives, 25*(3), 153–172.

Almond, D., Currie, J., & Duque, V. (2018). Childhood circumstances and adult outcomes: Act II. *Journal of Economic Literature, 56*(4), 1360–1446.

Anger, S., Kvasnicka, M., & Siedler, T. (2011, May). One last puff? Public smoking bans and smoking behavior. *Journal of Health Economics, 30*(3), 591–601. https://doi.org/10.1016/j.jhealeco.2011.03.003

ASH. (n.d.). *Action on smoking and health: Key dates in the history of anti-tobacco campaigning*. https://web.archive.org/web/20150119124658/http://www.ash.org.uk/files/documents/ASH_741.pdf

Atkinson, A. B., & Skegg, J. L. (1973). Anti-smoking publicity and the demand for tobacco in the U.K. *The Manchester School, 41*(3), 265–282. https://doi.org/10.1111/j.1467-9957.1973.tb00081.x

Bardsley, P., & Olekalns, N. (1999). Cigarette and tobacco consumption: Have anti-smoking policies made a difference? *The Economic Record, 75*(3), 225–240. https://doi.org/10.1111/j.1475-4932.1999.tb02452.x

Becker, J., Burik, C. A. P., Goldman, G., Wang, N., Jayashankar, H., Bennett, M., Belsky, D. W., Linnér, R. K., Ahlskog, R., Kleinman, A., Hinds, D. A., 23andMe Research Group, Caspi, A., Corcoran, D. L., Moffitt, T. E., Poulton, R., Sugden, K., Williams, B. S., Mullan Harris, K., ... Okbay, A. (2021, December). Resource profile and user guide of the polygenic index repository. *Nature Human Behaviour, 5*(12), 1744–1758. ISSN: 2397-3374. https://doi.org/10.1038/s41562-021-01119-3

Berridge, V. (2007). Medicine and the public: The 1962 report of the royal college of physicians and the new public health. *Bulletin of the History of Medicine, 81*(1), 286.

Bierut, L. J. (2010). Convergence of genetic findings for nicotine dependence and smoking related diseases with chromosome 15q24-25. *Trends in Pharmacological Sciences, 31*(1), 46–51.

Bitler, M. P., Carpenter, C. S., & Zavodny, M. (2010). Effects of venue-specific state clean indoor air laws on smoking-related outcomes. *Health Economics, 19*(12), 1425–1440. https://doi.org/10.1002/hec.1559

Blecher, E. (2008, July). The impact of tobacco advertising bans on consumption in developing countries. *Journal of Health Economics, 27*(4), 930–942. https://doi.org/10.1016/j.jhealeco.2008.02.010

Butler, N. R., & Goldstein, H. (1973). Smoking in pregnancy and subsequent child development. *British Medical Journal, 4*(5892), 573–575.

Carpenter, C. S. (2009). The effects of local workplace smoking laws on smoking restrictions and exposure to smoke at work. *Journal of Human Resources, 44*(4), 1023–1046. https://doi.org/10.3368/jhr.44.4.1023

Carpenter, C., & Cook, P. J. (2008, March). Cigarette taxes and youth smoking: New evidence from national, state, and local youth risk behavior surveys. *Journal of Health Economics, 27*(2), 287–299. https://doi.org/10.1016/j.jhealeco.2007.05.008

Carpenter, C., Postolek, S., & Warman, C. (2011, August). Public-place smoking laws and exposure to environmental tobacco smoke (ETS). *American Economic Journal: Economic Policy, 3*(3), 35–61. https://doi.org/10.1257/pol.3.3.35

Chaloupka, F. J., & Grossman, M. (1996, September). *Price, tobacco control policies and youth smoking*. Tech. rep., w5740. National Bureau of Economic Research. https://doi.org/10.3386/w5740

Colman, G., Grossman, M., & Joyce, T. (2003, November). The effect of cigarette excise taxes on smoking before, during and after pregnancy. *Journal of Health Economics, 22*(6), 1053–1072. https://doi.org/10.1016/j.jhealeco.2003.06.003

de Walque, D. (2010). Education, information, and smoking decisions: Evidence from smoking histories in the United States, 1940–2000. *Journal of Human Resources, 45*(3) 682–717.

DeCicca, P., Kenkel, D., & Mathios, A. (2008, July). Cigarette taxes and the transition from youth to adult smoking: Smoking initiation, cessation, and participation. *Journal of Health Economics, 27*(4), 904–917. https://doi.org/10.1016/j.jhealeco.2008.02.008

DeCicca, P., & McLeod, L. (2008, July). Cigarette taxes and older adult smoking: Evidence from recent large tax increases. *Journal of Health Economics, 27*(4), 918–929. https://doi.org/10.1016/j.jhealeco.2007.11.005

Dolan, C. V., Geels, L., Vink, J. M., Van Beijsterveldt, C. E. M., Neale, M. C., Bartels, M., & Boomsma, D. I. (2016). Testing causal effects of maternal smoking during pregnancy on offspring's externalizing and internalizing behavior. *Behavior Genetics, 46*, 378–388.

Doll, R., & Hill, A. B. (1950). Smoking and carcinoma of the lung. *British Medical Journal, 2*(4682), 739–748.

Doll, R., & Hill, A. B. (1954). The mortality of doctors in relation to their smoking habits. *British Medical Journal, 1*(4877), 1451.

Doll, R., & Hill, A. B. (1956). Lung cancer and other causes of death in relation to smoking. *British Medical Journal, 2*(5001), 1071.

Elsworth, B. L., Mitchell, R., Raistrick, C. A., Paternoster, L., Hemani, G., & Gaunt, T. R. (2019). *MRC IEU UK Biobank GWAS pipeline version 2.* MRC IEU. University of Bristol. https://doi.org/10.5523/bris.pnoat8cxo0u52p6ynfaekeigi

Etilé, F., & Jones, A. M. (2011). Schooling and smoking among the baby boomers – An evaluation of the impact of educational expansion in France. *Journal of Health Economics, 30*(4), 811–831.

Evans, W. N., Farrelly, M. C., & Montgomery, E. (1999, September). Do workplace smoking bans reduce smoking? *The American Economic Review, 89*(4), 728–747. https://doi.org/10.1257/aer.89.4.728

Evans, W. N., & Ringel, J. S. (1999). Can higher cigarette taxes improve birth outcomes? *Journal of Public Economics, 72*(1), 135–154.

Farrelly, M. C., Bray, J. W., Pechacek, T., & Woollery, T. (2001). Response by adults to increases in cigarette prices by sociodemographic characteristics. *Southern Economic Journal, 68*(1), 156–165. https://doi.org/10.1002/j.2325-8012.2001.tb00404.x

Farrelly, M. C., Nimsch, C. T., Hyland, A., & Cummings, M. (2004). The effects of higher cigarette prices on tar and nicotine consumption in a cohort of adult smokers. *Health Economics, 13*(1), 49–58. https://doi.org/10.1002/hec.820

Fertig, A. R. (2010). Selection and the effect of prenatal smoking. *Health Economics, 19*(2), 209–226.

Fisher, S. R. A. (1959). *Smoking: The cancer controversy: Some attempts to assess the evidence.* Oliver & Boyd Edinburgh.

Fleig, C. (1908). Influence de la fumée de tabac et de la nicotine sous la développement de l'organisme. *Comptes Rendus des Seances de la Societe de Biologie et de Ses Filiales, 64*, 683–685.

Forster, M., & Jones, A. M. (2001). The role of tobacco taxes in starting and quitting smoking: Duration analysis of British data. *Journal of the Royal Statistical Society: Series A, 164*(3), 517–547.

Frazier, T. M., Davis, G. H., Goldstein, H., & Goldberg, I. D. (1961). Cigarette smoking and prematurity: A prospective study. *American Journal of Obstetrics and Gynecology, 81*(5), 988–996.

Fry, A., Littlejohns, T. J., Sudlow, C., Doherty, N., Adamska, L., Sprosen, T., Collins, R., & Allen, N. E. (2017). Comparison of sociodemographic and health-related characteristics of UK Biobank participants with those of the general population. *American Journal of Epidemiology, 186*(9), 1026–1034.

Guillain, G., & Gy, A. (1907). Recherches exp['erimentales sur l'influence de l'intoxication tabagique sur la gestation. *Comptes Rendus des Seances de la Societe de Biologie et de Ses Filiales, 63*, 583–584.

Hammond, D. (2011, September). Health warning messages on tobacco products: A review. *Tobacco Control, 20*(5), 327–337. https://doi.org/10.1136/tc.2010.037630

Hansen, B., Sabia, J. J., & Rees, D. I. (2017, February). Have cigarette taxes lost their bite? New estimates of the relationship between cigarette taxes and youth smoking. *American Journal of Health Economics, 3*(1), 60–75. https://doi.org/10.1162/AJHE_a_00067

Hatcher, R. A., & Crosby, K. (1927). The elimination of nicotine in the milk. *Journal of Pharmacology and Experimental Therapeutics, 32*.

James, J. (Forthcoming). Smoking, information and education: The royal college of physicians and the new public health movement. *Journal of Policy Analysis and Management.* https://doi.org/10.1002/pam.22508

Jones, A. (1989a). The UK demand for cigarettes 1954–1986, a double-hurdle approach. *Journal of Health Economics, 8*(1), 133–141.

Jones, A. M. (1989b). A double-hurdle model of cigarette consumption. *Journal of Applied Econometrics, 4*(1), 23–39.

Jones, A. M. (1989c). A systems approach to the demand for alcohol and tobacco. *Bulletin of Economic Research, 41*(2), 85–106.

Jones, A. M. (1992). A note on computation of the double-hurdle model with dependence with an application to tobacco expenditure. *Bulletin of Economic Research, 44*(1), 67–74.

Jones, A. M. (1994). Health, addiction, social interaction and the decision to quit smoking. *Journal of Health Economics, 13*(1), 93–110.

Jones, A. M., & Labeaga, J. M. (2003). Individual heterogeneity and censoring in panel data estimates of tobacco expenditure. *Journal of Applied Econometrics*, *18*(2), 157–177.

Jones, A. M., Laporte, A., Rice, N., & Zucchelli, E. (2015). Do public smoking bans have an impact on active smoking? Evidence from the UK. *Health Economics*, *24*(2), 175–192. https://doi.org/10.1002/hec.3009

Kennaway, E. L., & Kennaway, N. M. (1947). A further study of the incidence of cancer of the lung and larynx. *British Journal of Cancer*, *1*(3), 260.

King, J. I. (1604). *A counterblaste to tobacco*. Robert Barker.

Kong, A., Thorleifsson, G., Frigge, M. L., Vilhjalmsson, B. J., Young, A. I., Thorgeirsson, T. E., Benonisdottir, S., Oddsson, A., Halldorsson, B. V., Masson, G. I., Gudbjartsson, D. F., Helgason, A., Bjornsdottir, G., Thorsteinsdottir, U., & Stefansson, K. (2018). The nature of nurture: Effects of parental genotypes. *Science*, *359*(6374), 424–428.

Kuehnle, D. (2019, September). How effective are pictorial warnings on tobacco products? New evidence on smoking behaviour using Australian panel data. *Journal of Health Economics*, *67*, 102215. https://doi.org/10.1016/j.jhealeco.2019.06.002

Levy, D. E., & Meara, E. (2006, March). The effect of the 1998 master settlement agreement on prenatal smoking. *Journal of Health Economics*, *25*(2), 276–294. https://doi.org/10.1016/j.jhealeco.2005.07.006

Lewitt, E. M., Coate, D., & Grossman, M. (1981). The effects of government regulation on teenage smoking. *The Journal of Law and Economics*, *24*(3), 545–570.

Lien, D. S., & Evans, W. N. (2005). Estimating the impact of large cigarette tax hikes: The case of maternal smoking and infant birth weight. *Journal of Human Resources*, *XL*(2), 373–392. https://doi.org/10.3368/jhr.XL.2.373

Lillard, D. R., Molloy, E., & Sfekas, A. (2013, January). Smoking initiation and the iron law of demand. *Journal of Health Economics*, *32*(1), 114–127. https://doi.org/10.1016/j.jhealeco.2012.08.006

Liu, M., Jiang, Y., Wedow, R., Li, Y., Brazel, D. M., Chen, F., Datta, G., Davila-Velderrain, J., McGuire, D., Chao, T. N., Zhan, X., 23andMe Research Team, HUNT All-In Psychiatry, Choquet, H., Docherty, A. R., Faul, J. D., Foerster, J. R., Fritsche, L. G., Elvestad Gabrielsen, M., ... Vrieze, S. (2019). Association studies of up to 1.2 million individuals yield new insights into the genetic etiology of tobacco and alcohol use. *Nature Genetics*, *51*(2), 237–244.

Lowe, C. R. (1959). Effect of mothers' smoking habits on birth weight of their children. *BMJ*, *2*(5153), 673–676. ISSN: 0007-1447. https://doi.org/10.1136/bmj.2.5153.673

Lührmann, M., & Wilson, T. (2018). *Long-run health and mortality effects of exposure to universal health care at birth*. Institute for Fiscal Studies.

MacLean, J. C., Kessler, A. S., & Kenkel, D. S. (2016). Cigarette taxes and older adult smoking: Evidence from the health and retirement study. *Health Economics*, *25*(4), 424–438. https://doi.org/10.1002/hec.3161

Meier, K. J., & Licari, M. J. (1997, July). The effect of cigarette taxes on cigarette consumption, 1955 through 1994. *American Journal of Public Health*, *87*(7), 1126–1130. https://doi.org/10.2105/AJPH.87.7.1126

Mills, M. C., Barban, N., & Tropf, F. C. (2020). *An introduction to statistical genetic data analysis*. MIT Press.

Monárrez-Espino, J., Liu, B., Greiner, F., Bremberg, S., & Galanti, R. (2014, October). Systematic review of the effect of pictorial warnings on cigarette packages in smoking behavior. *American Journal of Public Health*, *104*(10), e11–e30. https://doi.org/10.2105/AJPH.2014.302129

Noar, S. M., Francis, D. B., Bridges, C., Sontag, J. M., Ribisl, K. M., & Brewer, N. T. (2016, September). The impact of strengthening cigarette pack warnings: Systematic review of longitudinal observational studies. *Social Science & Medicine*, *164*, 118–129. https://doi.org/10.1016/j.socscimed.2016.06.011

Nonnemaker, J. M., & Farrelly, M. C. (2011, May). Smoking initiation among youth: The role of cigarette excise taxes and prices by race/ethnicity and gender. *Journal of Health Economics*, *30*(3), 560–567. https://doi.org/10.1016/j.jhealeco.2011.03.002

Pechstein, L. A., & Reynolds, W. R. (1937). The effects of tobacco smoke on the growth and learning behaviour of the albino rat and its progeny. *Journal of Comparative Psychology*, *24*, 459–469.

Pereira, R. D., Rietveld, C. A., & Kippersluis, H. van (2022). The interplay between maternal smoking and genes in offspring birth weight. *Journal of Human Resources*, 1020-11266R2.

Rantakallio, P. (1978a). Relationship of maternal smoking to morbidity and mortality of the child up to the age of five. *Acta Paediatrica*, *67*(5), 621–631.

Rantakallio, P. (1978b). The effect of maternal smoking on birth weight and the subsequent health of the child. *Early Human Development*, *2*(4), 371–382.

Register Office, General. (1960). (Vol. 1, pp. 1–167). Her Majesty's Stationery Office. https://web.archive.org/web/20150119124658/http://www.ash.org.uk/files/documents/ASH_741.pdf

Richon, L., & Perrin, M. (1908). Retards de dévelopment par intoxication tabagique expérimentale possibilité de la reprise de croissance après cessation de l'intoxication. *Comptes Rendus des Seances de la Societe de Biologie et de Ses Filiales*, *64*(March), 563–565.

Saffer, H., & Chaloupka, F. (2000, November). The effect of tobacco advertising bans on tobacco consumption. *Journal of Health Economics*, *19*(6), 1117–1137. https://doi.org/10.1016/S0167-6296(00)00054-0

Schneider, L., Klein, B., & Murphy, K. M. (1981). Governmental regulation of cigarette health information. *The Journal of Law and Economics*, *24*(3), 575–612.

Schoeneck, F. J. (1941). Cigarette smoking in pregnancy. *New York State Journal of Medicine*, *41*, 1945–1948.

Simpson, W. J. (1957). A preliminary report on cigarette smoking and the incidence of prematurity. *American Journal of Obstetrics and Gynecology*, *73*(4), 808–815.

Singleton, J. (2023). Going up in smoke: Tobacco and government policy in the age of austerity, 1945–50. *Twentieth Century British History*, hwad046.

Sloan, F. A., & Trogdon, J. G. (2004). The impact of the master settlement agreement on cigarette consumption. *Journal of Policy Analysis and Management*, *23*(4), 843–855. https://doi.org/10.1002/pam.20050

Sumner, M. T. (1971). The demand for tobacco in the U.K. *The Manchester School*, *39*(1), 23–36. https://doi.org/10.1111/j.1467-9957.1971.tb00365.x

The Tobacco and Genetics Consortium. (2010). Genome-wide meta-analyses identify multiple loci associated with smoking behavior. *Nature Genetics*, *42*(5), 441–447.

Wald, N., & Nicolaides-Bouman, A. (1991). *UK smoking statistics* (2nd ed.). Oxford University Press.

Walker, M. B., Tekin, E., & Wallace, S. (2009). Teen smoking and birth outcomes. *Southern Economic Journal*, *75*(3), 892–907.

Warner, K. E. (1977). The effects of the anti-smoking campaign on cigarette consumption. *American Journal of Public Health*, *67*(7). https://doi.org/10.2105/AJPH.67.7.645

Willson, J. R. (1942). The effect of nicotine on lactation in white mice. *American Journal of Obstetrics and Gynecology*, *43*(5), 839–844.

Woodhouse, P. (1971). Control of television advertising in Great Britain. *Food Drug Cosmetic Law Journal*, *26*, 328.

Wynder, E. L., & Graham, E. A. (1950). Tobacco smoking as a possible etiologic factor in bronchiogenic carcinoma: A study of six hundred and eighty-four proved cases. *Journal of the American Medical Association*, *143*(4), 329–336.

Yang, Q., Millard, L. A. C., & Smith, G. D. (2020). Proxy gene-by-environment Mendelian randomization study confirms a causal effect of maternal smoking on offspring birthweight, but little evidence of long-term influences on offspring health. *International Journal of Epidemiology*, *49*(4), 1207–1218.

Yen, S. T., & Jones, A. M. (1996). Individual cigarette consumption and addiction: A flexible limited dependent variable approach. *Health Economics*, *5*(2), 105–117.

Zweiniger-Bargielowska, I. (2000). *Austerity in Britain: Rationing, controls, and consumption, 1939–1955*. Oxford University Press.

APPENDIX A ADDITIONAL TABLES AND FIGURES

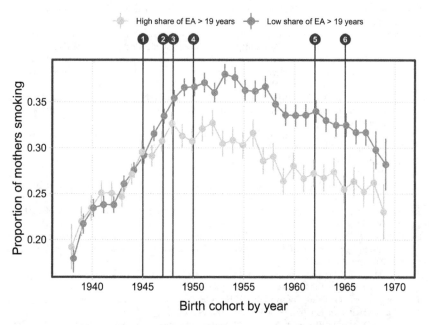

Fig. A1. SES Defined according to Frequency of Educational Attainment in 1951. *Notes:* (1) WW2 ends, (2) tax hike, (3) introduction of NHS, (4) first paper on smoking and cancer, (5) RCP report and (6) ban on TV advertising of cigarettes. Defines high education areas as districts with an above-median share of those who left education aged 20 years or older, taken across all districts based on the 1951 Census.

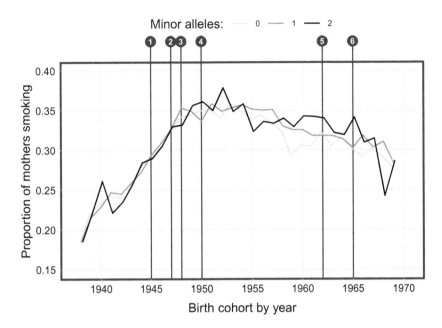

Fig. A2. Maternal Smoking by Offspring's RS16969968 Minor Allele Count; 1938–1969. *Notes:* (1) WW2 ends, (2) tax hike, (3) introduction of NHS, (4) first paper on smoking and cancer, (5) RCP report and (6) ban on TV advertising of cigarettes.

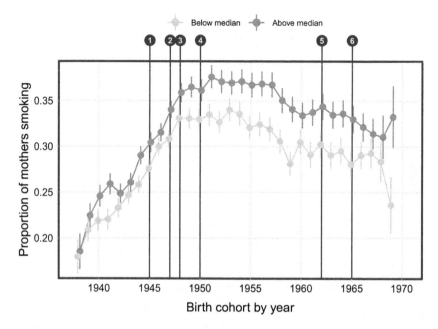

Fig. A3. Maternal Smoking by Offspring's Polygenic Index for 'Cigarettes per Day'; 1938–1969. *Notes:* (1) WW2 ends, (2) tax hike, (3) introduction of NHS, (4) first paper on smoking and cancer, (5) RCP report and (6) ban on TV advertising of cigarettes.

APPENDIX B GENETICS

Humans have 23 chromosome pairs in every cell apart from sex cells. Each pair contains a maternal and paternal copy inherited from the mother and the father, respectively. A single chromosome consists of a double-strand of deoxyribonucleic acid (DNA) containing a large number of 'base pairs': pairs of nucleotide molecules (referred to as the 'letters' A (adenine) that binds with T (thymine), and G (guanine) that binds with C (cytosine)) that together make up the human genome. Across a population, there will be locations in the genome where a single base pair has been replaced by a different one. Such variation is known as a single nucleotide polymorphism (SNP, pronounced 'snip') and is the most commonly studied type of genetic variation. When there are two possible base pairs at a given location (i.e. two alleles), the most frequent base pair is called the major allele, while the less frequent is called the minor allele. As humans have two copies of each chromosome, any given individual can have either zero, one or two copies of the minor allele at a given location.

STEPHANIE VON HINKE ET AL.

To identify specific SNPs that are robustly associated with a particular outcome of interest, so-called Genome-Wide Association Studies (GWAS) relate each SNP to the outcome. As there are more SNPs than individuals, the SNP effects cannot be identified in a multivariate regression model. Instead, a GWAS runs a large number of univariate regressions of the outcome on each SNP. These analyses have shown that most outcomes of interest in the social sciences are 'polygenic': they are affected by a large number of SNPs, each with a very small effect. To increase the predictive power of the SNPs, it is therefore custom to aggregate the individual SNPs into so-called polygenic indices, by constructing a weighted sum of the minor allele counts at each SNP, where the weight is the effect size obtained from a GWAS (after additionally accounting for correlations between SNPs).

We construct two measures of genetic predisposition to smoking. First, we focus on the single SNP RS16969968 on chromosome 15 (in the UK Biobank, we identify this SNP by position 78,590,583 [GRCh37/hg19]) and construct a variable counting the number of risk alleles each individual has at this location. We code A/T (the minor allele) as the risk allele such that smoking propensity increases with risk allele count. Second, we also use two polygenic indices from the PGI repository (Becker et al., 2021) to capture genetic predisposition for smoking aggregated across many SNPs. The PGI repository contains pre-computed polygenic indices for common outcomes in the UK Biobank. Becker et al. (2021) maximise the predictive power of the indices by meta analysing several large datasets. We focus on the indices for 'ever smoked' and 'number of cigarettes per day', allowing us to look at genetic predisposition across both the extensive and intensive margins. Becker et al. (2021) details the construction of the polygenic indices.[14]

To verify the predictive power of RS16969968 and the polygenic indices, we use a linear regression model to test how well they predict smoking outcomes in our UK Biobank sample. We QC the UK Biobank genetic data and identify individuals of European genetic ancestry using the procedure described in Elsworth et al. (2019). Our regressions control for sex and the first 20 genetic principal components, and we standardise the polygenic indices to have zero mean and unit variance in the sample. Since Becker et al. (2021) constructed the polygenic indices using a three-fold sample split with overlap in the GWAS discovery sample, we note that the standard errors in the regressions for the polygenic indices will be underestimated. However, the impact of this is negligible in our main analyses as we only use the polygenic indices to create an above/below median split of genetic predisposition.

---

[14]For background on how to interpret polygenic indices and on the PGI repository more generally, see also the FAQs for Becker et al. (2021) at https://www.thessgac.org/faqs

Table B1. Predictive Power of the Genetic Variables.

Dependent Variable:

	(1) Mother: Maternal smoking	(2) Child: Ever smoked	(3) Child: Number of cigs, current	(4) Child: Number of cigs, previous
Panel (a) – RS16969968 Minor Allele Count				
Child's RS16969968, minor alleles	0.005***	−0.005***	1.002***	1.043***
	(0.001)	(0.001)	(0.082)	(0.054)
Observations	334,573	334,573	21,986	77,927
Mean dep. var.	0.309	0.446	15.488	19.027
R^2	0.012	0.013	0.046	0.053
Incremental R^2	0.000	0.000	0.006	0.004
Panel (b) – Child's Polygenic Index for Ever Smoking				
PGI, ever smoked	0.053***	0.098***	0.366***	0.440***
	(0.001)	(0.001)	(0.057)	(0.038)
Observations	326,211	326,211	21,348	75,965
Mean dep. var.	0.309	0.445	15.516	19.034
R^2	0.025	0.052	0.041	0.051
Incremental R^2	0.013	0.039	0.001	0.002
Panel (c) – Child's Polygenic Index for Number of Cigarettes Daily				
PGI, number of cigarettes	0.021***	0.010***	1.277***	1.571***
	(0.001)	(0.001)	(0.055)	(0.037)
Observations	326,211	326,211	21,348	75,965
Mean dep. var.	0.309	0.445	15.516	19.034
R^2	0.014	0.014	0.063	0.072
Incremental R^2	0.002	0.001	0.023	0.023

Notes: Panels: (a) RS16969968 minor allele count, (b) polygenic index for ever smoking and (c) polygenic index for number of cigarettes daily. Columns: (1) smoking status of the mother around the time of birth, (2) the child ever having smoked, (3) the child's number of cigarettes smoked per day for current and (4) previous smokers. The number of cigarettes smoked per day is only available for current and past smokers, so the sample sizes are smaller for these outcomes. Uses QC'ed UK Biobank genetic data and individuals of European genetic ancestry, as described in Elsworth et al. (2019). Regressions control for sex and the first 20 genetic principal components. Polygenic indices are standardized to have zero mean and unit variance. $*p < 0.1$, $**p < 0.05$ and $***p < 0.01$.

Table B1 reports the regression results for the three genetic variables (panels) and four different smoking outcomes (columns) from the UK Biobank. We consider the smoking status of the mother around the time of birth (Column 1), the child ever having smoked (Column 2) and the child's number of cigarettes smoked per day for current (Column 3) and previous smokers (Column 4). Note that the number of cigarettes smoked per day is only available for current and past smokers, so the sample sizes are smaller for these outcomes. For each regression,

Table B1 also shows the incremental R^2, defined as the increase in R^2 when the genetic variable is included as a covariate.

Starting with maternal smoking in Column 1, we find that all three of the children's genetic variables predict whether the mother was smoking around the time of birth, giving supporting evidence to our use of the child's genetics as a proxy for the mother's. In Column 2–4, we examine how the child's genetic variables predict the *child's* outcomes, and we find that both polygenic indices positively predict 'ever smoking' as well as the number of cigarettes per day for both current and past smokers. Similarly, we see that RS16969968 also positively predicts number of cigarettes per day but shows a negative association with 'ever smoked'. We interpret this as RS16969968 being predictive of smoking intensity, rather than being predictive of the extensive margin, capturing whether or not the individual smokes.

BENCHMARKING CLINICAL PRACTICE ON TREATMENT GAIN INEQUALITY–PROBABILITY BOUNDS

Raf Van Gestel[a], Daniel Avdic[b] and Owen O'Donnell[a]

[a]*Erasmus University Rotterdam, The Netherlands*
[b]*Deakin University, Australia*

ABSTRACT

There is widespread concern about low adherence to clinical practice guidelines (CPGs) and the low adoption of new medical technologies. To assist the regulatory response, we propose benchmarking clinical practice on the lower bound on the probability that a recommended treatment/new technology achieves a better outcome. This inequality–probability bound can be estimated from marginal outcome distributions. We illustrate the approach by comparing Swedish cardiologists' adoption of drug-eluting stents (DESs) with the inequality–probability bound on this technology improving outcomes. A substantial fraction of cardiologists are below the benchmark.

Keywords: Healthcare; clinical practice; medical technology; guideline; adherence; evaluation; bound estimation; inequality–probability bound

1. INTRODUCTION

Clinical practice guidelines (CPGs) usually recommend uniform assignment of patients, possibly within a subgroup, to the treatment that clinical trials find to be most effective for the average patient. Low adherence to CPGs may signal inattention to evidence (Abaluck et al., 2020; McGlynn et al., 2003) and arouses concern given that treatment decisions based on clinical judgement have been shown to be inferior (on average) to mechanical application of a protocol (Abaluck et al., 2020; Currie & MacLeod, 2020; Groves et al., 2000; Manski, 2019; Meehl, 1954).

Recent Developments in Health Econometrics
Contributions to Economic Analysis, Volume 297, 229–239
Copyright © 2024 Raf Van Gestel, Daniel Avdic and Owen O'Donnell
Published under exclusive licence by Emerald Publishing Limited
ISSN: 0573-8555/doi:10.1108/S0573-855520240000297011

However, when there is a heterogeneous response to treatment, such that some patients would benefit from receiving the treatment that is inferior on average, deviation from uniform assignment to the treatment with the largest average effect is not necessarily inconsistent with maximisation of aggregate health outcomes. A physician with patient-specific information on expected treatment effectiveness could use it to improve overall outcomes by varying treatments across patients. Therefore, those responsible for evaluating clinical performance may be unsure whether non-adherence to guidelines is necessarily detrimental to patients (McGlynn et al., 2003; Rosenberg et al., 2015; Valle et al., 2015). The task of evaluators, who lack information on patient-specific treatment effectiveness, would be easier if they could compare the proportion of patients treated with the recommended treatment with a benchmark below which it is unlikely that deviation from the CPGs improves health overall.

We propose obtaining such a benchmark from the lower bound on the probability that the recommended treatment achieves a better outcome. The intuition can be conveyed with a simple example. Consider two treatments, A and B, with success probabilities for a binary outcome of 30% and 20%, respectively, in a defined patient population. In the extreme case in which the 20% of patients who would be successfully treated with B would also be successfully treated with A, 10% of the patient population would be strictly better off with treatment A. Treating less than 100% of patients with A, which would be the treatment recommended based on average effectiveness, would not necessarily jeopardise health maximisation. But treating less than 10% of patients with A would necessarily result in lower aggregate health and could not be attributed to physicians using information to select the treatment that has the greater expected outcome for each patient. This simple example demonstrates that the Boole-Fréchet lower inequality–probability bound, which can be estimated from marginal outcome distributions obtained from a clinical trial (Mullahy, 2018), can provide a useful benchmark against which to evaluate clinical practice.

We argue that these inequality–probability bounds have a number of potential uses in evaluating, informing and incentivising physicians. First, as the example illustrates, the lower probability bound on the gain from a treatment allows an evaluator to determine whether any deviation of clinical practice from uniform assignment to the treatment that is most effective on average could possibly be justified by physicians making use of patient-specific information. Second, a physician, or group practice of physicians, can be identified as a slow adopter of a new technology when the proportion of patients they treat with that technology is below the lower bound on the probability of benefiting from it. This is conservative because physicians may misallocate patients and yet still be above the lower bound on the proportion of patients treated with the recommended treatment that is consistent with still maximising aggregate outcomes. Third, inequality–probability bounds could be used to design physician feedback reports and provider payments. Rather than using arbitrary thresholds – for example, issuing information or warnings to the top X% of medicine prescribers – feedback or financial penalties could be triggered by data showing that a physician, or group of physicians, is approaching, or has fallen below, the benchmark proportion of patients treated with the recommended treatment given by the lower bound on the inequality–probability.

After deriving inequality–probability bounds from marginal distributions, we illustrate the approach by using published evidence to calculate bounds on the relative effectiveness of percutaneous coronary interventions (PCIs) to open clogged arteries. We compare the proportion of patients in Sweden treated with innovative PCIs with these bounds to assess whether clinical practice was, on average, attentive to available evidence while possibly utilising additional patient-specific information on treatment response. We calculate the share of Swedish physicians for whom the proportion of patients treated with the most effective PCI (on average) was below the lower bound on the probability of a patient benefiting from that treatment. This provides an estimate of the fraction of physicians practicing in a way that is inconsistent with using the available evidence to maximise patient outcomes.

2. METHOD

Consider treatments A and B that can each result in one of two outcomes: $y_k \in \{0,1\}$ and $k \in \{A,B\}$, where $y_k = 1$ is preferred. A clinical trial provides an unbiased estimate of the success probability with each treatment, $\Pr(y_k = 1)$, for the patient population. It may also provide unbiased estimates of conditional success probabilities, $\Pr(y_k = 1 \mid x_j = 1)$, where $x_j = 1$ identifies patient subpopulation j.

The problem faced by a regulator charged with evaluating clinical practice is to discern whether the preferred treatment – the one with the higher success probability – is sufficiently prescribed. The regulator must assess whether any observed deviation from uniform assignment to the preferred treatment could possibly be justified by a physician, or a group of physicians, making use of patient-specific information on treatment response. This task must be accomplished using only clinical (trial) evidence and the observed treatment patterns. The trial data provide estimates of the marginal outcome distribution under each treatment, possibly conditional on characteristics that define subpopulations. We assume, as a first approximation, that the regulator is only concerned about patient outcomes, with no consideration given to cost and safety.

As a starting point, take the situation in which the success probabilities are the same for all patients. Universal assignment to the treatment with the highest probability of success would then maximise the expected outcome of each patient. If the success probabilities were to differ between, but not within, subpopulations that are distinguished in the clinical trial evidence, then the assignment to treatment should be uniform within each subpopulation. When the success probabilities differ across patients within a subpopulation and physicians possess patient-specific information relevant to those probabilities, then deviation from universal assignment to the technology that is most effective on average can improve outcomes.

Consider the trivial case in which a physician is perfectly informed of the outcome that will be experienced by each patient under each treatment. This omniscient physician could ensure that some patients would have better outcomes than they would experience if treated consistent with evidence on the average treatment effect. No patient would be worse off (Appendix A). More generally, if a physician had imperfect patient-specific information on treatment response that went beyond trial evidence of conditional success probabilities for sub-populations, they could use the information to improve expected outcomes by deviating from uniform treatment assignment.

Suppose the regulator observes a physician prescribing a treatment other than the one with the higher (conditional) average success probability. This is not necessarily to the disadvantage of the physician's patients because $\Pr(y_A = 1) > \Pr(y_B = 1)$ does not imply $\Pr(y_A > y_B) = 1$. Provided the *inequality–probability* $\Pr(y_A > y_B)$ were less than one, then a physician with the ability to identify patients who would benefit from getting treatment B instead of A could obtain better outcomes by not prescribing A uniformly. The regulator would want to establish whether a physician's propensity to prescribe A is at least as high as $\Pr(y_A > y_B)$. If it is not, and the clinical trial sample is representative of the physician's patients, then deviation from uniform assignment to the more effective (on average) treatment cannot possibly be maximising the number of successful outcomes.

Without an estimate of the joint distribution of the outcomes, it is not possible to point identify the inequality–probability $\Pr(y_A > y_B)$. However, with estimates of the marginal distributions, it is possible to obtain sharp, best possible bounds on the parameter (Mullahy, 2018) (Appendix B):

$$\textit{Lower bound} : \Pr(y_A > y_B) \geq \max\{\Pr(y_A = 1) - \Pr(y_B = 1), 0\} \quad (1a)$$

$$\textit{Upper bound} : \Pr(y_A > y_B) \leq \min\{\Pr(y_A = 1), 1 - \Pr(y_B = 1)\} \quad (1b)$$

The lower bound arises from one extreme in which all patients that would be successfully treated with B would also be successfully treated with A. With this complete overlap, if treatment A is more effective on average, then the difference between the success probabilities of the two treatments is the probability that A is more effective than B. The upper bound captures the other extreme in which there is no overlap. Any patient successfully treated with B would not be successfully treated with A. Then, the probability that A is more effective than B is equal to the smaller of the success probability of A and the complement of the success probability of B.

Since the first extreme scenario of full overlap cannot be ruled out, it is conservative to use the lower bound on the inequality–probability to evaluate clinical practice. It is not possible to go below this lower bound in the proportion of patients treated with the more effective treatment and still maximise aggregate outcomes. Using estimates of the bounds obtained from clinical trial data, if a regulator were to observe a physician below the lower bound in prescription of

RAF VAN GESTEL ET AL.

the more effective treatment, then there would be sufficient evidence to deem that practice inconsistent with using patient-specific information to improve outcomes compared with those achievable with uniform assignment to the more effective (on average) treatment (Appendix C).

Treating a proportion with the more effective treatment that is above the upper bound on the probability of benefiting from that treatment does not necessarily imply that clinical practice is inconsistent with maximising the number of successful outcomes. For example, if technology B were entirely ineffective ($\Pr(y_B = 1) = 0$), then (1b) would be $\Pr(y_A = 1)$. However, uniform assignment of all patients to A would maximise the number of successes.

3. APPLICATION

We illustrate the application of inequality–probability bounds by evaluating the responsiveness of Swedish cardiologists to evidence on the comparative effectiveness of drug-eluting stents (DESs) in patients eligible for PCI. We use information on all interventional coronary procedures between 2002 and 2011 in the Swedish Coronary Angiography and Angioplasty Register ($N = 57,513$).

The first study on the effectiveness of DESs estimated that the one-year risk of a major cardiac event was reduced from 28.8% with a bare metal stent (BMS) to 5.8% with a DES ($P < 0.001$) (Morice et al., 2002). Using these estimates, the lower bound on the probability of avoiding a major cardiac event ($y = 1$) with a DES but experiencing such an event ($y = 0$) with a BMS is as follows:

$$Lower\ bound : \Pr(y_{\text{DES}} = 1, y_{\text{BMS}} = 0) \geq \max\{0.942 - 0.718, 0\} = 0.224$$

After publication of this evidence in 2002 and CE Mark approval of DESs for PCI in April of that year, cardiologists seeking to maximise their patients' chances of avoiding a major cardiac event within a year of surgery should have been using DESs in at least 22.4% of all PCIs. It took Swedish cardiologists only around 18 months to reach this lower bound (Avdic et al., 2019).

A 2006 study (Camenzind, 2006) raised doubts about the effectiveness of DESs. These concerns were quickly assuaged by evidence from a 2007 study (Stone et al., 2017) that DES improved rates of revascularisation, with the magnitude of effect depending on the type of drug coating used and the target vessel. The rate of revascularisation was estimated to be 23.6% with sirolimus-coated stents compared to 7.8% with BMS, 20% with paclitaxel-coated stents placed in a target lesion compared to 10.1% with BMS and 24.7% with paclitaxel stents in target vessels compared to 17.2% with BMS. Another 2007 study estimated that 13.3% of patients fitted with a DES died, suffered a myocardial infarction or required a reintervention compared with 26.3% of patients given a BMS (Kastrati et al., 2007). In response to this evidence, the American College of Cardiology (ACC) and American Heart Association (AHA) Task Force on Practice Guidelines issued an updated guideline for PCIs in December 2007 that confirmed effectiveness of DESs compared with

BMS. The Swedish National Board of Health and Welfare issued guidelines similar to those of the ACC/AHA at the same time.

Using the estimates from the two 2007 studies, we calculate that, compared with BMS, the lower bound on the probability that DESs would produce a better outcome varied from 0.075 to 0.158 for revascularisation, depending on the type of drug coating and the target vessel, and was 0.130 for avoidance of death, myocardial infarction and reintervention. Fig. 1 shows, by year, the fractions of Swedish cardiologists who used DESs for a proportion of PCI patients less than the lowest and the highest of the lower bounds for the revascularisation outcome – 7.5% (Low) and 15.8% (High), respectively. After the guideline update at the end of 2007, only 16% of cardiologists were using DESs at a rate below the lowest lower bound but 44% were below the higher of the lower bounds. Both fractions drop substantially in subsequent years. By 2011, there were no cardiologists using DESs for fewer than 7.5% of PCIs, and only 3% used DESs for less than 15.8% of PCIs.

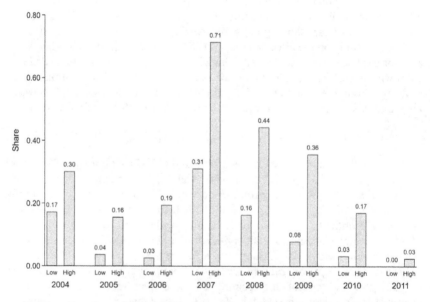

Fig. 1. Fraction of Swedish Cardiologists for Whom the Proportion of PCI Patients Treated With DESs Was Below the Lower Bound on the Probability of Benefiting From That Treatment in Terms of Revascularisation. *Source*: Authors' calculations from Swedish Coronary Angiography and Angioplasty Registry. *Note*: All registered interventional coronary procedures between 2004 and 2011. In total, there were 110,233 coronary interventions conducted by 149 cardiologists. *Low* (*High*) shows the fraction of cardiologists by year using DESs in less than 7.5% (15.8%) of all PCIs conducted. These are estimates of the lower bound on the (percentage) probability of DESs resulting in revascularisation while BMS does not (Stone et al., 2017).

4. DISCUSSION

There are a number of potential applications of inequality–probability bounds in the evaluation of clinical practice. A regulator can use them to determine, at the patient population level, whether any deviation from uniform assignment to the treatment that is recommended on the basis of average effectiveness could possibly be justified by physicians making use of patient-specific information. The bounds may also be used to identify physicians who are slow to adopt a new, more effective (on average) technology to a degree that cannot possibly be justified by use of patient-specific information on effectiveness. Evidence-based clinical practice could be encouraged by targeting physician feedback reports and incentives on the basis of performance relative to the lower bound on the probability of achieving a better outcome with the recommended treatment. Feedback reports could even refer to the lower bound inequality–probability as a benchmark, and incentives could be designed to reward performance above that benchmark or penalise any shortfall from it.

A major advantage over other measures is that inequality–probability bounds can be calculated even when information is scarce. They only require estimates of marginal outcome distributions that are available from clinical trials. Other approaches to evaluating clinical practice and the adoption of medical technology require objective and subjective patient characteristics, which are not easily gathered at large scale (Abaluck et al., 2020).

The approach does, however, have several limitations. Clinical decisions take more than one outcome into account. Other outcomes, patient safety and cost may all be considered. These may be legitimate reasons for deviation from the recommended treatment. Still, performance below the lower bound on the inequality–probability may trigger closer inspective of clinical practice to establish whether the deviation is justified by attention given to other outcomes, safety and cost.

We focused on the case with a binary outcome and two treatments. Inequality–probability bounds for continuous outcomes can be obtained by considering probabilities of the outcome exceeding a series of threshold values (Mullahy, 2018) although potential applications are more limited since the marginal distributions of continuous outcomes are seldom reported in clinical trials. With more than two treatments, the lower bound would be obtained by assuming that all patients who achieve a successful outcome with the recommended (most effective, on average) treatment would get the same outcome with all other treatments. However, this would likely deliver an uninformative bound. It may therefore be better to compare the recommended treatment only with the treatment that is the second most effective, on average.

Finally, physicians prescribing below the lower bound on the probability that the recommended treatment achieves the better outcome are necessarily inconsistent with health maximisation only if their patients are random samples of the population for which the treatment is recommended based on evidence obtained from a random sample of the same population. Although this is clearly unrealistic, the bound may remain a well-motivated threshold to identify deviant prescribers and follow-up with enquiries about the characteristics of their patients. If sufficient data were available, it may be possible to calculate case-mix adjusted bounds.

Healthcare agencies struggle to interpret and respond to low prescription of CPG-recommended treatments and low take-up of new technologies for which trials show that outcomes are improved. We propose to benchmark clinical practice against the lower bound on the probability that the recommended treatment/new technology achieves a better outcome. Prescription below this benchmark signals that outcomes could be improved by treating more patients with the recommended treatment. The benchmark is simple to calculate from clinical trial data and so is a pragmatic tool for evaluation. Beyond that, it could be used in the design of physician peer-feedback and outcome-based payment models to improve adherence to evidence and CPGs.

REFERENCES

Abaluck, J., Agha, L., Chan, D. C., Singer, D., & Zhu, D. (2020). *Fixing misallocation with guidelines: Awareness vs. Adherence*. NBER Working paper 27467.

Avdic, D., Propper, C., von Hinke, S., & Vikstrom, J. (2019). *Information shocks and provider responsiveness: Evidence from interventional cardiology*. Working paper.

Camenzind, E. (2006). Do drug-eluting stent increase death? *ESC Congress News*. https://scholar. google.com/scholar?hl=en&q=+Camenzind+E.+Do+drug-eluting+stent+increase+death% 3F+ESC+Congress+News.+Barcelona%2C+Spain%3B+2006

Currie, J., & MacLeod, B. W. (2020). Understanding doctor decision making: The case of depression treatment. *Econometrica, 88*(3), 847–878.

Groves, W., Zald, D., Lebow, B., Snitz, B., & Nelson, C. (2000). Clinical versus mechanical prediction: A meta-analysis. *Psychological Assessment, 12*, 19–30.

Kastrati, A., Mehilli, J., Pache, J., Kaiser, C., Valgimigli, M., Kelbaek, H., Menichelli, M., Sabaté, M., Suttorp, M. J., Baumgart, D., Seyfarth, M., Pfisterer, M. E., & Schömig, A. (2007). Analysis of 14 trials comparing sirolimus-eluting stents with bare-metal stents. *The New England Journal of Medicine, 356*, 1030.

Manski, C. (2019). *Patient care under uncertainty* (p. 184). Princeton University Press.

McGlynn, E. A., Asch, S. M., Adams, J., Keesey, J., Hicks, J., DeCristofaro, A., & Kerr, E. A. (2003). The quality of health care delivered to adults in the United States. *New England Journal of Medicine, 348*(26), 2635–2645.

Meehl, P. (1954). *Clinical versus statistical prediction: A theoretical analysis and a review of the evidence*. University of Minnesota Press.

Morice, M.-C., Serruys, P. W., Sousa, E., Fajadet, J., Hayashi, E. B., Perin, M., Colombo, A., Schuler, G., Barragan, P., Guagliumi, G., Molnar, F., & Falotico, R. (2002). A randomized comparison of a sirolimus-eluting stent with a standard stent for coronary revascularization. *New England Journal of Medicine, 346*(23), 1773–1780.

Mullahy, J. (2018). Individual results may vary: Inequality-probability bounds for some health-outcome treatment effects. *Journal of Health Economics, 61*, 151–162.

Rosenberg, A., Agiro, A., Gottlieb, M., Barron, J., Brady, P., Liu, Y., Li, C., & De Vries, A. (2015). Early trends among seven recommendations from the choosing wisely campaign. *JAMA Internal Medicine, 175*(12), 1913–1920.

Stone, G. W., Moses, J. W., Ellis, S. G., Schofer, J., Dawkins, K. D., Morice, M.-C., Colombo, A., Schampaert, E., Grube, E., Kirtane, A. J., Cutlip, D. E., Fahy, M., Pocock, S. J., Mehran, R., & Leon, M. B. (2017). Safety and efficacy of sirolimus-and paclitaxes-eluting coronary stents. *The New England Journal of Medicine, 356*, 998–1008.

Valle, C. W., Binns, H. J., Quadri-Sheriff, M., Benuck, I., & Patel, A. (2015). Physicians' lack of adherence to national Heart, lung, and blood institute guidelines for pediatric lipid screening. *Clinical Pediatrics, 54*(12), 1200–1205.

APPENDIX A: NON-UNIVERSAL ASSIGNMENT TO TREATMENT THAT IS MOST EFFECTIVE ON AVERAGE CAN IMPROVE OUTCOMES

Define $N_{10} = \sum 1(y_A > y_B)$, where (1) is the indicator function: the number of patients who get the good outcome ($y = 1$) with treatment A and the bad outcome ($y = 0$) with treatment B. Similarly, $N_{01} = \sum 1(y_A < y_B)$, and $N_{11} = \sum 1(y_B = y_A = 1)$. Let A be the more effective treatment on average: $N_{10} > N_{01} \Rightarrow \frac{N_{10} + N_{11}}{N} > \frac{N_{01} + N_{11}}{N} \Rightarrow \Pr(y_A = 1) > \Pr(y_B = 1)$, where N is the total patient population. Assigning every patient to A results in $N_{10} + N_{11}$ good outcomes. Assigning each patient to the treatment that is most effective for that patient results in $N_{10} + N_{01} + N_{11}$ good outcomes. Assigning up to $\sum 1(y_A = y_B) + 1(y_A < y_B) = N - N_{10}$ patients to the B – the least effective treatment on average – increases the total number of good outcomes and makes no one worse off relative to universal assignment to A.

APPENDIX B: DERIVATION OF BOUNDS ON THE INEQUALITY–PROBABILITY

The inequality–probability for treatment A better than B, $\Pr(y_A > y_B)$, is

$$\Pr(y_A = 1, y_B = 0) = 1 - [\Pr(y_A = 0, y_B = 0) + \Pr(y_A = 0, y_B = 1) + \Pr(y_A = 1, y_B = 1)]$$

This cannot be point identified without estimates of the joint probabilities on the right-hand-side. Set identification using estimates of the marginal outcome distributions is achieved by considering extreme cases in which joint probabilities reduce to marginal probabilities.

Positive lower bound. If there were no chance of B producing a better outcome than A, $\Pr(y_A = 0, y_B = 1) = 0$, then $\Pr(y_A = 1 | y_B = 1) = 1$ and $\Pr(y_A = 1, y_B = 0) = 1 - [\Pr(y_A = 0) + \Pr(y_B = 1)] = \Pr(y_A = 1) - \Pr(y_B = 1)$, which is the lower bound (1a) when A is the more effective treatment on average.

Zero lower bound. If treatment B is observed to be more effective on average, then $\Pr(y_A = 1, y_B = 0)$ is bounded below by zero, corresponding to the case in which there would be no chance of A producing a better outcome than B.

Upper bound I. If all patients who would get a good outcome with A would have a bad outcome with B ($\Pr(y_B = 0 | y_A = 1) = 1$), then $\Pr(y_A = 1, y_B = 1) = 0$ and $\Pr(y_A = 1, y_B = 0) = 1 - [\Pr(y_A = 0, y_B = 0) + \Pr(y_A = 0, y_B = 1)] = 1 - \Pr(y_A = 0) = \Pr(y_A = 1)$, which is the upper bound (1b) when $\Pr(y_A = 1) < 1 - \Pr(y_B = 1)$.

238 *Benchmarking Clinical Practice*

Upper bound II. If all patients who would get a bad outcome with A would have a good outcome with B ($\Pr(y_B = 1| y_A = 0) = 1$), then $\Pr(y_A = 0, y_B = 0) = 0$ and $\Pr(y_A = 1, y_B = 0) = 1 - [\Pr(y_A = 0, y_B = 1) + \Pr(y_A = 1, y_B = 1)] = 1 - \Pr(y_B = 1)$, which is the upper bound (1b) when $\Pr(y_A = 1) > 1 - \Pr(y_B = 1)$.

To obtain bounds on the weak inequality probability, note

$$\Pr(y_A \geq y_B) = \Pr(y_A = 0, y_B = 0) + \Pr(y_A = 1, y_B = 0)$$
$$+ \Pr(y_A = 1, y_B = 1) = 1 - \Pr(y_A = 0, y_B = 1)$$

Hence, the lower bound on $\Pr(y_A \geq y_B)$ is the complement of the upper bound on $\Pr(y_B > y_A)$. And the upper bound on $\Pr(y_A \geq y_B)$ is the complement of the lower bound on $\Pr(y_B > y_A)$. That is,

$$Lower\ bound : \Pr(y_A \geq y_B) \geq 1 - \min\{\Pr(y_B = 1), 1 - \Pr(y_A = 1)\} \quad (2a)$$

$$Upper\ bound : \Pr(y_A \geq y_B) \leq 1 - \max\{\Pr(y_B = 1) - \Pr(y_A = 1), 0\} \quad (2b)$$

APPENDIX C: ILLUSTRATIVE EXAMPLE OF USING BOUNDS TO EVALUATE CLINICAL PRACTICE

Table C1 shows treatment-specific outcomes for five hypothetical patients. Assume that these five patients and patients in a clinical trial sample are randomly drawn from the same population. Ignore the obvious small numbers problem, such that the distributions of outcomes over the five patients are expected to be the same as the outcome distributions in both the RCT sample and the population.

First, consider the outcomes y_A and y_B. Treatment A has the higher success probability, $\Pr(y_A = 1) = 0.4 > \Pr(y_B = 1) = 0.2$. Substitution of these marginal probabilities into Eqs. (1a) and (1b) gives bounds on the probability of A producing a better outcome than B.

$$Lower\ bound : \Pr(y_A > y_B) = \max\{0.6 - 0.4, 0\} = 0.2$$

$$Upper\ bound : \Pr(y_A > y_B) = \min\{0.6, 1 - 0.4\} = 0.6$$

A physician treats all five of the patients and prescribes A to only one of them. A regulator who observed the joint probability distribution of the outcomes, which is equivalent to observing all the information in the table, could point identify the

RAF VAN GESTEL ET AL. 239

Table C1. Hypothetical Outcome Distributions, Success Probabilities and Inequality Probabilities.

Patient	y_A	y_B	$y_{B'}$
1	1	1	1
2	1	0	0
3	1	0	0
4	0	1	0
5	0	0	0
$\Pr(y_k = 1), k \in \{A, B, B'\}$	0.6	0.4	0.2
$\Pr(y_A > y_k), k \in \{B, B'\}$		0.4	0.4
$\Pr(y_k > y_A), k \in \{B, B'\}$		0.2	0.0

inequality probability, $\Pr(y_A > y_B)$, at 0.4. Since that is larger than the proportion of patients given treatment A, such a regulator could immediately rule out that the physician maximises outcomes.

However, a regulator cannot observe the joint probability distribution. Since the proportion of patients given A (0.2) is on the lower bound of the inequality probability, a regulator who only observes RCT estimates of the marginal probabilities (as well as the physician's propensity to prescribe A and B) could not immediately rule out that the physician is using patient-specific information to maximise outcomes. In this way, the regulator gives the physician the benefit of the doubt and allows for the possibility that 2 of the first 3 patients would benefit from B and that the physician would have given A to the only patient among the first three that would not benefit from B. In every other case, a physician would not prescribe below the lower bound if outcomes are maximised. Hence, if a physician's, or group of physicians', propensity to prescribe a treatment that is more effective on average is below the lower bound on the probability of that treatment producing the better outcome, then this cannot possibly be justified by use of information on patient-specific treatment response.

Now, compare outcomes under treatment A with outcomes produced by treatment B'. A still has the larger success probability, on average. The bounds on the inequality–probability are as follows:

$$Lower\ bound : \Pr(y_A > y_{B'}) = \max\{0.6 - 0.2, 0\} = 0.4$$

$$Upper\ bound : \Pr(y_A > y_{B'}) = \min\{0.6, 1 - 0.2\} = 0.6$$

A physician observed to prescribe A to $1/5 = 0.2$ of all patients is below the lower bound on the probability that this treatment produces the better outcome and so cannot possibly be using patient-specific information to improve outcomes.

HIDDEN FIGURES: UNCOVERING QUANTITIES BEHIND ZEROS WITH ECONOMETRICS

Anirban Basu

University of Washington, USA

ABSTRACT

This chapter reviews the econometric approaches typically used to deal with the spike of zeros when modelling non-negative outcomes such as expenditures, income, or consumption. Relying on the assumptions of selection on observables for evaluating a policy or treatment, this chapter discusses other issues that arise with spikes of zeros in the data, including the analyst's choice between full information versus quasi-likelihood methods, considering whether observed zeros are true or masking more complex behavioural decisions, and dealing with zeros that arise due to self-selection. This chapter ends with discussions of empirical strategies to deal with these behavioural assumptions and a brief review of the literature where such strategies were employed.

Keywords: Zeros; non-negative outcome; behavioural assumptions; self-selection; empirical strategy

1. INTRODUCTION

Many economic outcomes are non-negative in nature. These typically include gross income, wealth (in some cases), patents, consumption expenditures and utilisations of commodities. The empirical distribution of these outcomes is usually skewed to the right (i.e. long tails) and often kurtotic (i.e. fat tails). Several statistical approaches (e.g. transformation models, non-linear method of moments, generalised linear models, etc.) have been developed to deal with these features (see Jones, 2000 for a review of related statistical models). However, special attention is sometimes needed to deal with another common part of such distributions – a spike in zeros. Often, alternate behavioural assumptions may be

---

Recent Developments in Health Econometrics
Contributions to Economic Analysis, Volume 297, 241–253
Copyright © 2024 Anirban Basu
Published under exclusive licence by Emerald Publishing Limited
ISSN: 0573-8555/doi:10.1108/S0573-855520240000297012

required to understand the economic rationale for why zeros were generated in the data, how they should be modelled, how the model parameters should be estimated, and how the results should be interpreted.

A key distinction is understanding whether the goal is to model the true zeros or some other hidden figures behind the zeros observed in the data. The data generation process for both the true zeros and the hidden figures can have rich behavioural content, which may trigger the use of some multi-part models and hurdles. However, uncovering the hidden figures and the marginal effects with respect to these hidden figures would require selection models (e.g. Heckman selection model) with appropriate exclusion restrictions. In this chapter, I briefly review some of these questions and solutions.

2. OVERVIEW OF STATISTICAL MODELLING OF NON-NEGATIVE OUTCOMES

To simplify concepts, let us focus on understanding the effect of one binary treatment variable, D, on a non-negative outcome, Y. For now, I assume that D was assigned (pseudo-) randomly across individuals, conditional on a set of observed covariates, X. Let the potential outcomes ($Y_j, j = 0, 1$) associated with each level of D be given as:

$$Y_j = \mu(X; \alpha_j) + U_j, j = 0, 1 \tag{1}$$

where α_j represents the parameter of the potential outcome models, and U represents a stochastic error term ($U \perp D|X$, where $\perp$ signifies statistical independence). These potential outcomes can be considered consumption outcomes generated based on some generic utility maximisation process conditional of D and X. An example would be understanding the effect of genetic therapy on emergency department-use expenditures or the impact of insurance coverage of nicotine patches on smoking. In both cases, assume that the choices of treatments (genetic theory or the coverage) were based on selection on a set of observed covariates, X.

The potential outcomes, being non-negative in nature, could include zeros. These zeros are considered corner solutions for maximisation of consumption utility (Jones, 1989a, 1989b). Statistically, having zeros in these outcomes is nothing special. They can usually be treated as any other value in the distribution of these outcomes. The observed outcome is given as follows:

$$Y = D \cdot Y_1 + (1 - D) \cdot Y_0 \tag{2}$$

Analysts never know the true functional form of $\mu()$. However, it is often assumed that the expectation of the observed outcome is typically non-linear with respect to D as long as $\mu()$ is a non-linear function. Therefore, the expectation of the observed Y can be empirically modelled as a function of D, allowing Y to follow any standard non-negative probability distribution functions such as

Poisson, Gamma or Exponential. Since Y is non-negative, its expectation is strictly positive, and hence, the typical mean function is given as:

$$E(Y|D, X) = h(\beta_0 + \beta_1 \cdot D + \beta_2 \cdot X) \tag{3}$$

and model parameters estimated via full-information maximum likelihood (FIML) or quasi-likelihood (QL) maximisation approaches (McCullagh, 1983; McCullagh & Nelder, 1989).

To understand the difference between FIML and QL, a quick review of distribution theory is needed. The shape of a distribution of random variables is characterised by a series of moments (m) (sometimes expressed as standardised moments by scaling with a power of the variance). For example, the first moment is the expected value, the second central moment is the variance and the third and fourth standardised moments are the skewness and kurtosis, respectively. There can be an infinite number of moments. A parametric distribution consists of one or a vector of parameters defined at the population level that completely specifies these moments. For example, a gamma distribution has two parameters, $\{a,b\}$, which in turn defines the moments, e.g. $m1 = a/b, m2 = a/b^2, m3 = 2/\sqrt{a}, m4 = 6/a$ and so on. A statistical model expresses functional forms for the first and second sample moments using a set of model parameters (e.g. β in Eq. (3), distinct from the distribution parameters). These model parameters or their functionals are typically the targets for inference. When we estimate these model parameters from the data at hand using a FIML approach, where a parametric distribution is specified, we link these model parameters to the structural parameters of the specified parametric distribution that specifies all the population moments. For example, in a log-linear model, one specifies an exponential mean model for the sample mean. For a FIML approach with, say, a log-normal distribution, this mean-model specification is followed to impose the full structure for all the moments of the parametric distribution onto the data at hand. When the data follow such a structure, we get a maximum likelihood estimator (MLE) for our statistical model parameters, generating the minimum variance estimator. However, if the data deviate considerably from the structure of the parametric distribution, then even when our mean (and variance model) may be correctly specified, MLE could be inconsistent.

In contrast, analysts often use the method of moments estimators (popular in economics) or QL estimators (popular in statistics) that relax the stringent FIML requirements (McCullagh, 1983; McCullagh & Nelder, 1989); Blough et al. (1999). A full parametric distribution is not explicitly specified for the dependent variable in these approaches. Instead, the sample moment models are set up to reflect a finite population moment following a specific distribution. Estimation of the model parameters then follows minimising some form of weighted least squares (Wedderburn, 1974). The advantage of these approaches is that if the specified sample moments models are correct, one will get consistent estimates for our model parameters. Therefore, these approaches are robust to misspecification of the underlying distribution function of the dependent variable. However, there are no free lunches. QL estimators are often inefficient compared to well-specified MLEs.

The QL approach was developed to estimate parameters linked to the exponential family of distributions, e.g. Exponential, Gamma, Poisson, etc. One

244   *Hidden Figures*

characteristic of this distribution family is that the second moment can often be
expressed as a function of a dispersion parameter and the first moment. Therefore, if we specify a mean model for the data, the QL approach uses this specification to define the population mean and variance. It then only imposes this
mean–variance relationship to the data at hand but not any structural relationships with the higher order moments that would be defined under a specific
parametric distribution.

2.1 Least Squares

Sometimes researchers use transformation models to avoid running non-linear
specifications for Eq. (3) (Box & Cox, 1964). For example, a common practice in
economics is to log transform a non-negative outcome so that the transformed
outcome can then be modelled linearly as a function of D, X and possibly their
interactions.

$$\text{Ln}(Y) = \beta_0 + \beta_1 \cdot D + \beta_2 \cdot X + \varepsilon \qquad (4)$$

Estimation can proceed following FIML or QL. For example, in FIML, one
can assume $\varepsilon \sim \text{Normal}(0, \sigma^2)$ and carry out a log-likelihood maximisation.
Alternatively, one can use minimise ordinary least squares (OLS), which represents a QL approach.

The challenges of interpreting the parameters of log-transformed outcomes
have been widely reported (Manning, 1998; Manning & Mullahy, 2001). Specif-
ically, such a model represents the conditional mean of the Log(Y), i.e. $E(\text{Ln}(Y)|$
D, X). This formulation represents the conditional geometric mean for the distribution of Y, not the arithmetic mean, which is the target for inference in Eq. (3).
Consequently, the marginal effects of D on the geometric mean of Y are directly
obtained from the regression parameters. Still, the marginal effect of D on the
arithmetic mean requires complex transformation processes (e.g. Duan's smearing
estimate, Duan (1983)) that can fundamentally rely on modelling all dependence
of all the higher order moments of Y on both D and X. Similar challenges arises
with other transformation approaches such as inverse hyperbolic sine.

Transformation models become even more challenging in the presence of zeros
in the data for Y. Typically, authors add an arbitrary constant to Y and then take
a log transformation. Alternatively, they use an inverse hyperbolic sine transformation that is similar to the natural log transformation but allows for zeros. A
recent paper by Mullahy and Norton (2022) shows that these transformation
models have an extra parameter generally not determined by theory but whose
values have enormous consequences for point estimates. As these parameters go
to extreme values, estimated marginal effects on outcomes' natural scales
approach those of either an untransformed linear regression or a normed linear
probability model. Chen and Roth (2023) explain why marginal effects from such
transformation models are not interpretable in the presence of zeros. Intuitively,
they show that the individual-level percentage effect is not well-defined for
individuals whose outcome changes from zero to non-zero when receiving

treatment. These papers suggest that if the goal of the analysis is to obtain consistent estimates for the marginal effects of, say, D on the conditional arithmetic mean, as in Eq. (3), then one should not rely on transformations, especially in the presence of zeros.

3. THE WORLD OF EXCESS ZEROS

The term 'excess zeros' is usually not clearly defined. In statistical terms, if the proportion of zeros in the data exceeds that implied by a specific distribution from the exponential family, data are presumed to be overdispersed (due to excess zeros). Overdispersion can occur due to other values in the data, and the designation of excess would vary based on the reference distribution (typically a Poisson distribution). Most often, when zeros lead to a bimodal distribution of the empirical data, analysts consider them to be excess. Mullahy (1997) describes them to be a consequence of unobserved heterogeneity.

3.1 True Zeros

An important feature of non-negative outcomes in specific applications is the presence of a significant density spike at zeros. These zero-inflated data arise from many individuals reporting/recording, for some reason, no consumption. Econometric modelling of this feature of the Y distribution often requires understanding the structural data-generating process (DGP) and specifying the target parameter of interest in the context of such a structure. The simplest assumption regarding such a DGP is that these zeros are all due to the results of a corner solution of a maximisation process, as described above. Under a DGP where the observed zeros are the 'true' zeros, the sample data can be modelled using the ML and QL methods described above. In some cases, a two-part model (TPM) may be used that conditionally separates the expectation of the dependent variable as:

$$E(Y|D, X) = \Pr(Y > 0|D, X) \cdot E(Y|D, X, Y > 0) \tag{5}$$

As the name suggests, this model can be estimated using two parts – the first part consists of a binary outcome of whether $Y > 0$ (Mullahy, 1998). A logistic or a probit model can be used for the first part, and either can be estimated following FIML or QL techniques. The second part models the expectation of Y given $Y > 0$. This part can be modelled with any of the FIML or QL approaches described in Section 2.

One FIML approach to this estimation involves estimating parameters for both parts of the models jointly. Based on Tobin's (1958) work, a tobit model was formulated where one explicitly considers the utility function underlying the observed choices. This latent utility function (Y^*) is assumed to follow a Gaussian distribution, Normal (μ^*, σ^2). The corner solutions arise as follows:

$$Y = 0 \text{ if } Y^* \leq 0$$
$$= Y^* \text{ if } Y^* > 0 \qquad (6)$$

Under this formulation, one can directly maximise a likelihood for Y^*, following observed data Y. Specifically, consider a linear mean model for Y^*: $\mu^* = E(Y^*|D,X) = \beta_0 + \beta_1 \cdot D + \beta_2 \cdot X$ and $Z^0 = -\frac{\mu^*}{\sigma}$. Then,

$$\Pr(Y > 0|D, X) = \Pr(Y^* > 0) = \left(1 - \Phi(Z^0)\right),$$
$$E(Y|Y^* > 0, D, X) = \left[\mu^* + \sigma \cdot \lambda(Z^0)\right], \text{and} \qquad (7)$$
$$E(Y| D, X) = \left(1 - \Phi(Z^0)\right) \cdot \left[\mu^* + \sigma \cdot \lambda(Z^0)\right],$$

where $\lambda(Z^0) = -\emptyset(Z^0)/(1 - \Phi(Z^0))$ is the inverse Mills ratio, $\emptyset()$ is a standard normal density function and $\Phi()$ is a standard normal cumulative distribution function. It is helpful to note that the Tobit model mirrors the principle of a TPM (as in Eq. (5)). Still, its estimation is based on a Gaussian likelihood function, accounting for the truncation of zeros in the second part.

There are primarily three advantages of a TPM over a Tobit model. One can specify different functional forms for the mean models of the two parts. These mean models can be non-linear in D and X. One does not have to formally deal with the truncation of zeros in the second part while using a QL approach.

3.2 Richer Behavioural Assumptions for Zeros

Zeros can often comprise richer behavioural assumptions than corner solutions for consumption decisions. Given the substantive context of the data, one must conceptualise and defend a richer DGP. Following Deaton and Irish (1984) and Jones's work (1989a, 1989b), I describe data on cigarette smoking behaviour where zeros may camouflage other underlying behaviours.

A survey of smoking behaviour often collects data using the question 'How many cigarettes have you smoked in the past 30 days?' or 'On how many of the PAST 30 DAYS did you smoke a cigarette?'. Of course, most national surveys of cigarette consumption will ask other related questions to fully understand the dynamic nature of cigarette behaviour. However, suppose one wants to model the above question in silo. In that case, one can easily perceive that some reported zeros may result from alternate DGPs rather than a corner solution of a consumption decision. Let's consider those alternative DGPs.

Two distinct behaviours could lead to zeros in reported data. An individual may be a never smoker, i.e. the reported zero is a manifestation of a distinct decision process on whether to smoke at all. Alternatively, an individual may be a smoker, but their consumption decision reached a corner solution of zero cigarettes last month for various reasons. For example, the individual may take a break and quit smoking for some time. These behaviours can be represented formally as:

Reported/observed outcomes (Y) represent $Y = P \cdot Y^{**}$, where P is the smoking participation decision, and Y^{**} is the latent potential consumption for everyone, irrespective of their smoking status.

ANIRBAN BASU

Participation Decision (driven by latent utility U):

$$U = g(D, Z; \alpha) + u = \alpha_0 + \alpha_1 \cdot D + \alpha_2 \cdot Z + u \tag{8}$$

such that $P = 1$ *if* $U > 0$, $P = 0$ otherwise. Z is a set of covariates affecting participation, which may or may not be different from X.

Among those who chose to participate, *Consumption Decision* (following Eq. (6)):

$$\begin{aligned} Y^{**} &= 0 \text{ if } Y^* \le 0 \\ &= Y^* \text{ if } Y^* > 0, \text{ and} \\ Y^* = h(D, X; \beta) + v &= \beta_0 + \beta_1 \cdot D + \beta_2 \cdot X + v \end{aligned} \tag{9}$$

A joint likelihood for the data under these DGPs is given as follows:
For data representing zeros:

$$\begin{aligned} L^0 &= \prod_0 [1 - \Pr(P = 1) \cdot \Pr(Y^* > 0 | P = 1)] \\ &= \prod_0 [1 - \Pr(U > 0) \cdot \Pr(Y^* > 0 | U > 0)] \\ &= \prod_0 [1 - \Pr(u > -g(D, Z; \alpha)) \cdot \Pr(v > -h(D, X; \beta) | u > -g(D, Z; \alpha))] \end{aligned} \tag{10}$$

For data representing non-zeros:

$$\begin{aligned} L^+ &= \prod_+ [\Pr(P = 1) \cdot \Pr(Y^* > 0 | P = 1) \cdot f(Y^* | Y^* > 0, P = 1)] \\ &= \prod_+ [\Pr(u > -g(D, Z; \alpha)) \cdot \Pr(v > -h(D, X; \beta) | u > -g(D, Z; \alpha)) \cdot f(Y^* | v > \\ &\quad -h(D, X; \beta), u > -g(D, Z; \alpha))] \end{aligned} \tag{11}$$

This set-up gave rise to the double-hurdle model in consumption economics (Blundell & Meghir, 1987; Jones, 1989a; Jones & Yen, 2000), where the first hurdle represented the participation decision, while the second hurdle represented the corner solution to the consumption decision. It is immediately clear from Eqs. (10) and (11) that the joint distribution of errors u and v is unknown, and additional information is required to identify the parameters of this likelihood function. However, certain behavioural assumptions can help restrict the dependence between errors u and v, and simply the likelihood, which can facilitate identification. I describe three such behavioural assumptions below.

3.3 Hidden Figures Behind Zeros

There is an additional layer of complexity when one believes that the observed zeros are masking hidden quantities. This usually arises in the context of the first hurdle. Even though the first hurdle represents the participation decision, a researcher may ask about potential consumption decisions by those who never smoke. The main reason why such questions become relevant and modelling the observed outcomes would produce biased results relates to self-selection bias.

248 *Hidden Figures*

Self-selection bias arises through many channels. One way it appears is when the observed outcomes represent a selected population segment, but we want to make an inference about the entire population. For example, suppose our (young adults) smoking data were collected by interviewing young adults in colleges. However, we would like to make inferences about the smoking levels of all young adults in the population, some of whom may not go to college. In such cases, even though one can infer the participation rate among any observably identical group of individuals in the sample, this quantity may not reflect the participation rate for an observably identical group in the population. One reason is that some of the zeros at the first hurdle in the sample may not be zeros at the population level. Consequently, even if one invokes the richer behavioural models in Section 3.2 and applies certain behavioural restrictions, modelling the observed outcome versus the potential outcome beneath the self-selection would require different empirical strategies.

Another way self-selection bias arises is during the evaluation of the effect of a treatment or policy, even when the treatment or policy was allocated in a random or pseudo-random manner in the sample. This is often known as the general-isability issue of randomised experiments.

In the previous two examples, the self-selection bias can affect not just zeros but every outcome level. In contrast, sometimes self-selection occurs even when we can obtain a representative population sample, mainly affecting zeros. Such self-selection bias can arise if outcomes for certain groups of people are censored due to endogenous selection into those groups. For example, one wants to evaluate the effect of a smoking cessation programme assigned randomly to a representative group of individuals. However, some individuals reside in counties with stringent public and workplace smoking bans. Compared to counties without such prohibitions, individuals living in the ban counties must have higher smoking inertia to overcome the shadow price of smoking and smoke the marginal cigarette. Consequently, we expect a larger spike in zeros in the smoking data for individuals residing in the ban counties. This does not invalidate the treatment effect estimate of the cessation policy, as the policy was randomly assigned. However, this treatment effect reflects the impact on the observed outcomes in the context of the current policies in place. Suppose the analyses aimed to estimate the full impact of the cessation policy without the encumbrance of other complementary policies. In that case, we must acknowledge that some of the observed zeros would represent non-zero quantities without these complementary policies.

3.4 Empirical Strategies With Behavioural Restrictions

- *First-Hurdle Dominance*
  The dominance restriction implies that individuals always smoke once the first hurdle is passed. Consequently, the second hurdle is irrelevant, and none of the zeros are generated via a consumption decision. This results in a simplification of the likelihood function in Eqs. (10) and (11):
  For data representing zeros:

$$L^0 = \prod_0 [\Pr(U \le 0)] = \prod_0 [\Pr(u \le -g(D, Z;\ \alpha))] \tag{12}$$

For data representing non-zeros:

$$\begin{aligned} L^+ &= \prod_+ [\Pr(U > 0) \cdot f(Y^* | P = 1)] \\ &= \prod_+ [\Pr(u > -g(D, Z;\ \alpha) \cdot f(Y^* | u > -g(D, Z;\ \alpha)))] \end{aligned} \tag{13}$$

If the goal is to estimate the effect of a covariate on the observed outcomes, then a two-part QL model or a Tobit model can be employed (See Section 3.1).

If the goal is to estimate potential consumption after accounting for certain self-selection behaviours, i.e. what would have the consumption levels of certain non-smokers if a smoking ban had not been in effect, a Heckman selection model can be employed (also known as the 'Heckit' model, Heckman, 1976, 1979). This model is identical to the standard Tobit model in Eq. (7) under the Gaussian distributional assumptions (except that the original Heckman model was conceptualised as a two-step estimator). The only difference is that the Tobit model is used for modelling the corner solution of a consumption decision. In contrast, the Heckit model is used to model participation and consumption decisions, where the latter does not have a corner solution. More importantly, Heckit recovers parameters for the potential consumption decisions if everyone had participated.

It is important to note that the identification in the Heckit model relies entirely on distributional assumptions. One needs sufficient variability of D and X, independent of the inverse Mills ratio, to consistently identify the regression parameters. Alternatively, the identification in the Heckit model can be much improved if one has an exclusion restriction (e.g. an instrumental variable) in the first-stage model for participation (Manning et al., 1987).

- *Independence*
The Independence assumption implies independence between the participation and consumption equations (technically, $u \perp v$). However, unlike the dominance assumption, corner solutions for consumption are allowed beyond participation. Here, the likelihood functions in Eqs. (10) and (11) simplify to:
For data representing zeros:

$$\begin{aligned} L^0 &= \prod_0 [1 - \Pr(U > 0) \cdot \Pr(Y^* > 0)] \\ &= \prod_0 [1 - \Pr(u > -g(D, Z;\ \alpha)) \cdot \Pr(v > -h(D, X;\ \beta)] \end{aligned} \tag{14}$$

For data representing non-zeros:

$$\begin{aligned} L^+ &= \prod_+ [\Pr(U > 0) \cdot \Pr(Y^* > 0) \cdot f(Y^* | Y^* > 0)] \\ &= \prod_+ [\Pr(u > -g(D, Z;\ \alpha)) \cdot \Pr(v > -h(D, X;\ \beta) \cdot f(Y^* | v > -h(D, X;\ \beta)))] \end{aligned} \tag{15}$$

When inferring observed outcomes, one can also use a two-part QL model or a Tobit model (See Section 3.1). However, these models alone cannot distinguish between the participation and consumption zeros from the corner solutions. One needs additional information to decompose the observed zeros into these two parts. For example, if one obtained data on whether individuals have ever smoked, they can use that as a proxy for the participation equation. In such a case, a three-part QL model, or a TPM, with the participation model being a binary model and the consumption equation being a Tobit model (also known as the Cragg model), can be used. To an extent, this is a double-hurdle model, but the independence assumption helps to identify the model using the data at hand.

- *Complete Dominance (Independence and Dominance)*
Finally, if one assumes both independence and dominance, the outcomes can be modelled directly using any single equation model, as in Eq. (3), and using a TPM. The zeros are deemed true, and no separate potential consumption decisions exist.

3.5 Marginal Effects

One of the challenges of using non-linear and multi-step estimators is calculating the marginal effects of covariates. These are no longer apparent by looking at the coefficients of any one or multiple regressions. Here, we focus on *incremental effects* (ξ) of a binary variable (D), which is the difference in the expected value of the target outcome between two levels of D, *marginalised* over the distribution of all other X in the model. Similar discussions for computing the average marginal effects for continuous variables can be found in Dow and Norton (2003).

Let the hat $()$ on a parameter or a functional of parameters indicate that those parameters have been estimated from the data at hand. Following Eq. (3) for a single equation model, an estimator for the incremental effect of D is given as:

$$\widehat{\xi} = \widehat{h}\left(\widehat{\beta}_0 + \widehat{\beta}_1 \cdot 1 + \widehat{\beta}_2 \cdot X\right) - \widehat{h}\left(\widehat{\beta}_0 + \widehat{\beta}_1 \cdot 0 + \widehat{\beta}_2 \cdot X\right) \tag{16}$$

This approach is also known as the method of recycled predictions, where one turns on and off the D indicator for everyone in the sample and predicts the expected outcomes for all, takes the sample average of the predictions and calculates a difference.

For TPM, the method of recycled predictions can be used to estimate incremental effects for each part of the model (Belotti et al., 2015). However, to obtain the incremental effects for the overall consumption, one must first compute the predictions for overall consumption for everyone in the sample under the two levels of D and then take the difference:

$$\begin{aligned}
\widehat{\xi} = {}& \widehat{g}\left(\widehat{\alpha}_0 + \widehat{\alpha}_1 \cdot 1 + \widehat{\alpha}_2 \cdot X\right) \cdot \widehat{h}\left(\widehat{\beta}_0 + \widehat{\beta}_1 \cdot 1 + \widehat{\beta}_2 \cdot X\right) \\
& - \widehat{g}\left(\widehat{\alpha}_0 + \widehat{\alpha}_1 \cdot 0 + \widehat{\alpha}_2 \cdot X\right) \cdot \widehat{h}\left(\widehat{\beta}_0 + \widehat{\beta}_1 \cdot 0 + \widehat{\beta}_2 \cdot X\right)
\end{aligned} \tag{17}$$

Interestingly, after accounting for participation, the Tobit and the Heckit models follow the same principle in computing the average incremental effects of D on overall (or potential) consumption.

Inference on these incremental effects is based on computing their variances, which can follow standard Taylor series approximations (e.g., Delta method) or non-parametric bootstrap approaches.

4. SELECTED EMPIRICAL APPLICATIONS

There is a large literature demonstrating the application of these methods. I highlight a few applications here. Blundell and Meghir (1987) used the double-hurdle model to estimate the Engel curve for clothing, the first hurdle arises from the observation that purchases of clothing are infrequent and that many households will not record any during the 2 weeks of the survey. Jones (1989a) applied double-hurdle models to study cigarette consumption data from the General Household Survey in the United Kingdom and separated participation from consumption decisions. He later used these models to panel data on cigarette consumption (Jones, 1989b). Yen and Jones (1996) expand on these models to incorporate the effect of addiction on participation and consumption. Grootendorst (1995) invoked both the dominance and the independence assumptions in modelling healthcare utilisation data using a TPM. Similar models were used by Street et al. (1999) to model pharmaceutical expenditures in Russia, by Laporte et al. (2008) to model healthcare utilisation in Canada and by Parente and Evans (1998) to model medical care use in the United States. Maciejewski et al. (2012) used a correlated TPM on specialty care expenditure data to relax the independence assumption between participation and consumption. However, they did not explicitly assume dominance. Deb et al. (2014) model healthcare expenditure dynamically, allowing for contemporaneous interdependence between the participation and the consumption equations through a copula model. However, they invoke the dominance option and use a single hurdle model, which they implement using a two-part specification. Greene et al. (2018) modelled the demand for illegal drugs using a double-inflated double-hurdle model that differentiated between nonparticipants, participant misreporters and infrequent consumers. They assume independence across these three equations.

Zweifel et al. (1999) modelled healthcare cost data using a two-step Heckman model and concluded that the main demographic driver of healthcare costs was time to death rather than age. Using similar data, Seshamani and Gray (2004) replicated Zweifel et al.'s results and showed that, when using a TPM, both time to death and age were significant predictors of healthcare costs. These analyses highlight the importance of proper interpretation of results from these models. The Heckman two-step is used to solve a self-selection issue where only those with longer time to death are likely to have non-zero expenditures. On the other hand, the TPM model observed costs without trying to correct for self-selection. Which model is correct would depend on the relevant question at hand. Another example of the use of the Heckman selection model is by Porterfield and Derigine (2011), which examined whether medical home use affected out-of-pocket expenditures in a special population. They appear to correct for a self-selection mechanism where some families used medical homes but reported zero expenditures in the self-reported data, and the authors intended to uncover the hidden figures behind these zeros. A similar approach was adopted by Wirtz et al. (2012) to model the effect of health insurance in Mexico on self-reported out-of-pocket expenditures on medicines.

5. CONCLUSIONS

Zeros in consumption data have rich economic content. Structural approaches to understanding the DGPs for these zeros, especially those driven by behavioural criteria, dictate the choice of econometric modelling and the role of hidden figures behind the zeros. Applied researchers should articulate the behavioural assumptions made and the target outcome for inference when selecting their econometric approach to modelling these data.

ACKNOWLEDGEMENTS

I thank Edward Norton and John Mullahy for their helpful comments – all opinions and errors and mine.

REFERENCES

Belotti, F., Deb, P., Manning, W. G., & Norton, E. C. (2015). Twopm: Two-part models. *STATA Journal, 15*(1), 3–20.

Blough, D. K., Madden, C. W., & Hornbrook, M. C. (1999). Modeling risk using generalized linear models. *Journal of Health Economics, 18*, 153–171.

Blundell, R. W., & Meghir, C. (1987). Bivariate alternative to the univariate Tobit model. *Journal of Econometrics, 33*, 179–200.

Box, G. E. P., & Cox, D. R. (1964). An analysis of transformations. *Journal of the Royal Statistical Society B, 26*, 211–252.

Chen, J., & Roth, J. (2023). Log with zeros? Some problems and solutions. *Quarterly Journal of Economics.* https://doi.org/10.48550/arXiv.2212.06080

Deaton, A., & Irish, M. (1984). Statistical models for zero expenditures in household budgets. *Journal of Public Economics, 23*, 59–80.

Deb, P., Trivedi, P. K, & Zimmer, D. M (2014, October). Cost-offsets of prescription drug expenditures: Data analysis via a copula-based bivariate dynamic hurdle model. *Health Economics, 23*(10), 1242–1259.

Dow, W. H., & Norton, E. C. (2003). Choosing between and interpreting the Heckit and two-part models for corner solutions. *Health Services & Outcomes Research Methodology, 4*, 5–18.

Duan, N. (1983). Smearing estimate: A nonparametric retransformation method. *Journal of the American Statistical Association, 78*, 605–610.

Greene, W., Harris, M. N, Srivastava, P., & Zhao, X. (2018, February). Misreporting and econometric modelling of zeros in survey data on social bads: An application to cannabis consumption. *Health Economics, 27*(2), 372–389.

Grootendorst, P. V (1995, May–June). A comparison of alternative models of prescription drug utilization. *Health Economics*, *4*(3), 183–198.

Heckman, J. (1976). The common structure of statistical models of truncation, sample selection and limited dependent variables and a simple estimator for such models. *Annals of Economic and Social Measurement*, *5*, 475–492.

Heckman, J. (1979). Sample selection bias as a specification error. *Econometrica*, *47*, 153–161.

Jones, A. M. (1989a). A double-hurdle model of cigarette consumption. *Journal of Applied Econometrics*, *4*(1), 23–39.

Jones, A. M. (1989b, March). The UK demand for cigarettes 1954–1986, A double-hurdle approach. *Journal of Health Economics*, *8*(1), 133–141.

Jones, A. M. (2000). Health econometrics. In *Handbook of health economics* (Vol. 1a). Elsevier.

Jones, A. M., & Yen, S. T. (2000). A box-cox double-hurdle model. *The Manchester School*, *68*(2), 203–221.

Laporte, A., Nauenberg, E., & Shen, L. (2008, October). Aging, social capital, and health care utilization in Canada. *Health Economics, Policy and Law*, *3*(Pt 4), 393–411.

Maciejewski, M. L, Liu, C. F, Kavee, A. L, & Olsen, M. K (2012, August). How price responsive is the demand for specialty care? *Health Economics*, *21*(8), 902–912.

Manning, W. G. (1998). The logged dependent variable, heteroscedasticity, and the retransformation problem. *Journal of Health Economics*, *17*, 283–295.

Manning, W. G., Duan, N., & Rogers, W. H. (1987). Monte Carlo evidence on the choice between sample selection and two-part models. *Journal of Econometrics*, *35*, 59–82.

Manning, W. G., & Mullahy, J. (2001). Estimating log models: To transform or not to transform? *Journal of Health Economics*, *20*, 461–494.

McCullagh, P. (1983). Quasi-likelihood functions. *Annals of Statistics*, *11*, 59–67.

McCullagh, P., & Nelder, J. A. (1989). *Generalized linear models* (2nd ed.). Chapman and Hall.

Mullahy, J. (1998). Much ado about two: Reconsidering retransformation and the two-part model in health econometrics. *Journal of Health Economics*, *17*, 247–281.

Mullahy, J. (1997). Heterogeneity, excess zeros, and the structure of count data models. *Journal of Applied Econometrics*, *12*, 337–350.

Mullahy, J., & Norton, E. C. (2022). Why transform Y? A critical assessment of dependent-variable transformations in regression models for skewed and sometimes-zero outcomes. *NBER Working Paper*, 30735.

Parente, S. T, & Evans, W. N (1998 Winter). Effect of low-income elderly insurance copayment subsidies. *Health Care Financing Review*, *20*(2), 19–37.

Porterfield, S. L, & Derigne, L. (2011, November). Medical home and out-of-pocket medical costs for children with special health care needs. *Pediatrics*, *128*(5), 892–900.

Seshamani, M., & Gray, A. (2004, April). Ageing and health-care expenditure: The red herring argument revisited. *Health Economics*, *13*(4), 303–314.

Street, A., Jones, A. M., & Furuta, A. (1999). Cost-sharing and pharmaceutical utilisation and expenditure in Russia. *Journal of Health Economics*, *18*(4), 459–472.

Tobin, J. (1958). Estimation of relationships for limited dependent variables. *Econometrica*, *26*(1), 24–36.

Wedderburn, R. W. M. (1974). Quasi-likelihood functions, generalized linear models, and the Gauss–Newton method. *Biometrika*, *61*, 439–447.

Wirtz, V. J, Santa-Ana-Tellez, Y., Servan-Mori, E., & Avila-Burgos, L. (2012, July-August). Heterogeneous effects of health insurance on out-of-pocket expenditure on medicines in Mexico. *Value in Health*, *15*(5), 593–603.

Yen, S. T., & Jones, A. M. (1996). Individual cigarette consumption and addiction: A flexible limited dependent variable approach. *Health Economics*, *5*(2), 105–117.

Zweifel, P., Felder, S., & Meier, M. (1999). Ageing of population and health care expenditure: A red herring? *Health Economics*, *8*, 485–496.

INVESTIGATING HEALTH OUTCOMES DEFINED BY MULTIPLE CHRONIC CONDITIONS

John Mullahy[a,b]

[a]*University of Wisconsin, USA*
[b]*University of Galway, Ireland*

ABSTRACT

Multiple chronic conditions (MCCs) have attracted significant public policy and clinical attention. Whether MCCs determine other important outcomes, or are themselves the outcomes of health-producing activities or interventions, metrics based thereon have potential to be useful indicators of the health of populations and of differences between and among the health of sub-populations. While the attention MCCs are attracting in various policy circles is impressive, MCCs' potential roles as indicators of population health and of how health determinants influence population–health outcomes have received less attention. The purpose of this chapter is to direct attention towards questions that involve considerations of chronic condition (CC) patterns as health outcomes; specifically, this paper hopes to advance the consideration of patterns of MCCs as indicators of individual and population health. Using data from the United States (US) Behavioural Risk Factor Surveillance System (BRFSS), the chapter explores whether both the 'intensity' (i.e. the number or count) of CCs as well as their 'composition' (i.e. the patterns of particular CCs) might be jointly of interest when considering the prevalence of MCCs in populations and how the nature of MCCs may vary across sub-populations of interest. It is seen that information about intensity tells an incomplete story about MCC health outcomes.

Keywords: Chronic conditions; multiple morbidities; multivariate outcomes; partial effects; count data

---

Recent Developments in Health Econometrics
Contributions to Economic Analysis, Volume 297, 255–270
Copyright © 2024 John Mullahy
Published under exclusive licence by Emerald Publishing Limited
ISSN: 0573-8555/doi:10.1108/S0573-855520240000297013

1. INTRODUCTION

1.1 Background

In population health, clinical and other policy contexts, much attention has been devoted in recent years to the phenomenon of multiple chronic conditions (MCCs). Sometimes called multimorbidity, the circumstance when an individual is affected at a point in time by more than one chronic condition has been associated with high burdens on the healthcare system in addition to the obvious personal and family burdens stemming from such poor health.

Understanding and assessing the state of, disparities in and temporal trajectories of population health outcomes relies on relevant conceptual characterisations of health as well as on measures and data that can reliably inform them. In the 2010 launch of its *Strategic Framework for Multiple Chronic Conditions*, the US Dept. of Health and Human Services proposed:

> The intention for this framework is to catalyze change within the context of how chronic illnesses are addressed in the United States – from an approach focused on individual chronic diseases to one that uses a multiple chronic conditions approach. (USDHHS, 2010)

A large and growing number of United States (US) adults of all ages is afflicted with multiple chronic conditions (MCCs): 80% ages 65+, 49% ages 45–64 and 18% ages 18–44, and racial/ethnic minorities suffer disproportionately from MCCs, especially the most complex MCCs (AHRQ, 2014; CMS, 2012; Schneider et al., 2009; Ward & Schiller, 2013). Beyond the real suffering and life challenges faced by individuals with MCCs, MCCs impose huge burdens on the US healthcare system – healthcare spending increases rapidly with the number of CCs – as well as on the economy more broadly due to early mortality and reduced productivity (AHRQ, 2014). Moreover, such concerns are not limited to the US. For instance, the European Union (EU) is sponsoring a major, multi-partner initiative, *ICare4EU* (www.icare4eu.org), whose goal is to generate care innovations for the growing number of Europeans who suffer with MCCs.

It is thus unsurprising that MCCs have attracted significant public policy and clinical attention. Beyond general concerns, considerations of MCCs have arisen prominently in contexts as diverse as clinical population health management (Mattke et al., 2015; Medicare Payment Advisory Commission (MedPAC), 2015), Medicare provider payment innovations (Edwards & Landon, 2014), comparative-effectiveness analysis (Tinetti & Studenski, 2011), regulatory approvals of new medical technologies (U.S. FDA, 2009), costs and cost containment (Machlin & Soni, 2013) and healthcare equity issues (CMS, 2015; See IOM, 2012, for a comprehensive discussion.)

1.2 MCCs as Health Outcomes

Whether MCCs are determining other important individual- or system-level outcomes, or are themselves the outcomes of health-producing activities or interventions, metrics based thereon have potential to be useful indicators of the health of populations and of differences between and among the health of subpopulations of interest. Yet, while the attention MCCs are attracting in various policy circles is impressive, MCCs' potential roles as indicators of population health and of how health determinants influence population–health outcomes have received less attention. This paper hopes to contribute to enhancing such attention.

Specifically, the purpose of this paper is to direct attention towards questions that involve considerations of CC patterns as health outcomes. The paper explores whether both the 'intensity' (i.e. the number or count) of CCs as well as their 'composition' (i.e. the patterns of particular CCs) might be jointly of interest when considering the prevalence of MCCs in populations and how the nature of MCCs may vary across subpopulations of interest.

It is suggested that information about intensity tells an interesting but incomplete story about MCCs. Consider that if one focuses on individuals suffering from three CCs, one finds in the sample studied in this chapter that the prevalence of individuals with cardiovascular disease, kidney disease and diabetes is virtually the same as that of individuals suffering from arthritis, chronic lower respiratory disease, and cancer. While it would be implausible to argue that the health status of these two groups is remotely similar, a measurement system that focuses only on CC counts would not distinguish them. This chapter hopes to advance the consideration of patterns of CCs as indicators of individual and population health.

The main hypothesis here is that there will be heterogeneity across sub-populations in the nature of the typical patterns of CCs observed controlling for the typical counts or intensities of CCs in those subpopulations. Importantly, even if there are no differences across subpopulations of interest in the average number of CCs or differences in the probabilities of a specific number of CCs, there may still be variation across such subpopulations in the patterns of CCs for a given count or average of CCs. The paper uses a US sample (described in Section 2) to document the extent to which such CC pattern variations may exist. Should such variations be identified and whether they are of policy, clinical or societal interest are for others to determine; the effort here is documentary.

The main analytical and translational challenge is that even when the number of CCs under consideration is relatively small, such an exercise is complicated by the fact that there will be many (specifically, 2^M) possible patterns of CCs to consider as outcomes (e.g. with $M = 7$ CCs, as in the examples considered here, there are 128 possible patterns). The dimension of the analytical space increases further when considering multiple determinants of such patterns. As such, once the data have become available, there is a trade-off between the straightforward approach of analysing averages or counts of CCs – as is typical in MCC research – and the arguably richer information yielded by consideration of specific patterns of CCs.

Using a graphical approach, the strategy pursued in this paper is novel in that it combines considerations of intensity and composition by examining the heteroge-neity of patterns and their determinant for any given count of CCs. While these ideas are operationalised here using data from the Behavioural Risk Factors Surveillance System (BRFSS), the intent is that the approaches suggested here can be used more broadly to document the chronic-condition-related health status of populations and differences therein between subpopulations and/or over time.

258   *Health Outcomes Defined by Multiple Chronic Conditions*

The plan for the remainder of the chapter is as follows: Section 2 describes the samples used for analysis. Section 3 describes the chapter's analytical approach and the data visualizations used to convey its findings. Section 4 presents the results. Section 5 offers discussion and conclusions.

2. MCCs: DATA AND SAMPLING

2.1 The Nature of Chronic-Condition Data

How individual-level information on CCs is elicited is a central consideration. For example, different survey or administrative (e.g. Medicare) data systems may yield information on CCs that is of a fundamentally different nature: self-reports ('Have you ever been told by a provider that you have ____?'), open-ended elicitations and healthcare-encounter-based (e.g. 'reason for visit') are three strategies prominent in this line of inquiry. See Machlin et al., 2014, for a useful discussion. While the analysis undertaken here uses measures of the 'Have you ever been told...' variety, the analytical approaches suggested here would appear equally applicable to other data systems (See also NQF, 2012).

Notwithstanding the modes of elicitation when describing the prevalence of MCCs in populations or subpopulations, the typical approach has been to determine from some predefined list of conditions how many such conditions affect an individual over some time window (including 'ever') and then reporting averages or frequencies across the relevant (sub)population (e.g. subpopulations defined by age ranges). See Goodman et al., 2013. While in daily-living and clinical contexts the particular chronic conditions that affect an individual are obvious and essential considerations, rarely have the specific patterns of MCCs – *which* CCs affect an individual – been studied per se when examining and summarising population-level data.

2.2 Data Used in This Analysis

The data used for this analysis are drawn from a combination of the 2011, 2013, 2015 and 2017 BRFSS samples. (In those years, the BRFSS provided greater detail on CCs than in the adjacent even-numbered years.) The present analysis restricts the age range to 25–69 (to better describe terminal schooling completion and to reduce threats of survivor bias). This results in a sample of $N = 1,255,523$ observations for which complete data are available.

In the BRFSS the survey, the question used is as follows: 'Has a doctor, nurse or other health professional EVER told you that you had any of the following?' For this analysis, the 13 CCs in the BRFSS are aggregated to $M = 7$ CCs:

(1) Cardiovascular disease (V)
(2) Arthritis (A)
(3) Depression (D)
(4) Kidney disease (K)
(5) Diabetes (B)
(6) Cancer (C)
(7) Chronic lower respiratory disease (R)

The paper uses the notation $h = [h_1, \ldots, h_M]$ to describe a health pattern, where each h_m is binary indicating the presence ($h_m = 1$) or absence ($h_m = 0$) of each of the M chronic conditions. For instance, $h = [0,1,1,0,1,0,1]$ describes the health state of an individual who reports arthritis, depression, diabetes and chronic lower respiratory disease (CLRD). With seven chronic conditions, there are $2^7 = 128$ possible combinations of CCs.

The paper considers how the intensity and patterns of CCs vary between subpopulations defined by gender and schooling. These estimated marginal effects should be interpreted as female relative to male and college graduates (16+ years of schooling attainment) relative to high school graduates (the latter defined by 12–15 years of completed schooling). Of course, the empirical results reveal associations, not causal relationships; the 'effects' terminology is convenient shorthand.

3. ANALYTICAL STRATEGY

3.1 Empirical Methodology

The main parameters of interest are the marginal effects on the CC patterns of a particular covariate x, defined for a binary x covariate as

$$m_h(x) = \text{Prob}\,(y = h|x_{\text{oth}}, x = x_1) - \text{Prob}\,(y = h|x_{\text{oth}}, x = x_0)$$

for each of the 2^M possible health outcome patterns h and where 'x' is variously gender (female, male) or schooling (highest schooling attainment college graduate vs highest schooling attainment high school graduate). Covariates other than x (x_{oth}) are age categories, race/ethnicity categories, year dummies, plus either gender or schooling. All 128 possible health patterns h are observed with positive frequency in the sample. The average marginal effect estimates presented here are obtained nonparametrically.[1]

3.2 Summarising MCC Marginal Effects

Encapsulating results for such a high-dimensional set of outcomes is challenging. To provide a parsimonious representation of the findings that still conveys the essence of the analysis with respect to the paper's main hypothesis, a series of heatmaps was produced. These data visualizations map colour schemes to the

---

[1]Since all the covariates and outcomes are binary then nonparametric marginal effect estimates are straightforward to obtain. Defining the 2^M scalar binary indicators $y_h = 1(y = h)$, then with covariates $x_1, \ldots, x_k$ the same nonparametric average marginal effect estimates will obtain from either of the Stata commands:

    npregress series yh i.(x1 x2 ... xk)

or

    regress yh x1##x2## ... ##xk, vce(robust)
    margins, dydx(*)

260   *Health Outcomes Defined by Multiple Chronic Conditions*

magnitudes and signs of the estimated $m_h(x)$ so that for any given level of the intensity or count of CCs ($S = 0,1,\ldots,7$ in this analysis; S denotes 'sum'), the range of estimated marginal effects for all the possible patterns of CCs corresponding to a particular count can be appreciated by examining the range of colours (orange for negative; blue for positive) and colour intensity (deeper shades indicate larger magnitudes) corresponding to that count. In essence, the chapter's main hypothesis is supported if there is a range of colours and colour intensities at each count value.

Note that for each count there are $\binom{7}{S}$ possible CC outcome combinations that correspond to that particular count S. For instance, for $S = 2$, there are 21 patterns ($h = [1,1,0,0,0,0,0]$, $h = [1,0,1,0,0,0,0]$, etc.), while for $S = 0$ and $S = 7$, only one pattern is possible ($h = [0,0,0,0,0,0,0]$ and $h = [1,1,1,1,1,1,1]$, respectively). Finally, it should be emphasised that the results presented here do not consider sampling variation. As such, some of what is depicted in the heatmaps is necessarily a reflection of such sampling variation. However, with a large sample size such concerns are perhaps of second-order importance.

4. RESULTS

4.1 Baseline Results

Summary statistics are presented in Tables 1 and 2, which show the sample frequencies of each CC (Table 1) and the marginal frequencies of the CC counts (Table 2). The frequency distributions in Table 2 are essentially the kind of summary information about CCs typically presented in population reports of MCCs.

4.2 Results for MCC Counts/Intensities

The first heatmaps presented (Fig. 1) are simple data visualizations of the associations of each covariate with the simple counts of CCs in the BRFSS sample (The rightmost columns in Table 2 present the corresponding numerical values).

Table 1. Marginal Sample Frequencies of Chronic Conditions.

Chronic Condition	Sample Frequency
Cardiovascular disease	0.52
Arthritis	0.29
Depression	0.21
Chronic lower respiratory disease	0.17
Cancer	0.12
Diabetes	0.11
Kidney disease	0.03

JOHN MULLAHY

Table 2. Sample Frequencies and Nonparametric Estimated Marginal Effects for Counts (S).

| S | Sample Frequency (×100) | Marginal Effect (×100) | |
		Gender	Schooling
0	28.48	−1.70	6.10
1	29.79	−3.85	4.14
2	21.25	−0.16	−1.28
3	12.20	2.12	−3.89
4	5.73	2.18	−3.20
5	2.05	1.09	−1.48
6	0.44	0.28	−0.35
7	0.05	0.03	−0.04

Deeper shades of orange signify large (in magnitude) negative associations while deeper shades of blue indicate increasingly large positive effects. Being female and not being a college graduate are associated with greater probabilities of higher levels (counts) of CCs.

It is useful to note here that the colour intensity tends to fade as the count of CCs increases, corresponding to smaller magnitudes of $Pr(y = h|x)$. This reflects the fact that the marginal count frequencies decline as the number of CCs increases (top panel of table) so that the corresponding effect magnitudes are necessarily smaller for larger counts of CCs.

4.3 Results for MCC Health Outcome Patterns

Turning to the paper's main results on the patterns of CCs, the heatmaps are presented in Figs. 2 (gender) and 3 (schooling). The top panel in each of these figures depicts the average marginal effects while the bottom panel depicts a normalised (or semi-elasticity) version where each effect is divided by the corresponding $Pr(S)$. All 128 estimated marginal effects appear in Table 3.

Note that if were there no variation in the magnitudes or signs of the estimated pattern effects *for a given count* or intensity, then each of the horizontal bars corresponding to $S = 0,1,...,7$ would be monochromatic. If only magnitude varied but not direction, then each bar would include only different shades of either orange or blue. If both magnitude and sign vary for a given S, then each bar will have different intensities of both orange and blue. As only one possible pattern corresponds to $S = 0$ $h = [0,0,0,0,0,0,0]$ and $S = 7$ ($h = [1,1,1,1,1,1,1]$), there can be no colour variation in these cases. Finally, the x-axes in these figures indicate the fraction of pattern associations of each particular sign and magnitude, ordered left to right from most negative to most positive.

First, consider the results for the gender effects in Fig. 2. The marginal effect heatmaps indicate a noteworthy negative association (deep orange) of being female with the probability of the 'no CC', – i.e. the 'healthiest' – pattern ($h = [0,0,0,0,0,0,0]$).

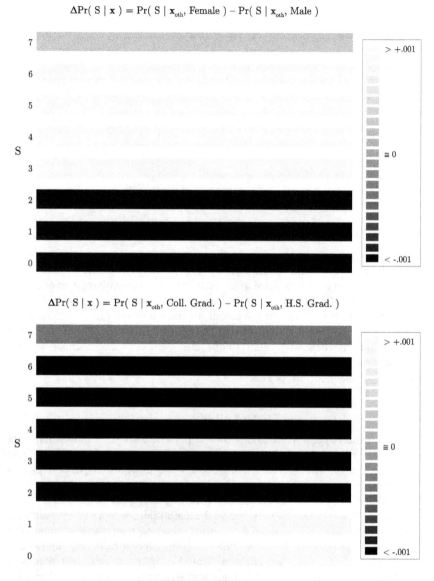

Fig. 1. Count Outcome Marginal Effect Point Estimates – Gender (Top Panel); Schooling (Bottom Panel).

For $S = 1$, the same figure shows a mixture of positive and negative associations, with the majority – in this case 5 of 7 – of the pattern associations being positive (i.e. probability increasing with being female). As the counts S increase, it is evident that being female contributes increasingly to the likelihoods of these more complex health

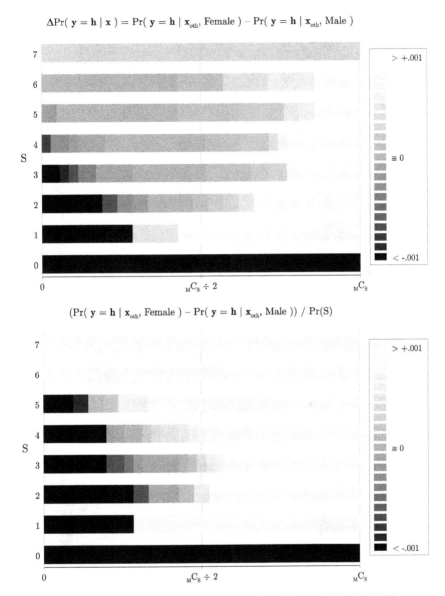

Fig. 2. Estimated Marginal Effects: Gender – Average Marginal Effects (Top Panel); Normalised Marginal Effects (Bottom Panel).

problems, with no negative associations estimated for any of the 22 patterns corresponding to $S \in \{6,7\}$.

The results for schooling, depicted in Fig. 3, suggest strong associations of health status with college completion. College completion has negative marginal

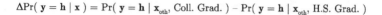

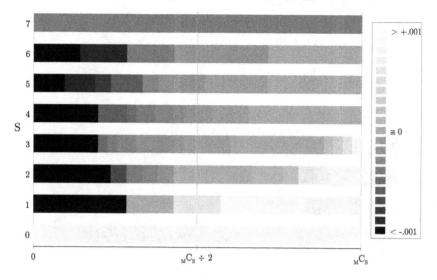

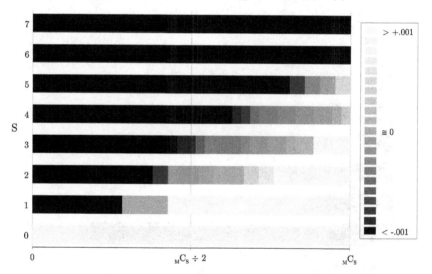

Fig. 3. Estimated Marginal Effects: Schooling – Average Marginal Effects (Top Panel); Normalised Marginal Effects (Bottom Panel).

effects on all 64 h patterns that correspond to $S \in \{4,5,6,7\}$. While the marginal effects for the patterns corresponding to $S \in \{1,2,3\}$ are a blend of negative and positive estimates, it is readily evident that the effects of college completion on complex health conditions are strongly negative, a result seen only coarsely in Fig. 1.

JOHN MULLAHY

Table 3. Sample Frequencies and Nonparametric Estimated Marginal Effects for 128 Health Patterns h – (Order of Elements in h is Cardiovascular Disease, Arthritis, Depression, Kidney Disease, Diabetes, Cancer and Chronic Lower Respiratory Disease).

h	Sample Frequency ($\times 100$)	Marginal Effect ($\times 100$)	
		Gender	Schooling
0000000	28.479	−1.701	6.096
1000000	16.627	−7.271	2.796
0100000	3.887	0.591	−0.178
0010000	3.423	2.079	0.062
0001000	0.144	0.057	−0.000
0000100	0.609	−0.273	−0.106
0000010	1.981	0.719	0.997
0000001	3.122	0.253	0.570
1100000	6.238	−0.885	−1.055
1010000	3.028	0.532	−0.034
1001000	0.230	−0.071	0.009
1000100	2.503	−1.452	−0.644
1000010	2.286	−0.477	0.845
1000001	2.297	−0.489	0.024
0110000	1.197	0.929	−0.317
0101000	0.049	0.020	−0.004
0100100	0.179	−0.033	−0.070
0100010	0.636	0.296	0.179
0100001	0.786	0.362	−0.186
0011000	0.057	0.053	−0.002
0010100	0.092	0.033	−0.038
0010010	0.332	0.302	0.082
0010001	0.869	0.621	−0.142
0001100	0.007	−0.003	−0.001
0001010	0.031	0.001	0.016
0001001	0.028	0.013	0.000
0000110	0.058	−0.016	−0.005
0000101	0.083	−0.002	−0.018
0000011	0.268	0.110	0.078
1110000	2.587	1.099	−1.064
1101000	0.187	−0.009	−0.039
1100100	1.570	−0.436	−0.847
1100010	1.380	−0.039	0.060
1100001	1.640	0.323	−0.770
1011000	0.089	0.026	−0.027
1010100	0.569	−0.014	−0.232
1010010	0.481	0.174	0.105
1010001	0.910	0.311	−0.325
1001100	0.136	−0.095	−0.055
1001010	0.074	−0.039	0.019
1001001	0.050	−0.007	−0.012

(Continued)

Table 3. (Continued)

h	Sample Frequency (×100)	Marginal Effect (×100)	
		Gender	Schooling
1000110	0.365	−0.159	−0.022
1000101	0.443	−0.073	−0.192
1000011	0.391	−0.010	0.030
0111000	0.039	0.034	−0.017
0110100	0.065	0.034	−0.035
0110010	0.222	0.210	−0.006
0110001	0.531	0.508	−0.349
0101100	0.006	−0.002	−0.002
0101010	0.017	0.005	0.002
0101001	0.018	0.012	−0.005
0100110	0.031	−0.001	−0.006
0100101	0.048	0.012	−0.022
0100011	0.159	0.107	−0.011
0011100	0.005	−0.000	−0.002
0011010	0.010	0.009	−0.003
0011001	0.016	0.015	−0.008
0010110	0.013	0.008	−0.005
0010101	0.034	0.019	−0.018
0010011	0.097	0.103	−0.025
0001110	0.003	−0.002	0.000
0001101	0.002	−0.001	−0.001
0001011	0.006	0.002	0.001
0000111	0.009	−0.001	−0.003
1111000	0.136	0.077	−0.056
1110100	0.798	0.165	−0.555
1110010	0.600	0.343	−0.120
1110001	1.514	1.036	−1.126
1101100	0.137	−0.036	−0.067
1101010	0.072	−0.027	−0.007
1101001	0.077	0.026	−0.046
1100110	0.336	−0.085	−0.125
1100101	0.583	0.122	−0.423
1100011	0.439	0.141	−0.166
1011100	0.050	−0.007	−0.033
1011010	0.027	0.008	0.002
1011001	0.040	0.016	−0.030
1010110	0.098	0.003	−0.024
1010101	0.238	0.090	−0.165
1010011	0.174	0.100	−0.058
1001110	0.030	−0.023	−0.007
1001101	0.032	−0.007	−0.018
1001011	0.017	−0.006	−0.001
1000111	0.084	0.000	−0.026
0111100	0.005	0.003	−0.002

JOHN MULLAHY

Table 3. *(Continued)*

	Sample	Marginal Effect ($\times$100)	
h	Frequency ($\times$100)	Gender	Schooling
0111010	0.010	0.008	-0.005
0111001	0.021	0.023	-0.018
0110110	0.016	0.011	-0.007
0110101	0.044	0.041	-0.038
0110011	0.117	0.134	-0.065
0101110	0.003	-0.000	-0.003
0101101	0.003	0.002	-0.001
0101011	0.006	0.004	-0.002
0100111	0.011	0.007	-0.005
0011110	0.001	-0.000	-0.001
0011101	0.002	0.001	-0.000
0011011	0.004	0.005	-0.002
0010111	0.004	0.004	-0.003
0001111	0.001	-0.000	-0.000
1111100	0.104	0.017	-0.067
1111010	0.055	0.024	-0.013
1111001	0.122	0.091	-0.099
1110110	0.197	0.065	-0.097
1110101	0.681	0.422	-0.619
1110011	0.433	0.379	-0.311
1101110	0.050	-0.018	-0.020
1101101	0.078	0.002	-0.065
1101011	0.034	0.010	-0.018
1100111	0.156	0.048	-0.086
1011110	0.015	-0.002	-0.001
1011101	0.027	0.007	-0.022
1011011	0.013	0.005	-0.006
1010111	0.048	0.025	-0.030
1001111	0.011	-0.005	-0.003
0111110	0.003	0.000	-0.002
0111101	0.004	0.003	-0.004
0111011	0.008	0.009	-0.006
0110111	0.009	0.010	-0.008
0101111	0.001	0.000	0.001
0011111	0.001	0.001	-0.000
1111110	0.037	0.005	-0.025
1111101	0.114	0.066	-0.096
1111011	0.053	0.041	-0.038
1110111	0.197	0.157	-0.164
1101111	0.032	0.009	-0.022
1011111	0.008	0.004	-0.003
0111111	0.001	0.002	-0.001
1111111	0.051	0.029	-0.040

It may be of interest to note that in some applications, an obvious alternative to nonparametric estimation is estimation of the conditional joint probabilities $\Pr(y = h|x)$ and their corresponding marginal effects using multivariate probit (MVP) (see Mullahy, 2016, 2017, for details). The estimation of marginal effects with MVP can be more computationally demanding since multidimensional cumulative normal probabilities must be repeatedly simulated. However, when not all 2^M possible outcome patterns are observed in the data MVP is still capable of estimating nonzero magnitudes for all 2^M conditional outcome probabilities, nonparametric estimation fails (or, viewed as an analogy estimator, estimates a joint probability equal to zero). Table 4 presents point estimates and associated standard errors for MVP models estimated using the same covariates as used to obtain the nonparametric estimates discussed above while Table 5 reports the estimated MVP error correlation matrix. The MVP estimates are obtained using the algorithm described in Mullahy, 2016.

Table 4. Multivariate Probit Parameter Point Estimates and Standard Errors.

	Outcome						
	V	A	D	K	B	C	R
Age 40–54	0.668	0.612	0.051	0.258	0.605	0.471	−0.006
	(0.003)	(0.004)	(0.004)	(0.008)	(0.006)	(0.006)	(0.004)
Age 55–69	1.26	1.13	0.035	0.508	1.04	0.962	0.087
	(0.003)	(0.004)	(0.003)	(0.007)	(0.006)	(0.005)	(0.004)
Female	−0.163	0.209	0.382	0.068	−0.076	0.157	0.211
	(0.002)	(0.003)	(0.003)	(0.005)	(0.003)	(0.003)	(0.003)
H.S. Grad.	−0.093	−0.186	−0.239	−0.164	−0.208	−0.011	−0.221
	(0.005)	(0.005)	(0.005)	(0.008)	(0.006)	(0.007)	(0.005)
Coll. Grad.	−0.263	−0.477	−0.441	−0.310	−0.492	0.033	−0.405
	(0.005)	(0.005)	(0.005)	(0.009)	(0.006)	(0.007)	(0.005)
White N/H	−0.110	0.084	0.201	−0.117	−0.312	0.386	0.014
	(0.003)	(0.003)	(0.003)	(0.006)	(0.004)	(0.004)	(0.003)
Year 2013	0.009	0.019	0.063	0.015	0.016	0.015	0.039
	(0.003)	(0.003)	(0.004)	(0.007)	(0.004)	(0.004)	(0.004)
Year 2015	−0.031	0.007	0.049	0.046	0.026	0.015	0.029
	(0.003)	(0.003)	(0.004)	(0.007)	(0.004)	(0.004)	(0.004)
Year 2017	−0.050	0.001	0.089	0.082	0.050	0.023	0.058
	(0.003)	(0.003)	(0.004)	(0.007)	(0.004)	(0.004)	(0.004)
Constant	−0.393	−1.25	−0.989	−2.06	−1.44	−2.26	−0.876
	(0.006)	(0.006)	(0.006)	(0.011)	(0.008)	(0.009)	(0.006)

Notes: (1) The outcome abbreviations are as follows: cardiovascular disease (V), arthritis (A), depression (D), kidney disease (K), diabetes (B), cancer (C) and chronic lower respiratory disease (R). (2) The reference age category is age 25–39. The reference schooling category did not complete high school. The reference time category is year 2011.

JOHN MULLAHY

Table 5. Multivariate Probit Estimated Correlation Matrix.

	V	A	D	K	B	C	R
V	1	0.29	0.27	0.29	0.48	0.11	0.20
A	0.29	1	0.37	0.26	0.23	0.14	0.30
D	0.27	0.37	1	0.26	0.21	0.12	0.31
K	0.29	0.26	0.26	1	0.33	0.20	0.20
B	0.48	0.23	0.21	0.33	1	0.07	0.19
C	0.11	0.14	0.12	0.20	0.07	1	0.12
R	0.20	0.30	0.31	0.20	0.19	0.12	1

Note: The outcome abbreviations are as follows: cardiovascular disease (V), arthritis (A), depression (D), kidney disease (K), diabetes (B), cancer (C) and chronic lower respiratory disease (R).

5. DISCUSSION AND CONCLUSIONS

The empirical results bear out the chapter's main hypothesis, namely that the manner in which CCs vary across important subpopulations is prominent and involves both variations in intensity (count) and variations in patterns for given intensities. To reiterate a point made earlier, even if there are no differences across subpopulations of interest in the average number of CCs or in the probabilities of specific counts or intensities of CCs, there may still be variation across such subpopulations in the patterns of CCs for a given count or average of CCs.

Having now identified that such variations exist, whether they are of policy or clinical interest is to be determined. Of course, no causal interpretation should be claimed for the marginal effects discussed above. Beyond this, however, what can be suggested is that future discourse about how MCCs are prevalent in populations and vary across subpopulations should be more attuned to the likelihood that the composition – along with the intensity – of the MCCs being considered will likely vary in interesting and potentially important ways.

Demonstration and discussion of the intensity of CCs and how it may vary in interesting and policy-relevant ways remain timely. The results reported here suggest, however, that at minimum, such discussions might perhaps be usefully nuanced by considerations of the kinds of pattern variations that this paper has found to be empirically important.

ACKNOWLEDGEMENTS

Thanks are owed to participants in the UW-Madison Health Economics Workgroup and in the fourth Italian Health Econometrics Workshop in Padova and to an anonymous referee for helpful comments and suggestions. Partial financial support by the Robert Wood Johnson Foundation's Evidence for Action Research Program (Grant No. 73336) is gratefully acknowledged.

REFERENCES

Agency for Healthcare Research and Quality. (2014). *Multiple chronic conditions chartbook*. AHRQ.

Centers for Medicare and Medicaid Services. (2012). *Chronic conditions among Medicare beneficiaries chartbook, 2012 Edition*. https://www.cms.gov/research-statistics-data-and-systems/statistics-trends-and-reports/chronic-conditions/downloads/2012chartbook.pdf

Centers for Medicare and Medicaid Services. (2015). *The CMS equity plan for improving quality in Medicare*. CMS, Office of Minority Health.

Edwards, S. T., & Landon, B. E. (2014). Medicare's chronic care management payment—Payment reform for primary care. *The New England Journal of Medicine, 371*, 2049–2051.

Goodman, R. A., Posner, S. F., Huang, E. S., Parekh, A. K., & Koh, H. K. (2013). Defining and measuring chronic conditions: Imperatives for research, policy, program, and practice. *Preventing Chronic Disease, 10*(April 25, 2013).

Institute of Medicine. (2012). *Living well with chronic illness: A call for public health action*. National Academies Press.

Machlin, S. R., & Soni, A. (2013). Health care expenditures for adults with multiple treated chronic conditions: Estimates from the medical expenditure panel survey, 2009. *Preventing Chronic Disease, 10*(April 25, 2013).

Machlin, S., Soni, A., & Fang, Z. (2014). *Understanding and analyzing MEPS household component medical condition data*. http://meps.ahrq.gov/survey_comp/MEPS_condition_data.pdf. Accessed on October 30, 2014.

Mattke, S., Higgins, A., & Brook, R. (2015). Results from a national survey on chronic care management by health plans. *American Journal of Managed Care, 21*, 370–376.

Medicare Payment Advisory Commission (MEDPAC). (2015). *Improving care for Medicare beneficiaries with chronic conditions*. Testimony of MEDPAC Executive Director Mark E. Miller, Senate Finance Committee. Accessed on May 14, 2015.

Mullahy, J. (2016). Estimation of multivariate probit models via bivariate probit. *Stata Journal, 16*, 37–51.

Mullahy, J. (2017). Marginal effects in multivariate probit models. *Empirical Economics, 52*, 447–461.

National Quality Forum. (2012, May). *Multiple chronic conditions measurement framework*. National Quality Forum.

Schneider, K. M., O'Donnell, B. E., & Dean, D. (2009). Prevalence of multiple chronic conditions in the United States Medicare population. *Health and Quality of Life Outcomes, 7*(Sept. 8, 2009).

Tinetti, M. E., & Studenski, S. A. (2011). Comparative effectiveness research and patients with multiple chronic conditions. *New England Journal of Medicine, 364*, 2478–2481.

U.S. Dept. of Health and Human Services. (2010, December). *Multiple chronic conditions: A strategic framework. Optimum health and quality of life for individuals with multiple chronic conditions*. https://www.hhs.gov/sites/default/files/ash/initiatives/mcc/mcc_framework.pdf

U.S. FDA, Dept. of Health and Human Services. (2009). *Guidance for industry: Patient-reported outcome measures: Use in medical product development to support labeling claims*. Food and Drug Administration.

Ward, B. W., & Schiller, J. S. (2013). Prevalence of multiple chronic conditions among US adults: Estimates from the national health interview survey, 2010. *Preventing Chronic Disease, 10*(April 25, 2013).

Printed in the USA
CPSIA information can be obtained
at www.ICGtesting.com
JSHW011336280824
68947JS00004B/58